Population and Society
in Western European Port-Cities,
c. 1650–1939

Liverpool Studies in European Population
General Editor DAVID SIDDLE

Population and Society in Western European Port-Cities, *c.* 1650–1939

edited by
RICHARD LAWTON and ROBERT LEE

LIVERPOOL UNIVERSITY PRESS

Published by
LIVERPOOL UNIVERSITY PRESS
4 Cambridge Street
Liverpool
L69 7ZU

British Library Cataloguing-in-Publication Data
A British Library CIP Record is available
ISBN 0–85323–435–3 cased
ISBN 0–85323–907–X paper

Typeset by Wilmaset Limited, Birkenhead, Wirral
Printed and bound in the European Union by
Creative Print and Design Limited, Ebbw Vale.

In Memoriam: Gunnar Fridlizius, an innovative scholar, an enthusiastic colleague, and a generous friend

CONTENTS

LIST OF FIGURES

LIST OF TABLES

PREFACE

One of the original aims of the Institute for European Population Studies was to concentrate research activities on the demography of urban areas and of the urbanization process. Urbanization was a critical element in European demographic change in the modern period, with unprecedented population growth associated directly with rapid urban expansion. Our earlier publication in this series (Lawton and Lee, 1989) examined key aspects of urban population change in a number of Western European countries. It focused on different aspects of urban growth, including the respective role of natural increase and in-migration in urban demographic development, the nature and impact of the migration process and the significance of urbanization for demographic change in modern Europe. The individual contributions highlighted the significant acceleration of large city growth from the early-nineteenth century onwards, the steepening of the downward curve of urban rank-size distribution, and the perceptible patterns of increasing European convergence: by the early-twentieth century Europe's cities were effectively dominated by national capitals, major ports and the central towns of the main industrial regions.

Recent research in historical demography has also highlighted the need for disaggregated analysis and the empirical testing of hypotheses on the basis of selected micro-level studies. An industrial or functional typology has been applied successfully in urban history in order to isolate common urban characteristics (Rodger, 1992) and the demographic profile of a city was, at least in part, a reflection of its function. Different city types can be associated historically with the role of different components in urban population growth and differences in occupational structure, social stratification and income distribution were reflected systematically in the demography of individual urban communities. If a clearer understanding of the nature of population processes in cities is essential to any analysis of demographic and social change in modern Europe, as a whole, the application of a sufficiently robust urban typology may well provide an important key for future research in this field.

This volume focuses explicitly on a port-city typology, providing a series of contributions on major commercial ports in Western Europe during the modern period. To this extent, the individual studies of Bremen, Cork, Genoa, Glasgow, Hamburg, Liverpool, Malmö, Nantes and Trieste offer an important insight into the population dynamics and development of Western European port-cities. Portsmouth, as a major naval base, evinced to an extreme degree many of the specific demographic characteristics of a port-city. The following chapters, therefore, contribute significantly to our understanding of the particular socio-economic and demographic characteristics of port-cities and their demographic régime. In terms of mortality, nuptiality and fertility, port-cities shared a number of common characteristics, including an inflated risk of epidemic infection and persistently high birth rates well into the early-twentieth century. Although urban demographic régimes in the nineteenth century were traditionally dependent on in-migration, many port-cities remained dispro-portionately dependent on migrant streams drawn from a more extended migration zone. Port-cities were also often dominated by shipping and port-related activities, with a local economy characterized by a high proportion of unskilled and casual labour, susceptible to both seasonal and cyclical unemployment. Moreover, as the individual contributions to this volume confirm, the demographic development of port-cities was frequently affected by other common factors of a socio-economic, cultural and political nature.

The choice of a port-city typology for this volume was a deliberate one. A number of factors reinforced the case for such a choice. First, urban development in Western Europe from the late-seventeenth century onwards was accompanied by the increasing predominance of port-cities. Secondly, the specific focus on ports reflected a long-standing and continuing tradition of research on the port-city of Liverpool, by colleagues in the Department of Geography (Lawton, 1953; 1989; Lawton and Pooley, 1976; Laxton, 1981) and Economic and Social History (Power, 1992; Belchem and Power, 1990; Hyde, 1971; Taplin, 1978; Marriner, 1982; Burton, 1989; Jarvis, 1991; Milne, 2000). This has been extended in the latter case by the development of the Docklands History Project, in conjunction with staff in the Department of Sociology, which has provided an important insight into various facets of life and industry in the dockside communities of Liverpool and Merseyside (Johnson and Moore, 1987; Ayers, 1988a; Johnson, 1989; Moore, 1989), just as the publications of the Liver Press have addressed a variety of social, ethnic, gender and political issues relating to the long-run development of Merseyside (Ayers, 1988b; Miller, 1988; Boyce, 1989; Wong, 1989; Davies et al., 1992; Murphy, 1995). Thirdly, the Institute for European Population Studies has sought to promote in recent years a series of interrelated studies of individual port-cities, which have been undertaken both in Liverpool (Compton, 1992; Sheard, 1994; Lewis, 1993) and in collaboration with colleagues in Germany (Urban, 1998; Leidinger et al., 1997; Lee and Marschalck, 1996; 1998) and Sweden (Kearns et al., 1989; Rogers and Nelson, 1989; Nelson and Rogers, 1992). A number of the present contributions were presented at an earlier interdisciplinary conference held at the University of Liverpool and have been revised for the purpose of this publication; others have been specifically commissioned for the current volume. By focusing on a distinct port typology, it is hoped that the volume will provide a useful contribution to the comparative analysis of urban population development in Western Europe during the period 1650 to 1939.

We would like to record our gratitude to the University of Liverpool, the Economic and Social Research Council and the Nuffield Foundation for providing support for the original conference. We also owe a very substantial debt of gratitude to all our contributors for their unstinting patience in accepting, without complaint, a protracted editorial process. Andrea Murphy has performed miracles in transforming undecipherable handwriting into legible typescript and Robin Bloxsidge, of Liverpool University Press, deserves our sincerest thanks for maintaining an unflagging interest in this publication and for continuing to promote the Liverpool Studies in European Population.

Richard Lawton, Marton, North Yorkshire
Robert Lee, Birkenhead

References

AYERS, P. (1988a), *The Liverpool Docklands. Life and Work in Athol Street*, Liverpool.

AYERS, P. (1988b), *Women at War. Liverpool Women 1939–45*, Liver Press, Birkenhead.

BELCHEM, J. C. and M. J. POWER (1993), 'Structural change, culture and class in early industrial Liverpool', in R. Schulze (ed.), *Industrie-Regionen im Umbruch. Industrial Regions in Transformation* (Veröffentlichungen des Instituts zur Erforschung der europäischen Arbeiterbewegung, Schriftenreihe A: Darstellungen, Bd.3), 119–45.

BOYCE, J. (1989), *Pillowslips and Gasmasks. Liverpool's Wartime Evacuation*, Liver Press, Birkenhead.

BURTON, V. (ed.) (1989), *Liverpool Shipping, Trade and Industry*, Liverpool.

COMPTON, P. J. (1992), 'Public health and mortality decline in late nineteenth-century Bordeaux', unpublished PhD dissertation, University of Liverpool.

DAVIES, S., P. GILL, L. GRANT, M. NIGHTINGALE, R. NOON and A. SHALLICE (1992), *Genuinely Seeking Work. Male Unemployment in Merseyside in the 1930s*, Liver Press, Birkenhead.

HYDE, F. E. (1971), *Liverpool and the Mersey. An Economic History of a Port: 1700–1970*, Newton Abbot.

JARVIS, A. (1991), *Liverpool Central Docks 1799–1905. An Illustrated History*, Bath.

JOHNSON, A. (1989), *Working the Tides. Gatemen and Masters on the River Mersey*, Liverpool.

JOHNSON, A. and K. MOORE (1987), *The Tapestry Makers. Life and Work at Lee's Tapestry Works, Birkenhead*, Birkenhead.

KEARNS, G., M. C. NELSON and J. ROGERS (1989), 'Portals of death. A research project', unpublished paper.

LAWTON, R. (1953), 'Genesis of population', in W. Smith (ed.), *A Scientific Survey of Merseyside*, Liverpool, 120–31.

LAWTON, R. (ed.) (1989), *The Rise and Fall of Great Cities. Aspects of Urbanisation in the Western World*, Belhaven Press, London.

LAWTON, R. and R. LEE (eds) (1989), *Urban Population Development in Western Europe from the Late-Eighteenth to the Early-Twentieth Century* (Liverpool Studies in European Population, 1), Liverpool.

LAWTON, R. and C. G. POOLEY (1976), *The Social Geography of Merseyside in the Nineteenth Century, Final Report to SSRC*, Liverpool.

LAXTON, P. (1981), 'Liverpool in 1801', *Transactions of the Historic Society of Lancashire and Cheshire*, **130**, 75–113.

LEE, W. R. and P. MARSCHALCK (1996), 'The dynamics of demographic change in a port-city context: Bremen, 1820–1910', in A. Bideau, A. Perrenoud, K.-A. Lynch and G. Brunnet (eds), *Les systèmes démographiques du passé*, Lyons, 123–38.

LEE, W. R. and P. MARSCHALCK (1998), 'Demographic change and industrialization in Germany, 1815–1914: Bremen in comparative perspective', *The History of the Family. An International Quarterly* (forthcoming).

LEIDINGER, B., W. R. LEE and P. MARSCHALCK (1997), 'Enforced convergence: political change and cause of death registration in the Hansestadt Bremen, 1860–1914?', *Continuity and Change*, **2**, 221–46.

LEWIS, F. (1993), 'The demographic and occupational structure of Liverpool: a study of the parish registers, 1600–1750', unpublished PhD dissertation, University of Liverpool.

MARRINER, S. (1982), *The Economic and Social Development of Merseyside*, London.

MILLER, A. (1988), *Poverty Deserved? Relieving the Poor in Victorian Liverpool*, Liver Press, Birkenhead.

MILNE, G. J. (2000), *Trade and Traders in Mid-Victorian Liverpool: Mercantile Business and the Making of a World Port*, Liverpool.

MOORE, K. (1989), *The Mersey Ship Repairers. Life and Work in a Port Industry*, Liverpool.

MURPHY, A. (1995), *From the Empire to the Rialto. Racism and Reaction in Liverpool 1918–1948*, Liver Press, Birkenhead.

NELSON, M. C. and J. ROGERS (1992), 'The right to die? Anti-vaccination activity and the 1874 smallpox epidemic in Stockholm', *Social History of Medicine*, **5** (3), 369–88.

POWER, M. J. (1992), 'The growth of Liverpool', in J. C. Belchem (ed.), *Popular Politics, Riot and Labour: Essays in Liverpool History 1790–1939*, Liverpool, 21–37.

RODGER, R. (1992), 'Urban history: prospect and retrospect', *Urban History*, **19** (1), 1–33.

ROGERS, J. and M. C. NELSON (1989), 'Controlling infectious diseases in ports: the importance of the military in central-local relations', in M. C. Nelson and J. Rogers (eds), *Urbanisation and the Epidemiologic Transition*, Uppsala, 1989, 83–108.

SHEARD, S. (1994), 'Nineteenth-century public health. A study of Liverpool, Belfast and Glasgow', unpublished PhD dissertation, University of Liverpool.

TAPLIN, E. L. (1978), 'Dock labour at Liverpool: occupational structure and working conditions in the late nineteenth century', *Transactions of the Historical Society of Lancashire and Cheshire*, **127**, 133–54.

URBAN, W. (1998), 'Die Stralsunder und die Choleraepidemien im 19. Jahrhundert', in W. R. Lee and W. Urban (eds), *Stadt und Bevölkerung bis zum Ende des 19. Jahrhunderts. Pommern im Vergleich*, Stralsund (forthcoming).

WONG, M. L. (1989), *Chinese Liverpudlians. A History of the Chinese Community in Liverpool*, Liver Press, Birkenhead.

Chapter 1

PORT DEVELOPMENT AND THE DEMOGRAPHIC DYNAMICS OF EUROPEAN URBANIZATION

ROBERT LEE and RICHARD LAWTON

Urbanization has been a critical component in European demographic change in the modern period and the scale of urban transformation has been extensive. By the early-seventeenth century only a fraction of Europe's population lived in cities or towns of over 10,000 inhabitants, but by the late-eighteenth century a substantial urban network, with a large and growing population, had been established. The nineteenth century, in turn, witnessed unprecedented population growth and rapid urban expansion, with a marked acceleration in large city growth (Lawton and Lee, 1989b). Moreover, initial variations in the pace and scale of urbanization in individual European states gradually gave way to a process of general convergence, with Europe's cities in the early-twentieth century largely dominated by national capitals, major ports and the regional capitals of highly industrialized regions.

But if an understanding of the nature of urban population processes is essential for an analysis of demographic and social change in modern Europe as a whole, the search for general explanatory models remains constrained by the continuing absence of detailed demographic studies of individual towns and cities. Recent research has not only challenged some of the basic assumptions concerning the alleged demographic costs of rapid urban growth, but has also highlighted the need for more disaggregated studies that allow the empirical testing of specific hypotheses on a micro-level. In particular a number of studies of individual European states (Lawton and Lee, 1989a) have pointed towards the existence of an identifiable typology of cities, with distinct demographic, economic and social characteristics, which represents a potential framework for examining key elements in urban population development in Western Europe.

The relevance of such an approach for historical population studies, particularly within a framework of an economic or occupational typology that distinguishes between communities dependent on textiles or heavy industry, great capital cities or seaports, was recognized at an early stage by Wrigley (1961). Significant demographic differences are visible within a European context, not only between high- and low-pressure demographic régimes, but also between specific socio-economic or occupational groups. Urban communities throughout Europe which depended primarily on coal-mining or heavy industry frequently registered high nuptiality and fertility rates, whereas textile manufacture, for example, was associated with low fertility (Haines, 1979). Large cities in the nineteenth century invariably suffered from high mortality and depended to a substantial degree for population growth on in-migration (Lawton, 1983). In both Germany and Sweden urban mortality was positively correlated with city size at least until the late-nineteenth century, and specific types of smaller-scale settlement, such as fishing communities, shared certain demographic characteristics (Kearns, Lee and Rogers, 1989; Lee, 1989).

The individual contributions to the present volume seek to explore the utility of an urban typology for examining the demographic dynamics of European urbanization by focusing on port-cities. The viability of such a typology, particularly in terms of comparative analysis within Western Europe as a whole, is reinforced by a number of hypotheses that effectively serve to integrate the individual micro-level studies of particular ports (Kearns, Nelson and Rogers, 1989). First, by the early-eighteenth century, if not earlier, Western Europe can be regarded as an effectively integrated area, with port-cities functioning as key connecting links in terms both of national and international trade and of capital and labour mobility (Konvitz, 1993). Secondly, despite important regional differences, at the start of the modern period Western Europe had developed a distinct epidemiological pattern which increasingly reflected the specific demographic impact of urban growth, of which the rapid expansion of port-cities and maritime commerce was an important component. Thirdly, port-cities, given their degree of interconnectedness, played an important role in the evolution of the general demographic régime of Western Europe. Not only did they function as significant transmitters of epidemic disease in the age of receding pandemics (Omran, 1971; Rogers and Nelson, 1989), but they were also a focal point for extensive migration and interchange both with their immediate hinterlands and their wider, international catchment areas. To this extent, changing conditions in port-cities arguably influenced the pattern of the epidemiological transition in Western Europe. Indeed, such an urban typology focusing specifically on the role of port-cities provides a means of pursuing some of the central issues connected with urban population development and demographic change in modern Europe as a whole.

By the seventeenth and eighteenth centuries urban development increasingly reflected a high degree of rationalization of economic activity between European towns (Hohenberg and Lees, 1985; Clark, 1984), primarily as a function of cumulative transport improvements. Even in the pre-industrial period marketing and trade were important factors affecting the pattern of urban expansion or decline, and ports, after capital cities, frequently recorded the greatest growth. Moreover, with the rapid expansion of specific trades, in particular the transatlantic trades, and the growth in the size of the merchant marine in many individual states (Johansen, 1992), the urban profile of

Western Europe was characterized by the increasing predominance of port-cities. Even in European regions of relative decline in the eighteenth century, such as Italy, ports still tended to develop at a faster rate than other cities and, despite the deceleration in French urban growth from the 1770s, port-cities remained unaffected by national population trends (Bairoch, 1988; Poussou, 1989). Maritime commerce was therefore a powerful factor behind European urbanization. Seaports accounted for almost 40 per cent of the world's great cities with more than 100,000 inhabitants in 1850 (Lawton and Lee, 1989b) and it was not until the mid-twentieth century that the role of port-cities in the European urban hierarchy was eclipsed by industrial towns and conurbations (Hohenberg and Lees, 1985).

The role of port-cities in the general process of urban development was particularly evident in a number of European states, for example, France, Germany, Holland, Ireland, Norway, Sweden and the United Kingdom (Lawton and Lee, 1989a). In Spain urbanization was essentially a coastal phenomenon: apart from the capital, Madrid, all the large cities (Barcelona, Cadiz, Malaga, Seville and Valencia) were on or near the coast (Alemanny, 1984; Fernández Armestoa, 1992). French ports—such as Bordeaux, Marseilles, Nantes and Rouen—were also important regional capitals, and many of the new towns of the late-seventeenth century, including Brest, Lorient, Cherbourg and Rochefort, had been created explicitly for naval purposes (Poussou, 1989). Rochefort, for example, was chosen for its remoteness, defensibility and size, as a suitable location for the building and fitting out of the French Atlantic fleet (Konvitz, 1978). During the eighteenth century maritime ports in France generally experienced the greatest population expansion (Meyer, 1983), particularly those situated on the Atlantic coast. In the Netherlands the port-cities of Amsterdam and Rotterdam registered rapid development and dominated the country's urban pattern. Gothenburg, the chief port of Sweden, was and remains the second city; and in Norway, which had a higher proportion of urban population in the nineteenth century than Sweden, towns were invariably coastal (Pounds, 1985). Ports were among the fastest growing urban communities in eighteenth-century France (until 1792), Germany and Spain, as well as in nineteenth-century Italy (Nadal, 1984; Poussou, 1985, p. 339; del Panta, 1989).

In the case of Britain a period of almost perpetual naval warfare in the eighteenth century undoubtedly benefited dockyard towns and fleet stations, such as Chatham, Falmouth, Harwich, Portsmouth and Rochester (Stapleton, chapter 7, below; Clark, 1984). Particularly from the 1740s Plymouth and Portsmouth witnessed striking population growth as a result of a significant increase in naval expenditure. With the rapid expansion of maritime trading, particularly the Atlantic and colonial trades, and the increasing competitiveness of manufactured products in international markets, many port-cities in Britain registered substantial population growth, so that by 1801, 21 of the 54 largest towns with more than 10,000 inhabitants were seaports (Lawton, chapter 4, below). Of the ten largest boroughs in England and Wales in 1851, five (Liverpool, Bristol, the City of London, Newcastle and Kingston-upon-Hull) were ports and in the course of the second half of the nineteenth century many of the major commercial ports, such as Liverpool, maintained population growth rates well in excess of the national average.

The relative importance of port-cities within the urban profile of Western Europe, as a whole, was reinforced during the nineteenth century. Although the structure of European trade was marked by the changing importance of Third World exports and a relative stability of imports from more developed countries, increasing diversification in international trade and improved technical organization contributed to a significant growth in trade activity (Bairoch, 1974). International ship movements, for example, increased at an annual rate of 4.7 per cent between 1872 and 1889 and the overall value of world trade rose by 4.8 per cent per annum between 1860 and 1890, despite cyclical influences (Von Juraschek, 1896). In the case of Genoa, as Felloni (chapter 3, below) indicates, sea-borne trade expanded at an annual rate of 12 per cent in the 1850s and 1880s. It is not surprising, therefore, that individual port-cities frequently registered intense population growth. For example, Malmö reported an annual increase in resident population of 12.4 per cent (1820–1914) (see Fridlizius, chapter 5, below), Kiel grew at an annual rate of 16.2 per cent (1867–1914) (Wulf, 1991), and Cardiff by a rate of 20.4 per cent per annum (1825–1871) (Daunton, 1977). The increasing predominance of the transatlantic trades, however, was accompanied by a relative decline in the importance of the Baltic and Mediterranean trading areas, at least during the late-eighteenth and early-nineteenth centuries, and a number of ports, such as Königsberg, Amsterdam, Stockholm and Venice, as a result, only registered weak population growth (Felloni, 1977; Söderberg et al., 1991).

However, the variance in the population growth rates of individual ports, particularly in the second half of the nineteenth century, indicates the extent to which international trade diversification was accompanied by further port specialization. This also heightened the distinction between first- and second-rank ports and reinforced the role of the major ports within the urban hierarchy of individual European countries. In most parts of Europe an increasing distinction became evident between leading ports, with improved dock facilities and a developed transport infrastructure to major industrial regions, and medium-sized or smaller centres of trading activity, often concentrating on coasting traffic (Clark, 1984). The rapid growth of first-rank ports in this context was often associated with an increased diversification in function and an accelerated domination of the surrounding hinterland.

Inevitably, significant differences existed between various types of ports. A functional classification must distinguish between a considerable variety of port types (Sargent, 1938; Morgan, 1952; Bird, 1963), including naval ports, with a small or negligible amount of commercial traffic, fishing and ferry ports, with the latter increasingly specialized in function (Derville and Vion, 1985, chapter V), entrepôt and free ports, as well as outports such as Cuxhaven and St Nazaire. The development of liner ports was also linked with the expansion of cargo traffic. The export of manufactures from North-West England, from Liverpool, for example, provided an inducement to many liner companies to sail from the same port, just as the increased emphasis on bulk imports including cotton, sugar and timber encouraged the development of the emigrant trade as a viable and profitable return cargo (Williams, 1989; Morgan, 1952).

Even within individual port categories certain differences were apparent. Among the English naval ports, for example, Plymouth was noted for a certain amount of commercial traffic, including passenger liners and coastal trade, whereas Portsmouth witnessed consistent attempts by the naval authorities to restrict commercial activity (Stapleton, chapter 7, below). In the case of Germany, the port of Kiel, although predominantly devoted to naval interests after 1865, still managed to retain its traditional transit trade with Sweden; Wilhelmshafen, on the other hand, was entirely a naval base (Jensen and Wulf, 1991; Maierhöfer, 1986). Similarly in France, although the economy of Brest remained highly dependent on the maritime fortress, the Second Empire witnessed a perceptible expansion of local commerce, whereas the increase in French overseas expeditions in the post-1815 period, including the conquest of Algiers, only served to reinforce the importance of the naval base at Toulon and left little room for the development of commerce and private industry (Le Gallo, 1976; Agulhon, 1980). In a broader context, river ports, such as Grenelle and Saint-Ouen in France, or resort-based ports, such as Brighton or Bognor Regis in England, cannot be strictly compared with major ports, such as Copenhagen, London or Stockholm, which maintained a multi-functional role as capital cities (Ratcliffe, 1985; Dale, 1976; Young, 1983). However, with the exception of the naval base of Portsmouth, all the contributions to the present volume focus on major commercial ports which expanded significantly in the late-eighteenth and nineteenth centuries; in this context Bremen, Genoa, Glasgow, Hamburg, Liverpool, Malmö, Nantes, Trieste and, to a lesser extent, Cork constitute a perceptible sub-group within the broader port-city typology.

THE DEMOGRAPHIC CHARACTERISTICS OF PORT-CITIES

The hypothesis that the demographic profile of a city is, at least in part, a reflection of its function suggests that different city types can be associated historically with the role of different components in urban population growth. Differences in occupational structure, social stratification and income distribution, which often varied according to city type, were also reflected systematically in the demography of individual urban communities. Within the German urban system of the nineteenth century, for example, although the level of fertility (I_g) and the birth rate were primarily influenced by regional factors and city location, both the proportion married (I_m) and overall fertility (I_f) were directly related to city function (Laux, 1983; 1989; Lee, 1978). Throughout the eighteenth and nineteenth centuries European port-cities often recorded an above-average rate of population growth and particularly in relation to the larger commercial ports (such as Bremen, Genoa, Glasgow, Hamburg, Liverpool, Malmö, Nantes and Trieste, which are the subject of individual contributions to the present volume), it is reasonable to posit the existence of a number of common demographic characteristics.

Mortality

Because of their transport links the mortality profile of port-cities reflected an increased risk of exposure, particularly to infectious diseases. They were often vulnerable to ship-borne infections and some of the dominant epidemic diseases of the nineteenth century were primarily coastal phenomena (Vincent, 1988). Indeed the development of steam ships may well have increased initially the risk of epidemic infection (Falliner, 1978). As Fridlizius (chapter 5, below) points out, streptococcal infection was first imported via port-cities which, in turn, then accelerated disease diffusion on account of their extensive transport links. Port-cities, therefore, functioned as connecting links within the distinct epidemiological pattern of Western Europe. Despite the imposition of both external and internal quarantine measures, Toulon witnessed the direct importation of the plague in 1720 from Marseilles (Agulhon, 1980; Bertrand, 1973) and the transmission of epidemic disease was often facilitated by a concern among the merchant élites of port-cities that restrictive measures aimed at isolating the sick should not disrupt trade unnecessarily (Cameron, 1984).

Certainly for many contemporaries there appeared to be a direct link between long-distance or overseas migration and the proliferation of epidemic disease in port-cities. Irish immigration into Cardiff and other mainland British ports in the late 1840s and early 1850s, for example, was closely associated with the local incidence of disease and Irish lodging-houses were known to have harboured cholera victims (Lewis, 1980). Cholera was inevitably spread along shipping routes, resulting in a disproportionate impact on port-cities such as Bilbao, Grimsby, Malmö and Nantes (Iturbe Mach, 1986; Gillett, 1970; Fridlizius, chapter 5, below; Cameron, 1984). In the cholera outbreak of 1832, for example, French ports had a higher case fatality rate than most inland towns and conditions in Dieppe were truly catastrophic (Becchia, 1990). The epidemic was also particularly severe in Cork, perhaps as a reflection of high population density (O'Brien, chapter 11, below). In Glasgow the disease claimed 3,000 victims between February and November (Gibb, chapter 2, below). The severity of the 1850 cholera epidemic in Stralsund led to the town's highest annual crude mortality rate for the whole of the nineteenth century (Urban, 1998). As a function of their transport links and high migration levels port-cities played an important role as transmitters of epidemic disease and changing conditions in these cities, in turn, influenced the pace of the epidemiological transition (Omran, 1971).

Ports such as Genoa (Felloni, chapter 6, below), Hamburg (Lindemann, 1990) and Southampton (Patterson, 1966) remained susceptible to wartime dislocation, particularly in the eighteenth century. A sudden or enforced reduction in living standards following the disruption of traditional trading links often had significant demographic effects, producing in the case of Rochefort a dramatic excess of deaths over births during the War of the Spanish Succession (Konvitz, 1978). Many of the Baltic ports, such as Pernau, Narva and Tallinn, were so seriously affected by the Great Northern War (1700–1721) that their demographic recovery was a long drawn-out process (Pullat, 1988; Pullat and Mereste, 1982). Maritime conflict could quickly erode commercial wealth dependent on the relatively fragile basis of colonial imports, particularly in cases such as Bordeaux where commercial expansion in the course of the eighteenth century had not been accompanied by any significant diversification in the employment structure of the city (Poussou, 1983). In this context, the Napoleonic Wars and the imposition of the continental blockade occasioned a major disruption of foreign trade and led to significant investment losses in such ports as Genoa and Trieste (see below, chapters 3 and 6). In general the prosperity of many ports rested by definition on a limited number of sectors that were subject to international markets and cyclical volatility in this context frequently had a pronounced impact on the demographic profile of port-cities, particularly in relation to mortality and nuptiality (Montanari, 1989).

Although not all port-cities conformed to the law of urban natural decrease (de Vries, 1984), many continued to register high levels of mortality well into the nineteenth century: Bordeaux, for example, recorded a significant mortality surplus between 1851 and 1872, as did Toulon in the period 1874–93 (Guillaume, 1969a, p. 240; Agulhon, 1980). Largely because of its polluted water supply, Marseilles witnessed the last major cholera epidemic in France in 1854 (Preston and van der Walle, 1978; Hohenberg and Lees, 1985), whereas the preconditions for the cholera outbreak in Hamburg in 1892, which killed almost 10,000 people within the space of six weeks, were a function of the specific economic, social and political structure of Germany's premier port-city (Evans, 1987). Glasgow was equally susceptible to fever epidemics and periodical mortality crises were often connected with high levels of cholera and typhus mortality (Gibb, chapter 2, below). Although crude mortality peaked in the period 1845–1849, there was no significant decline below the rates for the early-nineteenth century until the 1890s (Cage, 1987).

Throughout the first half of the nineteenth century Stockholm also revealed a demographic structure in which extremely high mortality was a key phenomenon and its port function undoubtedly contributed to high levels of population turnover and exposure to disease (Söderberg et al., 1991; Zacke, 1971). Glasgow and Liverpool frequently registered very high mortality rates and were perceived by contemporaries as particularly unhealthy cities, while Bordeaux, Marseilles, Nantes and Rouen, even at the end of the nineteenth century, recorded consistently high mortality rates from food- and water-borne diseases, well above the average for the eleven largest French towns (Compton, 1992).

Apart from the mortality consequences of increased exposure to epidemic diseases, as a function of trading links and migration streams, the predominance of unskilled or casual employment, in conjunction with residential overcrowding and poor quality housing, also contributed to relatively high death rates in many port-cities. At a disease-specific level major outbreaks of typhus frequently occurred in individual port-cities; in 1818, for example, approximately 33 per cent of Cork's population was infected with typhus fever (O'Brien, chapter 11, below) and in Glasgow, as Gibb indicates (chapter 2, below), it had an exceptionally high case fatality rate. These epidemics were often particularly severe in unskilled working-class areas of poor and insanitary housing, associated directly in the case of Cardiff and Liverpool with the prevalence of Irish immigrants and congested housing conditions (Lewis, 1980; Hardy, 1988). Tuberculosis mortality remained excessively high in the French ports of Boulogne and Nantes, with no significant decline in the latter case registered until the late 1920s (Oustric, 1983a, p. 236; Leroux, 1985). In both instances, a combination of factors typical of many cities in the nineteenth century, but particularly prevalent in European ports, contributed to this phenomenon. Extensive poverty remained a key characteristic of Boulogne, with over ten per cent of the port's population receiving public assistance in the 1890s, and the local concentration of tuberculosis mortality in Nantes reflected a level of over-crowding significantly in excess of the French national average.

High levels of infant and child mortality also tended to be a characteristic of many ports, whether in Hamburg-Altona (Gehrmann, 1994), Bordeaux (Guillaume, 1969b), Cardiff (Lewis, 1980), Dublin (Dickson, 1989) or in Trieste (Cattaruzza, chapter 6, below). Infant and child deaths constituted 54 per cent of total mortality in Glasgow in 1861 and between 40 and 60 per cent of all annual deaths in Liverpool in the mid-Victorian period. Although high infant mortality rates were commonly registered in many different types of urban community in nineteenth-century Europe, some port-cities appear to have been particularly vulnerable. Even at the end of the century Trieste still had an infant mortality rate of 22.26 (per 100 live births) (chapter 6, below), a figure only exceeded by a number of Baltic ports, including Danzig, Stettin and St Petersburg. High infant and child mortality rates in port-cities undoubtedly reflected the interaction of a complex set of economic, environmental and epidemiological variables. In Glasgow (chapter 2, below) and Trieste (chapter 6, below) severely congested living conditions and a high degree of residential segregation were critical factors, but a general absence of breast-feeding in the latter case, or poor infant health care in general, also contributed to high mortality levels (van Aalen, 1985). Many port-cities, perhaps reflecting their specific occupational structure, unbalanced sex ratios and population turnover, recorded unusually high illegitimacy ratios. Moreover, as in Glasgow, illegitimate infant mortality was often twice the legitimate rate, so that the extent of illegitimacy was a further important factor in the persistence of high overall infant mortality rates in many port-cities. From an epidemiological perspective, exposure rates to epidemic disease for both infants and children in seaports were noticeably higher than in other urban centres. As in the case of mid-nineteenth century Malmö (chapter 5, below) improved transport links aggravated existing exposure rates and contributed to the noticeable increase in child mortality between 1850 and 1880, just as high levels of in-migration in port-cities accelerated the spread of diseases affecting infants and young children (Lewis, 1980).

Shipping losses, particularly in ports which had a high dependency on fishing such as Boulogne, Grimsby or Lowestoft, exacted a high mortality toll and threatened the livelihood of many families (Oustric, 1983b; Gillett, 1970; Malster, 1982). In the eighteenth century piracy often had a similar effect (Cieślak, 1972) and the high mortality rate of British sea-captains involved in the slave trade confirms the implicit dangers of a seafaring career (Behrendt, 1990). The working conditions of seamen in the nineteenth century were particularly bad (Herkscher, 1903), especially for stokers on steam ships, and fatalities were disproportionately high (Kiupel, 1983). The opposition of shipowners to new safety requirements negated potential improvements to the hazards of the sea, as reflected in the annual loss of 470 sailors in Norwegian ports throughout the 1880s and 1890s (Gjølberg, 1978). The proliferation of unskilled and frequently dangerous jobs, connected primarily with cargo-handling and dock-related activities, contributed to high adult mortality and morbidity, specifically among male in-migrants, as the evidence from Bremen suggests (Lee and Marschalck, chapter 8, below). With the frequent preponderance in port-cities of large numbers of single young men, prostitution was common and in many naval ports, such as Portsmouth (chapter 7, below) or Toulon (Agulhon, 1980), it remained extensive despite selective efforts at municipal control: naval ports were also included among the eighteen 'protected districts' covered by the Contagious Diseases Acts in Britain of 1864, 1866 and 1869 (Smith, 1990). Indeed given the social composition and employment structure of many port-cities, such efforts were inevitably ineffective. The recorded incidence of prostitution in Boulogne during the first half of the nineteenth century increased noticeably (Oustric, 1983b) and by the 1890s eleven separate houses were regularly used by prostitutes in the port-city of Stralsund (Neumerkel, 1992, p. 18). Under such circumstances, it is not surprising that the recorded incidence of venereal disease was disproportionately high in port-cities, nor that adult mortality rates were accordingly inflated (Schönfeld, 1941; Tjaden, 1932).

The rapidity of city growth in many parts of nineteenth-century Europe was often accompanied by urban dislocation and distress. In this respect major ports, such as those examined in the individual chapters of this book, were not necessarily exceptional. However, within the urban hierarchy of Western European states, many of the major commercial ports, particularly those with strong links with the Atlantic and colonial trades, recorded above-average population growth rates, albeit at different points in time, which undoubtedly exacerbated the health risks of urban expansion. The individual demographic régimes of large ports were moulded by similar factors, with larger ports acting as reservoirs of disease (Fridlizius, chapter 5, below). An extended trading and communications network and high levels of in-migration aggravated the latent exposure risks of the indigenous population. Unavoidable constraints on residential development, particularly in naval ports, tended to reinforce the mortality consequences of urban congestion, while the specific occupational and socio-economic structure of major port-cities associated with an exceptional degree of social inequality, ethnic segregation, and susceptibility to periodic crises contributed to unusually high overall mortality rates and strengthened the persistence of a particularly high-pressure demographic régime in many of the seaports under examination (Guillaume, 1972; Fahy, chapter 10, below).

Nuptiality and fertility

The significance of city function can also be detected in relation to nuptiality and fertility (Laux, 1989). In port-cities nuptiality was often constrained by skewed sex ratios, in turn a function of gender-specific migration streams, urban structure and employment opportunities (Reher, 1989; Cattaruzza, chapter 6, below). The fishing industry, which flourished in many of the major commercial ports, had an insatiable demand for young crews: in Grimsby, for example, there were three apprentices in a crew of five, often provided directly from the workhouse by the local guardians (Gillett, 1970). Naval ports, such as Cartagena, Kiel, Portsmouth and Toulon, had an age- and sex-structure that continued to reflect a close dependency on naval affairs: *La Marine* in Toulon, including those employed in the arsenal and all naval personnel, accounted for almost half the port's total population in 1881 (Agulhon, 1980) and a similar situation existed in Brest (Le Gallo, 1976), Kiel (Wulf, 1991) and Portsmouth (Stapleton, chapter 7, below). Added to this, limited opportunities for female work, especially in specialist ports, reduced marriage opportunities and limited nuptiality rates. Average age at first marriage, whether in Glasgow or Toulon, was relatively late, despite the absence in port-cities of institutional or legal constraints on marriage that were still selectively applied in various regions and cities of Europe, particularly in the first half of the nineteenth century (Matz, 1980; Lynch, 1991). In the case of Bremen average age at first marriage rose during the course of the nineteenth century from 25.0 to 26.6 years (Marschalck, 1990). Moreover, in-migrants, who played a significant role in moulding the demographic dynamics of port-cities, also had a higher age at first marriage than the more established, indigenous population (Cage, 1987; Agulhon, 1980) and completed family size was perceptively smaller (Lee and Marschalck, 1998; see below, chapter 8).

By contrast, nineteenth-century port-cities were characterized by high birth rates and high fertility, which were intrinsically linked with contemporary employment structures. Sailors, at least in the seventeenth and early-eighteenth centuries, tended to marry at an early age and to select young brides (Boulton, 1990; Lewis, 1993). The predominance of casual, unskilled work arguably encouraged a high birth rate by truncating the earnings curve for men and by prioritizing the economic function of children, just as the limited opportunities for female employment, at least within the formal structures of port-city economies (see chapters 4 and 6, below), encouraged high fertility and a comparatively late onset of the secular fertility transition (Woods, 1984, 1987). Moreover, the larger commercial ports in general had a disproportionate distribution of occupations, such as riveters and ship-platers, as well as general labourers, which consistently registered the highest marital fertility rates (Haines, 1979; Lawton, chapter 4, below). The persistence of high rates of infant mortality in many port-cities, significant levels of in-migration and its youthful age structure, continued to encourage this tendency towards high birth rates into the early-twentieth century.

IN-MIGRATION

Although their demographic history can only be fully understood in terms of their regional location and their specific position within a national urban hierarchy, the population development of the major commercial ports of Western Europe in the eighteenth and nineteenth centuries was strongly influenced by a number of key demographic characteristics, one of which was a disproportionate dependency for population growth on in-migration and the specific configuration of migrant streams. Migration to a port-city may well have been a viable alternative to emigration, as O'Brien (chapter 11) argues for Cork, and this may explain why migration in Germany was most significant in commercial and service centres, particularly in the major ports (Laux, 1989). The population development in the nineteenth century of all the port-cities covered by this volume was undeniably dependent on a high and persistent level of in-migration. In the case of Genoa, for example (chapter 3, below), in-migration was the key determinant of demographic development; similarly, the growth of Glasgow in the period 1820 to 1850 was primarily a function of large-scale in-migration (Gibb, chapter 2, below). Fifty-three per cent of the registered increase in Bremen's total population between 1812 and 1914 (Marschalck, 1990; chapter 8, below) and 60 per cent in the case of Hamburg (1871–1910) (see Wischermann, chapter 9, below) was due to in-migration, reflecting the fact that economic growth in nineteenth-century Europe was invariably accompanied by increased migrant flows into the expanding centres of commerce and trade (Daunton, 1977). In many cases, as in Bordeaux, Toulon and Naples (Desgraves and Dupeux, 1969; Hohenberg and Lees, 1985; Agulhon, 1980), the level of in-migration rose over time. Port-cities, in any case, frequently had a large floating or transient population and if they offered additional functions, such as resort or bathing facilities, were also noted for seasonal migration patterns (Ruddel and Lafrance, 1985; Curtis, 1986; Young, 1983; Péronas, 1961). The nature and scale of in-migration in the course of the nineteenth century, in turn, played a key role in determining their overall demographic profile.

Variations in the frequency and range of the migration flows can systematically affect nuptiality and fertility both in the rural hinterland and in expanding urban areas (de Vries, 1984) and many port-cities, such as La Rochelle, frequently had a wide migration area at a comparatively early date (Péronas, 1961). In evaluating the broader significance of port-city in-migration, a number of points need to be made. First, as a function of their transport links, port-cities were often noted for the extent of long-distance immigration, as in the case of Bilbao (Shubert, 1990), as well as a more extended migration zone than other comparable urban centres (Hohenberg and Lees, 1985). Moreover, as a number of empirical case studies confirm, during the course of the eighteenth and nineteenth centuries port-cities tended to attract an increasingly higher proportion of their migrants from more distant locations (Agulhon, 1984; Konvitz, 1978). For example, long-distance migrants were particularly noticeable among Liverpool apprentices (Rawling, 1986). Secondly, as a result of the continuing importance of sea-borne transportation, port-cities tended to attract a significant proportion of overseas, or non-national, migrants, given that the final choice of destination was often a function of information availability disseminated through existing communication networks (Poussou, 1989; Poulain, 1990). At one level, a port such as Boulogne, dependent increasingly on cross-Channel passenger traffic, witnessed a significant growth in its resident foreign community during the first half of the nineteenth century (Oustric, 1983a, p. 208). In a more general sense, however, all port-cities, as a function of their overseas trading links, tended to develop a variegated ethnic structure. Although migration was often occupation- and age-specific, as in the case of the 'keelmen' in Newcastle or the Polish miners in the Ruhr (Ellis, 1984; Klessmann, 1978; Murphy, 1983), the particular migration traditions of port-cities resulted in a broader ethnic mix than was the case in other types of urban centres. Because of their international connections port-cities often tended to attract human capital and drained natural resources from relatively far-away regions (Hohenberg and Lees, 1985). As Felloni indicates (chapter 3, below), Genoa housed migrants from all over the Mediterranean; Trieste accommodated different Armenian, Greek, Jewish and Serbian 'nations' (chapter 6, below), and the attractiveness of port-cities in general was reinforced by their relative size and existing ethnic complexity in line with Ravenstein's law of migration that the larger the town, the greater the proportion of long-distance migrants (Dennis, 1984). The large-scale Irish immigration and settlement within the United Kingdom after the famine, for example, was most marked in port-cities, such as Liverpool, Glasgow, Cardiff and Hull, generating, in turn, a secondary diffusion effect in the hinterland of the major ports (Gillett and MacMahon, 1980; Lewis, 1980; Coney, 1989; Gibb, chapter 2, below; Devine, 1995). The distance-decay gradient of migration into Liverpool fluctuated on a decennial basis throughout the nineteenth century, but Ireland remained the main source of migrants, except during the depression of the 1880s (see below, chapter 4); by 1845 the Irish-born proportion of Glasgow's population already amounted to 25 per cent and if those of Irish extraction are included around one in three of the city's inhabitants were of Irish descent (Devine, 1988, p. 43). Similarly, immigrant Italian communities were most strongly represented in the French ports of Bordeaux, Marseilles and Nantes (Compton, 1992; Sewell, 1985; Leroux, 1985).

Most immigrant groups in nineteenth-century cities were characterized by a marked degree of residential segregation with initial settlement associated with low socio-economic status, poor housing and overcrowding. Only in exceptional cases, as in Hamburg, does it appear that new migrants were not subject to appreciable spatial segregation (see below, chapter 9). Immigrant groups, such as the Irish, undoubtedly had a profound effect on the long-term process of social and structural change in such port-cities as Glasgow and Liverpool (Neal, 1988; Lawton, 1991). They were often forced to rent the poorest available property, with occupancy rates in excess of the national average. Moreover, the sons of foreign-born workers, as in the case of the Italians in Marseilles, invariably suffered from very low rates of upward mobility (Sewell, 1981). As Anderson (1982) has indicated, individual ethnic groups had different traditions in relation to transience and mobility and the extent, nature and ethnic composition of in-migration in port-cities may well have increased the rate of intra-urban mobility (Lawton, 1989). The particular balance between the more stable or established social core of port-cities, as in Brest (Le Gallo, 1976) with its 'municipal caste', and migrant groups characterized by high mobility and low social status, undoubtedly affected the distribution of power in those communities, but the high degree of ethnic in-migration typical of many port-cities also reinforced their existing demographic profile. For example, migration was frequently linked with an increased incidence of disease, as in the case of the contemporary association of Irish immigration into Liverpool with inflated typhus mortality (Lawton, 1989), while the incidence of typhus in Cardiff was directly related to congested housing and Irish occupation (Lewis, 1980). Increased long-distance migration in this context was synonymous with a higher exposure risk, as Fridlizius notes below (chapter 5). In a more general sense, the low economic status of many ethnic groups within port-cities and their continuing dependency on casual, unskilled employment and poor quality housing had a negative effect on overall mortality trends and, in particular, on infant mortality.

THE LOCAL ECONOMY AND LABOUR MARKETS OF PORT-CITIES

The structure of migration flows into many port-cities in the course of the nineteenth century, however, also reflected a further specific characteristic of these urban communities that had substantial significance for their demographic development. Foreign trade was seldom by itself a sufficient cause for industrialization, although Barcelona became a key centre for the Spanish cotton industry (Thomson, 1992), while the linen industry and, to a lesser extent, cotton production were key factors in the growth of Belfast (Geary, 1981; Ollerenshaw, 1992) and Glasgow developed a pronounced industrial base (see chapter 2, below). However, with increasing functional specialization within the urban hierarchy of individual European nation states in the course of the nineteenth century, the local economy of many port-cities became disproportionately dominated by shipping and port-related activities. Many port-cities failed to sustain a strong and widely-based manufacturing industry and tended to concentrate on processing or refining imported raw materials, particularly colonial products and bulk cargoes. While ports invariably acted as centres for a variety of activities—from warehousing to trade, banking and insurance (Montanari, 1989; Ollerenshaw, 1992, p. 68)—port-related industries such as artisan-based cooperage, flour-milling, fish-canning, soap-boiling, sugar-refining, spice-grinding and, at a later stage, petroleum-refining predominated (Hohenberg and Lees, 1985). In Nantes, for example, the production of tinned food, biscuit-making, sugar-refining and rice-milling were well-established industries and the later development of the chemical industry was equally dependent on the port's import trade of natural phosphates and superphosphates (Leroux, 1985). Marseilles, with its transport links to North Africa and the Far East, particularly after the opening of the Suez Canal in 1869, attracted a broad spectrum of port industries, but soap-boiling and textile factories processing imported wool and cotton were particularly important (Chabaud, 1883; Pounds, 1985). Bordeaux became one of the centres for imported colonial sugar and, following the recovery of the port's economy after the dislocation of the Napoleonic period, 37 sugar refineries were in production by 1840 (Casey, 1981). In individual cases, such as Cardiff, effective industrial development was hindered by supply-side constraints (Daunton, 1977), but in most ports the increasing primacy of a trading and shipping function effectively crowded out the possibility of significant diversification into industrial manufacturing. Industrial undertakings in Cork, Bordeaux and Stralsund, for example, remained largely small-scale, reflecting a fragmented employment structure, and wool manufacture in Danzig collapsed from the early-eighteenth century onwards as shipping interests became more predominant (O'Brien, below, chapter 11; Lee, 1998; Hübner, 1925; Desgraves and Dupeux, 1969).

Although the present century has witnessed the development of industrial ports with the spatial relocation of the steel industry and the shore-based expansion of the chemical industry, as at Ellesmere Port and Nantes (Aspinall and Hudson, 1982; Leroux, 1985), throughout most of the nineteenth century only general port industries, such as flour-milling, feedstuffs, leather-tanning (as on Merseyside and in Bristol and Hull) and the processing of 'colonial' products, including sugar-refining at Liverpool and Nantes, tended to predominate (Morgan, 1952; Leroux, 1985; Smith, 1953). In Liverpool, which is not atypical of the situation prevailing in many major port-cities, it was noted that 'there is probably no city of anything like equal size in which so small a proportion of the population is maintained by permanent and industrial work' (Muir, 1907, p. 306). Although Glasgow was able to shift its sectoral emphasis throughout the nineteenth century from cotton production to the iron and engineering industries and, increasingly, to ship-building, it retained a narrow employment base noted by low wages and the persistence of labour-intensive methods of production (Rodger, 1976). Even when ports benefited from a perceptible diversification in their employment structure, particularly from the late-nineteenth century onwards, the new industrial sectors remained characterized by a low technological level and a continuing dependency on raw material imports, as Cattaruzza shows (see chapter 6, below).

In certain cases the extent to which port-based industries were directly related to the sea was very explicit. Ship-building became an important source of employment in ports such as Barcelona, Belfast, Bergen, Birkenhead, Bremen, Hamburg and Rostock, as well as on the Tyne, Wear and Clyde (Montanari, 1989; Armitage, 1992; Thowsen, 1973; Kuckuk and Roder, 1988; Sprandel, 1986; Bernitt, 1956), just as the development of ropery works in Grimsby, or nail-making in Nantes, betrayed a similar dependency on sea-related activity (Gillett, 1970; Leroux, 1985). The accelerated fleet construction programme in Germany before 1914 stimulated the proliferation of supply industries for anchors, chains and navigational equipment in Kiel (Wulf, 1991). Indeed, during the course of the eighteenth and nineteenth centuries the greatest European ports, on the whole, frequently became the chief ship-building centres both in Britain and on the Continent (Morgan, 1952).

Naval ports, in particular, evinced to an extreme degree the two key elements of a port-city economy. As already indicated, the naval authorities were often anxious to restrain competition from commercial enterprises and land-based employment was often dependent to a high degree on opportunities provided by the provisioning and servicing of the fleet. The merchants of Toulon, for example, were encouraged to concentrate on provisioning the local military establishment and, apart from extensive property investments, showed little inclination to diversify their commercial interests (Agulhon, 1980). Lorient and

Brest, in this context, had great difficulty in achieving long-run economic autonomy (Hohenberg and Lees, 1985). A privileged status in terms of victualling navy and army supply ships was a critical factor in Cork's prosperity in the late-eighteenth century, as O'Brien shows in chapter 11. But for many naval ports the extent of such dependency was often problematical. In the late-seventeenth and eighteenth centuries royal penury and naval recession had an immediate and adverse effect on the local economy of such naval ports as Rochefort (Konvitz, 1978) and the overall needs of the navy dictated the rhythm of economic development in Toulon and Portsmouth. In the former case, for example, naval personnel and their families accounted for 21 per cent of the port's total population by 1891 (Agulhon, 1980). The central importance of the naval arsenal, whether in British, French or German naval ports, often left virtually no room for the development of commerce and private industry or for any noticeable diversification within the local economy.

The nature and development of specific port-city economies were reflected in distinct similarities in the operation of their labour markets in the nineteenth century. In many ports the existence of a flexible pool of temporary manpower was traditionally viewed as the most effective way of meeting the fluctuating demand for dock labour. Many trades, whether coal exports from Newcastle or raw cotton imports into Liverpool, were, by definition, seasonal, as were many other port-based occupations such as fishing and ship-building (Williams, 1989; Dale, 1976). If Trieste, on the one hand, registered a long-term growth in the volume of shipping using its port facilities as Cattaruzza indicates (see chapter 6, below), other ports, such as Le Havre or Marseilles, were marked by an increasing degree of annual volatility in terms of the value and volume of goods handled (Desgraves and Dupeux, 1969). In addition to the high 'floating' population, especially in naval ports, the seasonal nature of port-city labour markets in general had important implications. Unskilled employment was predominant, constituting a distinctive secondary labour market accompanied by low wages, casualism, an absence of training, residential immobility and ethnic separateness, as in Liverpool (Anderson, 1991; Lawton, chapter 4, below). Low wages and casual labour remained associated with dock employment, as well as the building trades, because it was widely believed that it was 'both natural and essential' for a casual system of employment to apply in the port transport industry (Williamson, 1990; Jackson, 1973, p. 5). Dockers in Hull, for example, were known as 'lumpers' and were generally regarded as the most degraded of workers, 'treated more like brute beasts than rational beings' (Gillett and MacMahon, 1980, p. 281). The introduction of labour-saving methods of cargo-handling in Marseilles in the 1860s with the opening of a new *dock à l'anglais* effectively reduced dockworkers to little more than unskilled labourers (Sewell, 1988). In Liverpool the principal source of employment at the beginning of the twentieth century remained the handling of goods between ships, warehouses and the railway network, '...a function which is mainly performed by unskilled labour', including approximately

25,000 dockers (Muir, 1907; Anderson, 1991). High nominal wages attracted casual labour, with overall supply inflated by continuing in-migration. But the casualism of dock labour in many European ports was associated with a static earnings curve, high seasonal and cyclical unemployment and a fragility of working-class family budgets which allowed confidence men to flourish, such as the 'Gombeen men' in Liverpool offering small loans at extortionate rates (Taplin, 1978; Anderson, 1991). The continuing predominance of unskilled male work in port-city economies inevitably placed a premium on the earnings capacity of other family members. In Hamburg, for example, the earnings of children were often important for family survival (May, 1915) and in Boulogne ten-year-old children were commonly sent to sea (Oustric, 1983b). Although this was a common feature of many urban working-class communities in the nineteenth century, at least prior to the effective introduction of compulsory primary education, it was arguably more apparent in towns such as ports where casual employment was disproportionately high.

Of even greater importance, in this context, was the contribution of married women to the family economy, despite the fact that port-cities were noted for a general lack of female employment opportunities outside the sphere of domestic service. Although in fishing ports, such as Fleetwood, women could sometimes find specific niches in the labour market as 'braiders' (Curtis, 1986) and the growth of certain service industries or home-based clothing trades, such as stay-making in Portsmouth (chapter 7, below), provided employment for a segment of the reserve army of female labour, in most port-cities employment opportunities for women within the formal economy remained very limited (Guillaume, 1969b, p. 240). In Liverpool, for example, female employment opportunities remained few and far between and only a lower class of women was taken on irregularly 'at rough unskilled work such as sack mending' (Harrison, 1904). As a result, most women, whether in Liverpool or Toulon, were essentially dependent on exploiting limited income-earning opportunities in the informal economy (Ayers, 1990; Agulhon, 1980). In the case of Toulon, for example, despite the fact that some wives were able to find employment at the *Arsenal* as office workers or as nurses in the naval hospital, the majority remained dependent on the informal economy—such as taking in washing, or cultivating agricultural land in a neighbouring village—in order to avoid the ever-present risk of poverty (Agulhon, 1980. p. 298). Although sailors frequently had the reputation of being good providers (Ross, 1989), the periodic absence of men at sea not only reinforced the role of women as managers of the household budget, but also inevitably forced many women to exploit all available income-earning opportunities, whether on a casual or seasonal basis (Ayers, 1990; Gay *et al.*, 1977). Ports such as Boulogne often had a high proportion of widows with dependent children, but their employment in the local economy was constrained by trenchant middle-class opposition to the concept of female work (Lottin, 1983). The precarious economic basis of male power in many port-cities, in the context of insecure employment and largely seasonal trades, further strengthened the position of women when a wife's energy and skill was often the dividing line between a decent level of comfort and bare survival (Ross, 1989; Fahy, chapter 10, below).

The predominance of casual employment for men within a local labour market was linked at an early stage by social observers, such as Booth and Rowntree, to bad housing, insanitary conditions and ill health (Jackson, 1973). Although it is true in general that the process of urban expansion in nineteenth-century Europe seldom kept pace with the rise in population, resulting in visible shortages in housing, services and infrastructure (Montanari, 1989), the nature of port-city economies and their dependent labour markets undoubtedly aggravated these underlying conditions. Not only did 'casualism' persist, often with a grading system that consigned 'casual casuals' to the bottom of the labour recruitment system (Taplin, 1978), but port-cities frequently depended on only a limited number of sectors, all of which were subject to seasonal, as well as cyclical, trends and governed by international markets. In addition, a great deal of dock work and port-related employment was disproportionately dangerous and the accident rate, particularly in winter, was often high, contributing to excess male mortality in the age groups 25 to 30 and above (Johnson, 1988; Eggerickx and Debuisson, 1990; see above, pp. 8–9).

Given the particular nature of port-city economies, the prevalence of substantial downward mobility (Sewell, 1981), the relative absence of employment opportunities for women, at least within the formal economy, and an above-average dependency for population growth on long-distance migration from lower socio-economic groups, it is not surprising that the underlying demographic characteristics of European port-cities were reinforced in the nineteenth century. The probable health hazards associated with in-migration were recognized by contemporaries in early-nineteenth-century Nantes (below, chapter 10), mid-nineteenth-century Cardiff (Lewis, 1980), as well as in many other port-cities during this period. Liverpool, for example, was regarded, with some justification, as being notoriously unhealthy, with one of the highest mortality rates in England (Lawton and Lee, 1989b) and Glasgow evinced a close link between population density and death rates, particularly in relation to selected age groups (Cage, 1987). The volatility of a port-city economy geared to tidal rhythms, the additional insecurity facing many new young in-migrants, as well as the continuing uncertainty of employment, undoubtedly reinforced both instrumental and psychological drinking, as in the case of Boulogne where alcohol consumption was excessive, with significantly negative health consequences (Oustric, 1983b, p. 238). Similarly, the relative absence of formal employment opportunities for women and the continuing dependency on the adaptability of the family economy almost certainly encouraged both high birth rates and a delayed onset of the secular fertility transition (Dyrvik,

1988). To this extent, the character and nature of port-city economies in the nineteenth century had a tangible impact on demographic development.

SOCIAL CONDITIONS IN PORT-CITIES

In the absence of rigorous national or international comparisons focusing on key social indicators, it is problematical to generalize about prevailing social conditions in nineteenth-century port-cities. However, the individual contributions to the present volume highlight the extent to which many of the contemporary urban social problems in the nineteenth century were particularly acute in towns and cities dependent, to a high degree, on the port transport industry and related secondary-sector activities.

The extent of over-crowding and high urban population density in port-cities were frequently determined by the existence of distinctive land markets, as in both Bremen and Glasgow (Tidemann, 1907; Schwarz, 1976; Gibb, 1983), which, in turn, influenced the nature of residential development. However, many seaports appear to have suffered from excessive over-crowding in the course of the nineteenth century as a function of the spatial limitations of their sites, the specific nature of their migrant streams and the structure of their local economies. Nantes recorded one of the highest levels of urban over-crowding in France as late as the 1920s, closely followed by Marseilles; in the former case, a significant proportion of all accommodation in the *quartier* Barbin had no effective ventilation (Leroux, 1985). Extensive over-crowding was registered in Cork and Glasgow (as O'Brien and Gibb in chapters 11 and 2, below show), in Liverpool (Neal, 1988), as well as in Hull, where the working-class courts were of a 'very peculiar construction' (Gillett and MacMahon, 1980, p. 257). In this context, port-cities were arguably more prone to urban over-crowding and the social problems generated by an unresponsive housing market than many other types of nineteenth-century towns. The changing level of in-migration was the single most important factor determining fluctuations in housing demand and the 'housing problem' in many European countries, particularly in the second half of the nineteenth century, was largely a result of increased urban in-migration running ahead of housing supply (Lee, 1978; Tilly, 1991). Inevitably, there were marked differences historically in the natural and migrational components of population change in different types of town (Lawton, 1991), but port-cities, as indicated above, were often distinct, both in terms of the extent and persistence of their dependence for demographic growth on in-migration and in the nature and composition of their migrant streams. The origins and characteristics of in-migrants in turn affected not only the housing market of port-cities, but their overall social structure.

Whether in Hull or Marseilles migrants were often attracted to port-cities, not solely as a result of relative ease of access, but also because of the proliferation of casual and unskilled jobs (Gillett and MacMahon, 1980; Sewell, 1981). The willingness of many migrants to work for lower than customary wages gave them an important competitive edge, specifically in local labour markets dominated by casual employment. Low wages, however, were directly associated with poor quality housing and over-crowding. Moreover, given the importance of supplementary earnings for family members and the high relative cost of intra-urban transportation, the working class in port-cities was frequently forced to remain in the city centre where multiple opportunities existed for unskilled and casual employment (Sutcliffe, 1982; Wischermann, chapter 9, below), thereby reinforcing the highly localized nature of urban experience (Hardtwig and Tenfelde, 1990, p. 13; Wischermann, 1993, p. 164). The predominance of casual labour in port-cities, by definition, required residential proximity to the major sources of employment. The continuing uncertainty in port-city labour markets, together with high levels of in-migration and occasionally of out-migration (as in Glasgow in the 1870s and 1880s, see chapter 2, below), also increased the level of residential mobility. Even in a period when transiency was undoubtedly an integral aspect of the expected life-experience of most people (Anderson, 1982), the extent of mobility within individual port-cities was remarkable. In Kiel, for example, with a total population in 1914 of 225,161, approximately 80,000 individuals are known to have changed their residence within the city each year (Wenzel, 1978) and high levels of in-migration, typical of most port-cities in the period under consideration, were invariably associated with increased intra-urban mobility (Lawton, 1989).

A wider range of migrant origins evident in the case of port-cities as a whole throughout the nineteenth century was also associated with different degrees of residential segregation according to migrant group. In particular, the ethnic residential concentration of migrants and the differentiated social mobility of social, occupational and ethnic groups within the urban population tended to produce a high degree of segregation (Macdermott, 1977; Sewell, 1981). Specific patterns of segregation in port-cities were often the result of an interplay between ethnicity, socio-economic status and housing, and segregation or dissimilarity indices for such British port-cities as Cardiff, Hull and Liverpool confirm their particular status (Dennis, 1984). In Bordeaux urban expansion in the nineteenth century was accompanied by a heightened degree of social compartmentalization, as successive new elements in the workforce made up of building workers, port labourers and railway employees adopted residential patterns that were *très cloisonnées* (Guillaume, 1969a, p. 241). Seamen, in particular, often had a specific spatial distribution within a port-city, as in Boulogne, occupying a cohesive residential area separated from other parts of the town and using a distinct *patois des marins* (Oustric, 1983b, p. 244). Even in smaller ports, such as Stavanger, high intra-urban mobility could not disguise the existence of two separate urban communities delineated on the basis of economic and occupational criteria (Dyrvik, 1988). Rapid population growth and in-migration only served to aggravate existing socio-ethnic divisions in the course of the nineteenth century (Ruddel and Lafrance,

1985). The low status of many new in-migrants helped to create strong segregation which in many port-cities, given the composition of their long-distance migration streams, was reinforced by language and religious differences. Neighbourhood or street endogamy remained 'the rule' in many inner-city districts (Ross, 1989, p. 222). In the extreme case of Liverpool the high concentration of Irish settlement and the absence of a paternalistic culture facilitated the rise of popular Protestantism and meant that the 'fabric of working life was permanently scarred by open sectarian violence' (Neal, 1988, p. 253). More frequently, the acute social divisions, evidenced by Fahy in Nantes in the early-nineteenth century (see below, chapter 10) with a high proportion of *défavorisée* and wide variations in mortality according to social class, street and *quartier* (Leroux, 1985; Blum, 1990), presented an accurate picture of the extent of residential segregation and above-average income inequality prevalent in many European port-cities during this period (Ellis, 1984; Le Gallo, 1976).

Specific locational factors also tended to reinforce the predominant social conditions in port-cities. Port sites frequently constrained urban expansion, with naval ports, in particular, suffering from persistent physical limitations that aggravated over-crowding and housing density. Naval authorities were often reluctant to abandon the ramparts and fortifications that directly hindered effective expansion of the local housing market. Moreover, because of a significant floating population, high residential mobility and a large number of 'casual' poor (Davis, 1989), there was little incentive for radical housing reform. Toulon was known as a dirty city, Boulogne was characterized by persistent poverty and between 63 and 69 per cent of the tenements in the Tyne ports of Newcastle, South Shields and Tynemouth were officially classified as over-crowded in 1901 (Agulhon, 1980, p. 247; Oustric, 1983b, p. 246; Grace, 1977). Although there was a gradual increase in the proportion of houses with a bathroom in Hamburg towards the end of the nineteenth century (May, 1915), the traditional single-family house had been displaced completely by tenement blocks (*Mietskasernen*), many of four storeys or more (see chapter 9, below). Fifty-three per cent of the approximately 11,000 lodgings in Brest in 1906 simply consisted of one room; over 8,000 had only one window (Le Gallo, 1976, p. 305). Although individual naval ports benefited from the creation of dedicated housing to accommodate ship-yard workers, as was the case in Wilhelmshaven (Maierhöfer, 1986), most ports witnessed few attempts to improve working-class housing in contrast to the construction of 'worker cities' in such French manufacturing towns as Anzin and Mulhouse (Desgraves and Dupeux, 1969), or the provision of company housing in the mining communities of the Ruhr (Teuteberg and Wischermann, 1992, p. 259). Even in Hamburg, as Wischermann shows below (chapter 9), the trauma of the last major cholera epidemic of 1892 failed to generate substantive changes in housing policy and was followed by a continued dilatory approach to slum clearance and housing reform (Grüttner, 1983). Only in exceptional cases, as in

Liverpool, were port-cities in the forefront of corporation housing initiatives before 1914 (Dennis, 1984): in Glasgow, the City Improvement Trust was reluctant initially to build houses and had added only 2,199 new houses to the city's stock by 1914 (Butt, 1987, p. 47) and public-interest house construction remained insignificant in Hamburg in the period 1895–1912 (Teuteberg and Wischermann, 1992, p. 258).

However, perhaps as a reaction to the adverse social conditions typical of port-cities, significant socio-ethnic divisions and a persistence of low pay, both for seamen and port labourers as a whole (Gjølberg, 1978), family and kinship networks often remained of great significance. Indeed, despite broader patterns of social change, there was a perceptible strengthening in the role of the nuclear family in such ports as Marseilles in the second half of the nineteenth century. The nexus of kinship and neighbourhood was reinforced by the urban work patterns of port-cities, as well as by ethnicity (Hohenberg and Lees, 1985; Ayers, 1988; 1990) and the persistence of such strong cultural norms in turn influenced demographic behaviour, in particular fertility.

THE IDEOLOGY OF MERCHANT CAPITAL

A final characteristic of port-cities that distinguished them from other urban communities was the predominance of trade and commerce and the ideology of merchant capital. Urban élites, in general, are often regarded as having been outward-looking: the presence of foreign merchants and the network system of overseas trade undoubtedly stimulated the circulation of 'free ideas' and the propensity to assimilate external influences (Newman, 1985; Clark, 1984; Hohenberg and Lees, 1985; Agulhon, 1980). In this context, shipping links were frequently a favourable mechanism for the dissemination of new ideas (Le Gallo, 1976). For example, the merchants of eighteenth-century Dunkirk, with close trading links with Britain, rapidly adopted innovations in commercial practice and trade credit, just as the tradition of placing their sons in the counting houses of foreign merchants provided significant commercial and educational benefits for merchant families throughout Western Europe (Clark, 1981; Fridlizius, 1981). Many port-cities were effectively dominated by a relatively small, inter-connected merchant élite, such as the *corpo mercantile* in Trieste, as Cattaruzza notes below (chapter 6). In eighteenth-century La Rochelle, for example, approximately 90 merchant families provided economic and municipal leadership (Clark, 1981); Liverpool was dominated by a tight-knit group of roughly 25 merchants before 1750 (Clemens, 1976); Newcastle-upon-Tyne was controlled increasingly by an oligarchy from the Merchants' Company (Ellis, 1984); and merchants represented the largest group on the council of Southampton (Patterson, 1966). Guépin's analysis of the social structure of Nantes in the mid-1830s distinguished between eight main groups, but power was clearly exercised by the *grande bourgeoisie* who embodied the relative solidity of the merchant oligarchy (Leroux, 1984, p. 163; Fahy, chapter

10, below). Although noble landowning remained important in Boulogne, the port's development was taken forward by a dynamic bourgeoisie, dependent on trade and commerce, that dominated the local Chamber of Commerce in the nineteenth century (Oustric, 1983a). In naval ports, such as Brest, the structure of the urban élite was determined by the presence of a large number of naval officers and municipal affairs, both in the eighteenth and nineteenth century, were often dealt with jointly by the civilian and military bourgeoisie (Le Gallo, 1976).

Given the tendency for selective economic diversification in individual ports and the development of port-related industries which made the Italian ports of Genoa and Leghorn, for example, significant centres of manufacturing by the end of the nineteenth century (Pounds, 1985; Felloni, 1961), it would be false to assume the existence of a uniform ideology among the urban élites of port-cities. In eighteenth-century Danzig there was substantial local opposition to the liberalization of trade and the merchants of Dunkirk persisted with an increasingly problematical mercantilist concept of money (Cieślak, 1970; Teneur, 1966). At times the commercial élite itself could be seriously divided in the articulation and implementation of its specific interests: the late-nineteenth century witnessed a disruptive conflict between shipowners and coal exporters in Cardiff (Daunton, 1977); in Liverpool the proliferation of vested interests in the period 1858 to 1914, including shipowners, the railway companies and members of the Dock Board, increasingly represented 'an array of forces which were often harmful to the interests of Merseyside's growth' (Hyde, 1971, p. 132). In Brest the 'municipal caste' was frequently in conflict with another important group within the port's social élite, namely the judiciary (Le Gallo, 1976) and although there was a proliferation of bourgeois interest groups in Kiel from the 1870s onwards, with the foundation of a *Kommunalverein* (1871) and a *Bürgerverein* (1890), improved institutional cohesion within the local merchant community could not alter the continuing prioritization of the fleet, nor lift the restrictions on the development of commercial trade with Sweden (Wulf, 1991). In a different context, the traditional supremacy of the merchants in Rostock had been undermined by legal changes in 1770 (Olechnowitz, 1968). Moreover, in the course of the nineteenth century not all merchant élites in port-cities fully espoused the concept of free trade. If merchants in Bordeaux, Boulogne, Marseilles and La Rochelle were vociferous in their support for free trade, the *négociants* of Nantes vigorously opposed *libre échangisme* and the treaty of 1860 (Gille, 1959, pp. 146–47; Guillaume, 1969a; Oustric, 1983a; Leroux, 1984; Smith, 1980, pp. 80–81.)

However, as a whole, the ideology of merchant capital which dominated the local administration of most port-cities in the nineteenth century was characterized by a belief in the concept of the 'night-watchman' state, an adherence to *laissez-faire* and liberal economic principles (Wischermann, chapter 9, below) and an underlying commitment to avoid any unnecessary disruption to trade and commerce. In particular, the dominant élites of most port-towns and cities showed a constant concern over cash expenditures and were strongly opposed to increased local taxation (Dale, 1976; Le Gallo, 1976). In Hull, for example, 'the edge of local politics could become sharp, when it had to be tempered on the anvil of finance' (Gillett and MacMahon, 1980, p. 224). Inevitably, like their counterparts in other urban centres, the port-city middle class operated essentially within the constraints of the existing system as O'Brien argues below (chapter 11), but their parsimonious and penny-pinching approach to most forms of local expenditure, evident in many city governments, was often excessive (Spencer, 1986; Curtis, 1986). A restricted franchise often encouraged corruption, complacency and a clumsy adminis-tration in port-cities (Dale, 1976; Gillett, 1970; Patterson, 1966) to a degree that was far less typical of industrial towns (Dennis, 1984). Despite the gradual lifting of franchise restrictions in the course of the nineteenth century in many European states, port-cities such as Bremen, Hamburg and Lübeck remained dominated by quasi-oligarchies and the general trend towards a more efficient, or bureaucratic urban administration was less evident in such cases (Krabbe, 1985; Clark, 1984; Evans, 1987). Increased corporate organization and the dominance of business interests were important factors that encouraged the implementation of far-reaching socio-political initiatives by many German urban authorities, particularly after 1870, underpinned selectively by the establishment of local Administration Academies (*Verwaltungsakademien*) (Howe, 1913; Krabbe, 1985; Bolten, 1987). But few port-cities participated to any great extent in this process. Merchants in general, whether in Saint-Mâlo or Marseilles, remained ideologically opposed to urban planning and infrastructural investment (Hohenberg and Lees, 1985; Ruddel and Lafrance, 1985; Konvitz, 1978), and only in a few naval ports was it possible to formulate city extension plans (Wulf, 1991). Local tax revenues were to be used primarily for port and harbour improvements, to prevent soil erosion by the sea, or to promote the commercial interests of the town (Evans, 1987; Dale, 1976). Indeed, in the case of Bordeaux the modernization of the port's railway and transport connections was largely carried out against local opinion by government authorities and the state was forced to assume responsibility for a large part of the cost of dock construction due to the continuing opposition of the local Chamber of Commerce (Guillaume, 1969a). If high levels of population mobility and the existence of a stable urban core were synonymous, in general terms, with the development of significant inequalities in power (Anderson, 1982), the persistence of extensive in-migration and the predomi-nance of casual employment in many port-cities reinforced the ideology of merchant capital and affected the overall direction of social welfare policy.

Certainly the available empirical studies of port-cities confirm an unusually high dependency on philanthropy and charity and an absence of a collective commitment to social welfare provision except in specific circumstances, as in Wilhelmshaven, where the naval authorities made some provision for naval ratings and ship-yard workers (Meller, 1976; Fabi, 1984; Maierhöfer, 1986). In many European industrial towns, such as Elbeuf, where manufacturers were more dependent on a stable and skilled workforce, the urban élite from an early stage was prepared to adopt collective precautionary measures to restrict the spread of disease. In towns dominated by a single major employer there was also a willingness to provide improved welfare facilities for the working class (Becchia, 1990; Chaloner, 1950). But in most port-cities, in clear contrast, health strategies often remained individualistic in nature, dependent almost entirely on charitable institutions (Becchia, 1990; van Aalen, 1985; Gillett and MacMahon, 1980). In Bordeaux, for example, the level of charitable provision had traditionally been substantial with a high participation rate by prominent local merchant families in the *Société de Charité Maternelle* and the *Bureaux de Bienfaisance* (Guillaume, 1969b, p. 261). In Toulon during the 1750s 50 per cent of the local notables left legacies in their wills to the three main charitable institutions in the town (Agulhon, 1980) and leading merchants in Liverpool, although opposed to the creation of the Pierhead Baths in the 1820s because they threatened to encroach on valuable space for travellers and commerce, provided extensive voluntary support for charitable initiatives that were deemed to be more appropriate for improving the quality of civic life (Calvert, 1987; Lees, 1985; Simey, 1951). Although the city also established the first public wash-house in 1842, the requirement that such facilities should be 'self-supporting' and run on a class system led to an inefficient pricing policy and reduced usage. Similarly in Cork the middle-class reaction to the city's health problems in the first half of the nineteenth century was piecemeal, relying on temporary fever hospitals during years of crisis mortality rather than considering a more structured approach to improving the health conditions of the working class (O'Brien, chapter 11, below). Only ports such as Fleetwood, that were also resorts for the middle class, appear to have been seriously concerned with their health image (Curtis, 1986).

In this sense the primacy of trade and commerce was often inimicable to public health reform in the nineteenth century. On the one hand, Liverpool (recognizing its acute problems of health and sanitation) appointed Britain's first full-time Medical Officer of Health, Dr W. H. Duncan, in 1846 (Frazer, 1947; Warren and Francis, 1987) and Glasgow developed a sophisticated sanitary department after 1863 (White, 1983), yet, as in Hamburg or Hull, sanitary improvements were difficult to implement precisely because they directly harassed negligent landlords, necessitated higher levels of local taxation and were deemed to be of secondary importance to the further promotion of trade and shipping. Indeed, in many port-cities, such as Boulogne, Danzig or Toulon, there was little, if any, commitment to effective public health reform (Oustric, 1983b; Cieślak, 1970; Agulhon, 1980) as Fridlizius also shows for Malmö (below, chapter 5). Many of the smaller German Baltic ports (such as Memel and Tilsit) were still dependent on well water at the end of the nineteenth century (Grahn, 1883). In 1893 only 1,200 houses in Toulon were connected to a drainage system that discharged directly into the sea (Agulhon, 1980) and the sewerage problems of Glasgow were not resolved until 1888, when the construction of the underground railway by private contractors was only permitted by the council on the condition that this was accompanied by a remodelling of the sewerage system at no cost to the rate payers (Checkland, 1982). Port-cities, in general, showed little concern to protect health and in individual cases local councils actively opposed the implementation of public health legislation or fulfilled statutory obligations with something less than enthusiasm (Ruddel and Lafrance, 1985; Gillett, 1970; Compton, 1992). Although a rigorous comparative analysis of public health policy in port-cities with other types of towns in the nineteenth century is difficult to implement in the absence of a sufficient range of representative case studies (Sheard, 1994), it is perhaps significant that German ports, such as Königsberg, Hamburg and Kiel, had a below-average distribution of health care personnel in the late-nineteenth century (Hietala, 1987). Indeed the classic example of the negative consequences of the continuing adherence to a belief in the primacy of the 'night-watchman' state and the ideology of merchant capital can be found in Hamburg, where protracted failure to raise tax revenues in order to install sand filtration for the port's water supply led directly to over 10,000 fatalities in the last cholera epidemic of 1892 (Evans, 1987). More generally, as in the case of Marseilles, a delay in the improvement to the water supply of port-cities was accompanied by a persistence of high mortality rates from diarrhoeal disease (Preston and van der Walle, 1978). Despite a range of socio-economic factors that frequently aggravated contemporary urban health conditions, it was specifically in port-cities that ideology and political culture were arguably most resistant to the adoption of effective public health reform in nineteenth-century Europe.

CONCLUSION

The posited typology of port-cities that underpins the separate contributions to this volume is not simply a heuristic device, but an effective means of focusing on some of the central issues connected with urban development in Europe from the early modern period onwards and for examining key components in urban demographic change as a whole. However, despite the overall importance of port-cities within the general process of European urbanization, their population growth rates varied markedly. Although many ports registered high rates of population growth in the nineteenth century, this was not uniformly the case, and they seldom conformed to a common temporal pattern in individual European countries, as Lawton notes for England (chapter 4, below). The total population of Stralsund, for example, expanded by only 1.2 per cent per annum (1828–1862) reflecting a perceptible decline in the relative importance of Baltic trade (Engelsing, 1971), while during the period 1866 to 1901 annual demographic growth in Boulogne was a modest 0.6 per cent (Urban, 1998; Oustric, 1983b). Not only was the hinterland of individual ports, as a series of geographically disconnected areas, often politically determined, but the degree of economic diversification also varied significantly as the contrast between Genoa (Felloni, 1961) and Liverpool (Lawton, chapter 4, below) indicates. Specific ports, such as Marseilles, Hamburg and Trieste, enjoyed, at particular times, the benefits of 'free port' status, although often in the pre-industrial period as a function of political lobbying and corruption (Schaeper, 1988), and even in terms of port and harbour administration local institutional practice differed. Bristol, for example, remained a municipal port, whereas other British ports were often administered by public trusts (Morgan, 1952). Indeed given the differences between various types of ports it is not surprising that seaports as a whole fail to reveal a clearly specific demographic régime. In the case of Malmö, as Fridlizius indicates below (chapter 5), the significance of its port function was not apparent demographically until the mid-nineteenth century, when its character as a port decisively influenced mortality trends in the period 1850 to 1880.

However, it is increasingly recognized that distinct urban types were associated historically with different components in population growth. Port-cities had a particular range of common determining characteristics which justify the adoption of a port-city typology. Urban demographic régimes were traditionally dependent on in-migration, but whereas the relative contribution of natural population growth became more marked in various types of town during the course of the nineteenth century, many ports remained dispro-portionately dependent on migrant streams (Bairoch, 1988). Moreover, if the opportunities for in-migrants to achieve economic stability were a function of the existence of a diversified economy and a relatively homogeneous social structure, assimilation in ports would have remained problematical (de Vries, 1984).

In particular, the major commercial ports such as Bremen, Genoa, Glasgow, Liverpool, Malmö, Trieste, Hamburg and Nantes, discussed in the following chapters, shared important characteristics. Although they reflected many of the demographic features of large European cities in general, these ports frequently registered some of the highest population growth rates in the nineteenth century (del Panta, 1989). Cork also witnessed substantial population growth in the late-seventeenth and early-eighteenth centuries as a result of capturing a large proportion of the new Atlantic trade in barrelled meat and butter (Dickson, 1989). Although the rates of growth of naval towns seldom matched the expansion of commercial ports, Portsmouth, the sole naval port included in this volume, reflected certain of the common demographic features of port-cities in an extreme manner.

Port-cities were undoubtedly key connecting links in the economic integration of Western Europe, but they were also important as transmitters of epidemic diseases. Certainly given the importance of port-cities within the urban hierarchy of individual European states, both in the eighteenth and nineteenth centuries, their contribution to urban population development was significant, if varied. In Malmö, for example (chapter 5), the periodization of demographic change did not differ significantly from national trends in Sweden, whereas in other port-cities, such as Naples, the existence of a regionally distinct demographic régime was patently more marked (del Panta, 1989). Nevertheless, many of the major commercial ports evinced elements of a distinctive demographic régime. In particular, trading and transport links increased the risk of exposure to infectious diseases, contributing to the persistence of high age- and disease-specific mortality until well into the late-nineteenth century. Similarly, large-scale ports tended to share a common pattern of nuptiality and fertility, with skewed sex ratios contributing to a high average age at marriage and comparatively low nuptiality, although British ports, in general, were characterized by early and high marriage rates (Lawton, chapter 4, below). However, port-cities as a whole registered high fertility rates even in the early-twentieth century, which reflected a perceptible delay in the transition to widespread family limitation. But perhaps the most distinctive element in the demographic experience of the port-cities analysed in this volume was the extent, range and nature of their migration streams. As a direct function of extensive trading links, many ports attracted long-distance migrants from a wide area from an early date, which inevitably had important demographic as well as social consequences.

In terms of underlying socio-economic variables, nineteenth-century port-cities were also characterized by a number of common features, including the structure and nature of the local port economy, dependent labour markets and associated social conditions, long-distance in-migration and its ethnic composition, as well as the ideology of merchant capital that continued to influence social welfare attitudes and public health policy. While individual ports were unique in character, similarities in their demographic behaviour, irrespective of cultural differences, reinforce the case for employing a particular urban typology for analysing both their demographic characteristics and their impact on European urbanization. The use of a common framework of analysis based on a functional classification provides an important mechanism for isolating the key demographic features of specific types of urban communities (Rodger, 1992). Given the continuing paucity of rigorous empirical studies of nineteenth-century urban communities that examine the full range of relevant demographic, economic and social variables, a full appraisal of the validity of such a port-city typology must be deferred. Nevertheless, the individual contributions to this volume point to the opportunities that such a comparative analytical framework may offer for a more effective understanding of urban population development in Western Europe and for exploring the interaction between demographic development and socio-economic change in a comparative European context.

References

ABRAMS, L. (1992), *Workers' Culture in Imperial Germany. Leisure and Recreation in the Rhineland and Westphalia*, London.

AGULHON, M. (ed.) (1980), *Histoire de Toulon*, Toulouse.

ALEMANNY, J. (1984), *El puerto de Barcelona, Historia y Actualidad*, Barcelona.

ANDERSON, G. (1991), 'Inequalities in the workplace: the gap between manual and white-collar workers in the port of Liverpool from the 1850s to the 1930s', *Labour History Review*, **56** (1), 36–48.

ANDERSON, M. (1982), 'Indicators of population change and stability in nineteenth-century cities: some sceptical comments', in J. H. Johnson and C. G. Pooley (eds), *The Structure of Nineteenth Century Cities*, London, 283–98.

ARMITAGE, A. (1992), 'Shipbuilding at Belfast: workman, clerk and company, 1880–1935', in L. R. Fischer (ed.), *From Wheel House to Counting House: Essays in Maritime Business History in Honour of Professor P. N. Davies* (Research in Maritime History, No. 2, International Maritime Economic History Association), 97–124.

ASPINALL, P. J., and D. M. HUDSON (1982), *Ellesmere Port. The Making of an Industrial Borough*, Didsbury.

AYERS, P. (1988), *The Liverpool Docklands. Life and Work in Athol Street*, Liverpool.

AYERS, P. (1990), 'The hidden economy of dockland families: Liverpool in the 1930s', in P. Hudson and W. R. Lee (eds), *Women's Work and the Family Economy in Historical Perspective*, Manchester, 271–90.

BAIROCH, P. (1974), 'Geographical structure and trade balance of European foreign trade from 1800–1970', *Journal of European Economic History*, **3**, 557–608.

BAIROCH, P. (1988), *Cities and Economic Development. From the Dawn of History to the Present*, London.

BECCHIA, A. (1990), 'Des villes épargnées? L'épidémie de choléra de 1832 à Elbeuf', *Annales de Démographie Historique*, 53–70.

BEHRENDT, S. D. (1990), 'The captains in the British slave trade from 1785 to 1807', *Transactions of the Historic Society of Lancashire and Cheshire*, **140**, 79–140.

BERNITT, H. (1956), *Zur Geschichte der Stadt Rostock*, Rostock.

BERTRAND, J.-B. (1973), *A Historical Relation of the Plague at Marseilles in the Year 1720*, London (2nd edition).

BIRD, J. (1963), *The Major Seaports of the United Kingdom*, London.

BLUM, A. (1990), 'Mortalité différentielle du XVIIe au XIXe siècle. Espace et société', *Annales de Démographie Historique*, 13–22.

BOLTEN, J. (1987), *Hochschulstudium für kommunale und soziale Verwaltung in Köln, 1912–1929. Eine Studie zur Wiedereinrichtung der Universität zu Köln* (Studien zur Geschichte der Universität zu Köln, **4**), Cologne and Vienna.

BOULTON, J. (1990), 'London widowhood revisited: the decline of female remarriage in the seventeenth and early eighteenth centuries', *Continuity and Change*, **5**, 323–55.

BURTON, V. (ed.) (1989), *Liverpool Shipping, Trade and Industry*, Liverpool.

BUTT, J. (1987), 'Housing', in R. A. Cage (ed.), *The Working Class in Glasgow 1750–1914*, London, Sydney, Wolfeboro, 29–55.

CAGE, R. A. (1987), 'Population and employment characteristics', in R. A. Cage (ed.), *The Working Class in Glasgow 1750–1914*, London, Sydney, Wolfeboro, 1–28.

CALVERT, J. (1987), 'The means of cleanliness: the provision of baths and wash-houses in early Victorian Liverpool', *Transactions of the Historic Society of Lancashire and Cheshire*, **137**, 117–36.

CAMERON, I. (1984), 'Halifax and the cholera epidemic of 1866', *The Nova Scotia Medical Bulletin*, **63**, 149–53.

CASEY, J. D. (1981), *Bordeaux, Colonial Port of Nineteenth Century France*, New York.

CHABAUD, L. (1883), *Marseille et ses Industries. Les Tissus, la Filature et la Teinturerie*, Marseilles.

CHALONER, W. H. (1950), *The Social and Economic Development of Crewe 1780–1923*, Manchester.

CHECKLAND, E. O. A. (1982), 'Local government and the health environment', in E. O. A. Checkland and M. Lamb (eds), *Health Care as Social History. The Glasgow Case*, Aberdeen, 1–15.

CIEŚLAK, E. (1970), 'Einige Probleme der politischen und sozialen Auseinandersetzungen in Danzig in der Mitte des 18. Jahrhunderts', *Neue Hansische Studien*, **17**, Berlin.

CIEŚLAK, E. (1972), 'Les pirates d'Alger et le commerce maritime de Gdansk au milieu du XVIIIe siécle', *Revue d'Histoire, Economie et Société*, 110–15.

CLARK, J. G. (1981), *La Rochelle and the Atlantic Economy during the Eighteenth Century*, Baltimore and London.

CLARK, P. (1984), 'Introduction', in P. Clark (ed.), *The Transformation of English Provincial Towns, 1600–1800*, London, 13–61.

CLEMENS, P. G. E. (1976), 'The rise of Liverpool, 1665–1750', *Economic History Review*, **29**, 211–25.

COMPTON, P. J. (1992), 'Public health and mortality decline in late-nineteenth-century Bordeaux', unpublished PhD dissertation, University of Liverpool.

CONEY, A. P. (1989), 'Mid-nineteenth-century Ormskirk: disease, overcrowding and the Irish in a Lancashire market town', *Transactions of the Historic Society of Lancashire and Cheshire*, **139**, 83–111.

CURTIS, B. (1986), *Fleetwood: A Town is Born*, Lavenham.

DALE, A. (1976), *Brighton Town and Brighton People*, London and Chichester.

DAUNTON, M. J. (1977), *Coal Metropolis: Cardiff, 1870–1914*, Leicester.

DAVIS, J. (1989), 'Jenning's Building and the Royal Borough. The construction of the underclass in mid-Victorian England', in D. Feldman and G. Stedman-Jones (eds), *Metropolis London, Histories and Representations since 1800*, London, 11–40.

del PANTA, L. (1989), 'Population growth, urbanization and regional differentials in Italy during the nineteenth century (1796–1914)', in R. Lawton and R. Lee (eds), *Urban Population Development in Western Europe from the Late-Eighteenth to the Early-Twentieth Century*, Liverpool, 258–69.

DENNIS, R. (1984), *English Industrial Cities of the Nineteenth Century*, Cambridge.

DERVILLE, A. and A. VION (eds) (1985), *Histoire de Calais* (Collection Histoire des villes du Nord-Pas-de-Calais, **VIII**), Westhoek.

DESGRAVES, L. and G. DUPEUX (eds) (1969), *Bordeaux au XIXe siècle*, Bordeaux.

DEVINE, T. M. (1988), 'Urbanisation', in T. M. Devine and R. Mitchison (eds), *People and Society in Scotland, I, 1760–1830*, Glasgow, 27–52.

DEVINE, T. M. (1995), 'The urban crisis', in T. M. Devine and G. Jackson (eds), *Glasgow, Vol. 1: Beginnings to 1830*, Manchester and New York, 402–16.

de VRIES, J. (1984), *European Urbanization 1500–1800*, London.

DICKSON, D. (1989), 'The demographic implications of Dublin's growth, 1650–1850', in R. Lawton and R. Lee (eds), *Urban Population Development in Western Europe from the Late-Eighteenth to the Early-Twentieth Century*, Liverpool, 178–89.

DUPEUX (1981), *Atlas Historique de l'Urbanisation Française*, Paris.

DYRVIK, S. (1988), 'Economie ou culture? L'introduction de la prévention des naissances dans la ville de Stavanger, Norvège, 1900–1935', *Annales de Démographie Historique*, 127–39.

EGGERICKX, T. and M. DEBUISSON (1990), 'La surmortalité urbaine: le cas de la Wallonie et de Bruxelles à la fin du XIXe siècle 1889–1892', *Annales de Démographie Historique*, 23–41.

ELLIS, J. (1984), 'A dynamic society: social relations in Newcastle upon Tyne, 1660–1760', in P. Clark (ed.), *The Transformation of English Provincial Towns, 1600–1800*, London, 190–227.

ENGELSING, R. (1971), 'Die Häfen an der Südküste der Ostsee und der Ostwestverkehr in der ersten Hälfte des 19. Jahrhunderts', *Vierteljahrschrift für Sozial- und Wirtschaftsgeschichte*, **58**, 24–66.

EVANS, R. J. (1987), *Death in Hamburg. Society and Politics in the Cholera Years, 1830–1910*, Oxford.

FABI, L. (1984), *La carita dei ricchi. Povertà e assistenza nella Trieste laica e asburgica del XIX secolo*, Milan.

FALLINER, H. (1978), 'Zur historischen Entwicklung des Bremischen Quarantänedienstes', *Bremer Aerzteblatt*, **9**, 36–50.

FELLONI, G. (1961), *Popolazione e Sviluppo Economica della Liguria nel secolo XIX*, Turin.

FELLONI, G. (1977), 'Italy', in C. Wilson and G. Parker (eds), *Introduction to the Sources of European Economic History, 1500–1800*, London, 1–36.

FERNANDEZ-ARMESTO, F. (1992), *Barcelona. A Thousand Years of the City's Past*, Oxford.

FRAZER, W. M. (1947), *Duncan of Liverpool. Being an Account of the Work of Dr W. H. Duncan, Medical Officer of Health of Liverpool, 1847–1863*, London.

FRIDLIZIUS, G. (1981), 'Handel och sjöfart 1820–1870—förändringens tid', in O. Bjurling (ed.), *Malmö Stads Historia (1820–1870)*, **3**, Malmö, 289–541.

FRIDLIZIUS, G. (1984), 'Från spannmålstunnor till smördrittlar. Malmö handel och sjöfart 1870–1924', in O. Bjurling (ed.), *Malmö Stads Historia (1870–1914)*, **4**, Malmö, 395–522.

GAY, H., Y. GRAVA, J.-M. PAOLI and A.-M. VIGOUEUX (1977), *Histoire de Fos-sur-Mer*, La Calde.

GEARY, F. (1981), 'The rise and fall of the Belfast cotton industry: some problems', *Irish Economic and Social History*, **VIII**, 39–49.

GEHRMANN, R. (1994), 'Urbane Mortalitätsmuster 1720–1914 am Beispiel Berlin-Spandaus und Hamburg-Altonas', in H.-G. Haupt and P. Marschalck (eds), *Städtische Bevölkerungsentwicklung in Deutschland im 19. Jahrhundert. Soziale und demographische Aspekte der Urbanisierung im internationalen Vergleich*, St. Katharinen, 229–57.

GIBB, A. (1983), *Glasgow: The Making of a City*, Beckenham.

GILLE, B. (1959), *Recherches sur la formation de la grande enterprise capitalistes (1815–1848)*, Paris.

GILLETT, E. (1970), *A History of Grimsby*, Oxford.

GILLETT, E. and K. A. MACMAHON (1980), *A History of Hull*, Oxford.

GJØLBERG, O. (1978), 'A note on wages, standard of living and social stability among Norwegian seamen, 1832–1914', *Economy and History*, **21**, 13–28.

GRACE, R. (1977), 'Tyneside housing in the nineteenth century', in N. McCord (ed.), *Essays in Tyneside Labour History*, Newcastle Upon Tyne, 178–94.

GRAHN, E. (1883), *Die Art der Wasserversorgung der Städte des Deutschen Reiches mit mehr als 5000 Einwohnern*, Munich and Leipzig.

GRÜTTNER, M. (1983), 'Soziale Hygiene und soziale Kontrolle. Die Sanierung der Hamburger Gängeviertel 1892–1936', in D. Herzig, D. Langewiesche and A. Sywottek (eds), *Arbeiter in Hamburg, Unterschichten, Arbeiter und Arbeiterbewegung seit dem ausgehenden 18. Jahrhundert*, Hamburg, 359–71.

GUILLAUME, P. (1969a), 'L'économie sous le second Empire', in L. Desgraves and G. Dupeux (eds), *Bordeaux au XIXe siècle*, Bordeaux, 179–210.

GUILLAUME, P. (1969b), 'La société et la vie quotidienne', in L. Desgraves and G. Dupeux (eds), *Bordeaux au XIXe siècle*, Bordeaux, 239–66.

GUILLAUME, P. (1972), *La Population de Bordeaux au XIXe siècle*, Paris.

HAINES, M. R. (1979), *Fertility and Occupation: Population Patterns in Mid-Industrialisation*, New York and London.

HARDTWIG, W. and K. TENFELDE (1990), *Soziale Räume in der Urbanisierung. Studien zur Geschichte Münchens im Vergleich 1850 bis 1933*, Munich.

HARDY, A. (1988), 'Urban famine or urban crisis? Typhus in the Victorian city', *Medical History*, **32**, 401–25.

HARRISON, A. (1904), *Women's Trades in Liverpool*, Liverpool.

HERKSCHER, S. (1903), 'Die Lage der in der Seeschiffahrt Hamburgs beschäftigten Arbeiter', in Schriften des Vereins für Socialpolitik, Div. I, *Die Lage der in der Seeschiffahrt beschäftigten Arbeiter*, 2 Bd., Leipzig.

HIETALA, M. (1987), *Services and Urbanization at the Turn of the Century. The Diffusion of Innovations* (*Studia Historica*, **23**), Helsinki.

HOHENBERG, P. M. and L. H. LEES (1985), *The Making of Urban Europe, 1000–1950*, Cambridge, Mass., and London.

HOWE, F. C. (1913), *European Cities at Work*, London.

HÜBNER, H. (1925), 'Danzigs Handel von 1650 bis zum Weltkreig', in H. Bauer and W. Millach (eds), *Danzigs Handel in Vergangenheit und Gegenwart*, Danzig.

HYDE, F. E. (1971), *Liverpool and the Mersey. An Economic History of a Port, 1700–1970*, Newton Abbot.

ITURBE MACH, A. (1986), '1893: Ultima epidemia de cólera en Vizcaya. Algunos aspectos socio-económicos', *Ernaroa, Revista de Historia de Euskal Herria/Euskal Historiazko Aldizkaria*, **3**, 153–82.

JACKSON, M. (1973), *Labour Relations on the Docks*, London.

JENSEN, J. and P. WULF (eds) (1991), *Geschichte der Stadt Kiel*, Neumünster.

JOHANSEN, H. C. (1992), 'Scandinavian shipping in the late eighteenth century in a European perspective', *Economic History Review*, **XLV**, 3, 479–93.

JOHNSON, A. (1988), *Working The Tides: Gatemen and Masters on the River Mersey*, Liverpool.

KEARNS, G., W. R. LEE and J. ROGERS (1989), 'The interaction of political and economic factors in the management of urban public health', in M. C. Nelson and J. Rogers (eds), *Urbanisation and the Epidemiologic Transition* (Meddelande från Familjehistoriska projektet No. 9), Uppsala, 9–82.

KEARNS, G., M. C. NELSON and J. ROGERS (1989), 'Portals of death. A research project', unpublished paper.

KIUPEL, U. (1983), 'Selbsttötung auf bremischen Dampfschiffen. Die Arbeits- und Lebens-bedingungen der Feuerleute 1880–1914', in W. Dreschsel and H. Gerstenberger (eds), *Arbeitsplätze, Schiffahrt, Hafen, Textilindustrie 1880–1933* (Beiträge zur Sozialgeschichte Bremens, **6**), Bremen.

KLESSMANN, C. (1978), *Polnische Bergarbeiter im Ruhrgebiet, 1870–1954. Soziale Integration und nationale Subkultur einer Minderheit in der deutschen Industriegesellschaft*, Göttingen.

KONVITZ, J. W. (1978), *Cities and the Sea. Port-city Planning in Early Modern Europe*, Baltimore and London.

KONVITZ, J. W. (1993), 'Port functions, innovation and the making of the megalopolis', in T. Barker and A. Sutcliffe (eds), *Megalopolis: The Giant City in History*, London, 61–72.

KRABBE, W. R. (1985), *Kommunalpolitik und Industrialisierung. Die Entfaltung der städtischen Leistungsverwaltung in 19. und frühen 20. Jahrhundert, Fallstudien zu Dortmund und Münster* (Schriften des Deutschen Instituts für Urbanistik, **74**), Stuttgart.

KUCKUK, P. and H. RODER (eds) (1988), *Von der Dampfbarkasse zum Containerschiff. Werften und Schiffbau in Bremen und der Unterweserregion*, Bremen.

LAUX, H.-D. (1983), 'Structural and regional differences of natural population growth in German cities, 1850–1905', *Erdkunde*, **77**, pp. 22–33.

LAUX, H.-D. (1989), 'The components of population growth in Prussian cities, 1875–1905 and their influence on urban population structure', in R. Lawton and R. Lee (eds), *Urban Population Development in Western Europe from the Late-Eighteenth to the Early-Twentieth Century*, Liverpool, 120–48.

LAWTON, R. (1983), 'Urbanization and population change in nineteenth-century England', in J. Patten (ed.), *The Expanding City*, London, Chapter 7.

LAWTON, R. (1989), 'Population mobility and urbanization: nineteenth-century British experience', in R. Lawton and R. Lee (eds), *Urban Population Development in Western Europe from the Late-Eighteenth to the Early-Twentieth Century*, Liverpool, 149–77.

LAWTON, R. (1991), 'The role of migration in the development and structure of British cities in the nineteenth century', in M. Poulain *et al.* (eds), *Historiens et Populations. Liber Amicorum Etienne Hélin*, Louvain-la-Neuve, 359–90.

LAWTON, R. and R. LEE (eds) (1989a), *Urban Population Development in Western Europe from the Late-Eighteenth to the Early-Twentieth Century* (Liverpool Studies in European Population, 1), Liverpool.

LAWTON, R. and R. LEE (1989b), 'Introduction: the framework of comparative urban population studies in western Europe, c. 1750–1920', in R. Lawton and R. Lee (eds), *Urban Population Development in Western Europe from the Late-Eighteenth to the Early-Twentieth Century*, Liverpool, 1–26.

LEE, J. J. (1978), 'Aspects of urbanization and economic development in Germany, 1815–1914', in P. Abrams and E. A. Wrigley (eds), *Towns in Societies. Essays in Economic History and Historical Sociology*, Cambridge, 279–94.

LEE, W. R. (1989), 'Sailing through unchartered waters', in J. Rogers (ed.), *Kustbygd i förändring 1650–1950. Familj och hushåll i nordiska fiskesamhällen*, Uppsala, 123–30.

LEE, W. R. (1998), 'Forschungen und Hypothesen zur Bevölkerungsentwicklung europäischer Hafenstädte: Stralsund im Vergleich', in W. R. Lee and W. Urban (eds), *Stadt und Bevölkerung bis zum Ende des 19. Jahrhunderts. Pommern im Vergleich*, Stralsund (forthcoming).

LEE, W. R. and P. MARSCHALCK (1998), 'In-migrants in Bremen, 1850–1910: demographic and economic indicators of integration', in P. Bourdelais (ed.), *L'Intégration des Populations dans les Villes Industrielle*, Paris (forthcoming).

LEES, A (1985), *Cities Perceived. Urban Society in European and American Thought, 1820–1940*, Manchester.

LE GALLO, Y. (ed.) (1976), *Histoire de Brest*, Toulouse.

LEROUX, E. (1984; 1985), *Histoire d'une Ville et de ses Habitants, Nantes, Des Origines à 1914*, **Tome 1**; *Nantes de 1914–1939*, **Tome 2**, Nantes.

LEWIS, C. R. (1980), 'The Irish in Cardiff in the mid-nineteenth century', *Cambria*, **7**, 13–41.

LEWIS, F. (1993), 'The demographic and occupational structure of Liverpool: a study of the parish registers, 1660–1750', unpublished PhD thesis, University of Liverpool.

LINDEMANN, M. (1990), *Patriots and Paupers, Hamburg 1712–1830*, New York and Oxford.

LOTTIN, A. (1983), 'Boulogne au XVIII siècle: les débuts d'une nouvelle croissance', in A. Lottin (ed.), *Histoire de Boulogne-Sur-Mer*, Lille, 133–54.

LYNCH, K. A. (1991), 'The European marriage pattern in the cities: variations on a theme by Hajnal', *Journal of Family History*, **16**, 79–96.

MACDERMOTT, T. P. (1977), 'The Irish workers on Tyneside in the nineteenth century', in N. McCord (ed.), *Essays in Tyneside Labour History*, Newcastle upon Tyne, 154–77.

MAIERHOFER, H. (1986), 'Die Entwicklung des Kriegshafens Wilhelmshaven', in H. Stoob (ed.), *See- und Flusshäfen vom Hochmittelalter bis zur Industrialisierung*, Cologne and Vienna, 291–308.

MALSTER, R. (1982), *Lowestoft: East Coast Port*, Lavenham.

MARSCHALCK, P. (1990), 'Zur Bevölkerungsentwicklung Bremens im 19. Jahrhundert', in D. Petzina and J. Reulecke (eds), *Bevölkerung, Wirtschaft, Gesellschaft seit der Industrialisierung*, Dortmund, 45–55.

MATOVIC, M. R. (1984), *Stockholmsäktenskap. Familjebildning och partnerval i Stockholm, 1850–1890* (*Monografier utgivna av Stockholms Kommun*, **57**), Stockholm.

MATZ, K.-J. (1980), *Pauperismus and Bevölkerung. Die gesetzlichen Ehebeschränkungen in den süddeutschen Staaten während des 19. Jahrhunderts*, Stuttgart.

MAY, R. E. (1915), 'Kosten der Lebenshaltung und Entwicklung der Einkommensverhältnisse in Hamburg seit 1890', *Schriften des Vereins für Sozialpolitik*, **145**.

MELLER, H. E. (1976), *Leisure and the Changing City, 1870–1914*, London.

MEYER, J. (1983), 'L'Europe, et la mer de 1778 à 1802', in A. Corvisier (ed.), *L'Europe à la Fin du XVIIIe Siècle (Regards sur l'histoire moderne*, **55**), Paris, 167–222.

MONTANARI, A. (1989), 'Barcelona and Glasgow. The similarities and differences in the history of two port-cities', *Journal of European Economic History*, **18**, 171–89.

MORGAN, F. W. (1952), *Ports and Harbours*, London.

MUIR, J. R. B. (1907), *A History of Liverpool*, Liverpool.

MURPHY, R. C. (1983), *Guest Workers in the German Reich: A Polish Community in Wilhelmian Germany*, New York.

NADAL, J. (1984), *La poblacio espanola siglos XVI a XX*, Ariel.

NEAL, F. (1988), *Sectarian Violence. The Liverpool Experience, 1819–1914. An Aspect of Anglo-Irish History*, Manchester.

NEUMERKEL, A. (1992), *Zur Geschichte der Prostitution in Stralsund* (Sündische Reihe, **6**), Stralsund.

NEWMAN, K. (1985), 'Hamburg in the European economy, 1660–1750', *Journal of European Economic History*, **1**, 57–94.

OLECHNOWITZ, K. F. (1968), *Rostock von der Stadtrechtsbestätigung im Jahre 1218 bis zur bürgerlich-demokratischen Revolution von 1848/49*, Rostock.

OLLERENSHAW, P. (1992), 'Der Ubergang von der Heim – zur Fabrikarbeit in der Leinenindustrie Ulsters (1680–1870)', in K. Ditt and S. Pollard (eds), *Von der Heimarbeit in die Fabrik. Industrialisierung und Arbeiterschaft in Leinen- und Baumwollregionen Westeuropas während des 18. und 19. Jahrhunderts*, Paderborn, 53–77.

OMRAN, A. (1971), 'The epidemiologic transition. A theory of the epidemiology of population change', *Milbank Memorial Fund Quarterly*, **491**, 509–38.

OUSTRIC, G. (1983a), 'Un siècle de croissance économique (1815–1914)', in A. Lottin (ed.), *Histoire de Boulogne-Sur-Mer*, Lille, 197–232.

OUSTRIC, G. (1983b), 'Une société originale et variée', in A. Lottin (ed.), *Histoire de Boulogne-Sur-Mer*, Lille, 233–48.

PATTERSON, A. T. (1966), *A History of Southampton 1700–1914: Vol. I, An Oligarchy in Decline, 1760–1835* (Southampton Records Society, **XI**), Southampton.

PÉRONAS, L. (1961), 'Sur la démographie Rochelaise', *Annales E.S.C.*, **16**, 1131–40.

POULAIN, M. (1990), 'De la campagne à la ville: le compartement démographique des migrants', *Annales de Démographie Historique*, 71–74.

POUNDS, N. J. G. (1985), *An Historical Geography of Europe, 1800–1914*, Cambridge.

POUSSOU, J.-P. (1983), *Bordeaux et le Sud-Ouest au XVIIIᵉ Siècle*, Paris.

POUSSOU, J.-P. (1985), 'L'évolution et les structures démographiques de l'Europe à la fin du XVIIIe siècle', in A. Corvisier (ed.), *L'Europe à la Fin du XVIIIe siècle*, Paris, 329–71.

POUSSOU, J.-P. (1989), 'The population increase of French towns between 1750 and 1914, and its demographic consequences', in R. Lawton and R. Lee (eds), *Urban Population Development in Western Europe from the Late-Eighteenth to the Early-Twentieth Century*, Liverpool, 68–92.

PRESTON, S. H. and E. VAN DER WALLE (1978), 'Urban French mortality in the nineteenth century', *Population Studies*, **32**, 275–98.

PULLAT, R. (1988), 'Einige Entwicklungszüge der Wirtschaft und der Einwohnerschaft von Pernau im 18. Jahrhundert', in R. Melville *et al.* (eds), *Deutschland und Europa in der Neuzeit*, Wiesbaden, 300–13.

PULLAT, R. and U. MERESTE (1982), *Uber die Formierung der Tallinner Stadtbevölkerung im 18. Jahrhundert und die Rekonstruktion der Zeitreihen in der geschichtlichen Demographie (anhand der Kirchenbücher)* (Kölner Vorträge und Abhandlungen zur Sozial und Wirtschaftsgeschichte, **34**), Cologne.

RATCLIFFE, B. M. (1985), 'The business elite and the development of Paris: intervention in ports and entrepôts, 1824–1834', *Journal of European Economic History*, **14** (1), 95–142.

RAWLING, A. J. (1986), 'The rise of Liverpool and demographic changes in part of south west Lancashire, 1660–1760', unpublished PhD thesis, University of Liverpool.

REHER, D. S. (1989), 'Urban growth and population development in Spain, 1787–1930', in

R. Lawton and R. Lee (eds), *Urban Population Development in Western Europe from the Late-Eighteenth to the Early-Twentieth Century*, Liverpool, 190–219.

RODGER, R. (1976), 'Employment, wages and poverty in the Scottish cities 1841–1914', in G. B. Gordon (ed.), *Perspectives of the Scottish City*, Aberdeen, 25–63.

RODGER, R. (1992), 'Urban history: prospect and retrospect', *Urban History*, **19** (1), 1–33.

ROGERS, J. and M. C. NELSON (1989), 'Controlling infectious diseases in ports: the importance of the military in central–local relations', in M. C. Nelson and J. Rogers (eds), *Urbanisation and the Epidemiologic Transition*, Uppsala, 83–108.

ROSS, E. (1989), '"Fierce questions and taunts." Married life in working-class London, 1870–1914', in D. Feldman and G. Stedman-Jones (eds), *Metropolis London. Histories and Representations since 1800*, London, 219–44.

RUDDEL, D.-T. and M. LAFRANCE (1985), 'Québec, 1785–1840: problèmes de croissance d'une ville coloniale', *Histoire Sociale-Social History*, **XVIII**, 315–33.

SARGENT, A. J. (1938), *Seaports and Hinterlands*, London.

SCHAEPER, T. J. (1988), 'Government and business in early eighteenth-century France: the case of Marseilles', *Journal of European Economic History*, **17**, 531–57.

SCHÖLLER, P. (1978), 'Grundsätze der Städtebildung in Industriegebieten', in H. Jäger (ed.), *Probleme des Städtewesens im industriellen Zeitalter*, Cologne and Vienna, 99–107.

SCHÖNFELD, W. (1941), *Die Syphilis-Endemien an der deutschen Nord- und Ostseeküste im beginnenden 19. Jahrhundert* (Arbeiten der deutsch-nordischen Gesellschaft für Geschichte der Medizin, der Zahnheilkunde und der Naturwissenschaften, **28**), Greifswald.

SCHWARZ, K. (1976), 'Wirtschaftliche Grundlagen der Sonderstellung Bremens im deutschen Wohnungsbau des 19. Jahrhunderts—Das Beispiel der östlichen Vorstadt', *Bremisches Jahrbuch*, **54**, 21–68.

SEWELL, W. H. (1981), 'Social mobility in a nineteenth-century European city: some findings and implications', in T. K. Rabb and R. I. Rotberg (eds), *Industrialization and Urbanization: Studies in Interdisciplinary History*, Princeton, 83–100.

SEWELL, W. H. (1985), *Structure and Mobility. The Men and Women of Marseille, 1820–1870*, Cambridge.

SEWELL, W. H. (1988), 'Uneven development, the autonomy of politics, and the dockworkers of nineteenth-century Marseille', *American Historical Review*, **95**, 604–37.

SHEARD, S. (1993), 'Nineteenth century public health. A study of Liverpool, Belfast and Glasgow', unpublished PhD thesis, University of Liverpool.

SHUBERT, A. (1990), *A Social History of Modern Spain*, London.

SIMEY, M. B. (1951), *Charitable Effort in Liverpool in the Nineteenth Century*, Liverpool (reissued 1992 as *Charity Rediscovered: A Study of Philanthropic Effort in Nineteenth-Century Liverpool*, Liverpool).

SMITH, F. B. (1990), 'The Contagious Diseases Acts reconsidered', *Social History of Medicine*, **3** (2), 197–215.

SMITH, M. S. (1980), *Tariff Reform in France 1860–1900. The Politics of Economic Interest*, Ithaca and London.

SMITH, W. (ed.) (1953), *Merseyside. A Scientific Survey*, Liverpool.

SODERBERG, J., U. JONSSON and C. PERSSON (1991), *A Stagnating Metropolis. The Economy and Demography of Stockholm, 1750–1850* (Cambridge Studies in Population, Economy and Society in Past Time, **13**), Cambridge.

SPENCER, E. G. (1986), 'State power and local interests in Prussian cities: police in the Düsseldorf district, 1848–1914', *Central European History*, **19**, 293–313.

SPRANDEL, R. (1986), 'Der Hafen von Hamburg', in H. Stoob (ed.), *See- und Flusshäfen vom Hochmittelalter bis zur Industrialisierung*, Cologne and Vienna, 193–210.

SUTCLIFFE, A. (1982), 'The growth of public intervention in the British urban environment during the nineteenth century: a structural approach', in J. H. Johnson and C. G. Pooley (eds), *The Stucture of Nineteenth-Century Cities*, London, 107–24.

TAPLIN, E. L. (1978), 'Dock labour at Liverpool: occupational structure and working conditions in the late nineteenth century', *Transactions of the Historical Society of Lancashire and Cheshire*, **127**, 133–54.

TENEUR, J. (1966), 'Les commercçants dunkerquois à la fin du XVIIIe siècle et les problèmes économiques de leur temps', *Revue du Nord*, **48**.

TEUTEBERG, H. J. and C. WISCHERMANN (1992), 'Germany', in C. G. Pooley (ed.), *Housing Strategies in Europe, 1880–1930*, Leicester, London and New York, 240–67.

THOMSON, J. K. J. (1992), *A Distinct Industrialization. Cotton in Barcelona, 1728–1832*, Cambridge.

THOWSEN, A. (1973), 'Bergen—a Norwegian seafaring town', *Maritime History*, **3**, 3–34.

TIDEMANN, DR (1907), 'Wohnungswesen, Badewesen', in H. Tjaden (ed.), *Bremen in hygienischer Beziehung*, Bremen, 164–99.

TILLY, R. (1991), 'Cyclical trends and market response: long swings in urban development in Germany, 1850–1914', in W. R. Lee (ed.), *German Industry and German Industrialisation. Essays in German Economic and Business History in the Nineteenth and Twentieth Centuries*, London, 148–84.

TJADEN, H. (1932), *Bremen und die bremische Aerzteschaft seit dem Beginn des 19. Jahrhunderts*, Bremen.

URBAN, W. (1998), 'Die Stralsunder und die Choleraepidemien im 19. Jahrhundert', in W. R. Lee and W. Urban (eds), *Stadt und Bevölkerung bis zum Ende des 19. Jahrhunderts. Pommern im Vergleich*, Stralsund (forthcoming).

VAN AALEN, R. (1985), 'The start of infant health care in Amsterdam: medicalization and the role of the state', *The Netherlands Journal of Sociology*, **21** (2), 126–39.

VINCENT, B. (1988), 'Le choléra en Espagne au 19e siècle', in J.-P. Bardet and P. Bourdelais (eds), *Peurs et Terreurs face à la Contagion*, Paris, 43–55.

VON JURASCHEK, F. (1896), *Übersichten der Weltwirtschaft*, Bd. VI, 1885–1889, Berlin and Bern.

WARREN, M. and H. FRANCIS (1987), *Recalling the Medical Officer of Health Writings by Sidney Chare*, London.

WENZEL, R. (1978), *Bevölkerung, Wirtschaft, Politik im kaiserlichen Kiel zwischen 1870 und 1914*, Kiel.

WHITE, B. (1983), 'Public health and civic administration in nineteenth-century Glasgow', *Bulletin of the Society for the Social History of Medicine*, **32**, 37–39.

WILLIAMS, D. (1989), 'Bulk trades and the development of the port of Liverpool in the first half of the nineteenth century', in V. Burton (ed.), *Liverpool Shipping, Trade and Industry*, Liverpool, 8–25.

WILLIAMSON, J. G. (1990), 'Migrant earnings in Britain's cities in 1851: testing competing views of urban labour market absorption', *Journal of European Economic History*, **19** (1), 163–90.

WISCHERMANN, C. (1983), *Wohnen in Hamburg vor dem Ersten Weltkrieg* (Studien zur Geschichte des Alltags, Band **2**), Münster.

WISCHERMANN, C. (1993), 'Germany', in R. Rodger (ed.), *European Urban History. Prospect and Retrospect*, Leicester and London, 159–69.

WOODS, R. I. (1984), 'Social class variations in the decline of fertility in late nineteenth-century London', *Geografiska Annaler*, Series B, **66**.

WOODS, R. I. (1987), 'Approaches to the fertility transition in Victorian England', *Population Studies*, **41**, 283–311.

WRIGLEY, E. A. (1961), *Industrial Growth and Population Change* (Cambridge Studies in Economic History), Cambridge.

WULF, P. (1991), 'Kiel wird Grossstadt (1867 bis 1918)', in J. Jensen and P. Wulf (eds), *Geschichte der Stadt Kiel*, Neumünster.

YOUNG, G. (1983), *A History of Bognor Regis*, Chichester.

Chapter 2

INDUSTRIALIZATION AND DEMOGRAPHIC CHANGE: A CASE STUDY OF GLASGOW, 1801–1914

ANDREW GIBB

INTRODUCTION

In his statistical study of urbanization, *The Growth of Cities in the Nineteenth Century*, Adna Ferrin Weber (1899) considered the relative growth of London and Glasgow in relation to the national populations of England and Scotland, and described Glasgow's growth as exceptional. He attributed this to its great variety of natural resources and its fortunate location. It occupied the position of a great commercial centre like London, it had a climate favourable to textile-working, like Manchester, and it lay in the middle of a great coal and iron district, like Birmingham. He added to these aspects of initial advantage, each responsible for the initiation of phases of growth, the idea that the force of attraction of a centre was proportional to its mass. In other words, the concentration, and both the relative and absolute growth of population in terms of numbers and time, varied in direct relation to the size of the centre, thus providing an explanation for its pattern of growth directly related to industrial and commercial development. Agglomeration of industry and people increased as a function of scale economies in the nineteenth century and these scale economies acted as an in-built accelerator to the process.

The effects of these processes of industrial and commercial agglomeration on the dynamics of population, in terms of its components of change, its internal structures and its spatial behaviour, are directly observable. In the case of Glasgow, as in that of other large cities, the nineteenth century may be divided into two main phases in both industrial and population terms, corresponding to what Friedlander (1974) has described as the 'urban transition'. In the first phase, Glasgow developed a broad industrial base, with textile-working dominant and the industrial workforce concentrated around the small and medium-size industrial units of the city core, sustained and increased by large-scale waves of in-migration replacing the losses caused by high death rates from contagious disease. In the second phase, while the spectrum of industry remained broad, more narrowly specialized heavy industries rose to over-whelming dominance and large-scale production units sought peripheral locations, attracting migrants from a population growing more on the basis of natural increase than net migration.

In the general sequence of long-run development, Glasgow exhibits in the nineteenth century broad areas of comparison with British port-cities such as Liverpool. However, while major aspects of population dynamics were similar, the motivating forces underlying those experiences were different. The crux of the matter lay in the growth of port functions and their relative role in the economic development of individual cities. Whereas in the case of Liverpool the growth of the port to a great extent led the economy of the nineteenth-century city, spawning ancillary processing and manufacturing industries, Glasgow's situation was more complex, with the physical condition of the River Clyde inhibiting large-scale port development. Until relatively late in the eighteenth century the Clyde in its upper reaches was a broad and shallow stream, braided and impeded by sandbanks and islands. It was not until the 1770s, when a system of jetties constricted the flow of the river, enabling it with some dredging assistance to excavate its own channel, that vessels drawing six feet of water could reach Glasgow's harbour at the Broomielaw (Pagan, 1847, p. 97). Prior to this, navigation as far upstream as Glasgow had been so difficult that the city had been forced to lay out a harbour several miles downstream in 1668 and for well over a century Port Glasgow handled the bulk of the city's water-borne trade (Gibb, 1983, pp. 44, 55–61).

From 1790 the Forth and Clyde and the Monkland canals, effecting a junction at Port Dundas in northern Glasgow, and to a lesser extent the Glasgow-Ardrossan canal begun at Port Eglinton in the south of Glasgow in 1807, handled a growing proportion of the city's traffic, thereby relieving pressure on the river. Until approximately 1840 reclamation and dredging together provided an increasingly useful ship canal, but wharfage extension remained extremely limited. Only from the 1840s onwards did an extension of commercial wharfage take place on any scale, creating a large and efficient nineteenth-century harbour. However, these developments were relatively minor, compared with the burgeoning growth of the city's industry, and any observed similarity in comparative demographic experience between Glasgow and Liverpool owed more to common elements within the Victorian labour market. Factors such as casual employment and long working hours, combined with a lack of transport facilities, necessitated a close relationship between dwelling and workplace (Rodger, 1982, p. 42). A concentration of population as a function of scale economies was also a process common to all industrial cities in the nineteenth century, but this varied nationally according to the size of the urban unit, and between Scotland and England, reflecting the operation of a distinctive land market which produced higher population densities in Scottish central city areas (Rodger, 1982, p. 64).

INDUSTRIAL AND COMMERCIAL GROWTH: THE FIRST PHASE

The prosperity of eighteenth-century Glasgow had been developed upon the basis of an expanding range of trading contacts with Ireland, the continent of

Europe and the Americas. Tobacco had become the dominant trading commodity and its disappearance with the American War of Independence produced a shift of emphasis in terms of products, markets and sources of raw material supplies. From the 1780s linen and cotton textiles, sugar, coal, fish and chemicals were exported to European and Russian markets, and after 1800 Glasgow merchants established important trading contacts in South America, the Far East and Australasia (Jackson, 1995). In terms of trade, Tables 2.1 and 2.2 give an impression of the increasing number and tonnage of vessels arriving at Glasgow, as well as the growth in the Glasgow-registered merchant fleet up to 1840.

While the range of products passing through Glasgow increased, a single item attained overwhelming dominance. In 1807 six million kilos of cotton were imported, and its processing and manufacture were to dominate the economy of the West of Scotland until the 1860s. Cotton ushered in the textile phase of the Industrial Revolution and transformed the urban and peri-urban landscape with its mills, factories, bleachfields, printworks and workers' tenements. The invention of the steam condenser permitted urban concentra-

Table 2.1: *The number and tonnage of ship arrivals at Glasgow, 1796–1823.*

Tons	1796	1806	1810	1816	1821	1823
Under 60	1,209	1,228	1,279	1,994	2,969	2,608
60–80	117	394	633	72	1,016	873
80–100	–	49	99	176	264	204
Over 100	–	7	10	19	103	252
Total tonnage	55,980	80,683	101,316	115,008	199,482	190,507

Source: Letter to Thomas Telford, 1824. Clyde Reports, p. 15.

Table 2.2: *The number and tonnage of ships registered at Glasgow, 1810–1840.*

Year	Number	Tons	Average tonnage
1810	24	1,956	81.5
1815	59	4,829	81.8
1820	77	6.131	79.6
1825	111	14,084	126.8
1830	21	39,432	181.7
1835	297	54,335	182.9
1840	403	185,707	460.8

Source: After Marwick, 1909, Appendix II, p. 237.

tion and cotton textile-working joined the expanding range of industries exploiting the benefits of central city locations. The production of dyestuffs and chemicals for cloth-processing and the manufacture of steam engines and mill machinery were closely connected with textiles, but breweries, distilleries, potteries and bottleworks, brick and tile works, tanneries and foundries all increasingly provided employment possibilities. At the same time the construction of canals and railways, as well as improvement schemes for the River Clyde and its port facilities, increased the scale and rapidity of concentration and provided huge numbers of construction jobs. Industry was also involved in the internal colonization of previously residential areas in the heart of the city, creating an early garment district whose proprietors, in their dealerships, contributed to the influx of commercial functions which presaged the appearance of a central business district. The structural components of the emerging Victorian city were beginning to crystallize, and competing industrial, commercial and residential land requirements were starting to exert their pressures on central city space. Population movement became a function of industrial attraction, population location reflected fierce competition, and population experience was moulded by a dense concentration on scarce and expensive residential space.

POPULATION DYNAMICS: THE FIRST PHASE, 1801–1841

Any discussion of population dynamics in late-eighteenth- and early-nine-teenth-century Glasgow is complicated by varying definitions of the area comprising the city and its suburbs. Also, since the national census began only in 1801, figures prior to that date are less certain. Therefore, in Table 2.3 the population increase of 25.8 per cent between 1791 and 1801 is to be regarded as an indication of the scale of change, rather than as a completely accurate figure. However, the most remarkable feature is the steady and consistent increase from 1801 onwards, always over 30 per cent in any decennial census period, and latterly over 35 per cent, bringing the total population of the city to over 274,000 by 1841. While growth rates of this magnitude could have been sustained by natural increase, the high mortality levels of the period clearly point to net migration as the major source of new population.

Table 2.3 and Figure 2.1 indicate the beginnings of a trend which was to become much more pronounced during the second half of the nineteenth century, namely the increasing proportion of the Scottish population concentrating in the industrializing counties of West Central Scotland and Glasgow's rising share of that population. Between 1801 and 1841 the West Central share of the Scottish population rose from 20.9 per cent to 30.2 per cent, while Glasgow's population grew from 24.4 per cent of the West Central population in 1801 to 32.3 per cent by 1841 thus demonstrating a markedly more rapid rate of increase than the West Central counties as a whole. While the overall Scottish population growth rate for this period did not match that

Table 2.3: *Population growth and concentration in Scotland, West Central Scotland and Glasgow, 1801–1911 (in 1,000s).*

	Scotland		West Central Scotland			Glasgow			
Year	Total	Decennial increase (%)	West Cent. Scot. total	% of Scottish total	Decennial increase (%)	Glasgow total	% of Scottish total	% of West Cent. Scot. total	Decennial increase (%)
1801	1,625	–	340	20.9	–	83	5.1	24.4	25.8
1811	1,824	12.3	410	22.4	20.5	110	6.0	26.8	31.8
1821	2,099	15.1	520	24.7	26.8	147	7.0	28.2	33.1
1831	2,373	13.0	640	27.0	23.0	202	8.5	31.5	37.6
1841	2,602	10.4	790	30.2	23.4	274	9.7	32.3	35.5
1851	2,888	10.3	926	32.1	17.2	329	11.3	35.3	20.0
1861	3,062	6.0	1,060	34.6	14.4	395	12.9	37.3	20.0
1871	3,360	9.7	1,241	37.0	17.0	477	14.2	38.4	20.7
1881	3,735	11.2	1,460	39.1	17.6	511	13.6	35.0	7.1
1891	4,025	7.8	1,657	41.2	13.4	565	14.0	34.1	10.5
1901	4,472	11.1	1,976	44.2	19.2	761	17.0	38.5	13.4
1911	4,760	6.5	2,169	45.6	9.7	784	16.4	36.1	3.0
1912	Glasgow Boundaries Annexation Act					1,008	21.1	46.4	28.5

Sources: Cleland, 1828; Census Enumeration Abstracts, 1801–1911. Appendix to 1911 Abstract, 'Population of Area affected by Glasgow Boundaries Act 1912'.

of either the West Central Lowlands or Glasgow, decennial increases were
nevertheless high (see Table 2.3, column 2) and the sharp rise in growth rates at
the turn of the century may be explained by the introduction of smallpox
vaccination on an extensive and growing scale. From 1803 onwards smallpox
mortality fell rapidly; the high rates of the late-eighteenth century, when
smallpox constituted 15 per cent of all deaths in Scotland (Flinn, 1977, p. 15),
were replaced by high survival rates for children, with only two to three per cent
of all child deaths in Glasgow between 1805 and 1818 attributed to smallpox

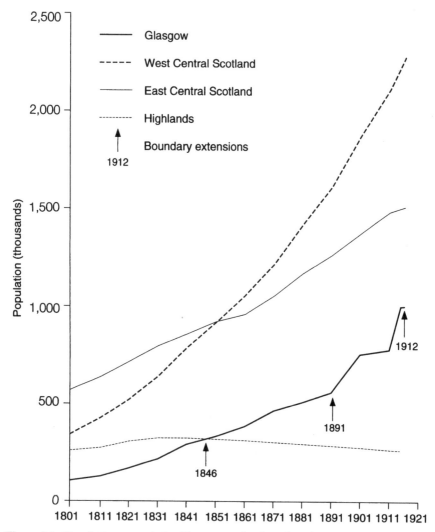

Figure 2.1: Population growth in Glasgow and selected regions, 1801–1914. *Source:*
Census Enumeration Abstracts, 1801–1921.

(Houston, 1988, p. 16). Before the implementation of civil registration of births and deaths from 1855 onwards, it is impossible to assess accurately the relative roles of natural increase and net migration in population growth, although rough calculations may be made from the 1841 and 1851 censuses. These broad indications reinforce the hypothesis that only sustained and large-scale in-migration could have produced Glasgow's high rates of increase in the first four decades of the nineteenth century.

MIGRANT SOURCES

Migrants of this early period may be identified as originating from three principal areas. The contiguous counties of West Central Lowland Scotland constituted the immediate hinterland of Glasgow and provided an initial source of migrants. In the 1780s and 1790s agricultural improvement schemes resulted in the enclosure of the former open fields and the replacement of multiple-tenancy farms, or hamlet clusters, by single farmsteads. The changing status of thousands of rural families left them with the choice of remaining on the land as hired labourers, often on a temporary basis, while drainage and construction schemes were carried out, or of migrating to the perceived security of a job in the developing textile centres. Rural skills in hand-loom weaving brought them ready employment in the villages of Calton, Anderston and Bridgeton, which were already beginning to be enveloped by Glasgow's urban spread, or later as factory hands in the new steam-powered mills in more central locations. By 1819 these migrants constituted over 40 per cent of the employed population of the weaving communities, which also increasingly offered employment opportunities for women (Cleland, 1828, p. 8; Whatley, 1995).

A second migrant stream derived from the Scottish Highlands (Withers and Watson, 1991). The collapse of the traditional bases of the regional economy, namely black cattle-rearing, fishing and the gathering of seaweed for chemical production, revealed a dangerous level of over-population on a very limited resource base. A steady trickle of migrants developed into a greater stream, pressed onwards by a harsh environment and by agricultural change, as some of the new ideas of improvement were taken up by the Highland landlords. These Highland families were different culturally from the Lowland migrants, with the majority being Gaelic speakers and Roman Catholics, as opposed to Lowland English-speaking Protestants, and a new ethnic group was therefore added to the city.

The third major element in the migrant stream derived from Ireland. Seasonal migrants from Ireland had been employed to bring in the Scottish harvest from the beginning of the eighteenth century and many of these joined the movements to the towns in the early stages of industrialization. After 1790 a combination of political unrest and industrial decline encouraged greater numbers of Irish to seek employment in the rapidly growing Scottish cotton industry, as well as in the construction of houses, factories, canals, docks and railways. The Irish-born proportion of Glasgow's population swelled from approximately 10 per cent in 1819 to 25 per cent in 1845, taking into account offspring born in Scotland (Handley, 1947, p. 55).

THE SPATIAL BEHAVIOUR OF MIGRANTS

The keynote of this early period was the concentration of migrants and, as Table 2.4 indicates, the inner-city parishes attracted large numbers of all migrant groups. The figures for 1819 do not show Scottish migrants, but the high percentage of lodgers in individual parishes may be taken as a rough proxy, reflecting the severe shortage of housing. The growing textile industry of Calton had attracted the largest number of migrants in 1819, as had the weaving centres of Anderston and Bridgeton; the group of inner-city parishes contrasted strongly in terms of migrant density with those of the outer city. By 1841 the deluge of migrants had overwhelmed available accommodation in the central area and migrants now constituted between approximately 40 and 60 per cent of the population of all city and suburban parishes. St Mary Tron, in this respect, clearly functioned as the principal reception area in the city. Table 2.4 also shows the high proportions of young people, many of them doubtless migrants, in every parish. In 1819 between 35 and approximately 46 per cent of the total population of all parishes was under 20 years of age: by 1841 this had risen in every case, with the exception of St Mary's parish, which reported a marginal decline from a very high figure. In an 1841 report compiled by the City Marshall and Superintendent of Police on over 1,000 destitute persons in the city, approximately 30 per cent were Irish, a proportion comparable to that within the total population, but over 63 per cent of those listed had been under 35 years of age on arrival in Glasgow (Miller, 1841). To propinquity was added fecundity, with inevitable consequences for population growth.

House-building had not managed to keep pace with the sharp rises in population brought about by high fertility levels and sustained in-migration, and the inevitable effect was a severe over-crowding of existing dwellings. A ratio of 4.4 persons per inhabited house in 1819 had risen to 4.6 in 1821, 4.8 in 1831 and to 5.2 by 1841 (Cleland, 1828, p. 9),[1] but the increase was spatially selective, both between and within parishes. While Outer High parish recorded a ratio of 4.9 in 1841, that of St Mary Tron registered 5.5, and in St John's parish in 1819 densities varied between 3.5 and 5.9 persons per house (Census of Great Britain, 1841; Cage and Checkland, 1976, p. 42). House construction focused principally on spacious and sanitary dwellings designed for the growing middle-class element in the city's population, moving out of the increasingly over-crowded and insanitary core to the new towns of the west end around George Square and Blythswood Hill, or to Laurieston on the south bank of the River Clyde (Gibb, 1983, pp. 95–100, Figure 5.iii).

1 Census of Great Britain, *Enumeration Abstract ... Scotland 1821, 1831, 1841.*

Table 2.4: *Migrants in Glasgow City and adjacent parishes, 1819 and 1841.*

	Parishes	1819				1841	
		% non-Scots	% Irish	% lodgers	% total pop. aged under 20	% non-Lanark-shire	% total pop. aged under 20
Inner	St Mary Tron	17.0	15.8	13.4	38.4	59.8	41.4
city	St John	15.8	14.5	10.2	41.7	41.2	46.2
	St James	14.7	13.3	11.7	39.0	39.2	43.3
	St Andrews	11.8	9.8	10.8	39.2	50.1	42.3
	College	11.0	9.7	12.3	37.7	43.6	43.9
Outer	St Enoch	7.7	6.1	12.5	35.2	51.0	39.8
city	Outer High	5.7	4.1	11.7	37.0	39.9	41.6
	St George	5.6	3.6	9.1	40.0	50.7	46.2
	St Mungo	4.6	4.4	5.8	46.4	44.2	45.6
	St David	4.3	1.8	12.7	34.5	47.1	42.3
Barony	Calton	21.7	20.5	11.4	43.9	54.8	47.8
	Anderston	13.9	12.7	11.4	43.1	53.5	46.2
	Bridgeton	12.1	11.3	11.4	44.6	40.6	50.4
	St Vincent	8.2	5.8	9.2	41.6	59.0 (Maryhill)	49.5
	Port Dundas	6.4	5.6	8.3	45.0	52.4 (Gorbals)	46.0

Sources: Cleland, 1828; Census of Great Britain (1841), *Enumeration abstract*.

For the working classes, available accommodation fell into three principal categories. First, along the backlands of burgage plots in the central area lay warrens of small and unhealthy apartments, lacking in sanitary facilities of even the most basic kind; into these the majority of migrants crammed themselves. Secondly, others found shelter in tiny 'made-down' cells in once-large apartments where middle-class demand had either failed to materialize, or from which it had departed. Finally, at the lowest end of the scale, thousands of in-migrants found that the only available shelters were rat-infested lodging houses, of which some 600–700 existed in the city, mainly in the old urban core (Laidlaw, 1956, p. 18). One of the earliest national surveys of living and working conditions provides a graphic description of central Glasgow in 1839.

I have seen human degradation in some of its worst phases, both in England and abroad, but I can advisedly say that I did not believe until I visited the wynds of Glasgow, that so large an amount of filth, crime, misery and disease existed on one spot in any civilised country.

The wynds consist of long lanes, so narrow that a cart could with difficulty pass along them; out of these open the 'closes', which are courts about 15 to 20 feet square, round which the houses, mostly of 3 stories high, are built; the centre of the court is the dung-hill, which is probably the most lucrative part of the estate to the laird in most instances, and which it would consequently be deemed an invasion of the rights of property to remove. The houses are for the most part let in flats, either to the lowest class of labourers or prostitutes, or to lodging keepers; these latter places are the general resort and favourite abodes of all those to whom a local habitation and a name are professionally inconvenient. They are likewise the resting place of outcasts of every grade of wretchedness and destitution. In the more costly of these abodes, where separate beds are furnished at the price of 3d per night, the thieves and prostitutes chiefly congregate...

In the lower lodging-houses, then, twelve and sometimes twenty persons of both sexes and all ages sleep promiscuously on the floor in different degrees of nakedness. These places are, generally as regards dirt, damp and decay, such as no person of common humanity to animals would stable his horse in ... It is my firm belief that penury, dirt, misery, drunkenness, disease and crime culminate in Glasgow to a pitch unparalleled in Great Britain. (Symons, 1839)

An 1841 police report on destitute persons in Glasgow refers to 'poor helpless children almost starving ... five children in fever ... no work—no bed ... beds only straw on floor ... house damp and very unhealthy ... five feet six inches only from floor to ceiling', and so on through an endless catalogue of human misery (Miller, 1841, pp. 2–10). By the 1830s rising grain prices, a trade and industrial recession, and changing industrial technology had brought unemployment to thousands and chronic hunger added to their hardship (Devine, 1995). Between 1814 and 1830 the living standards of the unskilled workforce fell markedly (Treble, 1988, p. 204). In 1831 there were 18,500 on relief,[2] constituting the most obvious element in a population under-nourished, over-crowded, exhausted by overwork and wide open to the ravages of disease.

MORTALITY CRISES

The net result of the conditions described above was not only a high endemic level of disease, but a recurrence, primarily in an urban context, of mortality crises associated with the spread of epidemic disease. Contagious diseases bred and proliferated through the airless, stinking warrens of the poorer districts and then erupted into wealthy and poor suburbs alike. Pools and streams of stagnant sewage contaminated already inadequate water supplies, making water-borne diseases common. Lice-infested houses, unhygienic bedding and soiled personal clothing encouraged the spread of typhus. Miserable accommodation sheltered pulmonary and infantile diseases. From 1816 onwards, recurrent epidemics of considerable magnitude devastated the central city, but

2 Statement on behalf of the Committee of Subscribers for promoting a change in the mode of assessment for the poor of the city of Glasgow, 1831.

these were only 'the higher peaks of an elevated table-land of disease, which was capable of maintaining an annual death-rate, oscillating frequently between 30 and 40 per 1,000, and of rising, in occasional years ... to 46 or 56 per 1,000' (Chalmers, 1930, pp. 2–3).

The availability of the Glasgow Bills of Mortality, to a limited extent, compensates for the lack of civil registration before 1855 and their data permitted Flinn (1977, pp. 388–96) to categorize crude death rates from certain infectious diseases between 1800–1810 and 1836–1842. In both periods, tuberculosis and bronchitis figured most prominently, accounting for 22.8 per cent and 16.1 per cent respectively of all deaths. Measles, smallpox and whooping cough hovered between 5 per cent and 7.5 per cent, and fever (including typhus, typhoid and scarlet fever in the second period) rose from 9.8 per cent to 16.1 per cent of all deaths. However, these averages either disguise the epidemic peaks or underestimate their chronological range. The typhus epidemic of 1818 raged unchecked for a year, producing a death rate for the city 42 per cent higher than the previous five-year average. Cholera first appeared in the city in 1832 and the virulence of the disease terrified its people. Three thousand of them died of the disease between February and November, including 79 per cent of all victims admitted to the Albion Street Cholera Hospital (Lawrie, 1832); but at the height of its ravages typhus accounted for twice as many victims, including over 30 per cent of all patients admitted to the Royal Infirmary in 1832 (Cowan, 1837, p. 7; Easton, 1832, pp. 97, 232, 441–42). In the third major typhus epidemic of the period, in 1837, a further 2,200 people died.

The public health response was limited, perhaps because political power prior to 1833 remained concentrated in the hands of a small, self-elected clique (Maver, 1994, p. 100). In the whole city south of the river there was only one doctor in 1832, as was the case in Anderston, while in Calton and Bridgeton there was none. Hospitals proved hopelessly inadequate in terms of coping with the flood of fever victims and many individuals remained at home to spread the disease. Quarantine attempts were crude and generally ineffective and centres of contagion such as public houses could not be closed.[3] The construction of temporary fever hospitals, the fumigation of thousands of homes and the burning of bedding, especially in lodging houses, also proved of little benefit (Cleland, 1828, p. 197). Little was done to provide fresh water supplies. Industrial pollutants and human effluent overwhelmed the crude sewerage system and few public wells remained untainted. Council committees failed to act on expert advice which advocated the tapping of the Monkland Canal, or the use of steam engines to raise water from the Clyde (Marwick, 1876–1908, Vol. VIII, pp. 266, 452–53; Vol. IX, pp. 161–90). Private water

---

3 For an insight into the limited extent of health provision in the early 1830s, see 'Remarks on the Proceedings of the Glasgow Board of Health', *Glasgow Medical Examiner*, Nos X and XI, January/February, 1832.

companies piped in limited supplies, but they were under no obligation to lay pipes into areas where it would not pay them to do so. As a result, the poorer districts, whose inhabitants could not afford the high water rates, were left without a fresh supply. A general clamour for the opening of additional wells in 1834 revealed that of the town's 30 existing wells, serving a population of over 200,000, only 14 were in good order (Marwick, 1910).

When the overall death rates are broken down into age-specific cohorts, mortality levels were highly concentrated and clearly appalling (Table 2.5). In particular, severely congested living conditions accelerated the spread of contagious diseases affecting children. Outbreaks of measles, and particularly smallpox, produced enhanced mortality levels for the under-fives, rising to 70 per 1,000 in 1821, and to 112 per 1,000 by 1841. The benefits of inoculation were offset by population growth, dirt, ignorance and hunger: the rate of mortality for the whole population rose from 1 in 41 in 1822, to 1 in 30 in 1828 and 1 in 24 by 1837, with a much increased population at risk, as fevers and pulmonary diseases, always under-registered and grossly accentuated by over-crowding, took a terrible and growing toll of both native inhabitants and the young and healthy migrant stream (Cowan, 1832; Watt, 1844). The combined effects of these factors on life expectancy may be seen in Table 2.6. At all ages both male and female life expectancy was lower, often significantly so, in the period 1832–1841 than in the period 1821–1827. The price for economies of scale and the logic of industrial location, together with a probable fall in average real wages between 1815 and 1839 (Cage, 1983, p. 178), was now being paid with a vengeance. The city was on the verge of choking on its own effluent and by the time of the 1841 census Glasgow was a city in the grip of an industrial and social crisis. In this respect, it deserved its notoriety as one of the unhealthiest cities in Britain (Devine, 1988, p. 48).

Table 2.5: *Age-specific death rates in Glasgow, 1821–1841 (deaths in each age group per 1,000 living in each age group, both sexes).*

Age group	1821	1831	1841
0–4	70.4	66.1	112.8
5–9	11.9	9.8	16.1
10–19	6.6	6.6	9.3
20–29	10.2	8.7	11.1
30–39	13.6	11.8	17.3
40–49	16.7	19.3	26.0
50–59	26.2	30.2	38.2
60–69	42.8	49.0	65.8
Over 70	117.1	151.2	160.6

Source: Flinn, 1977, Table 5.5.2, p. 378.

Table 2.6: *Life expectancy at various ages in Glasgow, 1821–1827 and 1832–1841 (in years).*

	Males		Females	
Age	1821–27	1832–41	1821–27	1832–41
0	34.12	n.a.	36.64	n.a.
10	42.27	37.40	45.24	39.94
20	35.13	30.96	38.07	33.57
30	29.40	24.90	31.23	26.90
40	23.16	19.45	24.71	21.07
50	16.86	14.53	18.31	15.86
60	11.29	9.89	12.79	11.10
70	6.75	5.95	7.93	6.80

n.a.: not available.
Source: Chalmers, 1894, Table XV, p. 39.

INDUSTRIAL AND COMMERCIAL GROWTH: THE LATER PHASE

In the second half of the nineteenth century, the textile industry faltered in the face of competition from both continental Europe and America, and the disruption of raw cotton supplies during the American Civil War brought severe contraction. In 1861 the 48,500 textile workers vastly outnumbered the 4,500 ship-building and metal-trade workers in Glasgow and Govan, but by 1911 ship-building, engineering and their allied trades accounted for 60,000 workers, while textiles could only muster 24,000. An increase in the number of power looms in the Glasgow area was accompanied by the eclipse of hand-loom weaving by the mid-1870s, and other sectors of textile production, including labour-intensive sewed muslin making, had also disappeared by the end of the century (Cage, 1987b, p. 3). One of the roots of industrial change lay in the large-scale expansion of cheap iron production, which acted as a stimulus to coal-mining and railway construction, and provided raw material for ship-building (Knox, McKinley and Smyth, 1993). Ready access to raw materials was, indeed, important but it was overshadowed by the climate of experimentation and innovation. New materials for construction and new methods of propulsion helped Glasgow's entrepreneurs to capture markets ahead of any rivals. Innovation in mechanical engineering also spread to railway locomotives, pumps, boilers, sugar-refining machinery, machine tools and other branches of engineering. Structural engineering, particularly of building frames, cranes and bridges, also developed rapidly. At the same time, the decline of the heavy chemicals sector matched that of its parent textile industry and revealed ominous indications of a growing over-dependence upon interlocking fields of heavy engineering. Massive capital investment in new plant and workshops drew whole new ranges of enterprises, specializing in

Table 2.7: *Gross and unit tonnages, 1841–1908 (in million tons): (a) ships using Glasgow Harbour; (b) Glasgow-registered ships.*

Date	a		b		
	Gross tonnage	Unit tonnage	Gross tonnage	Unit tonnage	Number of ships
1841	1.14	75.1	95,062	220.0	431
1861	1.5	93.5	218,804	332.2	679
1881	3.05	172.1	827,435	657.7	1,258
1891	3.37	209.1	1,316,809	835.5	1,576
1908	6.0	368.8	1,957,391	1,151.4	1,700

Source: Marwick, 1909, Appendix, Tables II and III.

dockyard construction and electrical apparatus, into the web dominated by ship-building. At the same time, the locational requirements of these industries, in terms of space, access to the river and to each other, produced new concentrations of heavy industry on the periphery of the city where extensive specialized districts developed dominated by large-scale industrial units. In the central area of the city, small foundries and metalworks declined, while between these an established inner ring of chemical and textile factories, as well as ironworks, remained in operation.

These new locational realities imposed demands on the spatial distribution of population, as did the large-scale improvements to the River Clyde and to the harbour of Glasgow. On the downstream section of the river, the construction of dry-docks for ship repair formed the boundary between the rapidly expanding ship-yards and the upper, commercial section of the river. Tidal basins were opened in the 1860s, 1870s and 1890s and provided badly needed off-river quay-space, while specialized mineral docks, cattle lairages and timber storage facilities transformed the River Clyde. It became a long ship-canal, wide and deep enough to permit the passage of ocean-going vessels to the port of Glasgow, with its modern dockside facilities, long rows of warehouses and waiting railways. Table 2.7 gives an indication of the rising scale of usage of the port of Glasgow, in terms of gross and unit tonnages of ships entering the harbour, as well as the growth in Glasgow-registered ships.

POPULATION DYNAMICS: THE LATER PHASE, 1841–1914

During the second half of the nineteenth and the early decades of the twentieth century Glasgow went through a demographic transition from a stage of dangerous imbalance, with population growth maintained only by large-scale migration, to a stage where growth was sustained on the basis of a lowered birth rate offset by the survival of a much higher proportion of infants and children, together with a greatly reduced level of net migration. The crucial processes during these decades were the beginnings of public health legislation and its implementation by the city authorities. At the same time Glasgow was a focus of broad spatial processes of population change within Scotland, consisting principally of Highland–Lowland and rural–urban transfers. In general terms, the West Central Lowland share of the Scottish population rose steadily and urban areas gained at the expense of rural districts, with the largest urban units, especially Glasgow, gaining most (see above, Table 2.3). As early as 1861 while the urban:rural population ratio for Scotland as a whole was 58:42 that of the West Central Lowlands was 80:20, demonstrating clearly the trend towards an overwhelming urban dominance which was to develop further during the next 50 years.

THE COMPONENTS OF DEMOGRAPHIC CHANGE

Any discussion of the relative roles of natural increase and net migration as components of population change in Glasgow is complicated by the operation of a third process, that of the absorption of peripheral population groups. However, while the three components are functionally linked it is possible to examine them separately and at different scales and, in doing so, a pattern of growth radically different from the earlier part of the nineteenth century may be discerned.

First, in terms of natural increase, Glasgow must be viewed in the context of its wider region, the West Central Lowlands. Of all Scottish regions, West Central exhibited the highest death rates in the second half of the nineteenth century[4], but it managed to maintain a rate of natural increase of 13–15 per 1,000, primarily on the basis of a birth rate which varied decennially between approximately 30 and 40 per 1,000. Such a high birth rate was a result of the best balanced sex ratio in Scotland, which produced high rates of marriage (Flinn, 1977, p. 41) and relatively good employment prospects, which allowed early marriage for both sexes (Anderson, 1996). As Glasgow was a major element in determining the population characteristics of the West of Scotland, it is not surprising that the city should closely echo these demographic patterns (Figure 2.2).

Significant divergences from the regional trend, such as the low rate of natural increase in the 1870s, can be explained by a phase of out-migration by fertile elements. The city's overall lower rate of natural increase between 1861 and 1910 was a function of Glasgow's greater efficiency as a killer of population. As public health measures took effect towards the end of the nineteenth and at the beginning of the twentieth century, the rates of natural increase of Glasgow and the West Central Lowlands began to converge.

Secondly, while the rate of natural population increase was maintained at a steady level, that of migration varied greatly, producing considerable

---

4 Census Enumeration Abstracts, 1861–1911.

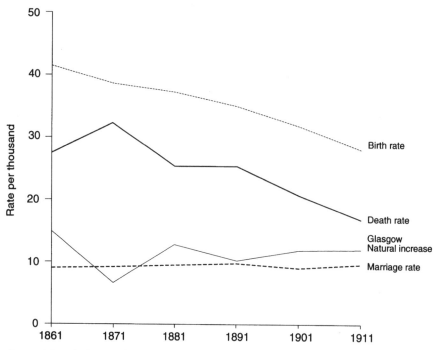

Figure 2.2: Vital rates in Glasgow, 1861–1911 (per 1,000). *Sources:* Cunnison and Gilfillan (eds), 1958, Appendix, pp. 794–95, 798; Census Enumeration Abstracts, 1861–1911.

irregularities in the city's overall growth rate. From 1841 to 1871 there was a large net inflow, while in the 1870s and 1880s out-migration was predominant (Anderson and Morse, 1993, p. 16). A resurgence of in-migration in the late 1890s was followed by an even steeper level of outflow lasting to the end of the period under consideration. This corresponded to a wider change in migration patterns in favour of emigration from the British Isles instead of urban in-migration.

To complicate matters further, the reduced in-migration flows into Glasgow in the 1870s and 1880s were not representative of the area as a whole, since suburban communities, where ship-building and engineering were booming, experienced sharp population increases (Gibb, 1983, p. 125). Table 2.8 gives some indication of Glasgow's migration pattern in relation to the broader characteristics of its suburban area, and of West Central Scotland as a whole, while Figure 2.3 shows the differential behaviour of the city core and periphery in one key decade, 1871–1881. For instance, in two ship-building areas, namely in Partick and Govan, the population rose between 1871 and 1881 from 17,000 to 36,000 and from 19,000 to 61,000, respectively. Thus within Greater

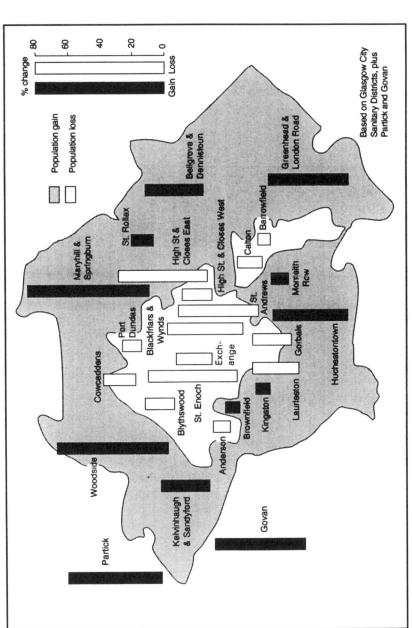

Figure 2.3: Population change in Glasgow, 1871–1881. *Source:* Russell, 1886, pp. 13–47.

Table 2.8: *Population change in West Central Scotland and Greater Glasgow, 1861–1910.*

Period	West of Scotland			Glasgow				
	Total %	Natural %	Balance %	Total %	Natural %	Balance %	Migration to Glasgow (000s)	Migration to suburbs (000s)
1861–1870	17.1	14.8	+ 2.3	20.8	11.5	+ 9.3	+ 41.0	+ 23.6
1871–1880	17.6	15.9	+ 1.7	2.3	11.3	− 9.0	− 38.0	+ 61.8
1881–1890	13.5	15.7	− 2.2	15.8	12.7	+ 3.1	− 11.0	+ 21.7
1891–1900	19.0	15.2	+ 3.8	10.2	13.6	− 3.4	+ 28.3	+ 9.3
1901–1910	9.8	15.0	− 5.2	1.1	11.8	− 10.7	− 82.6	− 7.4

Sources: Flinn, 1977, Tables 5.1.2 and 5.1.6, pp. 304–05, 312; Cairncross, 1953, p. 23.

Glasgow, an area which was constituted after various boundary changes and which may be viewed as the Glasgow migration region, the rates of migration and population growth fluctuated less than within the bounds of the older city. In the old city core population declined, partly as a result of the activities of the City Improvement Trust, which attempted to demolish large sections of Glasgow's central slums after 1866, and partly as a result of changing land use, as public buildings and offices for the growing central business district displaced residents. The periphery of the city, which contained the mass of recently erected tenements and industrial premises, attracted not only displaced central city residents but recent in-migrants.

THE SPATIAL BEHAVIOUR OF MIGRANTS

While population losses in the city core numbered 54,000 between 1871 and 1881, the gains in the peripheral districts stood at approximately 79,000, providing some indication of migrant preference for the newer tenement areas. However, migrant residential preference was as varied as the composition of the migrant stream which changed proportionally over time. The decade 1841–1851 continued the trend of extremely high rates of in-migration established during the previous 30 years, but from the 1851 peak, when almost 56 per cent of the population was not city-born, the level fell steadily throughout the later-nineteenth and early-twentieth centuries. Table 2.9 shows the birthplace of migrants to Glasgow and demonstrates the gradual rise in the proportion of Glasgow-born inhabitants. Among in-migrants Scots constituted the largest component, with the greatest contribution provided by short-distance migrants from the western and, to a lesser extent, the Eastern Lowlands. In the 1840s and early 1850s the failure of successive potato crops in Ireland and the resultant famines brought a sharp increase in the numbers of Irish immigrants. In 1848 arrivals from Ireland averaged over 1,000 per week, with Glasgow

Table 2.9: *The birthplace of Glasgow's inhabitants (in per cent), 1851–1911.*

Birthplace	1851	1861	1871	1881	1891	1901	1911
Scotland (exc. Glasgow)	34.68	30.04	34.52	31.56	29.89	*27.00	26.18
Ireland	18.17	15.69	14.32	13.12	10.57	8.87	6.73
England and Wales	2.51	2.63	3.06	3.16	3.36	3.72	3.81
Other	0.53	0.86	0.67	0.85	0.96	1.67	1.74
All migrants	55.89	49.22	52.57	48.69	44.78	*41.26	38.46
Glasgow-born	44.11	50.78	47.43	51.31	55.22	58.74	61.54

* Lanarkshire-born residents have been estimated at *c*.20,000 to give the Scottish total for 1901.
Source: Census Enumeration Abstracts, 1851–1911.

receiving 42,860 in the first four months of that year. This flood of migrants increased the overall Irish total by 90 per cent, constituting 7.2 per cent of the Scottish population in 1851 and 45.7 per cent of all migrants in the West of Scotland as a whole (Slaven, 1979, p. 143). Of these, 28.8 per cent were located in Glasgow where they formed 18.2 per cent of the city's population (Flinn, 1977, p. 456).

A small but steady trickle of English migrants grew in absolute numbers between 1851 and 1911, reflecting the rising number of skilled industrial jobs and especially the increased commercial opportunities in the city. In the decades around the turn of the century Italian migrants arrived; they mainly entered the service sector seeking employment in restaurants in particular and they were also concentrated in wholesaling and retailing. During the same period Russian and Polish Jews added to the ethnic diversity of the city, constituting a concentrated migration flow with a heavier than usual bias towards males. In 1911 around 65 per cent of this group were concentrated in the Western Lowlands with one-third of the total number in Glasgow, in both cases attracted by the opportunities to use their industrial skills (Flinn, 1977, p. 458).

Broad patterns of locational choice among migrants may also be discerned. The Italians initially located themselves in low-quality housing near the city core, but quickly spread to the new tenement districts of the industrial city and to the fringes of the commercial district where opportunities for business existed. The Polish and Russian Jews at first settled mainly in the Gorbals, where a Jewish community had existed since the Napoleonic wars. In 1879 the Jewish population numbered less than 1,000, but then expanded rapidly due to the new influx; many of the migrants found employment as mathematical and optical instrument makers, furriers, agents and manufacturers in the garment trade (Levy, 1958). This double connection, in terms of ethnic origin and occupation, was a mechanism of familiarization and entry used by every incoming group. Scots migrants, preferring to locate in the newer tenement areas, often moved in as lodgers or boarders with families from their own parish or region, and equally often are recorded as having the same occupation as, or a similar occupation to, members of the host family.[5] These social linkages were extended to the search for individual accommodation, with renters of long standing and good character approaching house factors on behalf of their erstwhile lodgers, thereby intensifying ethnic characteristics at a very localized scale (Morgan and Daunton, 1983, p. 277).

Irish immigrants showed a strong predilection for the densely-packed warrens of cheap housing in the central districts. The interlocking factors of relative poverty, low skill levels and the need for accessibility to the casual labour market combined to intensify and prolong the magnetic attraction of the central area, even after the large-scale demolitions of the 1860s and 1870s had reduced the number of low-quality houses available. An ageing group of residents, including large numbers of residual single-parent families with Glasgow-born heads, sure indicators of social decay (Lamont, 1976, pp. 49–50), shared the area with Irish migrants. The district around St Mary's or Tron parish, with a population 45 per cent Irish-born in 1851, still had 32 per cent Irish in 1881 after the considerable clearances in Tron, Bridgegate and the Wynds and the 1904 report on housing in the city noted the Irish preference for cheap central accommodation.[6] Outer areas, by contrast, had only small numbers of Irish; Kingston had 8 per cent and Kelvinhaugh and Sandyford only 6 per cent in 1881 (Russell, 1886, pp. 14, 20, 45). While a displacement of large numbers of Irish did take place, with Bridgegate and High Street (West) losing respectively 46 and 36 per cent of their Irish-born population between 1881 and 1891, movement was mainly to adjacent inner-city areas and to the new lodging houses erected by the City Improvement Trust in cleared areas (Lamont, 1976, pp. 125, 136–37; Cage, 1987a, pp. 69–70). Young single Irish males in particular found these institutions useful. In 1891 the Irish constituted 10.57 per cent of Glasgow's total population, but 20 per cent of its institutional population; they represented 29 and 38 per cent respectively of the population of model lodging houses and 'homes and refuges' (Russell, 1891, pp. 33–34).

In the second half of the nineteenth century, as Glasgow's industrial and commercial structure developed in scale and complexity and changing industrial requirements enforced new patterns of location, processes of social segregation produced a mosaic of distinctive social characteristics in the different areas of the city and its suburbs. As the central core deepened its residual social characteristics, highly skilled migrants were drawn to the new nodes of industry with their associated workers' tenements, while the lower

5 Manuscript Census Enumerators' Books: Kelvin and Dennistoun Registration Districts, 1891.
6 Glasgow Municipal Commission on the Housing of the Poor, 1904, Vol. 1, Minutes of Evidence,
   p. 4.

Table 2.10: *The growth of population in annexed Police Burghs, 1861–1911.*

Police Burghs	Type of Burgh	1861	1871	1881	1891	1901	1911	Date annexed
		Total Population						
Crosshill	residential	–	2,265	2,960	3,798			1891
Govanhill	residential	349	–	9,636	14,340			1891
Maryhill	industrial	3,717	5,835	12,884	18,134			1891
Hillhead	residential	–	3,718	6,648	7,738			1891
Pollokshields	residential	580	3,314	6,464	9,709			1891
Kinning Park	industrial	651	7,217	11,552	13,679	13,852		1905
Govan	industrial		19,200	49,560	61,589	76,532	89,605	1912
Patrick	industrial		17,707	27,410	36,538	54,298	46,849	1912
Pollokshaws	industrial		8,921	9,363	10,228	11,182	12,932	1912

Source: adapted from Tivy, 1958, p. 263.

middle classes and highly paid artisans created discrete areas of higher residential quality. As its core decayed, Glasgow sought to rationalize its municipal services and extend its rating base by absorbing these new, successful settlements. In 1846 the burghs of Anderston and Calton and the Barony of Gorbals were annexed, lying west, east and south of the city respectively. The next major extension took place in 1891, adding 6,000 acres of territory and over 90,000 people to the city. This represented a victory for the city in a hard-fought battle for independence by burghs created under the 1850 Police Act; in 1912 a further victory brought in another 6,000 acres and over 226,000 people (Gibb, 1983, p. 125). Table 2.10 shows the date of annexation and the character of the areas absorbed, in terms of their predominantly residential or industrial status, and demonstrates the effects of industrialization on rapid population growth and concentration, especially in Govan and Partick. The process of boundary extension therefore extended the range of urban social environments and their associated life-chances which eventually made up the city and at the same time absorbed large groups of population whose spatial, social and demographic structure was a reflection of the city in microcosm.

LIFE-CHANCES AND MORTALITY CRISES

The experience of the urbanization process in the early decades of the nineteenth century had been traumatic. Adam Smith's 1776 prophecy of workers brutalized by urban living had been borne out by Sir John Sinclair's description in 1825 of 'a servile, pallid and sickly race, brought up in the confined air of cotton mills' (Sinclair, 1825, p. 170). The terrible price in human misery of the inexorable logic of scale economies was making itself apparent,

Table 2.11: *Epidemic disease and the public health response in Glasgow, 1843–1910.*

	Disease		Public health response
1843	Relapsing fever: 1,398 deaths	1843	Police Act: Inspector of Cleansing (streets and public places) appointed.
1847	Typhus: 4,346 deaths	1846	Nuisance Removal (Scotland) Act.
1848/9	Cholera: 3,772 deaths	1848	Gravitation water supply to Gorbals (private).
1851	Typhus	1853	Compulsory infant vaccination (smallpox): not enforced.
1853/5	Cholera: 3,885 deaths	1855	Loch Katrine Act: Scottish Registration Act (compulsory registration of disease).
		1856	Nuisances Removal (Scotland) Act (amended).
		1857	Committee on Nuisances.
		1859/60	Loch Katrine Scheme—fresh water to city.
		1861	Police Act: Sanitary Department set up and Medical Officer of Health appointed.
		1863	'Ticketed' houses.
1864	Typhus: 1,138 deaths	1864	First municipal disinfecting and washing-house in High Street. Vaccination Act.
1865	Typhus: 1,177 deaths	1865	First municipal fever hospital in Parliamentary Road.
1866	Cholera: 53 deaths	1866	Police Act (sanitary clauses): City Improvements Act (housing).
		1867	Public Health (Scotland) Act.
1869	Typhus: 970 deaths	1870	Sanitary Department extended. Temporary fever hospital, Belvidere.
1870	Relapsing fever	1872	First reception house for families of typhus victims.
1873	Relapsing fever:* 228 deaths	1873	City Improvements Amended Act; vaccination station opened.
1875	Typhoid and enteric fever,* Camphill		
1877/8	Enteric fever,* West End	1878	Permanent smallpox hospital, Belvidere. First proper isolation.
		1878/84	Opening of district baths and wash-houses.
		1879	Dairies and Milkshops Order.

Table 2.11: *continued*

	Disease		Public health response
1880	Enteric fever,* North and Central	1880	City Improvements Amendment Act.
		1881	Free treatment for fever patients. Returns of vaccination defaulters; first refuse destructor (further provision in 1884, 1890, 1894, 1897, 1902).
		1883	Washing and disinfection station, Belvidere.
1884	Enteric fever,* hospitals	1889	Infectious Disease (Notification) Act.
1888	Scarlet fever,* Garnethill	1890	Housing of the Working Classes Act (Part V. Scotland). Glasgow Police Amendment Act (water closet provision).
1892	Scarlet fever,* Paisley Road	1892	Glasgow Building Regulations Act: Ruchill fever hospital started. Further Powers Act (smoke penalties).
1893/4	Scarlet fever,* Kelvinside	1894	First sewage purification unit, Dalmarnock; disinfection station, Ruchill.
		1897	Public Health (Scotland) Act: Glasgow Corporation (Improvements etc.) Act.
1900	Smallpox	1904	Sewage purification works, Dalmuir and Partick.
		1907	Notification of Births Act: Glasgow Infant Health Visitors Association.
		1908	Children Act.
		1910	Kinning Park and Shieldhall sewage purification works.
		1911	Health Insurance.
		1912	Notification of pulmonary tuberculosis.
		1914	Notification of all forms of tuberculosis.
		1915	Maternity and Child Welfare Schemes: Act for training and supervision of Midwives.

* infected milk source.

Sources: Chalmers (ed.), 1905, pp. 3, 19, 22, 55; Chalmers, 1930, pp. 7–12.

yet Glasgow's industrial revolution was barely under way and, for the working classes, the worst was yet to come. Growing awareness of the appalling living conditions and associated high death rates in over-crowded urban areas, together with the fear of a contagious diffusion of disease into higher-quality environments, finally provoked a response. Although sluggish and ineffective at first, the Victorian battle for public health gained vigour as the century drew to a close. Table 2.11 gives an impression of the increasing frequency and weight of legislation and official action, as well as their effects on the incidence of disease (see also Figure 2.4).

In Glasgow the large population increases of the early decades of the nineteenth century had overwhelmed housing and water supply alike, creating ideal conditions for the spread of disease. According to Russell:

> Though typhus did not arrest attention by an epidemic prevalence until 1818, it was in the city from the beginning of the century. Its subsequent history was that of an active volcano, periods of deceptive repose alternating with violent eruptions. For short intervals it smouldered in the wynds. When the steady influx of immigrants attracted by the prospect of work had reproduced a susceptible population, it burst out into an epidemic. Smallpox ... was scarcely ever entirely absent ... three severe epidemics of cholera ... 1832 ... 1848/9 ... 1853/4. An outbreak of relapsing fever in 1843 attacked more than a quarter of the inhabitants of the poorer districts. Underneath these periodic eruptions flowed a continuous condition of ill-health, which represented the chronic, as the former represented the periodic, results of precisely the same physical circumstances in the environment of the population. (Russell, 1895, p. 205)

Thus the second half of the nineteenth century began in Glasgow with a huge backlog of problems requiring curative rather than preventive effort, and the effectiveness of early public health measures was to a large extent negated by the continuance of old problems relating to sanitation and water supply, as well as by the appearance of a whole crop of new problems associated with the type and density of housing being constructed to meet the needs of a rapidly growing workforce. Table 2.12 indicates the broad course of changes in key variables and demographic rates between 1841 and 1911. Total population grew steadily in absolute numbers and, between 1841 and 1881, in terms of density per acre, with boundary extensions producing fluctuations in population density after that date. Overall death rates and mortality in the age group 0–5 closely followed similar patterns, with the first two census dates showing high levels and thereafter a steady reduction, interrupted by the anomalous year of 1871, when measles and smallpox epidemics raised both rates considerably. Infant mortality rates for the period exhibited a less dramatic reduction, but the 1914 levels are similar to those of Liverpool and Manchester (Figure 2.5), which admittedly had started at much higher levels than Glasgow. The public health response to infant mortality in these two English cities also followed a similar pattern, with measures aimed specifically

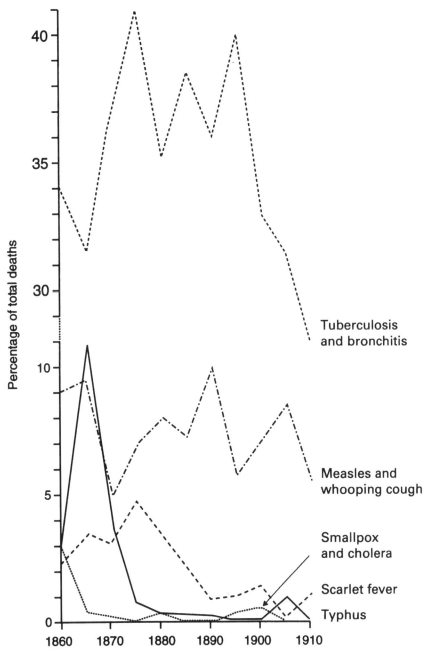

Figure 2.4: Percentage of total deaths from selected diseases in Glasgow, 1860–1910. *Sources:* Annual Reports, Registrar General for Scotland; Chalmers, 1914a, adapted from p. 212, 'Public health—vital statistics'.

Table 2.12: *Population density and death rates in Glasgow, 1841–1911.*

	Population (1,000s)	Density per acre	Death rate (per 1,000)	Death rate under 5 (per 1,000)
1841	274	50	31	156.8
1851	329	65	38	171.3
1861	395	78	30	137.8
1871	477	94	33	160.6
1881	511	97	28	104.9
1891	565	84	25	95.9
1901	761	93	21	83.8
1911	784	60	17	61.2

Sources: Cunnison and Gilfillan, 1958, Statistical Appendix Pt. 1, Table 9, p. 798; Flinn, 1977, Tables 5.5.2, p. 378.

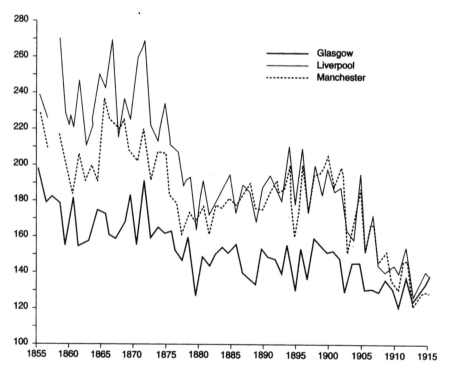

Figure 2.5: Infant mortality rate per thousand births in Glasgow, Liverpool and Manchester, 1855–1914. *Source:* Chalmers, 1930, p. 190.

at ante- and post-natal care coming into effect after the turn of the century (Table 2.11).

The official response to the growing problems of public health may be divided into three broad categories aimed, first, at water supply and sewage disposal, secondly, at personal and environmental cleansing, and finally at housing. Each one of these approaches affected particular groups of contagious disease and their general effects may be observed in Table 2.13 and Figure 2.4. In the period 1855–1875 the provision of fresh water supplies on a large scale from Loch Katrine attacked the principal breeding grounds of disease in the polluted waters of public wells and the River Clyde (Sheard, 1993, pp. 86–93). Completing the hydrological cycle, the cumulative provision of water closets in most of the housing stock and the use of impervious glazed clay pipes to take away sewage ensured the rapid removal of harmful effluents and a vast reduction of seepage into the water table. However, it was not until the opening of the Dalmarnock works in 1894 that the process of providing an effective system of sewage disposal and treatment was complete (Cage, 1987a, p. 68). Cholera demonstrated the most immediate downturn. In 1853, a virulent epidemic caused over 3,800 deaths, almost two-thirds of the total for the whole of Scotland. In 1866, with fresh water having been made available in the city over the previous six years, there were only 53 deaths. Some credit must also be given to the 1862 Glasgow Police Act, which authorized the creation of a Sanitary Department, as well as the energetic efforts of Dr W. T. Gairdner, installed in 1863 as the first of a series of Medical Officers of Health for the city. The provision of fever hospitals, such as Belvidere, provided isolation and treatment facilities (Russell, 1888a, p. 3; Lamb, 1982, p. 31; Dupree, 1993, p. 201), although smallpox was slow to decline because of delayed compulsory registration for vaccination in Scotland (introduced in 1863 compared with 1853 in England) and extremely lax enforcement of regulations. Smallpox epidemics continued to erupt and in the outbreak of 1900 to 1902 the death rate among unvaccinated patients was over 50 per cent, compared with only 9 per cent for those who had been vaccinated (Thomson and Fullarton, 1902).

Among endemic diseases, typhus was notable for its large-scale and periodic outbursts. Spread by lice breeding in unwashed clothing and bedding, as well as in the filthy conditions of sub-standard housing, it was tackled by a range of measures. Plentiful water supplies provided the possibility of more frequent washing, and the erection of central washing-houses for infected clothing and bedding had some effect. However, rapid and frequent reinfection was encouraged not only by the persistence of gross poverty in the city, which made recourse to 'Paddy's market', the huge used clothing market on the edge of Glasgow Green, a necessity, but also by the continued use of infected houses. The first of a series of Improvement Acts empowering municipal authorities to demolish congested slum property followed hard on the heels of Glasgow's worst typhus outbreak in 1864–65, during which districts such as Tron and Garngad suffered 33 and 27 cases respectively per 1,000 population

Table 2.13: *Quinquennial totals of deaths in Glasgow from major diseases, 1855–1914.*

	Diarrhoea, dysentery, cholera	Typhus	Enteric fever	Scarlet fever	Diphtheria	Measles	Whooping cough	Bronchitis, pneumonia	Phthisis, pulmonary tuberculosis	Smallpox
1855–1859	2,719	2,333	–	2,427	757	1,657	3,163	4,355	6,493	1,043
1860–1864	1,330	3,225	–	2,343	1,570	1,817	3,214	5,984	8,298	1,115
1865–1869	2,053	3,607	1,140	3,210	1,154	2,020	3,262	6,323	9,665	167
1870–1874	2,092	1,191	1,111	3,397	1,557	2,001	3,083	6,721	9,566	775
1875–1879	1,968	352	1,097	1,622	1,388	1,449	3,362	6,777	9,118	25
1880–1884	1,885	194	1,032	1,862	1,475	1,880	3,437	5,866	6,335	23
1885–1889	1,440	97	497	1,161	1,302	1,677	3,144	5,360	7,048	8
1890–1894	1,609	61	617	1,163	999	2,654	2,985	5,298	8,290	38
1895–1899	2,500	49	883	878	590	2,949	3,205	4,797	7,229	30
1900–1904	–	44	599	430	521	1,990	3,115	4,824	6,960	424
1905–1909	–	10	395	483	820	2,540	2,805	3,592	6,415	–
1910–1914	–	13	271	807	862	2,815	3,156	3,206	4,464	–

Sources: Chalmers, 1930, pp. 284, 298, 300, 311, 322, 337; Registrar General's Annual Reports for Scotland, 1855–1914.

(Gairdner, 1865, p. 8). Together with washing, disinfection and isolation facilities, these measures had brought typhus largely under control by the 1880s.

Among the group of endemic diseases which took a particular toll of young children, a random decline in the virulence of the scarlet fever streptococcus reduced its fatality level and by the 1870s it was in rapid decline. However, the same could not be said for measles, whooping cough, diphtheria and diarrhoeal infections; death rates from these diseases did not begin to decline until the turn of the century. Deaths of children under five as a proportion of total deaths within the city had dropped from over 50 per cent in the period 1855 to 1859 to approximately 45 per cent between 1860 and 1864; but from 1865 to 1869 the proportion rose again to 47.5 per cent and until 1890 the average for each five-year period never fell below 43.5 per cent (Nicol, 1891, p. 62). Just as five-year averages inevitably disguise extremes, such as the year 1861 when child deaths represented 54 per cent of Glasgow's total mortality (Strang, 1861, p. 17), so city-wide generalizations tend to hide concentrations of wretchedness in the poorer districts as reflected in infant death rates. In 1858 infant mortality was nearly double among illegitimate as opposed to legitimate children, while one in 13 illegitimate children was stillborn compared with one in 26 legitimate (Strang, 1859, p. 7). Ethnic differences also made themselves felt, especially in the early part of the period when death rates of children under five were heavier among Catholics than among the population as a whole, primarily because Catholics were less inclined to have their children vaccinated against smallpox. It was also noted that midwifery practices among Highlanders had a particularly negative effect on infant as well as maternal mortality (Strang, 1852, pp. 8–9).

The third avenue of assault on disease was directed towards Glasgow's housing. Statutes on cubic air space inside and clean air outside tenements were aimed at the most efficient group of contagious killers of the nineteenth century, the respiratory diseases, principally pulmonary tuberculosis, bronchitis and pneumonia. Declining mortality from other infectious diseases permitted more children to survive into adulthood, only to succumb to a wasting of their lungs through living in over-crowded houses and going outdoors to breathe polluted industrial air. Even in the 1860s nothing matched the killing power of these diseases. Their mortality rates in Glasgow rose steadily until general hygiene measures, as well as those aimed specifically at tuberculosis from the 1890s onwards, began to bring about perceptible reductions. However, while tuberculosis responded to official intervention, pneumonia and bronchitis proved to be much more resistant and frequent outbreaks of epidemic proportions continued to occur well beyond the turn of the century. While some of this tenacious refusal to respond to official action may be ascribed to variations in the virulence of the infecting organism (Chalmers, 1930, p. 95), there was no doubt in the minds of many observers active in the field of public health improvement in Glasgow about the importance of housing in the environmental equation (Checkland and Lamb, 1982).

> Glasgow stands alone with the highest death-rate, the highest number of persons per room, the highest proportion of her population occupying one-apartment houses, and the lowest occupying houses of five apartments and upwards ... These facts prove beyond a doubt that the predominant factor in the health of cities is the proportion of house-space to inhabitant. (Russell, 1887, p. 11)
>
> It is those small houses which give ... the striking characteristics of an enormous proportion of deaths in childhood, and of deaths from diseases of the lungs at all ages. Their exhausted air and poor and perverse feeding fill our streets with bandy-legged children. (Russell, 1888b, p. 14)

Available space within the city became over-crowded with houses, tenements and factories. Moreover, the tenements contained an excessive number of rooms and the rooms, in turn, were over-crowded with people (Gairdner, 1870, p. 249). However, the crude rises in population density hid wide intra-urban variations. In 1860 the extremes were represented by St Mary Tron, with 715 persons per acre, and Springburn, still mainly rural, with 15 persons per acre. Closer to the mean for the core and periphery were Blackfriars and the West End districts, which showed considerable disparity, not only in terms of population density but also in social characteristics (Table 2.14). Figures for 1871 and 1881 show that while the density range began to narrow, wide variations persisted in area death rates, and these death rates, in turn, were closely related to the proportion of one- and two-roomed houses in any area (Table 2.15). Public intervention in housing provision and in housing type was slow to materialize.

The early emphasis was on the eradication of the worst areas of contagion, with approximately 11,000 houses being demolished between 1866 and 1901 (Butt, 1971, p. 71): in the years immediately prior to the First World War a further 5,000 houses were cleared (Butt, 1987, pp. 41–47). However, only a limited number of properties were built or acquired by the local authority and approximately 35 per cent of Glasgow's houses still had no separate WCs by

Table 2.14: *Vital statistics for Blackfriars and West End Districts, 1860.*

	Blackfriars	*West End*
Population	10,577	2,972
Density per acre	328	34
% population under 5	13.6	9.1
Birth rate (per 1,000)	44	17
Death rate under 5 (per 1,000)	213	34
Death rate over 5 (per 1,000)	95	5.3

Source: Strang, 1861.

Table 2.15: *City sanitary districts: comparative population density (per acre) and mortality (per 1,000), 1871–1881, and the distribution of one- and two-room houses in 1881 (per cent).*

| No.* | Name | Density per acre | | Total death rate per 1,000 | | Death rate under 5 years | | 1-room | 2-room |
| | | | | | | | | (per cent) | |
		1871	1881	1871	1881	1871	1881	1881	1881
0	Blythswood	126	101	20.6	16.1	75.5	52.9	9.0	26
17	Kelvinhaugh and Sandyford	37	43	20.4	17.2	69.0	54.0	7.5	37
15	Woodside	81	134	25.5	20.9	90.0	64.2	20.0	43
9	Monteith Row	39	42	23.5	21.0	81.1	70.1	15.5	33
1	Exchange	123	96	22.0	21.7	78.8	67.4	18.0	38
19	Kingston	100	97	25.6	21.8	86.3	73.4	18.0	36
4	St Rollox	289	316	30.8	21.8	102.5	69.0	27.0	56
23/4	Springburn and Maryhill	17	26	28.4	22.4	84.7	68.6	31.0	59
5	Bellgrove and Dennistoun	37	47	29.4	23.1	94.5	72.3	32.0	44
12	St Enoch Square	93	44	31.3	24.4	109.6	87.7	24.0	34
21	Hutcheson Square	99	121	26.4	24.9	87.6	79.3	31.0	52
7	Greenhead and London Road	36	52	31.1	26.7	106.4	87.5	43.5	47
20	Laurieston	251	186	29.8	27.2	102.7	88.5	30.0	50
2	Port Dundas	73	64	33.9	27.3	126.1	83.5	28.5	63
18	Anderston	249	229	32.5	28.4	116.3	101.7	33.0	47
10	St Andrews Square	365	189	38.3	28.7	144.0	93.1	29.0	33
22	Gorbals	350	274	38.5	29.0	138.2	103.8	29.0	45
3	High St and Closes West	301	239	45.7	29.9	165.8	95.6	46.5	38
8	Barrowfield	245	233	31.2	30.3	108.2	103.3	47.5	46
13	Brownfield	337	348	38.3	30.7	138.9	99.3	24.0	56
11	Calton	388	335	36.7	30.9	124.5	108.4	43.0	66
16	Cowcaddens	316	249	33.9	32.0	116.1	116.6	45.0	47
6	High St and Closes East	351	155	40.7	37.8	148.9	128.5	53.0	33
14	Bridgegate and Wynds	408	223	42.3	38.3	166.1	138.7	49.0	35

* This table should be read in conjunction with the map of population change, Figure 2.3.

Table 2.16a: *House and room occupancy in Glasgow, 1911.*

Rooms (apartments)	% of housing stock	% of population	Persons per house	Persons per room
1	23.1	13.7	3.1	3.1
2	46.3	48.3	4.8	2.4
3	18.6	21.0	5.2	1.7
4	6.6	7.1	5.0	1.2
5	8.0	9.6	5.5	0.7

Table 2.16b: *Death rate (per 1,000) by age group and house size in Glasgow, 1912.*

Rooms	Under 1 year	1–5 years	10–15 years
1	187.0	39.0	4.5
2	143.5	28.5	3.0
3	114.5	16.5	2.0
4+	88.0	10.0	1.5
City	151.0	28.5	3.0

Sources: (a) adapted from Chalmers, 1916, p. 7; (b) adapted from Chalmers, 1914b.

1914 (Rodger, 1992, p. 110). Housing provision and management were left almost entirely to the private sector in which the type and level of provision, always minimal and subject to enormous fluctuation, reflected the play of market forces. Low levels of house-building encouraged severe over-crowding and even in boom times there was little alleviation, since the majority of apartments built during these periods were of only one or two rooms. Between 1862 and 1901 approximately 77 per cent of all new houses were of these types with the four-storey tenement block containing 6–20 housing units (Rodger, 1986; Gibb, 1982, pp. 7–8). Their clear and long-lasting effect on mortality is demonstrated in Tables 2.16a and 2.16b. The negative impact of poor quality housing was further compounded by a rising level of evictions in the late-nineteenth century, reflecting significant landlord–tenant friction and the domination of rent collection by house factors (Morgan and Daunton, 1983; Rodger, 1989, p. 61).

INDUSTRIAL AND DEMOGRAPHIC MATURITY

Between the turn of the century and the outbreak of the First World War Glasgow's industrial base reached maturity. It was by then characterized by extreme specialization in heavy industry, amounting almost to an industrial mono-culture, with a densely interlocked infrastructure within which innovation and diversification were greatly retarded (Gibb, 1983, pp. 115–17). In terms of urban development, industry is a fundamental component. Although the specific relationships between industrial and demographic change are invariably complex, it is possible to discern some important characteristics in pre-1914 Glasgow. In relation to population structure, Figure 2.6 shows considerable contrasts both in age and sex distribution between 1851 and 1911. In 1851 the population pyramid had a relatively broad base, with a rapid tapering in terms of older cohorts, typical of a population in the early stage of the demographic transition. Deep indentations in the 1–4, 5–9 and 10–14 age cohorts may be attributed to the baleful effects of the cholera and typhus epidemics in the late 1830s and 1840s, although without the ravages of typhus the base of the pyramid might have been significantly broader. By 1911 these characteristics had altered dramatically and the equilateral triangle form of the earlier pyramid had been replaced by a beehive shape. While its base is only marginally narrower than that of 1851, for reasons mentioned above, shallow indentations produced a slower tapering from cohort to cohort, indicating higher survival rates in all cohorts by 1911. The pyramid is that of a population which has recently attained mature status.

The changing relative roles of natural increase and net migration in the population development of Glasgow have already been discussed, but it is important to note that the stage of the demographic transition at which abrupt falls in the rates of natural increase were experienced lay only a decade in the future. Maturity in migratory characteristics is also indicated by the proportion of inhabitants locally born. Köllmann (1965) has discussed in a German context the relationship between the proportion of native-born in a city's population and the different stages in the urban transition process: with a proportion of native-born of 44 per cent in 1851, rising to 62 per cent by 1911, Glasgow was clearly well advanced. In terms of spatial behaviour, a centrifugal movement also points to maturity, and it must be concluded that between 1851 and 1914, especially from the 1870s onwards, Glasgow experienced a large part of the maturation phase of its urban transition, with important implications for its demographic fortunes. By 1914 its population was more stable. The migratory contribution was negligible, boundary extensions of any magnitude were now over and the population was maintaining itself by net reproduction. In terms of spatial behaviour, internal transfers within the mass of densely-packed tenement housing reflected class divisions, particularly on the basis of wage differentials within the working class, until the advent of large-scale public sector housing provision altered the geography of the city and instituted a new cycle of population dynamics.

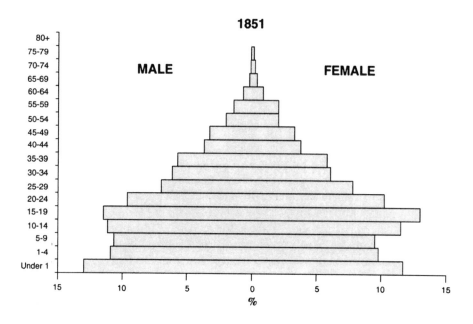

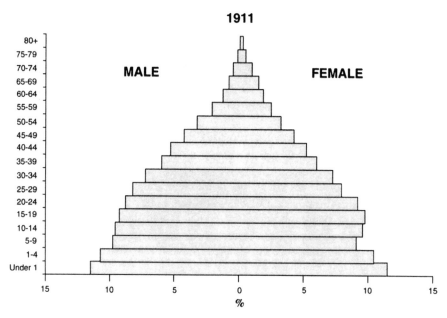

Figure 2.6: The age and sex distribution of Glasgow's population, 1851 and 1911. *Source:* Census Enumeration Abstracts, 1851 and 1911.

References

ANDERSON, M. (1996), 'Migration and nuptiality as interacting regulators of Scottish population growth, 1855–1914', in A. Bideau, A. Perrenoud, K.-A. Lynch and G. Brunet (eds), *Les systèmes démographiques du passé*, Lyon, 141–60.

ANDERSON, M. and D. J. MORSE (1993), 'High fertility, high emigration, low nuptiality: adjustment processes in Scotland's demographic experience, 1861–1914,' *Population Studies*, **47**, 5–25 and 319–43.

BUTT, J. (1971), 'Working-class housing in Glasgow, 1851–1914', in S. D. Chapman (ed.), *The History of Working Class Housing: A Symposium*, Newton Abbot.

BUTT, J. (1987), 'Housing', in R. A. Cage (ed.), *The Working Class in Glasgow 1750–1914*, London, Sydney, Wolfeboro, 29–55.

CAGE, R. A. (1983), 'The standard of living debate: Glasgow, 1800–1950', *Journal of Economic History*, **XLIII**, 175–82.

CAGE, R. A. (1987a), 'Health in Glasgow', in R. A. Cage (ed.), *The Working Class in Glasgow 1750–1914*, London, Sydney, Wolfeboro, 56–76.

CAGE, R. A. (1987b), 'Population and employment characteristics', in R. A. Cage (ed.), *The Working Class in Glasgow 1750–1914*, London, Sydney, Wolfeboro, 1–28.

CAGE, R. A. and E. O. A. CHECKLAND (1976), 'Thomas Chalmers and urban poverty: the St John's Parish experiment in Glasgow, 1819–1837', *Philosophical Journal*, 13 January.

CAIRNCROSS, A. K. (1953), *Home and Foreign Investment, 1870–1913. Studies in Capital Accumulation*, Cambridge.

CENSUS OF GREAT BRITAIN (1821, 1831, 1841, 1861–1911), *Enumeration Abstract ... Scotland*.

CHALMERS, A. K. (1894), *A New Life Table for Glasgow*, Glasgow.

CHALMERS. A. K. (ed.) (1905), *Public Health Administration in Glasgow: A Memorial Volume of the Writings of James Burn Russell*, Glasgow.

CHALMERS, A. K. (1914a), *Municipal Glasgow: its Evolution and Enterprises*, Glasgow.

CHALMERS, A. K. (1914b), *Public Health—Vital Statistics in Municipal Glasgow: Its Evolution and Enterprises*, Glasgow.

CHALMERS, A. K. (1916), *Health and Housing*, Glasgow.

CHALMERS, A. K. (1930), *The Health of Glasgow 1818–1925: An Outline*, Glasgow.

CHECKLAND, E. O. A. and M. LAMB (eds) (1982), *Health Care as Social History: The Glasgow Case*, Aberdeen.

CLELAND, J. (1828), *Statistical and Population Tables Relative to the City of Glasgow*, Glasgow.

COWAN, R. (1832), 'On the mortality of children in Glasgow', *Glasgow Medical Journal*, **V** (19), 353–61.

COWAN, R. (1837), *Vital Statistics of Glasgow, I. Statistics of Fever and Small Pox prior to 1837*, Glasgow.

CUNNISON, J. and J. B. S. GILFILLAN (eds) (1958), *The Third Statistical Account of Scotland*, Glasgow.

DEVINE, T. M. (1988), 'Urbanisation', in T. M. Devine and R. Mitchison (eds), *People and Society in Scotland I, 1760–1850*, Glasgow, 27–52.

DEVINE, T. M. (1995), 'The urban crisis', in T. M. Devine and G. Jackson (eds), *Glasgow. Vol. I: Beginnings to 1830*, Manchester and New York, 402–16.

DUPREE, M. W. (1993), 'Family care and hospital care: the "sick poor" in nineteenth-century Glasgow', *Social History of Medicine*, **6** (2), 195–212.

EASTON, J. A. (1832), 'Report of diseases among the poor of Glasgow', *Glasgow Medical Journal*, **V** (18).

FLINN, M. W. (ed.) (1977), *Scottish Population History from the Seventeenth Century to the 1930s*, Cambridge.

FRIEDLANDER, D. (1974), 'London's urban transition 1851–1951', *Urban Studies*, **11**, 127–41.

GAIRDNER, W. T. (1865), *Memorandum for the Chairman of the Sanitary Committee*, Glasgow.

GAIRDNER, W. T. (1870), 'On defects of house construction in Glasgow as a cause of mortality', *Proceedings of the Philosophical Society of Glasgow*, **VII**, 245–62.

GIBB, A. (1982), 'The development of public sector housing in Glasgow' (Centre for Urban and Regional Research, discussion paper), University of Glasgow.

GIBB, A. (1983), *Glasgow: The Making of a City*, Beckenham.

GLASGOW MEDICAL EXAMINER (1836), 'Remarks on the Proceedings of the Glasgow Board of Health', **X, XI**, January/February.

HANDLEY, J. E. (1947), *The Irish in Scotland 1798–1845*, Cork.

HOUSTON, R. A. (1988), 'The demographic regime', in T. M. Devine and R. Mitchison (eds), *People and Society in Scotland, I, 1760–1830*, Glasgow, 9–26.

JACKSON, G. (1995), 'New horizons in trade', in T. M. Devine and G. Jackson (eds), *Glasgow. Vol. I: Beginnings to 1830*, Manchester and New York, 214–38.

KNOX, W., A. MCKINLEY and J. SMYTH (1993), 'Industrialisation, work and labor politics: Clydeside, c. 1850–1990', in R. Schulze (ed.), *Industrieregionen im Umbruch (Industrial Regions in Transformation)* (Veröffentlichungen des Instituts zur Erforschung der europäischen Arbeiterbewegung, Schriftenreihe A: Darstellungen, Bd. 3), Koblenz, 196–226.

KÖLLMANN, W. (1965), 'The population of Barmen before and during the period of industrialisation', in D. V. Glass and D. E. C. Eversley (eds), *Population in History, Essays in Historical Demography*, London, 588–607.

LAIDLAW, S. (1956), *Glasgow Common Lodging-Houses and the People Living in Them*, Glasgow.

LAMB, M. (1982), 'The medical profession', in E. O. A. Checkland and M. Lamb (eds), *Health Care as Social History. The Glasgow Case*, Aberdeen, 16–43.

LAMONT, D. W. (1976), 'Population, migration and social-area change in central Glasgow, 1871–1891. A study in applied factorial ecology', unpublished PhD thesis, University of Glasgow.

LAWRIE, J. A. (1832), 'Report of the Albion Street Cholera Hospital', *Glasgow Medical Journal*, **V** (19), 309–31; (20), 416–29.

LEVY, A. (1958), 'The origins of Scottish Jewry', unpublished paper read before the Jewish Historical Society of England, 13 January.

MARWICK, J. D. (1876–1908), *Extracts from the Records of the Burgh of Glasgow*, Glasgow.

MARWICK, J. D. (1909), *The River Clyde and the Clyde Burghs*, Glasgow.

MARWICK, J. D. (1910), *The Water Supply of Glasgow*, Glasgow.

MAVER, I. (1994), 'Politics and power in the Scottish city: Glasgow Town Council in the nineteenth century', in T. M. Devine (ed.), *Scottish Elites* (Proceedings of the Scottish Historical Studies Seminar, University of Strathclyde, 1991–1992), Edinburgh, 98–130.

MILLER, H. (1841), 'Return showing ... particulars of ... destitute persons within the city of Glasgow', Glasgow.

MORGAN, N. J. and M. J. DAUNTON (1983), 'Landlords in Glasgow: a study of 1900', *Business History*, **XXV**, 264–86.

NICOL, J. (1891), *Vital, Social and Economic Statistics of Glasgow, 1885–1891*, Glasgow.

PAGAN, J. (1847), *Sketch of the History of Glasgow*, Glasgow.

RODGER, R. (1982), 'Rents and ground rents: housing and the land market in nineteenth-century Britain', in J. H. Johnson and C. Pooley (eds), *The Structure of Nineteenth-Century Cities*, London, 39–74.

RODGER, R. (1986), 'The Victorian building industry and the housing of the Scottish working class', in M. Doughty (ed.), *Building the Industrial City*, Leicester, 151–206.

RODGER, R. (1989), *Housing in Urban Britain 1780–1914*, Basingstoke.

RODGER, R. (1992), 'Scotland', in C. G. Pooley (ed.), *Housing Strategies in Europe, 1880–1930*, Leicester, London and New York, 105–31.

RUSSELL, J. B. (1886), *The Vital Statistics of the City of Glasgow*, Glasgow.

RUSSELL, J. B. (1887), 'The house in relation to public health', *Transactions of the Insurance and Actuarial Society of Glasgow, 2nd Series*, **5**.

RUSSELL, J. B. (1888a), *City of Glasgow Fever and Small-Pox Hospitals, Belvidere*, Glasgow.

RUSSELL, J. B. (1888b), *Life in One Room or some Serious Considerations for the Citizens of Glasgow*, Glasgow.

RUSSELL, J. B. (1891), *Old Glasgow and its Statistical Divisions*, Glasgow.

RUSSELL, J. B. (1895), *The Evolution of the Function of Public Health Administration as Illustrated by the Sanitary History of Glasgow in the Nineteenth Century*, Glasgow.

SHEARD, S. (1993), 'Nineteenth-century public health. A study of Liverpool, Belfast and Glasgow', unpublished PhD thesis, University of Liverpool.

SINCLAIR, J. (1825), *Analysis of the Statistical Account of Scotland*, I, Glasgow.

SLAVEN, A. (1979), *The Development of the West of Scotland: 1750–1960*, London.

STRANG, J. (1852), *Report on the Mortality Bills of the City of Glasgow and Suburbs for 1852*, Glasgow.

STRANG, J. (1859), *Report on the Vital, Social and Economic Statistics of Glasgow for 1858*, Glasgow.

STRANG, J. (1861), *Report on the Vital, Social and Economic Statistics of Glasgow for 1860*, Glasgow.

SYMONS, J. C. (1839), *Reports from Assistant Hand-Loom Weavers Commissioners.*

THOMSON, R. S. and R. FULLARTON (1902), 'A summary of statistics relating to vaccination and small-pox observed in the cases admitted to city of Glasgow Small-pox Hospital, Belvidere, between 10th April 1900 and 30th June 1901', *Proceedings of the Royal Philosophical Society of Glasgow*, **33**, 287–92.

TIVY, J. (1958), 'Population, distribution and change', in R. Miller and J. Tivy (eds), *The Glasgow Region*, Glasgow.

TREBLE, J. H. (1988), 'The standard of living of the working class', in T. M. Devine and R. Mitchison (eds), *People and Society in Scotland, I, 1760–1830*, Glasgow, 188–226.

WATT, A. (1844), *The Glasgow Bills of Mortality for 1841 and 1842*, Glasgow.

WEBER, A. F. (1899), *The Growth of Cities in the Nineteenth Century. A Study in Statistics*, New York.

WHATLEY, C. A. (1995), 'Labour in the industrialising city, c. 1660–1830' in T. M. Devine and G. Jackson (eds), *Glasgow. Vol. I: Beginnings to 1830*, Manchester and New York, 360–401.

WITHERS, C. W. J. and A. J. WATSON (1991), 'Stepwise migration and highland migration to Glasgow, 1852–1898', *Journal of Historical Geography*, **17**, 35–55.

Chapter 3

THE POPULATION DYNAMICS AND ECONOMIC DEVELOPMENT OF GENOA, 1750–1939

GIUSEPPE FELLONI

INTRODUCTION

The scholar analysing the historical population dynamics of Genoa will quickly notice its special and well-defined features.[1] From 1805 Genoa was the capital of a small regional state that had just over half a million inhabitants in 1777. From the second half of the eighteenth century its economy was mainly based on two activities: first, overseas investments, supplying most of the income of its aristocratic oligarchy; and, secondly, shipping and trade, pursued either on an independent basis or on commission for foreign merchants.

After the outbreak of the French Revolution and during the wars between France and other European powers, the majority of the city's overseas financial investments were lost due to the bankruptcy of state treasuries and private financial difficulties. In 1805 the Genoese State requested and obtained annexation by the French Empire, hoping to save at least the second mainstay of its economy, sea-borne trade. But this also failed due to the proclamation of the continental blockade in 1806 which destroyed Genoa's port activities almost completely (Tarle, 1928).

With the fall of Napoleon, the Genoese territory became part of Savoy, but this new political situation did not provide any immediate advantage. Investment losses during the Napoleonic Wars had been very considerable and the development of shipping and trade was obstructed until 1830 by the highly protectionist policy pursued by the Turin government. It was only in the 1830s that the tariff and customs policy was moderated and the Genoese economy began to recover its sea-borne trade, relying primarily on increased investment in the developing manufacturing sector. The successful results already obtained by English, Belgian and French manufacturers with innovative production technologies showed that industrial investment offered significant opportunities. An increasing number of Genoese entrepreneurs

---

1 This chapter is based on the results of a major historical research project on the population dynamics of Genoa in the nineteenth century; see Giuseppe Felloni (1961) for other on-going research on the period from the eighteenth to the twentieth centuries. Most of my research was based on official statistics and, for earlier periods, on ecclesiastical documentation, such as episcopal visitations and parish registers.

decided to move in this direction, followed by a growing number of tradesmen in Piedmont and Lombardy (Guglielmino, 1948).

At the beginning of the 1850s the take-off process was well established in Genoa, Turin and Milan, as the chief towns of Liguria, Piedmont and Lombardy respectively, and economic growth in the latter decades of the nineteenth century was sustained by industrial development in ferrous metallurgy, engineering and chemicals (del Panta, 1989, p. 264). The industrial revolution was beginning to change not only the economy of the three urban poles, but also that of the surrounding territories. The economic importance of Genoa was further boosted following the political unification of Italy in 1861 when the old regional customs borders were abolished and free trade was encouraged, thus leading to intensified commercial contacts with other Italian regions and the rest of the world. Stimulated by progressive industrialization and the increase in maritime traffic, Genoa's economy changed irreversibly and expanded in an unprecedented manner. On the eve of the First World War, Liguria—with Genoa as its centre—produced 40 per cent of Italian steel and the port dealt with one-third of the nation's shipping trade.

THE DEMOGRAPHIC DEVELOPMENT OF GENOA

In such a favourable economic environment it is not surprising that Genoa's population witnessed a dynamic expansion, as shown by census returns (Tables 3.1 and 3.2, Figures 3.1 and 3.2). From 1777 onwards statistics relating to the port-city's total population are available for an extended period, even though their quality tends to vary over time. Up to 1848–1850 they were usually produced by the parish priests and based upon data collected at Easter when they went around blessing people's homes. The data were collected on a nominative basis and not at the same time, but the information on the total number of souls can nevertheless be used as a satisfactory basis for calculating the indigenous or resident population. From 1861 onwards population data were derived from a nominative and simultaneous census controlled by the state and based on 'family forms' which were used to calculate both the population with the right of residence in Genoa as well as the population actually present (Instituto Centrale di Statistica, 1957–59).

Even if we allow for a certain margin of error in the earlier data, the growth in Genoa's population may be satisfactorily outlined, as long as we consider two important changes which took place in the urban environment in the course of time. First, there was a noticeable increase in population density within the traditional boundaries of the city. Around 1750 the urban boundaries of Genoa coincided almost exactly with the city walls of 1630–1633, enclosing an area of almost 1,038 hectares (Felloni, 1972, p. 1,077).[2] For

2 The figure of 1,038 hectares is based on surveys prior to 1861; it includes the port area and about 60 hectares of land outside the eastern walls, the so-called *Borgo Incrociati*, which had been separated from the city in 1818 and annexed to the suburb of San Fruttuoso.

Table 3.1: *Total population of Genoa, 1777–1936.*

Date	Town area to 1873	Area incorporated in 1874	Town area 1874–1925	Area incorporated in 1926	Town area from 1926
1777, Easter[a]	85,507				
1788, Easter[a]	87,637				
1806, Easter[a]	78,060	14,178	92,238	50,037	142,275
1822, Easter[a]	83,539	14,378	97,917	54,769	152,686
1827, Easter[a]	96,259	16,007	112,266	60,364	172,630
1838, Easter[a]	97,621	17,415	115,036	66,598	181,634
1848, Easter[a]	100,696[b]	19,272	119,456	72,858	192,314
1862, 1 Jan.[a]	127,735	24,111	151,846	87,019	238,865
1862, 1 Jan.[c]	127,986	23,362	151,348	83,665	235,013
1872, 1 Jan.[c]	130,269	31,400	161,669	97,877	259,546
1882, 1 Jan.[c]	139,366	40,149	179,515	110,698	290,213
1901, 10 Feb.[c]	169,343	65,367	234,710	159,927	394,637
1911, 10 Jun.[c]	173,633	98,588	272,221	179,648	451,869
1921, 1 Dec.[c]	190,408	125,809	316,217	237,782	553,999
1931, 21 Apr.[c]	192,759	153,878	346,637	261,459	608,096
1936, 21 Apr.[c]	191,648	167,820	359,468	271,878	631,346

[a] Resident population.

[b] Although officially attributed to 1848, the census of the town area within its pre-1873 boundaries was carried out in 1850; for Easter 1848 its estimated population was 100,184.

[c] Present population.

about two centuries only a small part of this area was actually inhabited, with Genoa's population fluctuating between 70,000 and 85,000. Further population growth after 1750 produced an increase in the number of inhabitants to almost 95,000 by 1798–99, but this figure underwent a drastic reduction during the Napoleonic period. From 1825 onwards there was once again an upward trend in total population which generated a considerable expansion of the built-up area, both spatially and in terms of housing density. Unlike past increases, which were transitory, the population growth which started in the mid-1820s continued for over a century. The urban population of Genoa grew significantly, reaching 100,000 inhabitants in 1848, 169,000 in 1900 and a maximum of almost 193,000 in 1931.

Secondly, urban growth was accompanied by suburban development. While vacant spaces within the city walls were gradually occupied, settlements in suburban areas grew considerably, particularly in the two adjacent valleys and along the coast. The growing links between the old city centre and the emergent suburbs were ultimately institutionalized by extending the urban boundaries of Genoa; six municipalities close to the eastern walls of the city were suppressed in 1874 and their 2,312-hectare territory was incorporated into the urban

Table 3.2: *Intercensal increases in the population of Genoa, 1777–1936 (average annual rates per 1,000 population).*

Period	Town area to 1873	Area incorporated in 1874	Town area 1874–1925	Area incorporated in 1926	Town area from 1926
1777–1788	2.3				
1788–1806	−6.1				
1806–1822	4.2	0.9	3.7	5.6	4.4
1822–1827	28.3	21.4	27.3	19.4	24.5
1827–1838	1.3	7.7	2.2	8.9	4.6
1838–1848	2.6[a]	10.1	3.8	9.0	5.7
1848–1862	19.7[a]	15.7	19.1	12.5	16.6
1862–1872	1.8	29.4	6.6	15.7	9.9
1872–1882	6.7	24.5	10.5	12.3	11.2
1882–1901	10.2	25.0	13.9	19.0	16.0
1901–1911	2.4	39.2	14.3	11.2	13.1
1911–1921	9.7	25.6	15.8	29.4	21.4
1921–1931	1.3	21.4	9.8	10.1	9.9
1931 1936	−1.2	17.3	7.3	7.8	7.5

[a] The rate has been calculated with reference to the population census of 1850.

municipality, thus extending its area to about 3,290 hectares.[3] Similarly, a further seven adjoining municipalities were also abolished in 1926, together with twelve on the western side of the city, and their 20,004-hectare territory became part of Genoa. This is how 'Greater Genoa', as it was known, had its origins, constituting an area of 23,479 hectares which has remained unchanged since then.[4]

Although the increase in population within the city walls was remarkable, the growth in the two territories annexed in 1874 and 1926 was even greater, accounting for an increase of 150,000 and 215,000 inhabitants respectively between 1820 and 1936. For the whole urban agglomeration of Genoa, a net increase of almost 480,000 inhabitants—three times the initial level—can be identified within the same period. Although it is difficult to evaluate the relative contribution of natural increase and net migration to this growth, it is important to explore the dynamics of these two phenomena and their relationship with economic trends.

3 For references to the territory of annexed communes, see 'Genova negli ultimi anni alla luce della statistica', *Genova, Rivista municipale*, **XI**, February 1933, p. 136. In general, the political unification of Italy in 1861 was followed by a new stage in the long-term evolution of many urban centres, characterized by their expansion beyond the old town walls. See Gambi (1982) and del Panta (1989, p. 263).

4 See del Panta, 1989, p. 263, *passim*. The figure includes the port area, which had been expanded in the meantime to 260 hectares.

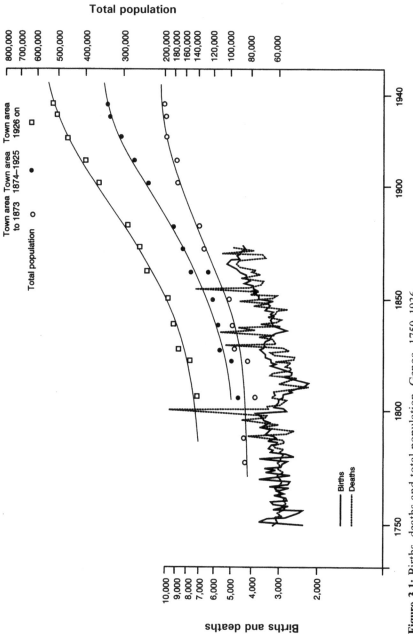

Figure 3.1: Births, deaths and total population, Genoa, 1750–1936.

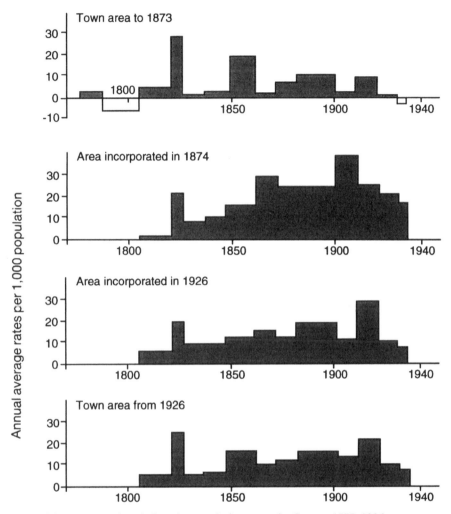

Figure 3.2: Intercensal variations in population growth, Genoa, 1777–1936.

The natural movement of Genoa's population prior to 1828 is hardly known, since the official statistics are incomplete and inconsistent. The only reliable data available refer to some of the town parishes, representing 53 per cent and 33 per cent of total births and deaths respectively in the period 1828–1837. This sample may be considered sufficiently representative for the city as a whole at least up to 1827 and provides the basis for the estimated figures on total births and deaths for the late-eighteenth and early-nineteenth centuries (see Figure 3.1). From 1828 onwards the natural population movement of Genoa is known in absolute and relative terms, even though this needs to be related to the

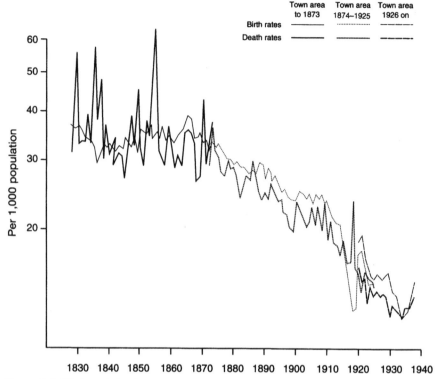

Figure 3.3: Birth and death rates (per 1,000 population) in Genoa, 1828–1936.

different phases of urban expansion and other historical events affecting the municipality (see Figure 3.3).

Figures 3.1 and 3.3 indicate the following aspects of Genoa's short-run demographic development which can be easily identified:

(a) a sharp increase in the death rate (or in the absolute number of deaths) due to famine (1770, 1789, 1811–1812, 1816–1817, etc.), epidemics (small-pox in 1829 and 1870; cholera in 1835–1837, 1845–1855, 1866–1867 and 1873; influenza in 1918), or war (the siege of 1800, the First World War);

(b) a reduction and gradual decrease in the frequency and amplitude of extreme mortality peaks;

(c) a drop in the birth and marriage rates (or in their absolute numbers) coinciding with the most severe famine periods and, conversely, an increase in the marriage rate after periods of extraordinarily high mortality.

The long-term demographic trends of Genoa can be summarized by reference to the following three points: first, within the area of the old city the birth rate slowly increased from an average of 33 per 1,000 inhabitants at the beginning of the nineteenth century to 37–38 per 1,000 in the 1860s; in the suburbs birth rates remained relatively stable at around that level at least from 1827. From 1870 onwards the birth rate started falling at an increasingly accelerated rate, both in the city and in the suburbs, until it reached 13 per 1,000 by the fourth decade of the twentieth century.

Secondly, for a long time the death rate was much higher within the city walls (around 33–34 per 1,000) than in the suburbs (where it fluctuated around 25 per 1,000). The highest urban mortality rates were recorded for the age groups 0–3 and 60 and over in the period 1870–1873, but the urban penalty was most pronounced in relation to the age groups 15–49 and 50–59, which recorded death rates twice those for the corresponding age groups in rural communities (see Table 3.3). Men were disproportionately affected by inflated urban mortality in these age groups, but women of working age also suffered from the same phenomenon. This was probably due to the adverse living conditions in the city and to the fact that the city hospital also accepted patients from the countryside, thereby inflating Genoa's overall mortality rate. After 1870 the death rate started falling everywhere, but this was particularly the case in the old city. The territorial differences between Genoa and the adjacent communes were gradually reduced, and by the 1930s the overall death rate was just under 13 per 1,000.

Thirdly, the balance between the birth and death rates within the city walls was almost always negative or only marginally positive. In the suburban settlements, however, there was a consistent surplus of births that fluctuated between 10 and 15 per 1,000 in those communes that were finally incorporated into 'Greater Genoa' in 1926. Data for the area incorporated in 1874 reveal a net population growth rate of 12.0 and 13.6 per 1,000 for the periods 1827–1837 and 1862–1872 respectively. This positive balance only began to diminish at the end of the nineteenth century: after 1931 it had fallen to below 5 per 1,000.

These observations are derived from Figures 3.1 and 3.3 and are confirmed by the data contained in Table 3.4, which presents the net intercensal population variation according to its constituent components—birth and death rates, and net migration rates (the balance between in-migration and out-migration). Separate data are reported for the walled city centre and the subsequently incorporated suburbs in order to place more emphasis on spatial variations.

Between 1822 and 1827 substantial population growth was reported for all areas: this was due to the considerable influx of migrants from the surrounding countryside where many Genoese had taken refuge during the Napoleonic period in order to avoid compulsory military service. It also represented a recovery from the adverse demographic impact of the famine years 1816–1817. The population growth of the city was also partly due to a considerable, but temporary, natural increase. This phenomenon, which was also observed in

Table 3.3: *Death rates by age group, Genoa district, 1860–1863, 1870–1873 and 1880–1883 (per 1,000 population in every age group).*

Age groups	Genoa		Rural communes	
	Male	*Female*	*Male*	*Female*
(a) Annual average 1860–1863				
Under 3	163.0	132.3	200.0	166.9
3–14	16.8	15.9	11.3	12.1
15–49	19.9	14.4	9.9	9.3
50–59	34.7	26.2	17.5	16.8
60 and over	90.9	87.0	61.5	70.1
All ages	32.5	28.6	28.9	25.7
(b) Annual average 1870–1873				
Under 3	219.8	192.6	145.2	132.4
3–14	20.6	20.3	14.2	14.4
15–49	18.4	15.8	9.4	9.7
50–59	39.7	25.0	16.7	16.1
60 and over	97.9	88.7	60.7	66.1
All ages	37.1	33.0	26.8	25.4
(c) Annual average 1880–1883				
Under 3	212.6	182.9	129.4	119.5
3–14	14.7	15.4	12.7	13.1
15–49	12.5	12.8	8.5	10.3
50–59	28.3	22.5	16.2	14.2
60 and over	74.9	66.6	57.8	59.7
All ages	26.9	25.3	25.8	24.8

other Italian regions such as Tuscany and Apulia, was caused by a short-term increase in the birth rate to 37.5 per 1,000 and a simultaneous, if more modest, fall in mortality to 32.4 per 1,000.

Apart from this period (1822–1827) the population dynamics of Genoa were mainly affected by two variables which had a differential impact over time and space: mortality crises and migration movements. Mortality crises had the most devastating effects on the city centre, while in the suburbs and surrounding rural territories they were less severe because the individual settlements were not so crowded and sometimes more scattered. An example is provided by the major cholera epidemics of 1835–1837 and 1854 (del Panta, 1979, p. 203), when the death rates were respectively 11.1 and 26.8 per

Table 3.4: *Vital and migration statistics for intercensal periods, Genoa, 1828–1936 (average annual rates per 1,000 population).*

Period	Town area to 1873		Area incorporated in 1874		Town area 1874–1925		Area incorporated in 1926		Town area from 1926	
1. Birth (b) and death (d) rates										
	b	d	b	d	b	d	b	d	b	d
1806–1822	33.1	34.5								
1822–1827	37.5	32.4								
1827–1838	33.5	39.6	39.9	27.9	34.4	37.8	36.9	23.5	35.3	32.7
1838–1850	32.9	33.3								
1850–1862	34.7	35.1								
1862–1872	35.7	32.5	39.3	25.7	36.3	31.3	39.3	24.5	37.4	28.8
1872–1882					31.3	29.9	36.2	25.7	33.2	28.3
1882–1901					26.6	24.3	33.1	22.3	29.2	23.5
1901–1911					24.0	21.3				
1911–1921					20.5	21.2				
1921–1931									15.5	13.6
1931–1936									13.0	12.6
2. Net population growth (a) and estimated net migration rates (b)										
	a	b	a	b	a	b	a	b	a	b
1806–1822	−1.4	+5.6								
1822–1827	+5.1	+23.2								
1827–1838	−6.1	+7.4	+12.0	−4.3	−3.4	+5.6	+13.4	−4.4	+2.6	+2.0
1838–1850	−0.4	+3.0								
1850–1862	−0.3	+20.0								
1862–1872	+3.2	−1.4	+13.6	+15.7	+5.0	+1.6	+14.8	+0.9	+8.6	+1.4
1872–1882					+1.4	+9.0	+10.5	+1.7	+4.9	+6.2
1882–1901					+2.3	+11.6	+10.8	+8.2	+5.7	+10.3
1901–1911					+2.7	+11.6				
1911–1921					−0.7	+16.6				
1921–1931									+1.9	+8.1
1931–1936									+0.4	+7.1

1,000 in the city and only 4.2 and 15.2 per 1,000 in the adjacent rural districts.

Due to the fact that mortality was generally high and occasionally reached crisis proportions, the city within the walls hardly ever recorded a natural population surplus and its population grew only because in-migration exceeded out-migration. This was the case throughout the period 1806–1866, with exceptionally high net migration rates contributing substantially to the city's growth between 1822 and 1827 and again between 1850 and 1862. Even as early as 1838 almost half of the city's population were in-migrants (del Panta, 1978, p. 87). Conversely, up to about 1890 the increased demographic growth of the suburbs was ensured to a far greater degree by the considerable natural increase of a young and vigorous population. Net population growth in the area incorporated into Genoa in 1874 had been particularly marked in two periods for which data are extant, namely 1827–1838 and 1862–1872, as a result of a significant surplus of births. In-migration was of secondary importance, except for the years 1862–1872, when a significant section of the indigenous population moved from the historical urban core to the adjacent eastern suburbs, probably as a response to an increase in rents and the contemporary crisis of the cotton industry. In the course of the late-nineteenth and early-twentieth centuries, however, the population growth of the suburbs also became increasingly dependent on in-migration (see below).

The significant demographic differences between the original city centre and its various suburban areas, clearly visible in Table 3.4, are also evident in an analysis of the sex and age distribution of Genoa's population. Migration mainly involved adult males and their relative proportion in any age group with respect to females of the same age is a good indicator of the scale and extent of in-migration. With respect to the age group 20–59 resident in the municipality of Genoa on 1 January 1862—at the end of a period of strong population growth—there were 110 males to every 100 females, while on 1 January 1871, following some years of out-migration, the ratio had dropped to approximately 103:100 (see Table 3.5). The relative surplus of men was particularly evident in 1862 in the age group 20–29 (142 per 100 women), reflecting the growth in employment opportunities offered by Genoa to young male migrants, particularly in unskilled or semi-skilled work (Davis, 1988, p. 101). In relation to the older age groups, however, both in 1866 and 1872, women were increasingly predominant, probably as a function of differential sex- and age-specific mortality.

From the last decade of the nineteenth century onwards the differences in the dynamics of population growth between the city centre and the adjacent suburbs slowly faded away, as the extent of natural increase gradually diminished and in-migration became increasingly important as the key determinant of demographic development. When considering the city as a whole, it can be stated that crisis mortality had practically disappeared after 1873 as a result of significant improvements in medical provision, urban public health and the nutritional status of the indigenous population. On the other hand, migration movements became more important and their short-term volatility now constituted the only element hampering the continuing population growth of Genoa.

When dealing with net migration trends, it must be kept in mind that they are the result of two simultaneous countervailing movements, namely in-

Table 3.5: *Total population by age group and sex (in per cent) and the male/female ratio in Genoa, 1862 and 1872.*

Age group	1862			1872		
	Male	*Female*	*M/F 100*	*Male*	*Female*	*M/F 100*
Under 9	16.6	18.3	97.9	17.3	17.7	96.2
10–19	16.5	18.3	97.7	17.8	18.5	95.1
20–29	25.3	19.2	142.4	20.2	18.9	106.0
30–39	15.1	15.7	104.5	15.6	15.5	99.6
40–49	11.2	11.3	113.7	12.5	11.8	104.3
50–59	8.0	8.3	104.3	8.5	8.6	97.6
60–69	4.7	5.7	89.9	5.3	5.7	92.0
70–79	2.1	2.5	93.7	2.3	2.5	88.3
80–89	0.4	0.6	74.7	0.5	0.7	75.2
90 and over	0.1	0.1	64.9	–	0.1	44.2
All ages	100.0	100.0	100.0	100.0	100.0	98.9
20–59			110.2			102.5

migration and out-migration. In the case of Genoa, the two phenomena may be followed on an annual basis from 1876 onwards—although with a few gaps—by using the entries relating to new residents in the registers of births, marriages and deaths and the recorded deletion of those who moved away. Figure 3.4 traces the migration streams over time and reveals the positive net migration balance which gradually led to a significant growth in the city's population, particularly after 1890. In relation to the town area as defined in 1874, the extent of net in-migration was particularly marked in the 1890s and in the first two decades of the twentieth century. But even after 1931, following the introduction of legislation to control further urban expansion which was reinforced subsequently in 1939, Genoa still recorded an appreciable net migration surplus (Ferro, 1973, p. 70).[5]

The data in Table 3.4 provide a synthesis of net migration rates for specified intercensal periods and Figure 3.4 records in-migration and out-migration on an annual basis for those years for which statistical information is available. In order to examine more precisely the overall impact of migration streams on Genoa's population, however, other data, including the classification of the urban population by place of origin, must be analysed. On the occasion of the 1921 census, following a phase of strong demographic development in Genoa, for every 1,000 people included in the census returns in the commune only 500 had been born there; 123 came from other communes in Liguria, 205 from

5 The effectiveness of such legislation has still to be proven.

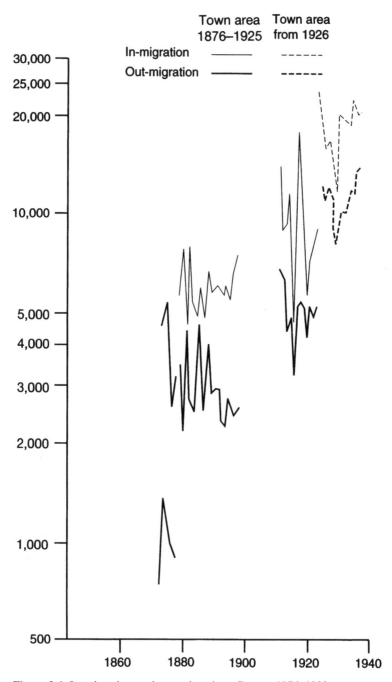

Figure 3.4: In-migration and out-migration, Genoa, 1876–1939.

northern Italy, 67 from the central regions, and 105 from southern Italy and the islands (Il Comune di Genova, 1925, p. 142).

This large number of strangers resident in Genoa can be explained by the enormous difference in economic opportunities which existed between the place of origin and the place of destination. From a theoretical perspective, such a difference may have been due either to a worsening economic situation in the place of origin or to better job opportunities (either real or assumed) associated with the place of destination. Both factors were important in determining the level of in-migration in the case of Genoa.

In-migration from Liguria, which was considerable if compared with the relatively small number of indigenous inhabitants in the region, was mainly due to the agricultural crisis which coincided with the onset of Italian industrialization and became particularly severe from the early 1870s onwards. This caused progressive depopulation of the inland areas and of wide coastal stretches along the Riviera. Similar factors also accounted for the extent of in-migration from northern Italy, even though in this case it was not due to a deep-seated agricultural crisis (as in the case of Liguria), but to the process of economic rationalization associated with the agricultural revolution. What is particularly striking in relation to the annual extent of in-migration into Genoa (see Figure 3.4) are the considerable and abrupt fluctuations, specifically in the years 1883, 1900, 1914, 1920 etc.

Given the volatility of in-migration, it is reasonable to argue that this level of annual variation was not primarily due to sudden changes in the intensity of push-factors operating in the place of origin, but rather reflected short-term improvements in the Genoese labour market and attendant increases in money wages. Such an impression is reinforced by the visible correlation, at least in the long run, between variations in the extent of net migration and the cyclical nature of economic development in the city of Genoa. The distinct phases of the economic life of the city, in turn, require a more extended discussion.

THE ECONOMIC DEVELOPMENT OF GENOA

Any analysis of the economic activity of a port-city, such as Genoa, must inevitably focus on the role of its sea-borne trade. As already indicated (see above, p. 74), the implementation of a more moderate customs and tariff policy from the 1830s onwards undoubtedly stimulated the port activities of Genoa. Sea-borne trade expanded at an average annual rate of 2 per cent throughout the 1830s and 1840s and then increased by 12 per cent annually in the 1850s with the onset of the industrialization process in Italy (see Table 3.6). Apart from a similar peak of annual growth in sea-borne trade in the 1880s, the second half of the nineteenth century and the early years of the twentieth century were characterized by an average annual growth rate in the port's shipping trade of four to five per cent. However, the First World War was marked by a sharp fall in shipping activity and although the early 1920s were

Table 3.6: *Maritime traffic in the port of Genoa, 1815–1889 (in tons).*

Five-year period	Annual average[a]
1815–19	378,651
1820–24	351,107
1825–29	333,227
1830–34	341,654
1835–39	357,449
1840–44	386,763
1845–49	444,120
1850–54	558,388
1855–59	654,719
1860–64	1,055,303
1865–69	1,203,428
1870–74	1,406,868
1875–79	1,621,868
1880–84	2,229,257
1885–89	2,869,600

Sources: Marchese, 1959, pp. 75–76; Felloni, 1961, p. 44.
[a] Ships arriving in Genoa.

characterized by a short-term recovery, the period between 1929 and 1939 witnessed an absolute stagnation in Genoa's sea-borne trade.

These distinct phases in the long-term development of the port's shipping activities directly affected the evolution of the city's population dynamics, as indicated in Table 3.1. However, there is one noticeable exception to this: during the First World War port activity was reduced by one-third, while Genoa's total population recorded a simultaneous growth of 16 per cent, primarily as a result of extensive in-migration.

This particular temporal disjuncture between the registered trends in the city's rate of population growth and the level of port activity, indicates that the demographic dynamics of Genoa cannot be explained solely in terms of the long-run development of its sea-borne trade. Increasingly, urban employment was determined by the structure and performance of Genoa's developing secondary sector, which, in turn, provided the basis for the port's shipping activities in general. By the early 1880s mining, manufacturing and construction already constituted the most important sources of employment in the city (see Table 3.7) and it was specifically these sectors as a whole, together with transport, which witnessed the most significant expansion in the period 1882 to 1936, as the relevant occupational census returns indicate.

The increasingly dominant role of industry as a source of employment in Genoa, in turn, influenced the scale and direction of contemporary migration

Table 3.7: *Economically active population by occupation, Genoa district, 1882 and 1936.*

	1882		1936	
	Number	%	Number	%
Agriculture, forestry and fishing	83,280	32.2	55,394	14.8
Mining, manufacturing and building	84,131	32.5	156,337	41.8
Transport	14,662	5.7	44,129	11.8
Trade, banking, insurance and private services	66,306	25.6	95,898	25.7
Public administration	10,385	4.0	22,033	5.9
Total	258,764	100.0	373,791	100.0

flows. For example, the considerable influx of in-migrants in the period 1850–1862 was undoubtedly due to the simultaneous and vigorous expansion in local industrial activity. Productive capacity in the cotton-spinning industry of the city in the 1850s increased three-fold and this period also witnessed the foundation and consolidation of Genoa's first significant iron and steel firms, including Robertson (1851), Taylor and Prandi (1846, reconstituted in 1852 as G. Ansaldo and Co.), as well as Agnese and Co. (1860). Similarly, the reduced extent of migration, particularly of in-migration in the 1860s and 1870s, can be attributed to the negative impact of free trade on many of Genoa's indigenous industries. The espousal of free trade by the Italian government created significant difficulties for local manufacturers, particularly in the cotton and iron and steel sectors, as it inevitably led to increased competition from British imports. Between 1858 and 1881, for example, the total tonnage of British ships using the port of Genoa increased markedly from 72,000 to 575,000 tons (Marchese, 1959, pp. 46, 48). However, the 1878 tariff provided moderate protection to a limited number of industries, thereby encouraging selective import substitution (Federico and Toniolo, 1991, p. 20) and the higher duties introduced in 1887 heralded a significant return to protectionism (del Vecchio, 1978; Zamagni, 1993, p. 117).

During the following years of the nineteenth century the further expansion of industrial activity in Genoa increasingly became the driving force of the city's economy. However, the emphasis shifted perceptibly from the textile industry to iron and steel production, whether connected with the development of the Italian railway network (Fenoaltea, 1983), ship-construction, or with the increasing needs of the local mechanical-engineering sector which by 1889–1890 employed 9,867 individuals within the boundaries of the city. During the First World War military requirements contributed to a further expansion in heavy industry which, in turn, generated a considerable increase in net in-migration at a time when port activity as a whole was undergoing a considerable short-term decline. It is clear, therefore, that in the long-run the population dynamics of Genoa were increasingly determined by industrial development within the city and the performance of individual industries within the secondary sector. Not only did the fishing industry (as well as other primary sector activities) decline significantly in the period 1882 to 1936 (see Table 3.7), but sea-borne trade, which historically had been the mainstay of the local economy, ultimately lost its primacy as the key determinant both of employment opportunities in the city and of Genoa's population dynamics.

References

DAVIS, J. A. (1988), *Conflict and Control: Law and Order in Nineteenth-Century Italy*, Basingstoke.

del PANTA, L. (1978), *Evoluziona Demografica e Popolamento nell'Italia dell'Ottocento* (1796–1914), Bologna.

del PANTA, L. (1979), 'Italy', in W. R. Lee (ed.), *European Demography and Economic Growth*, London, 196–235.

del PANTA, L. (1989), 'Population growth, ubanization and regional differentials in Italy during the nineteenth century (1796–1914)', in R. Lawton and R. Lee (eds), *Urban Population Development in Western Europe from the Late-Eighteenth to the Early-Twentieth Century*, Liverpool, 258–69.

del VECCHIO, E. (1978), *La via italiana al protezionismo*, Rome.

FEDERICO, G. and G. TONIOLO (1991), 'Italy', in R. Sylla and G. Toniolo (eds), *Patterns of European Industrialization. The Nineteenth Century*, London and New York, 197–217.

FELLONI, G. (1961), *Popolazione e sviluppo economico della Liguria nel secolo XIX*, Turin.

FELLONI, G. (1972), 'Le circoscrizioni territoriali civili ed ecclesiastiche nella repubblica di Genova alla fine del secolo XVIII', *Rivista storica italiana*, **LXXXIV**.

FENOALTEA, S. (1983), 'Railways and the development of the Italian economy to 1913', in P. O'Brien (ed.), *Railways and the Economic Growth of Western Europe*, London, 49–120.

FERRO, G. (1973), *Movimenti di popolazione nella regione ligure 1951–1971*, Genoa, Bozzi.

GAMBI, L. (1982), 'L'evoluzione storica delle città in Italia fino agli inizi del nostro secolo: eventi urbanistici e lovo rapporti con gli eventi demografici', in S.I.D.E.S., *La demografia storica delle città italiane*, Bologna, 21–46.

GUGLIELMINO, E. (1948), 'Genova dal 1814 al 1849. Gli sviluppi economici e l'opinione pubblica', *Atti della Regia Deputazione di Storia Patria per la Liguria, Serie del Risorgimento*, **IV**.

IL COMUNE DI GENOVA (1925), 'Lo sviluppo della popolazione di Genova', *Bollettino municipale mensile*, **V**, February.

INSTITUTO CENTRALE DI STATISTICA (1957–59), 'Le rilevazioni statistichi in Italia dal 1861 al 1956', *Annali di Statistica*, **VII**, 5, 6, 7, 8.

MARCHESE, U. (1959), *Il porto di Genova dal 1815 al 1891* (Archivio Economico dell'Unificazione Italiana, series I, **IX**), Rome.

TARLE, E. (1928), *Le blocus continental et le Royaume d'Italie – La situation économique de l'Italie sous Napoleon Ier d'après des documents inédits*, Paris.

ZAMAGNI, V. (1993), *The Economic History of Italy, 1860–1990*, Oxford.

Chapter 4

THE COMPONENTS OF DEMOGRAPHIC CHANGE IN A RAPIDLY GROWING PORT-CITY: THE CASE OF LIVERPOOL IN THE NINETEENTH CENTURY

RICHARD LAWTON

INTRODUCTION

While typologies of cities provide a useful framework for population studies, they present considerable problems. Most urban centres are multi-functional, definitions of dominant function usually being based on the most easily accessible criterion of census occupational data (Nelson, 1955; Laux, 1989). Other—perhaps more crucial—factors in demographic behaviour, such as social class, cultural characteristics (for example, ethnicity, religion, levels of education) and income are seldom easily available.

Moreover, the statistical bases of such classifications are usually very crude and the differences within a class in social, structural and demographic characteristics may be greater than those between different classes. Contrasts in demographic experience over time, in different regional settings, and in the wide differences (especially in the provision of non-basic industries and service activities) between small and large cities within particular types of town suggest that the advantages of such an approach to spatial demographic analysis may be greatly outweighed by the disadvantages. Nevertheless, demographic behaviour between particular socio-economic groups *is* different: coal-mining and heavy industrial communities have had, historically, high nuptiality and fertility (Haines, 1979); factory textile areas were generally characterized by low fertility; and large nineteenth-century cities had high mortality and substantially depended for growth on migration (Lawton, 1983). Such striking differences in demographic régimes are universally recognized. Contrasting demographic behaviour also produces distinctive population structures between particular sections of the community within individual towns and, at a broader scale, between different 'types' of town or region which also reflect environmental contrasts (at work and home) and differences in economic, social and individual behaviour. These are the very stuff of explanation in population studies.

In his comprehensive analysis of nineteenth-century urban growth in England and Wales, Brian Robson (1973, pp. 94, 127), while essentially concerned with growth rates over time and their effects on the ranking and distribution of towns, frequently alludes to the contrasts between different types of town in the temporal and spatial patterns of urban growth: for example, the early boom of the northern textile and metal-working areas and the much later growth of the towns within the South-East; or the impact of 'different factor endowments' on growth in specific areas of the 'growth impulses' in a sequence of growth industries—cotton, wool, iron and coal. Jan de Vries (1984, p. 263) argues that the 'new urbanization' in Europe of the late-eighteenth to early-nineteenth century was due, in considerable measure, to urban growth from below as new technology promoted industrial cities. He regards Europe's urban systems as being integrated 'not so much through vertical links between cities at different levels in an administrative or marketing hierarchy as *via* horizontal links—competitive relationships among function-ally differentiated cities of several different sorts'. In such developments, port-cities played a significant and distinctive part.

THE DEVELOPMENT AND POPULATION CHARACTERISTICS OF PORT-CITIES

Ports assumed considerable importance in urban growth in the seventeenth and eighteenth centuries, particularly those involved in Atlantic trade (de Vries, 1984, p. 257). Among the maritime trading and industrial nations of Western Europe, Britain was an early beneficiary of such growth: by 1801, of its 54 towns with populations of 10,000 or over, 21 were ports; by 1851 there were 26 out of 68; by 1881, 28 out of 71; and by 1911, 26 out of 72. By mid-century these 'port-towns' included 12 of over 50,000 population, and there were 22 of over 100,000 by 1911.[1] Moreover, among the great 'world cities'—those of more than 100,000 population in 1850 and one million in 1950—nearly two-fifths and over three-fifths, respectively, were seaports (Lawton, 1989).

The extent to which places may be described categorically as 'ports' is problematic. Two approaches may be suggested: first, in terms of the relative importance to their economies of trade and shipping; secondly, in terms of port-related economic activities. However, categorization of port-cities must be, to a considerable extent, subjective and take account of other activities which will have different implications for population structure and trends in particular towns: thus specialist naval bases tend to have imbalanced, young male-dominated populations; fishing ports may well have many male heads of household absent at censuses; while the proportion of maritime-related activities, dominated by male employment, will differ considerably between a port such as Liverpool, with many men employed in shipping, transport and on

1 The list of those included in 1911 is Aberdeen, Belfast, Birkenhead, Bristol, Cardiff, Dundee, Edinburgh/Leith, Gateshead, Glasgow, Greenock, Hull, Ipswich, Kings Lynn, Liverpool, Manchester/Salford, Middlesbrough, Newcastle-upon-Tyne, Newport, Plymouth/Devonport, Portsmouth, Southampton, South Shields, Swansea, Tynemouth, Wallasey and Yarmouth (see Mitchell and Deane [1962], *passim*).

the docks, and Glasgow, with both port employment and a wider range of manufactures from textiles to ship-building and heavy engineering (see Gibb, chapter 2, above).

Such diversity creates problems for comparative studies. Nevertheless, most ports—large or small—had above-average proportions employed in shipping, cargo-handling and transport. Different groups often dominated particular jobs: Irish Catholics as stevedores and dock porters, but Protestant 'Orange-men' as carters in Liverpool, for example. Larger ports had considerable commercial employment ranging from shipowners, merchants and brokers to tally- and office-clerks and warehousemen, and involving professional skills in banking, finance, insurance and law. This transactional role, and the external networks which it generated, is indeed of considerable economic and demo-graphic significance for port-cities, often exceeding their regional linkages and creating an unusually diverse and wide-ranging 'coming together of peoples, cultures, and cities' (Gottmann, 1990, p. 16). Nevertheless, in all ports (especially the larger general cargo ports) industry has been of con-siderable significance. It is usually dominated by the processing of imported commodities (grain, oilseeds and fats, sugar, livestock, tobacco, timber, chemicals, ores and fertilizers) and by secondary industries based on their refined products—foods, jams, paint, soaps, cattle-cake, oils and chemicals. In many places, older crafts (clock-making and pottery in Liverpool, for example) often gave way to expanding dockside industries during the nine-teenth century, and skilled manufacturers, other than in maritime engineering and instrument making, were under-represented although, in the specialist ship-building towns of Clydeside and North-East England and naval ship-building centres such as Barrow in Furness and Birkenhead, population trends and characteristics were dominated by the fortunes of a more narrowly-based economy.

Hence most nineteenth-century ports were dominated by semi- and unskilled workers, with relatively low proportions of artisans and women in the industrial workforce. Even in the commercial sector most employees, especially male clerks, were poorly paid (Anderson, G., 1976). Employment—like the port economy—was particularly unstable, with imports and exports quickly reflecting fluctuations in the national and international economy and with day-to-day activities in the docks influenced by the vagaries of weather, shipping and transport. In a workforce maintained at a level to cope with peaks of activity, under- and unemployment were high, especially in unskilled, casual jobs.

Such conditions were a recipe for poverty and class conflict. There were sharp divisions between a small mercantile and professional élite and a large unskilled proletariat, with only a small skilled artisanate. That class structure was reflected in the strongly contrasted social areas of such major ports as Glasgow, Liverpool, Hull and Bristol (and, indeed, as between the East and West Ends of London) which differed substantially from the more varied socio-economic structures of Birmingham (Vance, 1967) or Leeds (Ward, 1980).

SOME DEMOGRAPHIC CHARACTERISTICS OF ENGLISH PORT-CITIES

Socio-economic differences might be expected to have been reflected in the demographic characteristics of port-cities in general and of particular groups or communities within them. Extensive external connections and influences were apparent in their patterns of migration, and in the greater incidence of certain cause-specific morbidity and mortality (for example, from plague, cholera and typhus, often known as the 'Irish fever'). Internal influences— especially economic contrasts reflected in working, housing and environmental conditions—in turn influenced patterns of disease and mortality; while household and family structures were influenced by employment and work patterns, for example, the effect of absent household heads in those areas of large port-cities and especially in smaller maritime communities (such as fishing and packet ports) dominated by sea-going men.

In the absence of a full-scale analysis and faced by a diversity of local conditions, it is difficult to be more than speculative over the precise effects of such influences on the population structure and demographic characteristics of nineteenth-century port-cities. In this short account it is possible only to put forward some general propositions, to discuss the characteristics of the population dynamics of selected English ports from the mid-nineteenth to the early-twentieth century and, more fully, to outline some of the demographic and social characteristics of mid-Victorian Liverpool, an archetypal large port-city.

Exposure to external influences is reflected particularly in migration streams which introduce into the host population a variety of cultural influences and social attitudes which may substantially affect demographic behaviour. In the case of Britain, one of the most powerful of such influences was that of the Irish. The communication of a disease such as typhus, the incidence of which was high in Dublin and Belfast, may well have contributed to its relative virulence in port-cities with substantial Irish migration (such as Liverpool or Sunderland) and to its persistence after it had declined substantially in most English cities (Luckin, 1984). However, as Ward (1971) has pointed out for American cities, the adaptability of different migrant groups to city living varied considerably, not least as related to their previous experience of urban living. Certain rural migrants seem to have been particularly vulnerable to endemic urban disease, not least tuberculosis, although the extent to which this was a result of the vulnerability of particular groups (including the Irish), rather than their poverty, is difficult to establish.

Transmitted social norms and variations in the sex ratio among migrant groups may also be carried over into marital behaviour and be reflected in differential fertility, although the precise relationships and influences are complex and may owe more to employment structure (both for men and women) which reflect internal rather than external characteristics (Anderson, M., 1976; Woods and Hinde, 1985). Thus, the possible impact of 'absent' spouses on the birth rate was probably offset by the relatively early age of marriage among many sea-faring communities, not least among fisher-folk (Summers, 1990).

Marital behaviour certainly influences fertility levels. The extent to which port-cities often carry relatively high levels of fertility into the post-fertility transition may owe less to ethnic origins (at least after the second generation of migrant families) than to occupational structure. Robert Woods (1984) has shown that marked variations in marital fertility within London in the later-nineteenth century reflected differences in social structure, with high fertility in London's East End linked to the casual labour market (with its workforce surpluses and opportunities for adolescent earnings as well as substantial Irish and Jewish immigration). These differences persisted: thus in 1931, of the top 14 of London's 28 boroughs in magnitude of gross reproduction rate (GRR) 10 were riverside areas in the East End (Charles and Moschinsky, 1938). Similar conditions affected many of the larger port-cities and, as in Liverpool, the ports of North-East England and Glasgow, were reflected in rates of fertility above the national average well into the twentieth century. In the period 1911–1931, Charles and Moschinsky (1938, p. 151) specifically relate high fertility to large proportions of Irish migrants in a number of port-cities, notably on Merseyside and in North-East England: with much higher proportions of new migrants, such influences may have been more general in the nineteenth century.

Moreover, as Haines (1979) has shown in his analysis of the fertility data from the 1911 census of England and Wales, occupations which were numerous in port-cities, such as general labourers and ship platers and riveters, were among those with the highest marital fertility: these two groups had fertility ratios of 131 and 132, respectively, standardized at 117 and 121 as compared with 100 for England and Wales as a whole. Perhaps the most suggestive evidence is that provided by Glass (1938, Tables X and XI) of gross reproduction rates between 1861 and 1911 and their relative magnitude for 1911 and 1931 as calculated by Charles and Moschinsky (1938, Table II). Of the 20 county boroughs in England and Wales with the highest GRR in 1911, ten were ports, though it must also be noted that six of them were also in heavy industrial areas (five in North-East England). In contrast, of the 30 lowest GRRs in the county boroughs, only two were in port areas and one (Wallasey) was essentially a middle-class dormitory suburb predominantly of people working in commerce and business in Liverpool. One of the factors identified in high fertility, a low percentage of occupied women, is certainly typical of most port-cities: in 1911, all but one of 20 ports out of a total of 83 boroughs were in the lower half of the range of the percentage of adult women in work and only three (West Ham, Liverpool and Bristol) above that range in 1931. Robert Woods' more recent analysis certainly bears out that evidence and shows that, in the generation after the onset of the fertility transition, many English ports were above the levels of fertility predicted for urban areas in general (Woods, 1987, pp. 303–07 and Figure 7).

Reference has been made to the role of migration in bringing external influences to the shaping of the demographic characteristics of port-cities. Jan de Vries (1984, chapters 9 and 10), reviewing the particular role of migration in the growth of European cities between 1500 and 1800, has argued that although migrants may have been more susceptible to urban disease and often married later (and had fewer children) than established urban inhabitants, their 'reproduction value' was such that they did contribute to natural growth, certainly in the nineteenth century. De Vries shows that migration played a crucial role in urbanization before 1800 as the 'mediator of economic and demographic forces' since 'city populations rose or fell *despite* the behaviour of ... vital rates ... because of the enormous impact of migration' (de Vries, 1984, p. 199). Although the debate on the precise demographic significance of migration as against natural increase or decrease in the growth of cities up to the mid-nineteenth century continues (Woods, 1989), it is clear that deaths generally exceeded births in the inner areas of all large cities, and especially in port-cities, up to the mid-nineteenth century. Indeed, at times of major epidemics of cholera and typhoid there were sharp increases in natural losses (see below, p. 108). More detailed work is needed to isolate those risks of high mortality attributable to 'port-related' diseases as against the generally high levels of mortality in large nineteenth-century industrial cities. But there can be little doubt that ports provided some of the unhealthiest urban environments and had some of the lowest life expectancies of any British cities of that era.

From the mid-nineteenth century, however, rapid growth depended less on the rate of urbanward migration than on the role of migration in relation to urban/rural differentials in fertility and mortality (de Vries, 1984, pp. 231–34). Nevertheless, in the working-class districts of port-cities, high mortality continued to offset generally high fertility, and migration continued to contribute substantially to population growth.

While large ports share the migration characteristics of most large cities, in two respects they are often distinctive. First, they draw on a wider range of migrants, including proportionately more from overseas and of different ethnic origins. While this is a lesser feature, of even large British port-cities, than of American cities of the late-nineteenth century, nevertheless the special tabulations of overseas-born in the 1911 census suggest a particular role attributable to overseas immigration related to the nature of trade connections, a factor of importance in relation to the demography of minority groups in later-nineteenth-century Britain (see below, p. 119).

Secondly, since the hinterlands of large port-cities were often more extensive, not least because of their access to widespread overseas and internal communications networks, perceived distances from the potential hinterland were foreshortened, nationally and internationally. Moreover, the nature of their activities promoted a somewhat greater 'floating' population of migrants attracted by their larger casual labour markets than in many manufacturing towns. There are insufficient detailed studies of urban migrational hinterlands and the composition of particular groups of movers to substantiate this generalization, but one brief analysis of selected towns in North-West England in the period 1851 to 1901 suggests that Liverpool's range of attraction was greater than that of most inland towns (Lawton and Pooley, 1992, pp. 130–33).

POPULATION TRENDS AND COMPONENTS OF CHANGE IN ENGLISH PORT-CITIES, 1851–1911

The functional definition of ports discussed above (pp. 92–94) presents difficulties in the analysis of population trends from censuses and civil registers. Smaller ports are often most dominated by shipping and trade, but frequently cannot be separated, statistically, from the rural registration districts in which they lie. At the other extreme, London (always Britain's largest general port) and most other large ports such as Liverpool (the leading exporter for much of the nineteenth century) and Glasgow (see chapter 2, above) cannot simply be classified as port-cities. This part of the analysis is therefore restricted to 11 leading ports of England and Wales, excluding London, Manchester (an inland port only after the completion of the Manchester Ship Canal in 1894), Goole (also an inland port) and specialist naval bases (Plymouth, Portsmouth and Chatham), one of which, Portsmouth, is the subject of chapter 7, below.[2]

In one of a series of substantial analyses of nineteenth-century population, Thomas Welton (1900) calculated the growth of population in 30-year phases between 1801 and 1891 for individual towns, including port-towns and others classified as ports in this chapter (Table 4.1, which also includes Plymouth, Portsmouth, Chatham and Yarmouth for comparison). Without exception, the index of growth during this period exceeded that for England and Wales, commonly by a factor of over two. The large general ports (including Liverpool, Bristol, Hull and Southampton) showed sustained growth exceeding the national level, although the lead of Liverpool over its southern rivals

---

2 The basic list was compiled from data in Sir David J. Owen (1939) and J. Bird (1963). In order of average annual value of trade, 1936–1938, they are (£m): Liverpool (320.1), Hull (89.1), Southampton (66.7), Bristol (31.5), Newcastle and Tyne Ports (28.6), Swansea (21.3), Grimsby and Immingham (19.0), Cardiff (15.6), Middlesbrough (12.5), Dover (12.5) and Newport (8.3). Among those excluded, Plymouth had a substantial tonnage (especially inflated by calls from passenger liners) in addition to its naval base, while a number of 'packet ports' (Harwich, Holyhead, Newhaven, Fishguard and Folkestone) had trade valued between £4m and £3.5m; other specialist ports (e.g. Sunderland, Blyth and Port Talbot) handled considerable tonnages of coal and ores.

Table 4.1: *Population growth in selected port-towns in England and Wales, 1801–1891.*

Port-town	Population (000s)		% change			Index of change
	1801	*1891*	*1801–1831*	*1831–1861*	*1861–1891*	*1891:1801*
Liverpool	89.1	873.0	150.5	151.2	55.6	9.80
Bristol	70.4	304.9	76.3	47.8	66.1	4.33
Newcastle	46.2	310.4	68.7	103.1	96.1	6.72
South Shields	11.0	78.4	70.3	87.9	122.5	7.13
Tynemouth	13.8	49.5	75.7	43.3	42.3	3.59
Hull	31.9	205.1	78.2	80.1	100.4	6.43
Cardiff	2.7	141.3	169.0	497.3	230.2	52.33
Southampton	10.5	92.0	130.5	153.8	50.1	8.76
Swansea	10.7	91.9	99.4	115.7	100.1	8.59
Middlesbrough	0.6	76.1	28.4	2,581.3	280.6	126.83
Grimsby	1.9	56.4	156.3	157.6	346.6	29.68
Newport	1.9	55.9	316.2	250.3	101.2	29.42
Dover	8.0	32.1	95.0	65.7	31.0	4.01
Total of '11 ports'	298.7	2,367.0	–	–	–	7.92
Portsmouth	44.5	184.7	41.6	86.4	57.3	4.15
Plymouth	43.3	157.7	75.0	69.3	23.0	3.64
Chatham	22.6	83.1	53.1	60.5	49.3	3.68
Yarmouth	16.8	49.6	47.9	42.1	41.0	2.95
England and Wales	8,893.0	29,003.0	56.3	44.4	44.5	3.26

Note: Newcastle, together with South Shields and Tynemouth, forms a single unit (Tyne ports) in subsequent analysis.
Source: Welton, 1900, pp. 527–89.

(including London) and Europe-orientated ports (including Hull) declined somewhat in the late-nineteenth century. The most rapidly growing 'new ports' of the Victorian period included those essentially involved in the coal and iron industries such as Cardiff, Swansea, Newport, Middlesbrough and the Tees ports, and—to a substantial degree—the Tyne ports: they also involved big fishing ports (for example, Hull and Grimsby), although a comparison with Yarmouth (which Welton described as 'unprogressive' in growth) indicates that this was due in part to the continuing concentration of the fishing industry. Rates of growth in the naval towns were generally slower than in the late-eighteenth and early-nineteenth centuries, sometimes falling below the national level. Indeed, other than a generally substantial expansion in commercial ports, there is no obvious common temporal pattern in rates of port population growth.

Some of the most rapid rates of growth in British port-cities—not least in terms of migration—were undoubtedly achieved in the late-eighteenth and early-nineteenth centuries. This accords well with a model of the evolution of British ports described by Bird (1963) from a primitive nucleus to extension and elaboration of their quayage systems, including dock construction (the first three of his six phases of port development), which was reached in some ports such as London, Liverpool and Hull by the end of the eighteenth century and in other major ports (including Southampton and Bristol) by early- to mid-Victorian times. Coupled with the vast expansion of trade, the continuing expansion of the physical fabric of ports, the development of cargo handling and transportation, the processing of raw materials and the growth of commerce all contributed to rapid population expansion as labour continued to be drawn to Victorian port-cities.

The extent to which such growth was due to natural change or to migrational gain may be calculated after the initiation of vital registration in England and Wales in 1837 and with some precision from the 1850s. Table 4.2 summarizes the components of population growth between 1851 and 1911 for the 11 ports, with three selected naval ports and one fishing port for comparison. The areas for which these data are calculated include those registration districts dependent on and, by 1911, substantially linked by work journeys to the port in question. Thus the port of 'Liverpool' incorporates the registration districts of Liverpool, Toxteth Park, West Derby, Birkenhead and Wirral (Figure 4.1); Bristol, those of Barton Regis (Clifton), Bedminster, Keynsham and Long Ashton; Hull, of Sculcoates; Southampton, of South Stoneham; and so on. Conversely, some 'new ports' were included in their more extensive registration districts, often with substantial rural hinterlands, until they were accorded separate status later in the nineteenth century (for example, Grimsby and Middlesbrough).

While there are considerable differences between individual ports in rates of growth and in their components of change, the aggregate for the 11 selected ports indicates a faster rate of growth than for towns in general and for any other 'type' of town over the same period, other than that in selected colliery districts (Welton, 1911; Lawton, 1983). Only two, Dover and Bristol (both of which resemble the slower-growing southern English towns), recorded substantially below-average growth as compared with both the group of ports and national trends, but Bristol's growth accelerated in the late-nineteenth century as regional development in Britain shifted southwards. In contrast, Liverpool's growth, like that of its hinterland, had decelerated by the end of the century. Dover shared the characteristics of some of the older southern and naval ports (for example, Plymouth) in its relatively slow total growth, its modest natural increase and its net migrational loss.

With these exceptions, the rate of natural increase in ports between 1851 and

Table 4.2: *Components of population growth in selected port-towns, England and Wales, 1851–1911.*

Port area	Population (000s)		Population change 1851–1911					
			Total increase		Natural		Migrational	
	1851	1911	No. (000s)	%	No. (000s)	%	No. (000s)	%
Liverpool	468.7	1,150.6	681.9	145.5	510.7	109.0	171.2	36.5
Bristol	203.4	429.2	225.8	111.6	233.8	114.9	-7.9	-3.9
Tyne ports	189.2	637.5	448.3	236.9	357.3	188.8	91.0	48.1
Hull	95.4	297.1	201.7	211.4	147.7	154.8	53.9	56.5
Cardiff	46.5	281.5	235.2	505.8	130.9	281.5	104.3	224.3
Southampton	50.1	169.8	119.7	238.9	77.9	155.5	41.8	82.8
Swansea	38.4	147.9	109.5	285.2	86.0	224.0	23.5	61.2
Middlesbrough[a]	20.9	180.2	159.3	762.2	116.7	558.4	42.6	203.8
Grimsby[b]	34.3	123.8	89.5	260.9	58.2	169.7	31.2	91.0
Newport	44.5	152.9	108.4	243.6	81.0	182.0	27.4	61.6
Dover	28.3	51.9	23.6	83.4	27.2	96.1	-3.6	-12.7
Total (11 ports)	1,219.7	3,622.6	2,402.9	197.0	1,827.4	149.8	575.5	47.2
Portsmouth[c]	89.0	263.7	174.7	196.3	118.8	133.5	55.9	62.8
Plymouth[d]	102.4	194.7	92.3	90.1	88.8	86.7	3.5	3.4
Chatham[e]	42.8	112.5	69.7	162.9	55.1	128.7	14.6	34.1
Yarmouth[f]	47.0	104.2	57.1	121.5	59.1	125.7	-2.0	-4.3
All towns[g]	9,956.0	24,585.9	14,629.9	146.9	12,539.5	125.9	2,090.4	21.0

[a] Middlesbrough is included under Guisborough registration district until 1871 and comparisons include both districts up to 1911.
[b] Grimsby is included under Caistor registration district until 1891: both districts are included up to 1911.
[c] Portsea Island and Alverstoke registration districts.
[d] Plymouth, East Stonehouse and Stoke Damerel (Devonport) registration districts.
[e] Medway registration district.
[f] Yarmouth includes Mutford registration district.
[g] Total for 130 towns (73 'Northern' and 47 'Southern' + London) (see also Lawton, 1983, Table 4, p. 200).
Source: Censuses of England and Wales, 1861–1911.

Figure 4.1: Registration districts and sub-districts of Merseyside, 1841–1911 (Howard Street and Dale Street were amalgamated before the 1891 census and Islington added to them before 1901: St George and St Thomas were amalgamated before 1891).

1911 was at or above the rate for all towns, and in newer ports, such as Cardiff, was conspicuously so. This was primarily due to very high birth rates although, particularly in the case of Liverpool, these were sometimes offset by high—and at times excessive—mortality. In contrast, natural change in Yarmouth and the three naval bases was close to, or below, the general level for all towns. While the dependence on migration was much more variable, all the major ports except Dover and Bristol experienced substantial net gains which in decades of rapid increase exceeded the natural increase, especially in the newer ports.

Indeed, some continued to be more dependent on migration for growth than on natural increase (high though this was in most cases) until the later-nineteenth century: Newcastle and Southampton until 1861; Liverpool until 1871; and Middlesbrough and Cardiff until 1891. These contrasts have substantial implications in terms of their differing individual demographic and socio-economic characteristics, which have yet to be fully analysed for other than a few British ports.[3] As an example of certain facets of this aspect of the demography of the population dynamics of ports in their nineteenth-century development, the case of Liverpool is now analysed.

LIVERPOOL: A CASE STUDY

In the late-eighteenth and early-nineteenth centuries Liverpool experienced one of the most explosive phases of growth of any British city. Population grew by 40 per cent in the 1790s, an estimated two-thirds of it from migrational gain (Laxton, 1981). Similar levels of growth persisted into the 1830s, with a peak rate of increase between 1811 and 1821 (45.8 per cent), a

Table 4.3: *The population of Merseyside, 1801–1911.*

Year	Liverpool Borough	Liverpool registration district	Toxteth Park[b]	West Derby registration district[c]	Birkenhead[d]	Wirral registration district
1801	77,653	77,653	2,069	9,925	463	9,410
1811	94,376	94,376	5,864	13,208	579	10,013
1821	118,972	118,972	12,829	19,530	1,025	12,191
1831	165,175	165,175	24,067	28,991	3,737	17,340
1841	286,487[a]	223,003	41,295	47,385	10,777	31,784
1851	375,955	258,236	61,334	91,945	30,804	57,157
1861	443,938	269,742	69,284	156,561	61,420[a]	18,420[a]
1871	493,405	238,411	85,842	257,008	79,307	23,507
1881	552,508	210,164	117,028	359,275	103,426	27,928
1891	517,980	156,981	128,387	444,403	130,591	39,623
1901	684,958[a]	147,407	136,230	529,684	165,111	44,316
1911	746,421[a]	128,673	136,140	613,374	210,516	61,821

[a] Indicates boundary change in preceding decade.
[b] Registration sub-district to 1871; registration district from 1881.
[c] Excluding Toxteth Park.
[d] Registration sub-district to 1851; registration district from 1861.
Sources: Census of Great Britain, 1851; Censuses of England and Wales, 1861–1911.

3 In addition to the studies of Portsmouth and Glasgow contained in chapters 7 and 2, work on aspects of the population development of port-cities has been conducted for Cardiff by Martin J. Daunton (1977); Kingston upon Hull, by P. A. Tansey (1973); Newcastle, by M. Barke and M. J. Buswell (1980); and Sunderland, by R. C. Fox (1980).

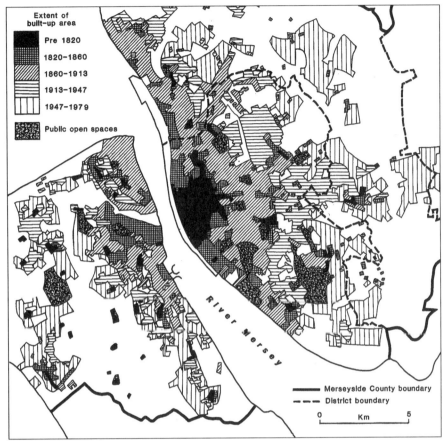

Figure 4.2: Growth of the built-up area of Merseyside to 1979. *Source:* Gould and Hodgkiss, 1982, Figure 1.3.

feature which it shared with most major British cities. The population of the Borough of Liverpool grew five-fold between 1801 and 1851, from 78,000 to 376,000, and had doubled to 946,421 by 1911 (Table 4.3). There were four boundary extensions as the dock system grew and the built-up area advanced behind it (Figures 4.2 and 4.3). The planned development across the river at Birkenhead from 1826 and the subsequent growth of ship-building and, from the 1840s, of the dock system created a new town of 24,333 inhabitants by 1851, which had grown to 130,794 by 1911. Thus, from early Victorian times a Merseyside conurbation emerged, increasingly united by steam ferries from 1817 and then from 1886 by under-river rail crossing, with a prime focus on the port, its activities and the impressive central business district of Liverpool.

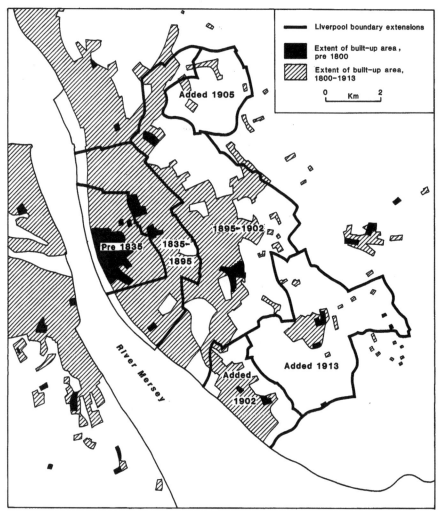

Figure 4.3: Growth of Liverpool, 1835–1913. *Source:* Gould and Hodgkiss, 1982, Figure 1.1.

Male employment in Liverpool was dominated by the traditionally casual and largely unskilled occupations. In mid-Victorian times, general dock and warehouse labour together accounted for 22.3 per cent of all males over 20, in contrast to London, also with a traditionally large dock labour force, with only 10.9 per cent (Table 4.4). Transport-related employment and ocean navigation formed the second most important occupational group in nineteenth-century Liverpool. The relative lack of choice within the labour market is emphasized by the paucity of large-scale manufacturing industry onMerseyside: for example, metal manufacture, engineering and toolmaking provided relatively few jobs in Liverpool as compared with Birmingham or Manchester. Commerce and urban services, however, provided more jobs in Liverpool than in many other towns, and its commercial functions a similar percentage to those of London. Female work in Liverpool was restricted: 65.7 per cent of women over 20 recorded no occupation in the census of 1871, and far and away the most important job for the remainder was domestic service (Table 4.4). The textile and clothing trade was much smaller than in many other towns of North-West England and, apart from shopkeeping and school-teaching, there were few service jobs for women and girls until the early-twentieth century.

Among the individual sectors of employment, transport-related activities expanded most rapidly in Liverpool in the second half of the nineteenth century, not only in the booming railway sector but also on the docks and in road transport. Commerce benefited from both the national expansion in tertiary employment and Liverpool's continuing pre-eminence as a port. Though employment in manufacturing and toolmaking experienced relative and absolute increases in employment during the period, both were relatively small-scale activities on Merseyside. Moreover, from the 1840s, iron manufacture and the construction industry declined relatively in employment; ship-building was gradually eliminated in Liverpool and concentrated in Birkenhead; in addition, a dramatic decline occurred in small-scale craft industries. Hence, in the nineteenth century a high and, in many parts of the region, a growing proportion of Merseyside's workforce was employed in unskilled trades with an emphasis on casual labour.

THE DEMOGRAPHIC PROFILE OF NINETEENTH-CENTURY LIVERPOOL

These basic physical and economic facts provide the background to a highly distinctive population geography, yet one which reflects many of the *general* features of large nineteenth-century commercial cities in Britain. The extent to which they may also be identified as peculiar to port-cities relates rather more to the social structure and the nature and origins of Liverpool's workforce than to any highly distinctive demographic régime.

POPULATION DYNAMICS

The overall population growth rate in Liverpool between 1851 and 1911 was rather less than for large British cities in general, including London (Table 4.2). The principal reason for this was its relatively modest rate of natural increase which, at 109 per cent, was almost identical to Manchester's 107 per cent, but behind those for London (134.2 per cent), Leeds (131.4 per cent), Birmingham (176.3 per cent) and Sheffield (182.2 per cent): while close to Bristol's natural increase over the same period (114.9 per cent), it was far

Table 4.4: *Occupational structure of Liverpool and selected towns, 1871.*

A: Male employment (as a percentage of occupied men over 20 years)

Occupational group	Liverpool Borough %	Manchester and Salford %	Birmingham %	Bristol %	London %	England and Wales %
Public service and professions	5.2	5.4	3.8	6.8	8.8	6.6
Personal and domestic service	2.9	2.4	2.1	3.4	5.2	3.5
Commerce	7.5	8.0	4.6	5.9	7.6	3.4
Rail and road transport	5.5	5.5	3.2	3.5	5.8	3.1
Ocean and inland transport and docks	21.4	6.4	2.9	7.0	6.4	3.7
Manufacturing industry	33.9	48.6	64.0	44.0	41.8	40.8
Building	8.8	11.0	7.9	12.1	11.0	8.4
General labour	10.2	5.5	5.5	10.5	6.6	7.3
Other (including agricultural)	4.3	7.0	5.7	6.2	6.1	22.8
Independent	0.3	0.2	0.3	0.6	0.7	0.4
Numbers employed (total over 20 years)	131,198	128,955	87,165	43,777	842,793	5,866,168

Table 4.4: *Continued.*

B: *Female employment (percentage of all women over 20 years)*

Occupational group		Liverpool Borough %	Manchester and Salford %	Birmingham %	Bristol %	London %	England and Wales %
Public service and professions		1.4	1.0	1.2	2.0	2.1	1.6
Personal and domestic service		15.6	13.1	10.0	17.5	18.3	13.9
Commerce		1.9	1.4	1.1	1.2	0.8	0.6
All transport		0.3	0.3	1.5	0.1	0.1	0.1
Manufacturing industry		12.9	27.7	22.2	20.3	17.7	17.0
Other (including agricultural)		0.7	1.3	0.8	1.2	1.0	2.5
Independent		1.6	1.0	1.1	3.5	2.8	2.2
Total in employment	%	34.3	45.8	37.9	45.8	42.7	37.9
	numbers	49,406	68,774	35,937	26,369	436,913	2,449,601
Wives in household work	%	65.7	54.2	62.1	54.2	57.3	62.1
	numbers	94,745	81,245	53,919	31,255	585,506	4,014,044
Total (women over 20 years)		144,151	150,019	94,856	57,624	1,022,419	6,463,645

behind such ports as Newcastle (142.0 per cent), Hull (151.2 per cent) and Southampton (155.5 per cent).

The reasons for this relatively modest natural increase lay in the generally high levels of mortality in Liverpool throughout the nineteenth century which, despite high birth rates, kept natural increase in check in the crowded inner-city and dockside wards where, from the 1840s, death rates were twice those of the suburbs even in 'healthy' years, and not uncommonly were three to four times as great. This was reflected in one of the highest mortality rates in England, ranging from 31 per 1,000 in the 1830s and 1840s to 71 per 1,000 in the Irish famine and typhus epidemic year of 1847.[4] Despite better sanitation and improving public health from the 1870s, mortality was consistently one-quarter to one-third above the national rate throughout the years 1850–1910, and the gap between healthier suburb and crowded slum often two-and-a-half times. In relation to epidemic and intestinal disease, Liverpool's mortality was one-and-a-half times the national rate and chest diseases were 60 per cent higher. Both were reflected in very high child and infant mortality, which accounted for 40–60 per cent of deaths in mid-Victorian times.

Inevitably there was a wide gap in life expectation between Liverpool and the 'healthy districts' identified in the Reports of the Registrar General: for example, in the 1840s a staggering 19 years between Liverpool (25 years at birth) and Surrey (44 years), and of 10 or more years even in 1911–12 (Glass, 1964). Liverpool's death rates were 50–100 per cent higher than the crude national rates throughout this period, and generally 20–30 per cent above them even in the relatively healthy suburbs of West Derby (Table 4.5). Moreover, despite improvements in housing and health conditions—reflected in a decline in both morbidity and mortality figures—the adverse ratio between Liverpool and national death rates in 1901–1911 was higher in the city centre than in mid-Victorian times and still adverse (and little improved) in both inner (Toxteth) and outer (West Derby) suburbs. This was particularly so in terms of infant mortality: in 1890, the ratio between Liverpool registration district (one of the worst in the country) and 'healthy districts' of England and Wales increased progressively from 150.3 in the first month of life, to 492 between nine and twelve months. Liverpool's infant mortality rates were, in general, three times the national level.

The reproduction rates of port-cities varied widely, as noted above. Ports in

4 The problems are abundantly evidenced in the data and reports from Dr W. H. Duncan, the Medical Officer of Health (the first in Britain) appointed under the Liverpool Sanitary Act of 1846, who in 1840 described Liverpool as 'the most unhealthy town in England'. The first full-scale evaluation of Duncan's data on morbidity and mortality and his methods of analysis is being carried out by Paul Laxton and Gerry Kearns in connection with a project funded by the Wellcome Trust to prepare an edition of Duncan's correspondence to be published by Cambridge University Press, the context of which is described in Laxton (1993). For a general account of Duncan's work and its place in the history of English public health, see Frazer (1947, 1950).

Table 4.5: *Birth and death rates in Liverpool registration districts and England and Wales, 1841–1911.*

Decade	England and Wales			Liverpool R. D.			Toxteth R. D.			West Derby R. D.		
	Birth rate per 1,000	Death rate per 1,000	Natural change (% per decade)	Birth rate per 1,000	Death rate per 1,000	Natural change (% per decade)	Birth rate per 1,000	Death rate per 1,000	Natural change (% per decade)	Birth rate per 1,000	Death rate per 1,000	Natural change (% per decade)
1841–1851	32.6	22.4	10.2	42.6	43.3	−0.7	51.2	38.2	13.0	48.8	36.1	12.7
1851–1861	34.2	22.2	11.9	34.9	34.0	0.9	42.1	27.4	14.7	44.2	28.1	16.0
1861–1871	35.2	22.5	12.7	35.4	36.4	−1.0	46.0	34.3	11.7	50.1	33.2	17.0
1871–1881	35.4	21.4	14.0	33.0	31.6	1.4	45.0	29.4	15.6	34.6	21.2	13.4
1881–1891	32.5	19.1	13.4	28.5	28.9	−0.4	38.2	25.1	13.2	41.2	24.4	16.8
1891–1901	29.9	18.2	11.7	32.6	32.3	0.3	32.7	23.1	9.6	36.4	22.1	14.3
1901–1911	27.2	15.4	11.8	34.2	28.7	5.5	29.7	19.3	10.4	34.7	18.9	15.8

Sources: Decennial Censuses of Population for Britain 1851 and for England and Wales, 1861–1911, and Registrar General's Annual Reports for England and Wales.

North-East England had some of the highest urban fertility levels in the later-nineteenth century (Glass, 1938). Among the larger ports, Liverpool (along with Bootle and, to a lesser extent, Birkenhead) had high reproduction rates, as did Hull. In contrast, Bristol had relatively low reproduction rates. Yet despite its generally high birth rates, Liverpool registration district had a very adverse rate of natural growth: as compared with England and Wales, the borough and even its suburbs generally lagged behind (Figure 4.4). High birth rates continued into the inter-war years, producing a late fertility transition in a population with large numbers in the lower social classes and a relatively high proportion of Catholic families. From the First World War until the 1960s, standardized birth rates were 11–30 per cent above the national level andthe general fertility rate was 13 per cent higher (Gould and Hodgkiss,1982, chapter 11). Hence, as its health and mortality experience improved, Merseyside's

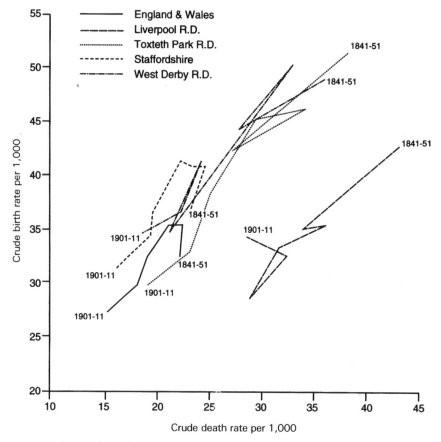

Figure 4.4: Decadal trends in birth and death rates in Liverpool's registration districts and in comparative areas, 1841–1911.

natural growth gradually moved above the national rates, especially in the inner areas of the conurbation.

These general characteristics conceal a good deal of internal demographic diversity. Between 1801 and 1841 rapid population growth occurred on north Merseyside, due to both rapid in-migration and moderate natural increase. Despite high death rates, especially in dockside areas, the older parts of Liverpool registration district grew at between 20 and 40 per cent in each decade, as compared with a growth of over 80 per cent per decade in the new suburban areas such as the former villages of Everton, Kirkdale and Toxteth. Similarly, Birkenhead, Wallasey and Tranmere on the Wirral all began to attract population. In contrast, many surrounding townships, both on the Wirral and north Merseyside, experienced stagnation or population loss as urban growth attracted labour from adjacent rural areas.

From 1841 to 1871 rapid population growth extended to all parts of suburban Merseyside, with gains of over 40 per cent per decade from Crosby in the north to Garston in the south, including West Derby and Walton, due to a combination of moderate natural increase, except in Liverpool registration district, and massive in-migration (Figure 4.5). Much of that in-movement was from adjacent rural areas of persistent natural increase of population associated with out-migration, the classic features of areas of rural/urban migration. By 1851, however, population growth in the decaying inner residential areas of Liverpool was grinding to a halt; three of its inner wards lost population in 1851–1861, and in 1861–1871 all seven wards within the parish of Liverpool showed an absolute decline in population. This trend, common to inner areas of all large cities, was due to a combination of very high mortality and relatively low birth rates, as reflected in low natural increases or, in certain areas, natural decrease and a net outflow of migrants to newly developing suburbs. In Liverpool registration district only the high-status Mount Pleasant area continued to have an inward balance of migration to 1871. The details are exemplified in the analysis of components of change in the area's registration sub-districts during the decade 1861–1871 (Figure 4.6).

Between 1871 and 1911 the most rapidly growing areas extended further north and south along both sides of the Mersey and, from 1891, reached inland to Fazakerley, Allerton and Wavertree. Meanwhile, population growth in the older Liverpool suburbs of Everton, Kirkdale and Toxteth Park slackened to between 5 and 20 per cent per decade after 1881, as compared with previous decennial rates of over 80 per cent. Out-migration from central Liverpool continued and, from 1881 onwards, older suburbs also lost population by migration to the new outer ring of residential areas.

Because of relatively high rates of natural increase between 1881 and 1901, Toxteth, West Derby and Everton maintained their population levels, but from the decade 1901–1911 (Figure 4.7) out-migration exceeded natural increase as these older suburbs declined in population. Similarly, out-migration occurred in Wirral; central Birkenhead lost population by out-migration from 1871

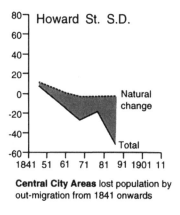

Central City Areas lost population by out-migration from 1841 onwards

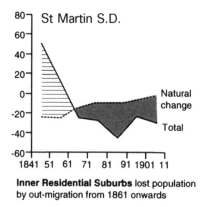

Inner Residential Suburbs lost population by out-migration from 1861 onwards

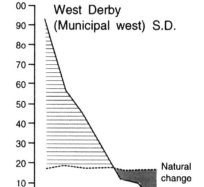

Newer Residential Suburbs grew to 1881, gaining population from the inner city and elsewhere but thereafter lost population by out-migration

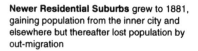

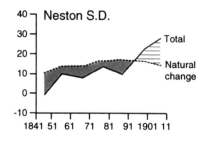

Peripheral Areas suffered rural depopulation to 1891 but by 1890s developed as commuter suburbs and gained population by in-migration

Figure 4.5: Natural and net migrational components of population change in selected registration sub-districts of Merseyside, 1841–1911. *Sources:* Censuses of Great Britain, 1841 and 1851, and of England and Wales, 1861–1911, and Registrar General's Annual Reports.

onwards, and suburban growth expanded to encompass peripheral townships such as West Kirby, Heswall and Neston; only the remoter rural parishes experienced net migrational loss. By the late-nineteenth century Merseyside increasingly drew the bulk of its migrational gain from outside the region.

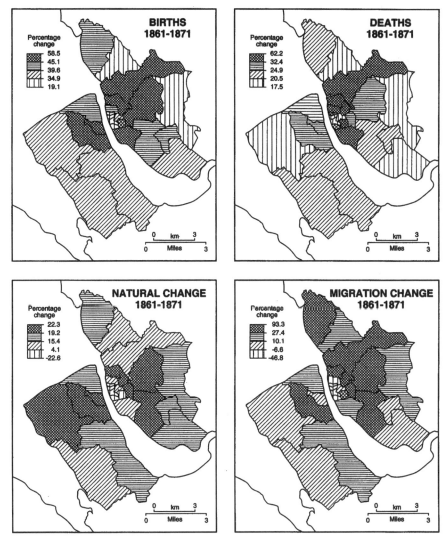

Figure 4.6: Components of population change on Merseyside, 1861–1871, by registration sub-districts (the percentage change for the decade is given by quartiles for crude birth and death rates and for natural and net migrational change). *Source:* Census of England and Wales, 1871 and Annual Reports of the Registrar General.

Although there was still a deal of intra-regional redistribution of population from centre to suburb and between suburbs, the port's far-flung links gave it a wide migrational hinterland. Such population trends are typical of most expanding industrial towns of the nineteenth century: an initial phase of rapid population increase and the development of early residential suburbs close to

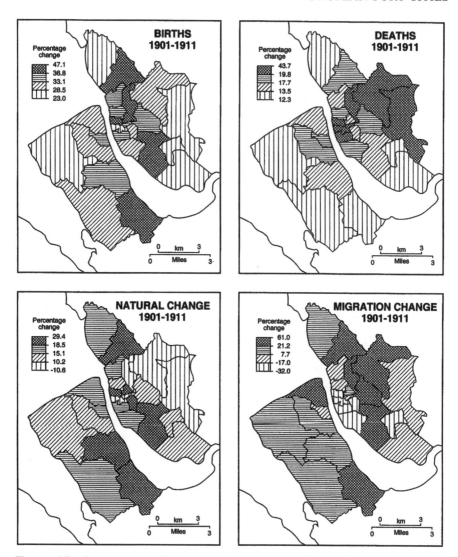

Figure 4.7: Components of population change on Merseyside, 1901–1911, by registration sub-districts (decadal percentage changes by quartiles are not directly comparable in absolute values with those for 1861–1871 in Figure 4.6). *Sources:* Census of England and Wales, 1911 and Annual Reports of the Registrar General.

the eighteenth- and early-nineteenth-century nucleus was quickly (in Liverpool between 1841 and 1871) followed by a second phase when suburban growth expanded and adjacent rural areas fed population to the city, helping to offset natural decrease in the core. A third phase, in the final quarter of the nineteenth century, saw a slackening of growth in increasingly unattractive inner residential areas into which the zone of out-migration extended from mid-Victorian times. Many areas, still in the rural periphery in 1871, were swallowed up by urban growth and attracted migrants from considerable distances, not least from other major urban regions.

The rapid growth of population from 286,487 in 1841 to 493,405 in 1871 owed more to migration than natural growth, with a migration gain of 211,685 in Liverpool's three registration districts as compared with 96,992 from natural increase. Despite very high mortality among many of the poorest immigrants, it was to a large extent through their large growth potential that between 1871 and 1911 the borough's population increased to 746,421. During these years there was a natural increase in these three registration districts of 138,330, compared with a migrational loss of 14,950, mainly through dispersion of population from city centre and older suburbs to the outer residential areas. This is reflected in the population of the Merseyside region, which increased from 354,244 in 1841 to 684,075 in 1871, and to over 1.15 million by 1911. However, census birthplace statistics, adjusted for mortality, suggest a migrant flow of almost 60,000 to Liverpool in every decade between 1851 and 1911, except during the depressed 1880s. These distinctive demographic trends are illustrated in Figure 4.5 for sub-districts of the city centre, the inner and outer suburbs and the periphery.

THE CHARACTERISTICS OF LIVERPOOL MIGRANTS

In 1851 49.4 per cent of Liverpool's population was born outside Lancashire. There were already within the city large migrant groups that were culturally, economically and socially distinctive: the Irish-born formed 22.3 per cent of the borough's population; the Welsh 5.4 per cent; and the Scots 3.7 per cent. A 10 per cent sample of households from the 1871 census enumerators' books confirms the demographic, occupational and social distinctiveness of different migrant groups. The Irish, dominated by semi-skilled and unskilled workers, were strongly clustered in dockside areas and experienced high fertility and mortality rates. The Welsh and Scots tended to have smaller families and were relatively more numerous in skilled manual and non-manual jobs. Many other groups of long-distance migrants were associated with particular industrial and commercial skills. Such occupationally selective migration provided an important feature of inter-urban movement often associated with residential clustering, especially among culturally or socially distinctive groups of migrants, which left a lasting impression on Liverpool's social character, as in many English port-towns.

The structure of such migrant communities, especially in areas where they formed a high proportion of households, could have significant demographic consequences. Cross-tabulations built up from a sample study of the census enumerators' books for mid-Victorian Liverpool show that in 1871 the age-structure of 11,455 household heads reflected changes in the pattern of migration to the city (Lawton and Pooley, 1976). Short-distance migrants were over-represented among those over 50, suggesting heavy migration from the local region in the 1830s and 1840s. In contrast, recent migration from newer areas of supply (such as London and Warwickshire) was reflected in an over-representation of the young (15–34) and younger middle-aged (35–46). Similarly, the high proportion of Irish household heads aged 50–64 reflected high in-migration of 20–40-year-olds in the famine years of 1845–1847.

The structure of Liverpool households also suggests differences in the pattern of life-cycle migration. Most short-distance migrants were single or married couples without children, a large proportion of whom had entered Liverpool households as lodgers or servants. In contrast, many long-distance migrants were married couples who had arrived with children either by direct movement (typical of the Scots) or via other areas (for example from South Wales, Warwickshire and London).

Occupational skills perhaps exert the greatest control over the distance of movement and mobility experience of migrants. Migration theory postulates that fluctuations in labour demand in both destinations and areas of origin and in places of competing opportunity are reflected in the characteristics of different occupational groups: longer-distance migrants tend to possess greater skills and higher socio-economic status; short-distance movers from nearby rural areas often entered the urban labour market as unskilled and relatively low-status workers. The Liverpool 1871 sample shows that Irish household heads were predominantly unskilled (mainly dockworkers or general labourers), most of whom had come direct to their nearest large labour market and attracted also by historic trade links and an already established Irish community. In contrast, the Welsh, again with close and long-standing links between North Wales and Liverpool, transferred such rurally derived skills as quarrying to the building industry, but many were also prominent in maritime activities, retailing and domestic service. The Scots, especially those from Clydeside, brought specific occupational skills to the metal and machine industries, and to ship-building and repairing: but they also included a substantial high-status professional and managerial group, including doctors, manufacturers (especially in port-based processing industries) and merchants, the latter often in similar types of trade to those of Liverpool. Migrants from other regions were often occupationally distinctive: for example, many from the West Midlands were metal workers; while a substantial proportion of those from London were commercial and professional workers.

One of the most significant aspects of migration to cities was the extent to which migrational patterns and behaviour varied between different migrant streams. To some extent, these may be related to the demographic and economic characteristics common to all migrants; but there were also distinctive differences in the composition and characteristics of different cultural and regional groups, which partly reflected their areas of origin and partly the degree to which different migrants were assimilated into a particular urban life-style. The wider range of migrant origins in large port-cities—which tend to have a greater proportion of longer-distance migrants and a wider range of origins—included distinctive ethnic groups from a variety of overseas areas which are of particular interest in studies of both demographic and socio-economic aspects of population development.

It is difficult to study the characteristics of migrants before, in the process of (in the case of stage migration), and after migration to the city. Some inferences on the role of various groups may be made from an analysis of migrant streams as related to demographic and economic changes in areas of origin and destination. But the main evidence of the extent to which migrants from different areas were or were not different in characteristics and the part they played in the life of the towns to which they came must be based on detailed cross-tabulations from census enumerators' books and other nominal data. Socio-economic status (as linked to employment and housing), family and household structure (which may reveal marriage patterns and, through children's birthplaces, family and migrational history), links with kin and home area (where relatives or lodgers are present in the household), and—where families can be traced between censuses—patterns of intra-urban mobility (which may be of interest in the study of assimilation into urban society) are some of the key themes in the study of both mobility processes and the part played by different groups in shaping social and residential patterns within nineteenth-century cities.

As a major port, Liverpool's migrant communities were characteristically diverse in origin (Table 4.6) and in their demographic, socio-economic and family structure. Differences in the time within the family life-cycle of movement and in changes in family status during the migration process account for some of the differences in demographic and family structure between Liverpool's migrant communities. Their occupational structure was a powerful factor shaping choice of residential area and social linkages (Pooley, 1977). In mid-Victorian Liverpool, the Irish were mainly—though by no means exclusively—employed in casual, unskilled work and tied by the needs of access to the docks, where labour was hired by the half-day, and to low-cost, poor-quality housing areas (Papworth, 1982). Forty-two per cent of all Irish households in the 1871 sample were headed by dock and warehouse workers who were markedly concentrated in dockside residential areas. In contrast, the Welsh had a much wider range of occupations and were found in a much wider range of society and of residential areas: some close to the city centre (for those in retailing and maritime-related activities); some in better working-class areas near the south docks where there were many Welsh artisans and builders; and many in the mainly Protestant 'decent' working-class bye-law suburbs of the Everton area, where many clerks and skilled workers lived (Pooley, 1983). Scottish households contained many skilled ship-building and engineering workers living in the newer dockside residential areas of north Liverpool, as

Table 4.6: *Birthplaces of the population of Liverpool borough, 1851–1901.*

Birthplace by region (of England) and country	Percentage of enumerated population					
	1851	*1861*	*1871*	*1881*	*1891*	*1901*
Lancashire (including Liverpool)	50.3	55.6	58.7	62.6	68.9	72.3
Adjacent counties (Cheshire, Yorkshire and Cumbria)	7.6	6.8	6.5	5.9	5.4	5.4
Northern and Midland England	3.4	3.1	3.4	3.2	3.2	3.2
Southern England	4.7	4.5	4.6	4.6	4.2	4.0
Ireland	22.3	18.9	15.6	12.9	9.1	6.7
Wales	5.4	4.8	4.3	3.9	3.4	3.0
Scotland	3.7	4.0	4.1	3.7	3.0	2.5
Islands in British seas (mainly Isle of Man)	1.0	0.8	0.8	0.8	0.7	0.7
Overseas (British and foreign subjects)	1.4	1.4	1.9	2.0	1.9	2.2
Total population of Liverpool (000s)	376.0	443.9	493.4	552.5	518.0	685.0

Note: The percentages do not total 100 because of the non-statement of birthplace by a small portion of enumerated population.

Sources: Birthplace tables of the Censuses of Great Britain, 1851 and of England and Wales, 1861–1901.

well as a strong group of professional and mercantile families who lived mainly in the high-class residential suburbs of south Liverpool.

Particular demographic features associated with individual migrant groups, whether these relate to stages in the life-cycle that reflect the period of migration or to social and behavioural characteristics, are likely to be concentrated within particular social areas. In mid-Victorian Liverpool, degrees of segregation varied. The Irish emerge as strongly segregated, while the Welsh and Scots are distinguished residentially from each other and from English- and locally-born people. Whether for reasons of culture or class status, there seems also to have been limited social intermixing, even within residential areas of varied background. Marriages were mainly within the same ethnic group, strongly so in the case of the Catholic Irish. Exogamous marriage outside the ethnic group was mainly with local or other English-born, except for fairly frequent marriages between Scots and Irish partners.

Lodgers or servants tended to reside with people from the same area as the household head and there was relatively little mixing of Irish, Scots and Welsh within such households. The Welsh had firm links with churches located almost wholly within strongly Welsh residential areas and which, through services and meetings conducted in Welsh, helped to preserve their language and culture as well as to foster social contacts among all sections of Welsh society. Residentially more dispersed than other ethnic groups, culturally they were strongly focused. The Irish were strongly segregated, residentially: positively in relation to housing and work, and negatively because they were discriminated against by other groups in jobs, housing and social status. Hence a strong sense of identity was generated within a close-knit community supported, in the case of the Catholic Irish, by the parochial system and, later, its associated schools. Thrown together by adverse housing, working and environmental conditions, their strong residential and cultural identity echoes that of the ethnic ghettos of American cities (Ward, 1989).

Over time, while the distinctiveness of smaller groups was often lost as social, residential and job mobility created different types of community and residential areas within the city, that of very strong and/or distinctive groups (for example, the Irish, the Jews and coloured immigrants) was preserved. In Liverpool, as in all large port-cities, one important aspect of such social sub-systems (which often have distinctive demographic characteristics) was that of foreign immigrants. Detailed information on this topic is meagre in British censuses, other than in the special tabulations carried out for selected towns and areas in 1911. At that date the Borough of Liverpool had some 12,580 foreign-born residents and 3,015 British citizens from tropical areas with which the port had long-standing trade (Table 4.7). While most of them were of European or English-speaking origin, they included small groups from South Asia (many of them seafarers) and one of the oldest-established Chinese communities in Britain (Wong, 1989). The latter has persisted and, at least up to the Second World War, was focused on the edge of the central business district around Pitt Street and Great George Square.

Similarly, contacts with West Africa, born of the slave trade and persisting through trade in vegetable oils, created an old-established black community in the Lower Parliament Street–Granby Street area that was subsequently added to by small numbers from other parts of tropical Africa and the Caribbean. Many of today's coloured community in Liverpool have been established for several generations. Yet this has not prevented their experiencing social and economic discrimination similar to that of more recent immigrants, a salutary warning against assumptions about assimilation—whether cultural, social or demographic—which the longer residence of established ethnic communities in port-cities might have been thought to promote (Ben-Tovim et al., 1992).

CONCLUSION

Although the notion that the population development of port-cities in the nineteenth and early-twentieth centuries had distinctive and common features is an attractive one, the analysis in the preceding pages does not establish any one clear demographic régime. Many of the characteristics of British ports, such as their high general and infant mortality, are common to most other large cities of the period (Lawton and Lee, 1989), although high specific

Table 4.7: *Birthplaces of overseas-born from tropical areas enumerated in Liverpool, 1911.*

Birthplace	Resident in Liverpool	Resident in Liverpool as a percentage of those resident in England and Wales
I *All colonies and dependencies*	3,015	1.9
Indian, Pakistan and Ceylon	916	1.4
As a % of I	30.4	
Rest of tropical Asia	268	6.5
As a % of I	8.9	
Tropical Africa	140	5.7
As a % of I	4.6	
West Indies and Caribbean	198	1.8
As a % of I	6.6	
II *All foreign*	12,580	3.4
Tropical Asia	52	2.8
As a % of II	0.4	
Tropical Africa	126	3.9
As a % of II	1.0	
Tropical Latin America	233	2.5
As a % of II	1.9	

Source: Census of England and Wales, 1911; Birthplace tables.

mortalities, such as those relating to epidemic diseases such as cholera entering Britain from abroad, are certainly distinctive. However, the impact of an employment structure heavily dependent on transport- and port-related industries and dominated by unskilled casual labour was a social and economic force that increased the vulnerability of port populations to many of the killer diseases of the period.

These wider socio-economic factors were also reflected in the generally high levels of fertility and the late transition to family limitation of an unskilled manual labour force that dominated the working-class areas of port-cities, although again these were shared with the populations of towns and regions dominated by heavy industry. Nor were the early and high marriage rates—reflecting employment structures, work patterns and wage rates which, through their early peaking, encouraged early marriage and large families—confined to ports: they were frequently shared by other areas with male-dominated employment structures.

Indeed, of the social and cultural characteristics that influenced demographic behaviour during the rapid rise of port-cities and provided a substantial part of their internal population structure and growth potential, their substantial and diverse migrant populations remain the most distinctive. While this aspect of demographic and social history must be considered in the specific context of the individual port, not least in relation to the precise periods and rates of peak population growth, migrant origins and characteristics and the scale and nature of their external linkages are a common thread running through the demography of all port-cities. Thus, the impact of migrant communities on Liverpool has its parallels in London (not least in the East End dockland areas); in Glasgow, Hull, Cardiff or Bristol; and even in smaller, more specialist ports such as those of the Tyne and Wear. The precise ingredients in the mix—for example the proportions of Irish, Jewish or other overseas immigrants—coloured the experience of individual places differently, but gave many common features to their population structure.

As with many questions relating to the demography of communities in periods of rapid change, the differences *within* individual nineteenth-century port-cities of Britain were often as great as those *between* them. The testing of such propositions, one of the objectives in this and other chapters in this book, requires much greater depth of analysis than is possible from the present state of demographic knowledge and a much greater range of case studies of both individual towns and types of area than is at present available.

References

ANDERSON, G. (1976), *Victorian Clerks*, Manchester.

ANDERSON, M. (1976), 'Marriage patterns in Victorian Britain', *Journal of Family History*, **1**, 55–78.

BARKE, M. and M. J. BUSWELL (1980), *Historical Atlas of Newcastle upon Tyne*, Newcastle upon Tyne.

BEN-TOVIM, G. S., M. CONNOLLY, P. TORKINGTON and K. ROBERTS (1992), *Black Youth in Liverpool*, Liverpool.

BIRD, J. (1963), *The Major Seaports of the United Kingdom*, London.

CHARLES, E. and P. MOSCHINSKY (1938), 'Differential fertility in England and Wales during the past two decades', in L. Hogben (ed.), *Political Arithmetic: A Symposium of Population Studies*, London, chapter 3.

DAUNTON, M. J. (1977), *Coal Metropolis: Cardiff 1870–1914*, Leicester.

de VRIES, J. (1984), *European Urbanization, 1500–1800*, London.

FOX, R. C. (1980), *The Demography of Sunderland 1851* (Occasional Paper 1), Department of Geography and History, Sunderland Polytechnic.

FRAZER, W. M. (1947), *Duncan of Liverpool. Being an Account of the Work of Dr. W. H. Duncan, Medical Officer of Health of Liverpool, 1847–1863*, London.

FRAZER, W. M. (1950), *A History of English Public Health 1834–1939*, London.

GLASS, D. V. (1938), 'Changes in fertility in England and Wales', in L. Hogben (ed.), *Political Arithmetic: A Symposium of Population Studies*, London, chapter 4.

GLASS, D. V. (1964), 'Some indicators of differences between urban and rural mortality in England and Wales and Scotland', in J. Ferguson (ed.), *Public Health and Urban Growth*, Centre for Urban Studies, University College London, Report No. 4, 51–55.

GOTTMANN, J. (1990), 'The opening of the oyster shell', in J. Gottmann and R. A. Harper (eds), *Since Megalopolis. The Urban Writings of Jean Gottmann*, Baltimore and London.

GOULD, W. T. S. and A. G. HODGKISS (1982), *The Resources of Merseyside*, Liverpool.

HAINES, M. R. (1979), *Fertility and Occupation: Population Patterns in Mid-Industrialisation*, New York and London.

LAUX, H.-D. (1989), 'The components of population growth in Prussian cities, 1875–1905 and their influence on urban population structure', in Richard Lawton and Robert Lee (eds), *Urban Population Development in Western Europe from the Late-Eighteenth to the Early-Twentieth Century*, Liverpool, 120–48.

LAWTON, R. (1983), 'Urbanization and population change in nineteenth-century England', in J. Patten (ed.), *The Expanding City*, London, chapter 7.

LAWTON, R. (ed.) (1989), *The Rise and Fall of Great Cities. Aspects of Urbanization in the Western World*, London.

LAWTON, R. and W. R. LEE (eds) (1989), *Urban Population Development in Western Europe from the Late-Eighteenth to the Early-Twentieth Century*, Liverpool.

LAWTON, R. and C. G. POOLEY (1976), *The Social Geography of Merseyside in the Nineteenth Century* (Final Report to SSRC), Liverpool.

LAWTON, R. and C. G. POOLEY (1992), *An Historical Geography of Britain, 1740–1950*, London.

LAXTON, P. (1981), 'Liverpool in 1801', *Transactions of the Historic Society of Lancashire and Cheshire*, **130**, 73–113.

LAXTON, P. (1993), *Statistics and Public Health: The Methods of W. H. Duncan M.D. 1805–1863*, unpublished conference paper.

LUCKIN, B. (1984), 'Evaluating the sanitary revolution: typhus and typhoid in London, 1855–1900', in R. I. Woods and J. Woodward (eds), *Urban Disease and Mortality in Nineteenth-Century England*, London.

MITCHELL, B. R. and P. DEANE (1962), *Abstract of British Historical Statistics*, Cam-bridge.

NELSON, H. J. (1955), 'A service classification of American cities', *Economic Geography*, **31**, 189–210.

OWEN, SIR DAVID J. (1939), *Ports of the United Kingdom*, London.

PAPWORTH, J. D. (1982), 'The Irish in Liverpool, 1835–1871: family structure and residential mobility', unpublished PhD thesis, University of Liverpool,

POOLEY, C. G. (1977), 'Residential segregation of migrant communities in mid-Victorian Liverpool', *Transactions, Institute of British Geographers*, New Series **2**, 364–82.

POOLEY, C. G. (1983), 'Welsh migration to England in the mid-nineteenth century', *Journal of Historical Geography*, **9**, 287–305.

ROBSON, B. T. (1973), *Urban Analysis*, London.

SUMMERS, D. W. (1990), 'Demographic evolution in the fishing villages of East Aberdeenshire, 1696–1880', *Scottish Geographical Magazine*, **106**, 43–53.

TANSEY, P. A. (1973), 'Residential patterns in the nineteenth-century city, Kingston upon Hull, 1851', unpublished PhD thesis, University of Hull.

VANCE, J. E. Jr (1967), 'Housing the worker: determinative and contingent ties in nineteenth-century Birmingham', *Economic Geography*, **43**, 95–127.

WARD, D. (1971), *Cities and Immigrants*, London.

WARD, D. (1980), 'Environs and neighbours in the '"two nations"': residential differentiation in mid-nineteenth-century Leeds', *Journal of Historical Geography*, **6**, 133–62.

WARD, D. (1989), *Poverty, Ethnicity and the American City, 1840–1925. Changing Conceptions of the Slum and the Ghetto*, Cambridge.

WELTON, T. A. (1900), 'On the distribution of population of England and Wales and its progress … 1801–1891', *Journal of the Royal Statistical Society*, **63**, 567–89.

WELTON, T. A. (1911), *England's Recent Progress; an Investigation of the statistics of Migration, Mortality, etc.*, London.

WONG, M. L. (1989), *Chinese Liverpudlians. A History of the Chinese Community in Liverpool*, Birkenhead.

WOODS, R. I. (1984), 'Social class variations in the decline of fertility in late nineteenth-century London', *Geografiska Annaler*, Series B, **66**, 29–38.

WOODS, R. I. (1987), 'Approaches to the fertility transition in Victorian England', *Population Studies*, **41**, 283–311.

WOODS, R. I. (1989), 'What would one need to know to solve the '"natural decrease in early modern cities" problem?', in Richard Lawton (ed.), *The Rise and Fall of Great Cities*, London.

WOODS, R. I. and P. R. A. HINDE (1985), 'Nuptiality and age at marriage in nineteenth-century England', *Journal of Family History*, **9**, 119–44.

Chapter 5

THE MORTALITY DEVELOPMENT OF A PORT-TOWN IN A NATIONAL PERSPECTIVE: THE EXPERIENCE OF MALMÖ, SWEDEN, 1820–1914

GUNNAR FRIDLIZIUS

INTRODUCTION

Malmö is a port-town situated on the south part of the Swedish west coast (Figure 5.1). With about 250,000 inhabitants, it is the third largest town in Sweden. In 1820, when this investigation begins, it had a population of 6,700 rising to 25,000 by 1870 and to 85,000 by 1914, with a rate of growth considerably in excess of that of most other Swedish towns, especially prior to 1870. Malmö was the chief town for the export of the Scandinavian grain surplus (Fridlizius, 1981; 1984a; 1990), exports of which began to increase as early as the second half of the eighteenth century, the main destinations being Gothenburg, Stockholm and the towns of the Gulf of Bothnia. Following the repeal of the British Corn Laws, this internal trade was increasingly replaced by a growth in exports for the English market. In the late-nineteenth century, butter replaced grain as the main export product and the town became one of the main ports in Sweden for exporting this commodity. Imports tended to consist of colonial goods from Copenhagen, Stettin and other German towns, together with coal and manufactured goods from England. Foreign trade during this period was a means by which intensive economic development spread from a perceptible centre, in the first place England, to outlying parts of the world. The process of 'give and take', brought about by foreign trade between highly industrialized and less developed areas, assumed an exceptional importance for economic growth, not least for the urban area under immediate consideration. Did this growing trade function of Malmö also mean that the town became a focal point for the import of different diseases which then spread over the whole country? Or did Malmö, as a port-town, develop a special demographic pattern in relation to mortality levels and trends during the period under consideration? These are the main questions that will be confronted in the present chapter.

From a methodological point of view, an attempt is made here to address these questions by employing a long-run analysis; for the whole period a relatively homogeneous mortality series has been constructed, taking into consideration not only the age-specific development of mortality in Malmö,

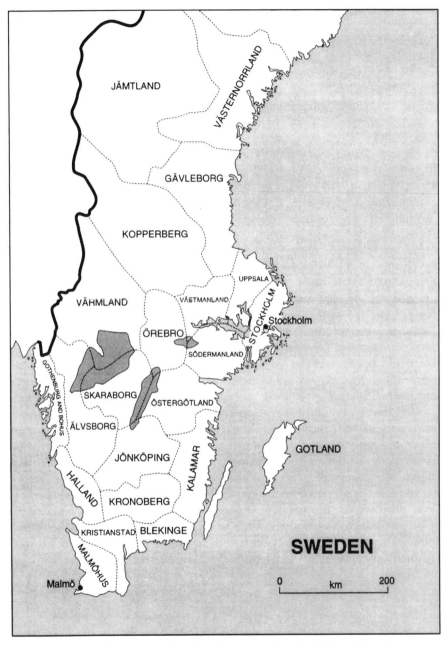

Figure 5.1: The division of Sweden into counties (excluding Västerbotten and Norrbotten).

but also focusing on disease- and sex-specific trends. Relevant comparisons are provided by a similar mortality series that has also been constructed for Stockholm, the urban and rural areas of Sweden, and the rural areas of Malmöhus.[1] In order to explore long-term changes in mortality, cause of death data for the mid-eighteenth century (1751–1770) have also been examined on a disaggregated basis. As a result, the analysis of mortality trends between 1820 and 1914 provides a suitable basis for developing a number of specific points of direct relevance to the issues addressed in the present volume.

This work has encountered considerable difficulties, especially concerning the cause of death series which shows considerable gaps over time. In addition, changes in the nomenclature and classification of diseases and the specification of age groups, as well as other shortcomings in the archival material, have had to be confronted. A detailed discussion of these issues is provided in Appendix 5.I and the cause of death series is presented in Tables 5.13 and 5.14. Nevertheless, we have been able to generate a series of data sets rich enough to permit an extended analysis of complex mortality changes over time and perhaps also a quantification of the particular factors contributing to these changes.

In terms of Sweden's demographic history in the nineteenth century, three distinct periods are frequently isolated, which represent important different phases in the Swedish mortality decline during the transition period (Fridlizius, 1984a). The decrease in mortality during the period 1821–1850 is essentially a continuation of a development which started in the late-eighteenth century. In its initial phase this was caused to a great extent by epidemiological factors beyond human control. During the second period, between about 1850 and 1880, mortality levels were increasingly affected by a multiplicity of factors and the mortality decline evident in some age groups was dramatically reversed, a development which has been interpreted as a last manifestation of the great epidemic cycles which characterized pre-industrial society. It is only during the third and final period, after about 1880, that we can speak of a sustained mortality decline. This periodization, however, is based on the mortality development of rural Sweden. How relevant is it in terms of the new material presented in this chapter? Is the hypothesis also relevant for urban areas? How does it fit the case of the port-city of Malmö? These are other important questions that we will try to answer in the following contribution.

---

1 For the purpose of this analysis it is also important to know that up to about 1860, 90 per cent of Sweden's population was rural and that Stockholm accounted for about one-third of the population of the urban area. This meant that Stockholm had an outstanding role among the towns of Sweden. In 1820 Stockholm had a population of 75,600, while Gothenburg, the second largest town, had only 16,500 inhabitants: Malmö, with 6,700 inhabitants, was the sixth largest town within the Swedish urban hierarchy.

THE EARLY MORTALITY DECLINE, 1821–1850

Although clearly unsatisfactory in terms of analysing mortality changes over time, the crude death rate can, however, give a rough indication of general trends. The picture that emerges for the period 1821–1850 is that of a decrease in mortality of about 20 per cent in rural areas (Figure 5.2). For the urban areas we can generally posit an unchanged level, although the extreme values of the last decade complicate the picture somewhat. The developments in crude mortality rates in the three main areas under consideration occurred in the context of a significant variation in initial mortality levels. In the 1820s the mortality of Stockholm and the county towns was respectively 100 and 40 per cent higher than that of the rural areas. In the latter case the further decrease in mortality in the period 1821–1850 was a continuation of a process that had started in the late-eighteenth century and had developed relatively homogeneously in the different counties of Sweden (Fridlizius, 1979; 1984b).[2] However, regarding Stockholm and the county towns the picture is more uncertain: in these areas there was hardly any change in mortality levels.[3] We have no figures for Malmö from the eighteenth century, but this general trend in crude mortality implies that there was a continuously widening gap between the urban and rural areas during the period under consideration. But how did the particular age groups contribute to overall mortality trends and what possible factors account for their divergent roles?

Infant mortality

To a certain extent, the crude mortality pattern throughout the period 1821–1850 is repeated in this age group. However, for the rural areas the decrease is

---

2 Note, however, that in this preliminary survey (1979) the figures for Stockholm in the period 1774–1794 are about 12 per cent too low.
3 If the mortality levels for 1751–1770 are taken as the base line of 100, the registered crude death rates by 1821–1830 generate index figures as follows:

Region	Crude death rate 1751–1770 (per 1,000)	Index 1821–1830
Stockholm	45.1	99
County towns	31.3	98
Rural Sweden	27.4	82
Total Sweden	28.3	85

For the eighteenth century there are no separate mortality series for rural Sweden, urban Sweden and the county towns. However, as mortality data exist for Sweden, Stockholm, four towns (Linköping, Norrköping, Karlshamn and Lund), as well as for nine counties, it has been possible to generate approximate mortality figures for these regions for the period 1751–1770: see also Appendix 5.I.

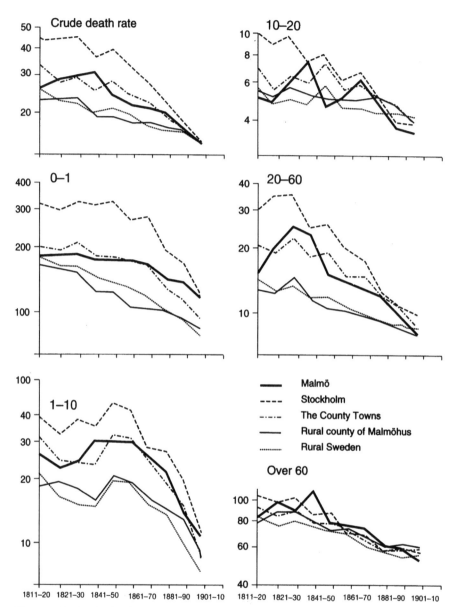

Figure 5.2: Crude death rates and age-specific mortality rates per 1,000 for Malmö, Stockholm, the county towns, the rural county of Malmöhus and rural Sweden, 1811–1820 to 1901–1910. *Sources:* Statistiska Centralbyrån (SCB) Tabellverket, MS; *Bidrag till Sveriges Officiella Statistik* (*BiSOS*) A and K.

somewhat more rapid; for the urban areas there was a stagnation or a slight increase, with the latter most pronounced in the case of Stockholm (Figure 5.2). Concerning the period up to the 1820s the mortality development of the different regions did not diverge from that of overall mortality, although a clear decline was evident in the urban areas.[4]

Any attempt to analyse the factors determining these levels and trends in infant mortality must take into consideration the cause of death pattern and registered changes over time. For the whole period from 1749 to 1830 the Swedish population statistics provide data on age at death and cause of death for different levels of aggregation. For many reasons, however, these statistics are difficult to utilize, in particular because of the vagueness and inaccuracy of cause of death diagnoses (see Appendix 5.I). This is especially relevant in relation to infant mortality, where a high proportion of deaths was attributed to a large group of diseases including convulsions, stroke, violent death and unknown illnesses. The problems posed by the unreliability of contemporary diagnosis are demonstrated, for instance, by the great differences in mortality from these diseases in the individual regions of Sweden (Table 5.13). However, by examining the relative structure of infant mortality and by applying the disease classification of the 1870s when cause of death diagnosis was finally carried out by trained doctors, it is reasonable to conclude that this group of diseases must have been synonymous to a large extent with the pneumonia-diarrhoea complex. This implies that about 60 per cent of infant mortality—somewhat higher for the towns, somewhat lower for the rural areas—was attributable to this group of diseases, with diarrhoea and pneumonia accounting for about 65 and 35 per cent respectively of this total. Mortality from epidemic infections and congenital diseases was responsible for a high proportion of the remaining infant deaths. This disease-specific pattern of infant mortality is of central importance for the following analysis.

The many factors which contributed to infant mortality at that time are well known: they included, for example, the generally poor health of pregnant mothers, bad childcare and breast-feeding habits. The latter were a result of

---

4 In relation to infant mortality, and using the same method of calculation as in note 3 above, we can obtain the following figures for the main regions under consideration:

Region	Infant mortality rate 1751–1770 (per 1,000)	Index 1821–1830
Stockholm	388	70
County towns	262	73
Rural Sweden	200	81
Total Sweden	210	80

Table 5.1: *Urban and rural deaths, 1751–1770 and 1821–1830. Rural deaths = 100: a = 1751–1770; b = 1821–1830.*

Age group	0–1		1–10		10–20		20–40		40–60		Over 60		Total	
	a	*b*	*a*	*b*	*a*	*b*	*a*	*b*	*a*	*b*	*a*	*b*	*a*	*b*
Malmö	–	114	–	119	–	94	–	177	–	170	–	112	–	121
Stockholm	194	170	198	199	151	188	226	325	204	276	112	129	167	197
County towns	159	118	152	163	101	131	125	178	128	176	105	125	120	136

Note: For 1751–1770 Stockholm is compared with rural Sweden; the county towns (Linköping and Norrköping) with the county of Östergötland. For 1821–1830 Malmö is compared with the county of Malmöhus; Stockholm and the county towns with rural Sweden.
Source: SCB Tabellverket, MS.

ignorance, and a lack of both knowledge and time. Bad personal and public hygiene, as well as inadequate housing, were also critical factors.[5]

However, in relation to the urban–rural infant mortality differential, it is clear that this was a result of differences in exposure rates rather than in nutritional status (Table 5.1). Urban over-crowding, combined with extremely unsanitary conditions, increased the risk from gastro-enteritic diseases in the towns, which were caused by bacteria as well as by viruses and could be diffused in several ways—by direct contact and droplet infection, but also by water, air, food and flies. Irrespective of the source of infection and the character of the micro-organism, the result was the same: diarrhoea associated with digestive disorders, often followed by death. In addition, there was a strong synergy between the diseases: diarrhoea decreased the immunity of infants and they became easier victims of pneumonia.

The sensitivity of the towns in this respect is reflected in the seasonality of deaths. In relation to Stockholm peak mortality for the age group 0–10 years occurred in July and August when the risk from gastro-intestinal disorders was greatest (Figure 5.3). This specific peak was also evident in Malmö and the county towns, although in these cases it was considerably attenuated; for the rural areas such a peak simply did not exist: indeed, in the latter three areas the most marked mortality peak occurred instead in March and April, which was primarily due to the prevalence of deaths from different forms of bronchitis and pneumonia. Environmental conditions also meant that mortality was sensitive to short-term changes in climate. Thus a comparison of changes in infant mortality and changes in climate (temperature) during the 1820s in

5 For a critical review of different interpretations of the causes of high infant mortality in Western Europe, see Lee (1988).

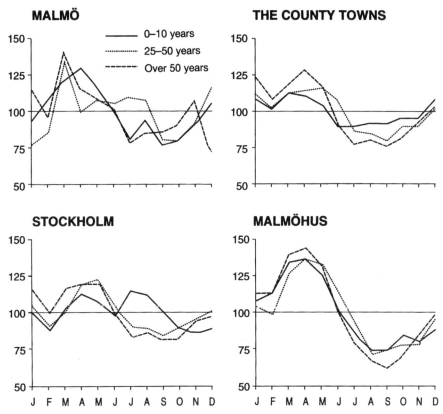

Figure 5.3: The seasonality of deaths in Malmö, the county towns, Stockholm and the rural county of Malmöhus, 1821–1830. *Source:* SCB Tabellverket, MS.

Malmö reveals a significant correlation which does not emerge if harvest data (prices) are used as the independent variable.[6]

What, then, of the original hypothesis which postulated the existence of an exogenous factor that determined the initial decline in Swedish mortality, only to be superseded by a multi-faceted complex of factors? An analysis of the mortality decline separating deaths from epidemic infections from deaths from other diseases reveals a more rapid fall in the incidence of deaths for the former group up until the 1820s (Table 5.2).[7]

6 See note 10 below.
7 Concerning Malmöhus County (RM) and rural Sweden (R) in Table 5.2, the figures for the eighteenth century also include the towns. This, however, has only a marginal effect on the result. If diphtheria had been noted among the registered causes of death for the period from 1751 to 1770, the decrease in epidemic infections in relation to other diseases would have been further accentuated (see also Appendix 5.I).

Table 5.2: *Changes in infant and child mortality from different diseases, 1751–1770 and 1821–1830, in Stockholm (S), Malmöhus County (RM) and rural Sweden (R).*

Cause of death	Age group					
	0–1			1–5		
	S	RM	R	S	RM	R
Epidemic infections	54	61	60	37	48	37
Other diseases	72	67	91	81	85	79
Total	70	66	84	65	64	58

Note: Index 1751–1770 = 100. Rural Sweden index 1779–82 = 100; see also footnote 7.
Source: SCB Tabellverket, MS.

   Despite the relatively unimportant role of epidemic infections in total infant mortality, their decline was sufficiently substantial to explain a considerable part of the fall in overall infant mortality, at least for rural Sweden. Moreover, a fall in smallpox mortality was a major component of this decline (Sköld, 1996), as will be explained later, and this undoubtedly tends to support the original hypothesis.

   Concerning the period after 1830, for which we have no cause of death data, the pattern of development is more uncertain. In regard to death rates in the age group 1–5 years, where infectious diseases played a more dominant role, it may be realistic to assume a limited, but continued, decline in mortality from epidemic infections. However, a significant proportion of the decrease was arguably related to the diarrhoea-pneumonia complex, which reflected primarily the impact of different environmental factors on this age group. It is equally possible that official breast-feeding campaigns also began to show a positive result, at the same time as better knowledge led to improvements in childcare. It might also be necessary to take into consideration a factor beyond human control, namely the transition to a milder climate in comparison with the earlier decades of the nineteenth century (Fridlizius, 1984a). Those factors that contributed to the mortality decline in rural areas, however, must also have operated in the towns. But in urban areas their positive effects were arguably counter-balanced by a deterioration in living conditions for significant elements of the population. In such a context, it is clear that few improvements in infant mortality rates could be expected in Swedish towns until the problems of over-crowding, poor sewerage and inadequate water supply had been resolved.

Child mortality

The mortality pattern of this age group agreed in several respects with that of infants. In both cases urban death rates either remained static or registered a slight increase until the mid-nineteenth century, while rural Sweden registered a parallel decline in age-specific mortality which started simultaneously in the late-eighteenth century (Figure 5.2).[8] In contrast to infant mortality, deaths from epidemic infections constituted the most important group in the cause of death panorama, while the diarrhoea-pneumonia complex was less prominent (see Table 5.13). Equally, there was a more rapid fall in child mortality from epidemic infections than from other diseases (Table 5.2). Up until 1820 more than 80 per cent of the mortality decline in rural areas and about 70 per cent of the fall in mortality in Stockholm in the age group 1–5 years can be attributed to the diminished role of epidemic infections.

In the mid-eighteenth century (1751–1770), at least in rural areas, smallpox deaths accounted for about 40 per cent of total child mortality (see Table 5.13). Stockholm, however, reveals somewhat lower figures. By 1821–1830 the role of smallpox was on the whole negligible. We have argued elsewhere that the decline in smallpox mortality must have had its roots in a changing host–parasite balance, possibly as a result of a spontaneous decrease in the virulence of the disease. Vaccination, which became compulsory in Sweden in 1816, only hastened a development already in progress (Fridlizius, 1984a).

The negative consequences of smallpox, however, were not limited to childhood; in different ways, the legacy of smallpox had life-long implications for each generation. It could be seen in the great number of blind, deaf and crippled people who constituted the army of beggars during the eighteenth century (Högberg, 1983). Nor was it limited to easily discernible disabilities; possibly those who survived smallpox suffered from reduced immunity to other diseases and therefore had less resistance to different infections. When mortality from smallpox decreased, so also did mortality and morbidity from different secondary diseases. The result was better health for children in

---

8 For child mortality and using the same method of calculation as in note 3 above, we can obtain the following index figures for the regions under examination:

Region	Child mortality 1751–1770 (per 1,000)	Index 1821–1830
Stockholm	48.2	67
County towns	36.7	73
Rural Sweden	25.0	65
Total Sweden	26.4	66

Table 5.3: *Causes of death and their age distribution, 1821–1830, in Malmö, urban Sweden and rural Sweden (in per cent).*

Malmö	Under 1	1–5	5–10	10+	Total
Whooping cough	49	46	5	–	100
Scarlatina	28	45	21	6	100
Measles	17	70	12	1	100
Diphtheria	25	42	8	25	100
Typhoid fever	5	15	8	72	100
Total	22	13	4	61	100

Urban Sweden	Under 1	1–5	5–10	10+	Total
Whooping cough	51	42	6	1	100
Scarlatina	19	39	23	19	100
Measles	22	56	16	6	100
Diphtheria	37	19	6	38	100
Typhoid fever	3	5	3	89	100
Total	20	11	3	66	100

Rural Sweden	Under 1	1–5	5–10	10+	Total
Whooping cough	57	38	5	–	100
Scarlatina	25	40	17	18	100
Measles	33	45	13	9	100
Diphtheria	21	23	8	48	100
Typhoid fever	5	8	5	82	100
Total	25	12	4	59	100

Source: SCB Tabellverket, MS.

general, a development that was also influenced positively by initial improvements in infant care. This had a distinct cohort effect as children went through life with a better resistance against different diseases. This thesis seems to be supported by the clear cohort pattern evident in the secular mortality decline in Sweden (Fridlizius, 1989).[9] Thus the disappearance of smallpox was of much

9 In arguing that the Swedish mortality decline during the nineteenth century was cohort-influenced, I have suggested that an improved state of health during childhood resulted in a better overall physical condition. This was inherited by the cohort, giving it an improved resistance to diseases of different kinds. It is clear, however, that the passage through life of different cohorts did not always occur in accordance with the preconditions established during

greater significance than can be concluded simply in terms of its proportional contribution to the overall mortality decline. Undoubtedly there must be some truth in the suggestion that the disappearance of smallpox was followed by a new, more benign, epidemic era.

However, significant short-term changes still influenced the disease spectrum. In relation to Malmö, almost every year during the 1820s was characterized by its special disease: measles was rampant in 1823, 1825 and 1829; scarlatina in 1822 and 1823 (accompanied by diphtheria); typhoid fever occurred in 1828 and remained persistent throughout the rest of the decade. These short-term changes in the virulence of individual epidemic infections followed their own laws and were largely unaffected by variations in climate and nutrition.[10]

With the exception of typhoid fever, mortality from infectious diseases was concentrated in those aged below 10 years. Table 5.3 gives a more detailed picture of this pattern, which was already evident in the mid-eighteenth century and persisted during the following century. This, in turn, indicates the early existence within Sweden of a well-integrated market which is confirmed by evidence of a generally homogeneous price structure characterized by simultaneous regional changes (Jörberg, 1972)

Adult mortality

The working age groups, however, demonstrated no significant change in their mortality level until the 1840s when all regions witnessed an initial fall in age-specific mortality (Figure 5.2). Stockholm reached this stage after a perceptible increase in adult mortality from the late-eighteenth century onwards. In relation to the county towns the picture is more uncertain, although the larger towns probably followed a similar pattern. The rural areas, however, registered

---

childhood. During the nineteenth century we can observe some great deformations. They extended over decades and affected different age groups. The 'alcoholic deformation' was evident between 1820 and 1850 and struck the male cohorts in their working ages. In Stockholm this deviation from the expected mortality pattern had considerable force. A marked deformation also occurred in the late-nineteenth and early-twentieth century. It affected the age group 10–30 years and was connected with the specific epidemic pattern of tuberculosis.

10 Changes in mortality from different epidemic infections were correlated with changes in temperature in Gothenburg (*Historisk Statistik för Sverige*, 1959); the price of rye is derived from Jörberg (1972), *passim*.

a slight decrease in relation to the mortality levels of individuals of working age.[11]

These developments occurred in the context of great differences in adult mortality levels in the three main regions under consideration. In the age group 25–50 years the mortality of Stockholm was about 70 per cent higher than that of the county towns, including Malmö, which, in turn, registered a similar urban penalty in comparison with rural regions. This is the most pronounced urban–rural mortality differential so far found during any period of Swedish history and among any individual age group.

Not unexpectedly there is a clear correlation between the level of adult mortality and the size of town. However, the level and pattern of mortality was also affected by another factor: the outstanding role of Stockholm in the mortality panorama. An analysis of mortality in the small county towns surrounding Stockholm, particularly in Södermanland, reveals mortality rates considerably above the average for Swedish county towns as a whole.[12] Perhaps this represents a sort of diffusion effect generated by intensive migration between Stockholm and its hinterland. To a varying degree this structure is repeated in most of the age groups. However, it appears to have been most pronounced in the adult ages, possibly due to the important role played by phthisis in the contemporary disease spectrum (see Appendix 5.I).[13]

The mortality from phthisis in the counties surrounding Stockholm was about twice as high as in the regions in the periphery. Thus Gothenburg, Sweden's second largest town, had a lower mortality from phthisis than the small towns in central Sweden.[14] This pattern was already evident in the eighteenth century, although the 'high mortality' of the central region was not

---

11 For adult mortality (25–50 years) and using the same method of calculation as in note 3 above, the following figures can be obtained for the main regions:

Region	Adult mortality rate 1751–1770 (per 1,000)	Index 1821–1830
Stockholm	27.4	126
County towns	17.1	123
Rural Sweden	13.1	93
Total Sweden	13.9	99

12 Thus the mortality rates per 1,000 in the age group 25–50 during the period 1821–1830 were as follows: Stockholm—35.0; the towns of the county of Södermanland—24.3; the towns of Scania—15.8; Gothenburg—21.0: see SCB, Tabellverket, MS.

13 For a broader survey of this disease, see Puranen (1984), *passim.*

14 For the towns of the counties of Stockholm, Uppsala, Södermanland, Ostergötland, Jönköping, Malmöhus and Elfsborg in 1823–1827, the crude mortality rates per 1,000 from phthisis were 4.18, 5.89, 5.25, 3.93, 2.33, 2.66 and 2.16 respectively. The crude mortality rate for Stockholm was 7.78 and for Gothenburg 3.33 per 1,000: see Statistiska Centralbyrån Tabellverket, MS.

Table 5.4: *Urban causes of death in Sweden in 1821–1830 for the age group 25–50.*

	Malmö	Urban Sweden	Stockholm
Typhoid	290	238	300
Phthisis	222	332	532
Inflammation fever	75	142	200
Dropsy	130	300	488
Stroke/violent death	312	383	550
Accidents	512	225	263
Total	188	230	329

Index: rural cause of death = 100.
Note: Malmö is compared with the county of Malmöhus; urban Sweden and Stockholm with rural Sweden.
Source: SCB Tabellverket, MS

quite as apparent as it became in the following century.[15] In reality Stockholm functioned as an enormous phthisis reservoir, which pumped out infectious diseases by means of an intensive migration between the town and its hinterland. Malmö was situated outside this 'high-mortality' area and because of its smaller size it could only generate to a lesser degree a similar dynamic of disease diffusion.

The 1820s witnessed a culmination of deaths from phthisis, which had been an important cause of rising mortality during the previous decades, particularly in the towns, and especially in the case of Stockholm. Phthisis, together with violent deaths, became the most urban-related cause of death during the period under consideration (Table 5.4). The surprisingly high mortality from phthisis in the higher age groups may perhaps have been a result of the bad state of health prevalent in these years. Physical stress, whatever the cause, also meant poor immunity from disease. This, in turn, raised the possibility of a higher incidence of an opportunistic disease such as phthisis by increasing the chances for the activation of latent microbes.[16]

However, the interpretation of the adult mortality pattern will be incomplete and perhaps misleading, if we do not take into consideration the sex differentials which were particularly important in the case of urban

15 For 1796–1800 the crude mortality rates per 1,000 from phthisis for the counties of Stockholm, Uppsala, Södermanland, Ostergötland, Jönköping, Malmöhus and Halland were 2.53 (2.89), 1.87 (2.30), 2.43 (2.48), 2.15 (1.87), 1.11 (1.18), 1.14 (1.37) and 0.90 (1.49) respectively. The figures in brackets refer to the period 1823–1827: see SCB Tabellverket, MS.

16 Puranen (1984) suggests that such high mortality must be cohort-influenced, as a result of higher mortality during an earlier period. However, this does not appear to have been the case on the basis of our material.

communities in Sweden. As can be seen from Tables 5.5 and 5.6, excess male mortality in the age group 25–50 was about 140, 100 and 20 per cent respectively for Stockholm, urban Sweden and rural Sweden. In relation to Malmö the figure was 134 per cent.

It has been suggested that increasing excess male mortality in rural areas was caused primarily by the enormous consumption of alcohol at that time. This would have been even more the case in an urban context (Fridlizius, 1988). In the towns alcoholic beverages were readily accessible and the taverns in Stockholm, for example, were innumerable. Evidence has shown that both disease and death due to the consumption of alcohol are directly correlated to access and that an environment which encourages collective interaction functions as an important incentive for an increased consumption of alcoholic beverages. Insecure conditions for many urban workers must have been a further stimulus to drinking. This insecurity, however, was not only economic in character. It was also the insecurity felt by the immigrant countryman having to face a new urban environment where self-confidence could be temporarily enhanced by the drinking of spirits. This was also true in terms of establishing a relationship with women, including the many unmarried young girls in the towns. Often there were quite practical reasons for drinking. Men drank because they froze at their work place or in cold barracks or lodgings. Sometimes a schnapps was the easiest way to take the edge out of hunger. Alcoholics and large consumers of alcoholic beverages are known to have been more exposed to disease and death than other adult groups. On the whole there were few causes of death where the potential role of alcohol can be totally excluded. The low excess male mortality from tuberculosis, however, is surprising, since it was a disease sensitive to alcohol. One explanation of this phenomenon might be that pregnant women also constituted a disproportionate potential risk group with respect to this disease (Puranen, 1984).

In trying to explain the huge adult mortality hump in Swedish towns attention must be concentrated not only on the excessive consumption of alcoholic beverages but also to a larger extent on labour market conditions. That the pre-industrial labour market was disadvantageous for males appears to have been a general rule. Insecurity with regard to job opportunities, poor housing conditions, with several lodgers in one room, and an insufficient diet were factors which left many males in social and economic penury. This was bound to have fostered high mortality rates. Many women, on the other hand, earned their living as domestic servants and were likely to have enjoyed better living and working conditions than was normally the case for men. Some recent estimates indicate a lower poverty ratio for women than for men in Swedish urban communities, although in rural areas the situation was the reverse (Söderberg, 1982).

In summary, it can be established that the early secular decline in mortality was concentrated in the infant and child age groups, specifically in the rural areas of

Table 5.5: *Sex-specific mortality rates for different causes of death in Malmö and Stockholm, 1821–1830.*

	Malmö					Stockholm				
	1–10	*10–25*	*25–50*	*50+*	*Total*	*1–10*	*10–25*	*25–50*	*50+*	*Total*
Phthisis	64	121	208	172	159	87	131	238	193	169
Inflammation fever	139	777	515	177	242	103	211	336	250	191
Remittent fever	64	155	136	228	135	90	175	214	153	137
Typhoid fever	87	272	285	208	189	130	205	295	236	221
Dropsy	98	–	125	80	77	130	174	182	126	128
Stroke/violent death	40	–	201	760	135	104	178	286	192	141
Accidents	–	1,250	580	547	557	274	633	648	680	572
Total	95	271	234	146	134	106	167	239	167	146

Note: Index: female = 100.
Source: SCB Tabellverket, MS

Table 5.6: *Sex-specific mortality rates for different causes of death in urban Sweden and rural Sweden, 1821–1830.*

| | Urban Sweden | | | | | Rural Sweden | | | | |
	1–10	*10–25*	*25–50*	*50 +*	*Total*	*1–10*	*10–25*	*25–50*	*50 +*	*Total*
Phthisis	94	118	195	163	149	82	73	117	123	107
Inflammation fever	101	185	210	173	160	109	107	140	127	120
Remittent fever	102	148	163	143	160	109	100	112	117	110
Typhoid fever	113	198	235	177	179	95	87	118	121	107
Dropsy	100	144	158	123	150	117	87	80	95	84
Stroke/violent death	100	152	250	205	150	119	117	189	158	137
Accidents	597	597	850	532	590	197	490	775	491	328
Total	105	154	207	142	134	108	105	119	114	111

Note: Index: female = 100.
Source: SCB Tabellverket, MS

Sweden. Urban districts registered a more modest fall until 1820, if at all, followed by a period characterized either by relatively stable or slightly rising mortality rates, depending on the actual size of the town. The analysis of disease-specific mortality trends supports the idea of a strong exogenous influence during the initial phase. It was only after this period that a cause of death pattern emerged which reflected the impact of environmental factors. The mortality pattern of Malmö, on the whole, conformed to this general picture. At least up until the mid-nineteenth century Malmö's role as a port-town does not appear to have influenced appreciably either its level or trend of mortality. The next period from 1850 to 1880, however, was to witness a significant change in this respect.

A RELAPSE INTO AN OLD PATTERN, 1850–1880?

During this period all the defined regions showed a long-term decline in overall mortality. The fall was most pronounced in Stockholm and least evident in the rural regions, while the county towns, including Malmö, occupied a middle position. However, this homogeneous pattern was not reflected in the age-specific mortality series. Of all the periods examined, the decades between 1850 and 1880 revealed the most disparate mortality pattern in this respect (Figure 5.2). In the urban regions three distinct patterns stand out: the level of infant mortality remained stable; child mortality evinced a strong increase producing a temporary peak which was not eliminated until the end of the period; and the working age groups benefited from a relatively strong fall in mortality. This picture was largely repeated in the rural areas, except for the fact that infant mortality continued the decline which had been evident in the earlier periods.

Infant mortality

Overall the growing predominance of multi-causal determinants of the general mortality decline, evident in the period 1821–1850, became increasingly marked. This was particularly the case in relation to the relative role of the diarrhoea-pneumonia complex of diseases. Personal hygiene was improved through a better access to soap and cotton clothes, and it was during the 1850s that Malmö merchants began to invest in cotton-mills and soap manufacturing. The cold and draughty houses both in the town and its hinterland also became warmer and healthier due to the increasing imports of coal from England purchased in return for exported grain. The official campaigns for better infant care were intensified and there was a significant increase in the number of midwives and doctors. The health of women in confinement gradually improved and this was reflected in a decline in adult mortality which, in turn, meant an increase in the birth weight and general health of children. These developments not only provided better immunity and ensured a lower

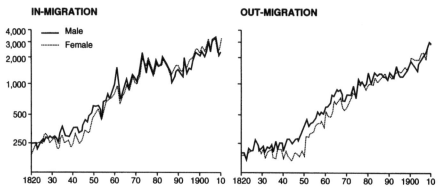

Figure 5.4: Migration in Malmö, 1820–1910 (in absolute numbers). *Source:* Malmö Stadsarkiv, Kyrkoböcker (church registers).

mortality during the first year of life, but they also had a synergistic effect in later life.[17]

Many of these factors affected both rural and urban areas. In the latter case, however, they were counterbalanced by chronically bad sewerage and water-supply, in combination with over-crowding, problems which were accentuated by large-scale in-migration from the end of the 1840s (Figure 5.4). In addition, early industrialization reduced the possibility for many women of providing satisfactory childcare. In the Swedish towns, with many unmarried women, there was also the problem of large numbers of illegitimate and badly-nursed children.

Child mortality

The conundrum of increasing child mortality in Sweden during the third quarter of the nineteenth century has long been observed, especially as the contemporary process of socio-economic development does not indicate any fall in the standard of living.[18] The well-known population statistician Gustaf

17 Fogel (1988) has argued that the range of intra-uterine occurrences that undermined nutritional status and raised mortality rates during infancy and early childhood has been unjustly neglected.

18 In relation to economic development, see especially Jörberg (1972) and Schön (1985). Sandberg and Steckel (1988) put forward an alternative interpretation. Their main arguments for a pessimistic view of economic development are: (1) a fall in the height of soldiers born from the end of the 1830s; (2) an increase in child mortality from the late 1840s; (3) the assumption that this increase was 'associated with diseases whose outcome is closely related to nutritional levels'; and (4) an increasing share of children in the population by the middle of the century, a phenomenon that was especially pronounced in the 'West of Sweden' which constituted 65.5 per cent of the total population in 1840. However, their conclusion is difficult to support. In relation to the first two points, during the 1840s most of the age groups under consideration showed a decrease in mortality. Not until the 1850s and 1860s is there evidence of a great mortality hump.

Sundbärg (1913) once thought that smallpox had been replaced by new infectious diseases and from a medical point of view the occurrence of such 'new' diseases has indeed been noticed at the same time as the 'old' diseases became more virulent and aggressive (Bergman, 1963). It is possible that these authors implicitly assumed that the increase was a result of an autonomous, epidemiological development and this particular idea has been articulated in a recent study of the Swedish mortality decline during the nineteenth century (Fridlizius, 1984a). The increase in the 1850s is seen as a last manifestation of the great epidemic cycles which characterized pre-industrial society. Our analysis of the cause of death panorama during the period provides further support for this hypothesis.

As can be seen from Table 5.7 there was a rising death rate from epidemic infections, while mortality from other diseases went down. In the former category, scarlatina and diphtheria were clearly dominant (Table 5.8): in the urban areas these two 'new' diseases together accounted for 80 per cent of child

Table 5.7: *Urban Sweden: changes in mortality from different diseases between 1821–1830 and 1875–1880.*

	Under 1	*1–5*	*5–10*
Epidemic infections	62	145	139
Other diseases	86	73	60
Total	83	94	86
Scarlatina	262	777	433
Diphtheria	132	533	525
Measles or whooping cough	38	55	21

Note: Index: 1821–1830 = 100.
Source: SCB Tabellverket, MS; *BiSOS* K.
Unfortunately there are no adequate figures for the 1850s or 1860s.

Sandberg and Steckel only present height figures up to 1854. As the height of the soldiers seems to have increased during the third quarter of the nineteenth century compared with the second, this increase happened during the mortality hump. Thus, instead we must ask the following question: why did the height of soldiers decrease at the same time that child mortality declined and rise again when child mortality increased? In relation to the third point, a study of the cause of death panorama shows that it was dominated by scarlatina and diphtheria, diseases that are not closely associated with nutrition. Finally, the Swedish population experienced a significant change in its age structure over time. Thus, the dependency ratio of children under 15 years in relation to the age group 15–60 years was actually lowest around 1850, standing in the rural 'North', 'East' and 'West' at 57.5, 53.3 and 57.3 per cent respectively. At the regional level there is a considerable similarity concerning these different points. The thesis of Sandberg and Steckel of bad times in Sweden in the mid-nineteenth century has also been criticized in terms of the use of the dependency ratio by Johan Söderberg (1989).

Table 5.8: *Crude death rates per 1,000 from different epidemic diseases, 1861–1870.*

	Malmö	Urban Sweden	Rural Sweden
Scarlatina	1.52	1.07	0.67
Measles	0.64	0.58	0.43
Diphtheria	0.88	0.80	0.52
Whooping cough	0.47	0.28	0.28
Typhoid fever	1.52	1.00	0.47
Dysentery	–	0.07	0.08

Source: *BiSOS* A and K, 1861–1870.

mortality from epidemic infections in the period 1875–1880 and about 38 per cent of the total mortality of this age group (Table 5.14). This can be compared with a relative contribution to child mortality of 18.0 and 5.2 per cent respectively in the period 1821–1830. It is possible, however, that the mortality figures from scarlatina are underestimated and diphtheria similarly over-estimated, as many deaths registered as having been caused by diphtheria were actually due to scarlatina. The difficulties in making a correct diagnosis are understandable, as the streptococcal infections were invariably accompanied by a broad spectrum of symptoms. On the whole, there are few microbes that give rise to so many pathological conditions as streptococcal microbes. In the countryside mortality from both diseases was certainly underestimated, as many priests neglected these 'new' child diseases.[19] In addition, scarlatina in particular exhibited various complications and was accompanied by secondary diseases, which, if they led to death, were frequently registered under other headings in the official statistics. It is important to note, however, that both scarlatina and diphtheria are not generally sensitive to changes in nutrition. Furthermore, they both belong to a group of diseases that can change in virulence over time.

Why, then, did this epidemic pattern develop during the period 1850–1880? Did it emerge as a result of increased diffusion possibilities for bacteria within the population, or was it a consequence of the appearance of a more aggressive streptococcal variant against which the population had no immunity? In both cases an important factor must have been increased migration between and within individual countries, caused in the first place by the expansion of trade and better communications.[20] At the beginning of the 1850s Malmö, for example, obtained its first regular steamboat lines and some years later the

19 See, for instance, *BiSOS* A, 1877, p. XVII.
20 Concerning migration from Malmö, see Bengtsson (1990) and Fridlizius (1990).

Table 5.9: *Causes of death and their age distribution: Malmö, 1861–1870 and urban Sweden, 1875–1880 (per cent).*

	Malmö				
	Under 1	*1–5*	*5–10*	*10+*	*Total*
Scarlatina	9	65	23	3	100
Diphtheria	14	69	15	2	100
Measles	20	65	10	5	100
Whooping cough	51	49	–	–	100
Bronchitis	40	23	1	36	100
Pneumonia	5	18	5	71	100
Digestion	45	24	1	30	100
	Urban Sweden				
	Under 1	*1–5*	*5–10*	*10+*	*Total*
Scarlatina	10	59	22	9	100
Diphtheria	10	62	21	7	100
Measles	24	61	11	4	100
Whooping cough	52	43	5	–	100
Bronchitis	46	16	2	36	100
Pneumonia	21	15	5	59	100
Digestion	64	10	1	25	100

Source: Malmö: *BiSOS* A and K; Urban Sweden: *BiSOS* K.

construction of the first railway line from Malmö was started. In addition, rapid urbanization increased the exposure risk to different diseases which was also enhanced by the development of elementary schools, a danger that the authorities during this period were well aware of.

The fact that the port-towns were first affected by this new epidemic pattern indicates that the streptococcal infection was probably imported, thereby lending support to the hypothesis that this period witnessed a change in the virulence of individual diseases. The towns on the Swedish west coast, in particular, displayed high mortality rates, a fact which points to the probability that England played a key role in exporting these 'new' childhood diseases. Thus, mortality from scarlatina and diphtheria in Malmö for the age group 1–5 during the period from 1861 to 1870 was significantly higher than the average for Swedish towns as a whole (see Table 5.9) which, in turn, had an excess mortality of about 60 per cent in comparison with the countryside. Despite the fact that the available data on disease-specific mortality for rural Sweden are not particularly robust, the picture of scarlatina as a specifically urban-related disease is indisputable. Moreover, this pattern is on the whole repeated in the case of diphtheria (Table 5.8).

Adult mortality

What, then, about the third distinct mortality pattern during the period, namely the homogeneous mortality decline among adults of working age which was visible in all the specified regions? It is first of all necessary to examine a further epidemic wave caused by the periodic outbreaks of cholera in the earlier years of the period between 1850 and 1880. On the whole, the appearance and diffusion pattern of this disease was a result of a similar mechanism that determined the spread of scarlatina, although it affected different age groups. In contrast to scarlatina, cholera was not endemic in Sweden. It came from abroad in seven distinct waves during the 1850s and last occurred in 1866. To a very high degree the epidemic was concentrated in the port-towns. Although cause of death data are relatively limited for the 1850s, our calculations show a crude mortality rate of 3.2 and 0.45 per 1,000 for urban and rural Sweden.[21] This can be compared with a mortality rate from scarlatina and diphtheria of 1.87 and 1.19 per 1,000 for the urban and rural areas of Sweden respectively during the period 1861–1870.

Considering the fact that the scarlatina and diphtheria epidemics lasted for three decades, it is perhaps surprising that they attracted so little attention compared with cholera. However, scarlatina and diphtheria were essentially childhood diseases and contemporaries were accustomed to great variations in child mortality, which they regarded as being more or less inevitable (see Table 5.9). To this may be added the fact that the development of cholera was particularly awful in the eyes of contemporaries. The infection primarily affected adult persons: in the towns 76 per cent of cholera mortality was concentrated in the age groups over 25 years; in the countryside the figure was 71 per cent. The infection was initially spread largely through contaminated water and sometimes through infected food. Flies also played an important role in transmitting infection. This explains why the cholera epidemics were most serious in the slum areas of the towns and were often concentrated in the summer period. The inexplicable outbreaks of cholera in places unconnected with the main focal points of infection were probably due to the role of individual carriers of the disease.

Despite an exposed position from the point of view of communication links—Malmö had relatively heavy maritime traffic with Russia, Prussia, Denmark (Copenhagen) and England—the town got off relatively lightly. Its cholera mortality figures were thus much lower than those of Stockholm and Gothenburg. The registered deaths from cholera during the 1850s were the

---

21 See further *BiSOS* A, 1851–1860. As the first wave of cholera during the period 1850–1880 actually arrived in 1850, an average has been calculated for the years 1850–1859.

result mainly of the epidemic of 1850, although minor cholera waves appeared in 1853, 1857 and 1859. Not surprisingly, the epidemics primarily hit the poor in the slum districts of the town. The authorities could not do very much to prevent the epidemics. Both the contagious nature of the disease and its diffusion process were unknown, even if some doctors suspected that the water supply may have played a role in determining its course. However, during the course of the 1850s there was an increase in knowledge concerning different methods that could be employed to limit the spread of the disease. Hospitals were founded and contemporaries began to be aware of the necessity to isolate infected persons.

However, the cholera epidemics could only cause a temporary break in the continuous decrease in mortality that had started in the 1840s (Figure 5.2). In relation to disease-specific trends, the decline in mortality from a number of diseases developed in a similar way, with only small variations between the main regions of Sweden.

In many ways this simultaneous decline may be more mysterious than the increase in child mortality during the same period. The nature of socio-economic development, discussed earlier, did not provide an adequate basis for a continuing mortality decline from the 1840s onwards. The only general factor that could have affected this simultaneous decrease was the reduced consumption of alcohol, a result of new legislation on the consumption of spirits introduced at the beginning of the 1850s. We have defended the thesis that an increase in the consumption of alcoholic beverages led to excess male mortality in early-nineteenth-century Sweden. Thus, a decline in alcohol consumption ought to have worked in the reverse direction. Modern research has shown that a decline in consumption quickly results in a fall in mortality from alcohol-related diseases. In terms of the cohort mortality pattern, the earlier 'deformation' of the male cohorts in the working age groups now began to disappear, a trend which undoubtedly supports this argument. As the alcohol factor primarily affected the mortality of males and only to a small degree influenced female mortality, the overall effect of this process must have been of more limited importance.

However, if we leave aside the proposed periodization and analyse instead the mortality decline from a cohort-specific point of view, the fall in mortality no longer seems so mysterious. What we can observe is a process by which the first generations after the disappearance of smallpox now reached working age; they were healthier, with an improved immunity to different diseases and with better possibilities of withstanding various stress factors than their immediate predecessors. A decline in mortality was the result. The cohort thesis is based on data for Sweden as a whole. In relation to the towns, especially Stockholm, the picture is more complicated. The parallelism in the mortality decline of the different regions, however, does suggest that a similar mechanism was also operating in urban areas.

The complex mortality pattern during this period, particularly in the 1850s,

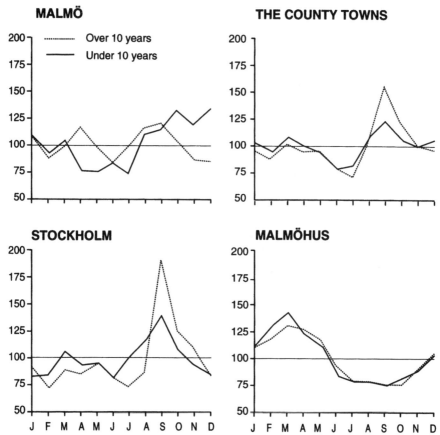

Figure 5.5: The seasonality of deaths in Malmö, the county towns, Stockholm and the rural county of Malmöhus,1851–1859. *Source:* SCB Tabellverket, MS.

is also mirrored in the seasonality of death. As can be seen from Figure 5.5, the seasonality pattern for the period 1851–1859 diverged radically from that of 1821–1830. The previous peak during spring was now replaced by a new one during September. This was the case for both the general age groups (under and over ten years) examined in this context.

In summary, therefore, the development of Swedish mortality in the period from 1850 to 1880 revealed an extremely complicated pattern. In interpreting this pattern we have to take into consideration both exogenous as well as environmental factors, which operated selectively in a cohort- and time-specific manner. If the visible trends in child mortality are taken as characteristic for the whole period, we can no doubt speak of a return to an old mortality pattern. As far as Malmö was concerned, during this period its function as a port-city undoubtedly influenced its mortality pattern for the first and, as we will see, for the last time.

TOWARDS A SUSTAINED MORTALITY DECREASE, 1881–1914

During this period we find for the first time a fall in overall mortality, as well as in the different age-specific series; this trend was visible both in the rural and urban regions (Figure 5.2). Another important characteristic of the mortality decline during this period was the fact that it was clearly more rapid in the urban than in the rural areas: by the end of the period, for the first time in history, overall urban mortality was lower than that of rural areas. Not until after the Second World War did the pendulum swing back again.

Infant mortality

In rural areas the decline in infant mortality continued on the whole at the same rate as during the previous period. The long-term pattern of infant mortality was increasingly the result of complex environmental factors and this was the case particularly in the decades immediately prior to 1914. In this context it is difficult to give priority to any specific factor as the main determinant of infant mortality trends during this period. In relation to the towns, however, a different pattern stands out. After a slight decrease in mortality, evident in the previous period, a rapid decline started around the 1880s which was much more precipitous than that of the rural areas.

The crucial factor in this rapid fall in urban infant mortality must have been the extensive improvements in water supply and sewerage in the towns during the period. This helped to reduce the frequency of gastro-intestinal disorders and resultant secondary diseases. A decline in mortality was the result. This suggestion is supported by developments in the cause of death panorama. In this context respiratory diseases and diseases of the digestive system accounted for nearly 60 per cent of all infant deaths in the urban areas between 1875 and 1880 (Table 5.14). As the diagnosed main causes of death, they were responsible respectively for 20.6 and 36.8 per cent of all recorded deaths. By 1911–1914 their shares had fallen to 19.5 and 21.5 per cent respectively. This constituted a mortality decrease of nearly 75 per cent from gastro-intestinal disorders, a much higher fall than that recorded for other causes of death. Moreover, on the basis of the analysis of the earlier decline in infant mortality, this is likely to have produced a cohort effect, positively affecting subsequent trends in age-specific mortality for later age groups.

It is clearly out of the question to attribute such a rapid fall in infant mortality to better nutrition and childcare. Breast-feeding customs were often less developed in the new industrial towns; nor was the substitute food of better quality. It has been suggested that an increased use of milk may have been a crucial factor in the decline in infant mortality (Beaver, 1973; Atkins, 1992). If this had been the case, Malmö would have been in an excellent position, situated in a region where the transition to dairy farming was most advanced and with excellent railway connections with its hinterland. However, the limited evidence we have concerning this topic does not support this suggestion; nor does the actual decline in infant mortality in Malmö which revealed a pronounced lag in comparison with the trend in other county towns. On the contrary, an increased reliance on dairy milk for infant feeding would have promoted the spread of bovine tuberculosis (Höjer, 1934).

However, the emphasis on environmental reform as a key determinant of urban infant mortality trends during this period also implies an increased difference between the mortality levels of particular towns. The successful implementation of extensive sanitation improvement programmes was due in part to natural prerequisites and, to a far greater degree, to the amount of money and energy mobilized by the local administration. The marked lag in the infant mortality decline evident in the case of Malmö was certainly the result of the hesitant implementation of improvement programmes for water supply and sewerage. This was partly due to difficult drainage conditions in the port, given its low-lying and waterlogged position, and partly due to a lengthy bureaucratic decision-making process.[22] The very high mortality from diseases of the digestive system even at the end of the period under consideration, which was 120 and 65 per cent higher in Malmö than in Stockholm and the towns respectively, undoubtedly supports this hypothesis.

Child mortality

At the beginning of this period epidemic infections were the main cause of death for this age group, accounting for about half of total child mortality. At the end of the period their share had declined to about 25 per cent. This rapid fall in mortality from epidemic infections is illustrated in Table 5.10.

Why, then, did epidemic infections decrease so rapidly, so that children as a whole benefited from a more rapid mortality decline than any other age group during this period? An examination of the development of mortality from this group of diseases shows that between 1875–1880 and 1911–1914 scarlatina and diphtheria accounted for 88 per cent of the decrease, whooping cough and measles for about nine per cent, and dysentery and typhoid fever for the rest. Thus it was the case that those diseases which had contributed significantly to the rapid increase in child mortality in the previous period had now almost disappeared.

We have argued that the earlier increase in the relative incidence of scarlatina was due to the appearance of a new, more aggressive streptococcus variant. Thus, the rapid decrease must have been a result of either a diminution in the virulence of the streptococcal micro-organisms or of a gradual increase in the population's resistance to such kinds of bacteria. A similar argument can also be presented concerning the mortality decrease from diphtheria. It is impossible at this stage to determine which of these two possible explanations is the more feasible.

---

22 This lengthy process can be followed in the yearly reports of the district medical officer in Malmö.

Table 5.10: *Urban Sweden: mortality from epidemic infections and other diseases in different age groups, 1875–1880, 1881–1890, 1891–1900, 1901–1910 and 1911–1914.*

	1875–1880	1881–1890	1891–1900	1901–1910	1911–1914
0–1					
Epidemic infections	100	97	96	59	37
Other diseases	100	77	64	50	46
1–5					
Epidemic infections	100	80	54	24	18
Other diseases	100	84	69	50	39
5–10					
Epidemic infections	100	61	47	16	14
Other diseases	100	94	76	68	65
Total					
Epidemic infections	100	77	48	23	53
Other diseases	100	85	76	68	65

Note: Index: 1875–1880 = 100.
Sources: Adapted from *BiSOS* K, 1875–1910 and SOS, Dödsorsaker, 1911–14.

The much slower decline in mortality from measles and whooping cough can be seen in another perspective. In general neither of these two diseases exhibits changes in virulence, but they seem to be more sensitive to changes in the standard of living than scarlatina and diphtheria. Probably the new mortality levels from measles and whooping cough reflected a general improvement within the population's health which altered the immunological balance between the human hosts and the parasites. Whatever the cause of the decline in disease-specific mortality, this development not only meant that the diseases became more harmless; it also implied that the risk of serious complications and sequelae diminished which resulted in a further improved state of health for children. One undoubted component in this development was the overall beneficial effect generated by the decreasing frequency of serious gastro-intestinal diseases among infants. In conjunction with other factors affecting the mortality decline of children, this had a cumulative impact that influenced the whole cohort. It is significant, therefore, that Malmö registered its last epidemic peak from dysentery in 1882, from scarlatina in 1883 and from

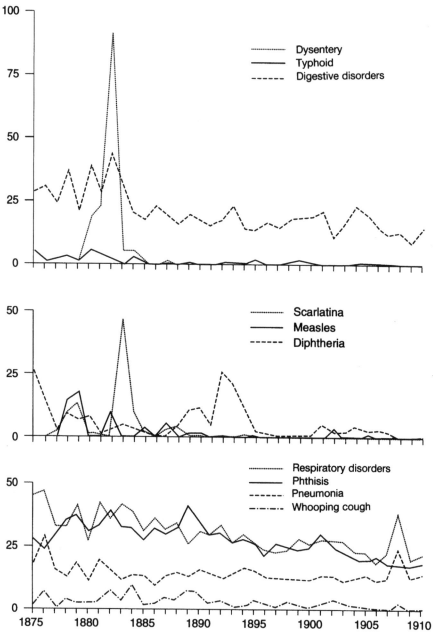

Figure 5.6: Crude death rates from different diseases in Malmö, 1875–1910 (per 100,000). *Source: BiSOS* A, 1875–1910.

diphtheria in 1895–96, although the trend in mortality from measles and whooping cough was more even (Figure 5.6).

Adult mortality

The general reduction in mortality benefited people of working age in urban areas much more than those in rural areas. Between 1875–1880 and 1901–1910 the mortality rates for the age group 20–60 years in Malmö, Stockholm, the county towns and the rural areas fell by 40, 45, 45 and 15 per cent respectively. This meant that the extent of the mortality decline in Malmö was approximately the same as for Swedish towns in general. At the end of the period under consideration the difference in the level of mortality between the rural and urban areas had either disappeared or had diminished considerably (Figure 5.2).

Even during this period the mortality decline was characterized by a cohort effect that must also have influenced the rapid fall in mortality in the towns. I have not, as yet, been able to calculate the precise significance of this phenomenon. However, we also find during this period a marked cohort deformation (or unusually high mortality levels), extending over several decades and accentuated in the age groups between 10 and 30 years (Fridlizius, 1989). In this case a study of the cause of death panorama indicates that we need to focus attention on a single disease, namely phthisis. As tuberculosis was the dominant cause of death in the age groups in question, the mortality pattern of this disease affected to a high degree the age-specific mortality figures.

As shown in Table 5.14 the share of tuberculosis mortality in overall adult mortality between 1875–1880 and 1901–1910 increased strongly. This pattern is even more striking as its relative share of total mortality in the age groups 40–60 and over 60 fell during the same period. A more detailed picture of this surprising development is given in Table 5.11. I cannot find any environmental factors that might explain this simultaneous development in all Swedish regions, both rural as well as urban (Fridlizius, 1988). This development of tuberculosis implies, however, a concentration of phthisis mortality in those age groups where, from a biological point of view, phthisis was most deeply rooted. Perhaps we have to assume that some still unknown epidemiological factors were responsible for this shift in the age-specific profile of tuberculosis mortality. The disparate behaviour of phthisis in the different age groups, however, is concealed in the overall mortality figures which indicate that deaths from phthisis declined at the same rate as mortality from other diseases. The relatively low crude death rate for phthisis in Malmö, compared with Swedish towns as a whole, is well known from the earlier periods and its causes were probably the same.

Another interesting pattern in the cause of death panorama during the late-nineteenth and early-twentieth century was the rapid increase in circulatory diseases. How much this was simply a result of better diagnosis is difficult to

Table 5.11: *Urban Sweden: mortality from phthisis and other diseases and total mortality for different age groups, 1875–1880, 1881–1890, 1891–1900, 1901–1910 and 1911–1914.*

	1875–1880	1881–1890	1891–1900	1901–1910	1911–1914
5–10					
Phthisis	100	91	64	45	36
Other diseases	100	75	61	37	32
Total	100	77	61	38	32
10–20					
Phthisis	100	100	94	100	81
Other diseases	100	71	59	51	44
Total	100	79	68	65	54
20–40					
Phthisis	100	94	79	79	82
Other diseases	100	75	58	49	46
Total	100	82	68	60	59
40–60					
Phthisis	100	90	65	54	44
Other diseases	100	91	75	70	81
Total	100	91	72	66	72
Over 60					
Phthisis	100	77	49	31	28
Other diseases	100	91	94	92	105
Total	100	89	89	84	96
All					
Phthisis	100	88	70	64	58
Other diseases	100	83	72	61	58
Total	100	84	72	62	58

Note: Index: 1875–1880 = 100.
Sources: Adapted from *BiSOS* K, 1875–1910 and SOS, Dödsorsaker, 1911–14.

say. In all events, it reflects a new and distinct phase in the epidemiological transition, characterized by the increasing predominance of degenerative diseases due to stress and man-made factors.

Finally, how did sex-specific mortality develop during this period? Did the new industrial town of the late-nineteenth century provide a similar advantage for females as we have noticed for the pre-industrial town? As can be seen from Table 5.12, excess male mortality by 1911–1914 had considerably decreased in all regions compared with the period 1821–1830. Possibly a reduced consumption of alcohol may be given credit for a considerable role in this development, although changes in employment structure and occupational status are other factors in this complicated pattern. In relation to the urban areas (Figure 5.7) and the age group 25–30 there was an excess mortality for married females in relation to both unmarried females and married males, but

Table 5.12: *Sex-specific mortality rates from phthisis and other diseases, and total mortality in different age groups in Malmö, urban Sweden, Stockholm and rural Sweden, 1911–1914.*

Age group	Malmö						Urban Sweden					
	1–10	*10–20*	*20–40*	*40–60*	*60+*	*Total*	*1–10*	*10–20*	*20–40*	*40–60*	*60+*	*Total*
Phthisis	104	38	72	115	86	78	85	96	106	151	147	108
Other	121	166	150	190	134	134	125	132	167	166	116	113
Total	119	122	113	173	131	131	118	106	135	135	117	112

Age group	Stockholm						Rural Sweden					
	1–10	*10–20*	*20–40*	*40–60*	*60+*	*Total*	*1–10*	*10–20*	*20–40*	*40–60*	*60+*	*Total*
Phthisis	71	90	151	223	222	155	72	61	79	81	122	80
Other	115	103	153	188	120	111	105	118	122	114	105	103
Total	112	97	151	195	122	117	104	95	102	107	107	100

Note: Index: female = 100.

Sources: Malmö Årsbok; Berättelse om allmänna hälsotillståndet i Stockholm; SOS, Dödsorsaker.

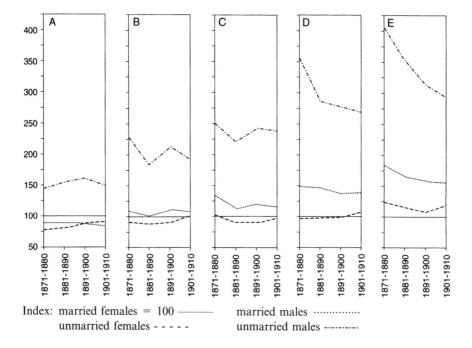

Index: married females = 100 ———   married males ··············
       unmarried females - - - - -   unmarried males ----·--·-

Figure 5.7: Urban Sweden: age-specific mortality rates for the age groups 25–30 to 45–50 according to sex and civil status, 1871–1880 to 1901–1910. Age groups: A = 25–30, B = 30–35, C = 35–40, D = 40–45, E = 45–50. *Source: BiSOS* A, 1871–1910.

at the same time they had a pronounced mortality advantage in comparison with unmarried men. In the higher age groups excess mortality among unmarried men became more accentuated, while the excess mortality of married women in comparison with married males was transformed into a mortality advantage. The conventional picture of a significantly adverse situation for married women in the early industrial town—primarily as a result of repeated pregnancies and a double work burden—is hardly confirmed by the Swedish data. The situation of a married woman was not significantly worse than for her unmarried counterpart, and much better than that of both married and unmarried men. This means that whereas in rural areas the dividing line in terms of mortality was to be found between married and unmarried people, in the town it was located between the two sexes (Fridlizius, 1988).

It has been suggested that Sweden after about 1880 entered an era of sustained economic growth (Rostow, 1960). Perhaps it was not an accidental occurrence that this was accompanied by a simultaneous and sustained decline in mortality. These two processes were more or less connected, particularly as the disease panorama in Sweden was increasingly dominated by degenerative and man-made diseases.

CONCLUSION

In order to identify and quantify different factors in the development of Swedish mortality during the nineteenth century this chapter has analysed various mortality series, focusing in particular on age-, disease- and sex-specific trends. The complex pattern which emerges from this disaggregated analysis is further accentuated when mortality trends are examined from a cohort-specific perspective. Such an approach emphasizes the need to pay particular attention to the changing pattern of diseases during childhood and the cumulative cohort effect of mortality improvements from specific diseases.

Our analysis supports the hypothesis that the development of Swedish mortality during the nineteenth century occurred in three distinct steps. The initial phase of the first stage of the mortality decline was caused by factors primarily beyond human control. This was followed by a period when mortality trends were determined by a multi-faceted complex of factors. A second stage witnessed a temporary halt to the earlier decline, at least for certain age groups, as a result of the appearance of new, uncontrolled waves of epidemics, partly of a pandemic character. A third phase witnessed a continuing decline in mortality which was obviously determined and sustained by factors connected with the emergence of a new industrial society in Sweden.

The development of mortality in Malmö was on the whole similar to that of the general pattern. It was only during the second period between 1850 and 1880 that its character as a port-town influenced mortality trends. Other temporal variations from the average mortality pattern of the Swedish county towns as a whole may be attributed to other factors, unrelated to Malmö's maritime role.

Having studied in this chapter the mortality development of Sweden on the basis of aggregate data, focusing in particular on urban and rural areas and the two cities of Malmö and Stockholm, we have been able to reach a number of general conclusions. The next step will be to produce a further disaggregation of the available demographic series in order to facilitate a study of long-run mortality trends, although employing a similar methodology to the one applied in this analysis. Particular attention will be paid to problems relating to infant mortality, causes of death and mortality conditions in the late-eighteenth century.

Table 5.13: *Mortality per 1,000 from different causes of death in different age groups, 1751–1770, 1821–1830, for Malmö (M), Stockholm (S), urban Sweden (U), rural Sweden (R) and the rural county of Malmöhus (RM).*

(1) Age group 0–1

Cause of death	1751–1770		1821–1830				
	S	RM	M	S	U	RM	R
Smallpox	25.3	32.5	0.4	1.7	1.5	0.9	1.5
Scarlatina	–	–	5.4	0.8	1.3	1.6	0.7
Measles	6.1	2.8	4.9	4.4	5.3	7.9	6.9
Diphtheria	–	–	6.2	2.5	2.2	3.8	1.3
Whooping cough	9.2	11.0	7.8	11.6	10.8	13.9	13.6
Typhoid fever	0.4	0.3	4.5	2.1	2.17	0.7	1.5
Dysentery	1.7	0.5	–	0.2	0.5	–	0.7
Epidemic infections	*42.7*	*47.1*	*29.2*	*23.3*	*23.7*	*28.8*	*26.2*
Phthisis	0.3	0.1	0.4	1.8	0.7	0.2	0.3
Pneumonia	31.8	7.6	1.2	15.8	11.6	6.5	17.0
Fever fits	13.7	4.1	3.3	3.0	3.4	3.6	3.1
Pine away disease	1.5	0.7	4.5	30.9	17.7	9.3	11.0
Convulsions	–	–	13.6	20.3	31.2	45.1	27.3
Stroke/violent death	203.5	10.4	30.9	150.5	99.2	12.2	34.5
Unknown	75.4	157.0	89.3	3.5	14.3	40.7	24.4
Other	15.1	10.0	4.6	22.9	14.2	9.6	16.2
Total	384.0	237.0	177.0	272.0	216.0	156.0	160.0

Table 5.13: (continued)

(2) Age group 1–5

Cause of death	1751–1770		Cause of death	1821–1830				
	S	RM		M	S	U	RM	R
Smallpox	22.0	20.5	Smallpox	–	0.1	0.3	0.2	0.3
Scarlatina	–	–	Scarlatina	2.6	0.9	0.9	0.9	0.4
Measles	2.9	2.3	Measles	6.0	3.6	4.5	4.6	3.0
Diphtheria	–	–	Diphtheria	3.5	1.8	1.2	2.4	0.4
Whooping cough	3.0	2.8	Whooping cough	2.2	3.7	3.1	3.8	2.9
Typhoid fever	0.6	0.2	Typhoid fever	4.4	0.8	1.4	0.7	0.8
Dysentery	0.7	0.4	Dysentery	–	0.1	0.2	–	0.5
Epidemic infections	29.2	26.2	Epidemic infections	18.7	11.0	11.6	12.6	8.3
Phthisis	0.9	0.1	Phthisis	0.6	1.5	0.6	0.1	0.2
Pneumonia	8.0	3.0	Inflammation fever	1.7	4.7	3.7	2.6	4.2
Fever fits	8.8	2.8	Remittent fever	0.2	3.1	2.7	1.8	1.6
Pine away disease	1.4	0.7	Rickets	1.6	5.4	4.1	2.7	2.4
Stroke/violent death	15.3	1.1	Stroke/violent death	4.0	19.1	12.3	0.7	2.8
Other	15.6	11.6	Other	5.9	6.9	4.9	8.5	6.1
Total	79.2	45.5	Total	32.7	51.7	39.9	29.0	25.6

Table 5.13: (continued)

(3) Age group 5–10

Cause of death	1751–1770		Cause of death	1821–1830				
	S	RM		M	S	U	RM	R
Smallpox	4.6	5.3	Smallpox	0.2	0.1	0.1	0.1	0.1
Scarlatina	–	–	Scarlatina	1.4	0.6	0.6	0.5	0.4
Measles	0.5	0.6	Measles	1.1	1.1	1.4	1.2	0.4
Diphtheria	–	–	Diphtheria	0.5	0.7	0.4	0.5	0.1
Whooping cough	0.3	0.4	Whooping cough	0.3	0.5	0.5	0.5	0.3
Typhoid fever	0.2	0.2	Typhoid fever	2.8	0.8	1.0	0.6	0.5
Dysentery	0.2	0.4	Dysentery	–	0.1	0.1	0.6	0.2
Epidemic infections	5.8	6.9	Epidemic infections	6.3	3.9	4.1	4.0	2.0
Phthisis	0.7	0.2	Phthisis	0.7	0.6	0.4	0.2	0.2
Pneumonia	1.7	1.2	Inflammation fever	0.4	1.5	1.3	1.0	1.2
Fever fits	3.4	1.7	Remittent fever	0.4	0.8	1.1	0.9	0.6
Pine away disease	0.6	0.1	Rickets	1.1	1.4	1.1	0.9	0.4
Stroke/violent death	2.5	0.4	Stroke/violent death	0.4	2.3	1.8	0.2	0.8
Other	4.9	3.4	Other	1.9	3.1	2.8	1.4	1.9
Total	19.6	13.9	Total	11.2	13.6	12.6	8.6	7.1

Table 5.13: *(continued)*

(4) Age group 10–25

Cause of death	1751–1770	
	S	RM
Epidemic infections	0.7	1.2
Phthisis	1.6	0.5
Pneumonia	0.7	1.0
Fever fits	4.0	2.2
Ague fits	0.4	0.3
Dropsy	0.9	0.3
Pine away disease	0.1	0.5
Accidents	0.6	0.2
Other	2.4	1.4
Total	11.4	7.6

Cause of death	1821–1830				
	M	S	U	RM	R
Epidemic infections	2.6	2.2	1.8	1.5	1.1
Phthisis	1.0	2.4	1.5	0.8	0.7
Inflammation fever	0.4	1.5	0.9	0.6	0.9
Remittent fever	0.1	0.3	0.6	0.5	0.4
Dropsy	0.3	1.0	0.6	0.2	0.2
Pine away disease	0.3	0.3	0.2	0.2	0.2
Stroke/violent death	0.1	0.9	0.6	0.1	0.3
Accidents	0.7	1.1	1.0	0.3	0.5
Other	0.7	1.6	1.0	1.1	0.9
Total	6.2	11.3	8.2	5.3	5.2

Table 5.13: *(continued)*

(5) Age group 25–50

Cause of death	1751–1770		Cause of death	1821–1830				
	S	*RM*		*M*	*S*	*U*	*RM*	*R*
Epidemic infections	0.6	0.8	*Epidemic infections*	4.2	3.9	3.1	1.6	1.3
Phthisis	7.6	1.6	Phthisis	4.4	10.1	6.3	2.0	1.9
Pneumonia	1.6	2.6	Inflammation fever	0.9	3.8	2.7	1.2	1.9
Fever fits	8.9	2.7	Remittent fever	0.3	1.4	1.4	0.7	0.7
Ague fits	1.1	0.3	Dropsy	0.8	3.9	2.4	0.6	0.8
Dropsy	2.0	0.6	Pine away disease	2.7	1.0	1.1	0.6	0.4
Pine away disease	0.5	0.8	Stroke/violent death	1.1	3.3	2.3	0.3	0.6
Child bed fever	1.3	1.1	Child bed fever	0.3	0.7	0.6	0.7	0.6
Accidents	0.7	0.3	Accidents	2.5	2.1	1.8	0.5	0.8
Other	3.3	2.3	Other	2.0	4.3	2.4	1.9	1.5
Total	27.6	13.1	Total	19.2	34.5	24.1	10.1	10.5

(6) Age group 50 +

Cause of death	1751–1770		Cause of death	1821–1830				
	S	*RM*		*M*	*S*	*U*	*RM*	*R*
Epidemic infections	0.8	1.1	Epidemic infections	4.4	4.5	3.9	2.5	2.4
Phthisis	13.7	4.2	Phthisis	6.2	16.4	10.7	4.4	4.9
Pneumonia	9.0	6.8	Inflammation fever	1.2	5.6	5.5	3.8	6.6
Fever fits	12.3	3.1	Remittent fever	0.4	2.0	2.9	1.9	2.1
Ague fits	1.4	0.3	Dropsy	2.5	7.4	5.0	2.4	2.7
Dropsy	3.6	1.6	Pine away disease	7.5	4.5	4.0	2.1	1.7
Pine away disease	1.2	1.1	Stroke/violent death	2.3	10.0	6.4	1.1	2.3
Stroke/violent death			Old age	34.5	15.2	21.5	29.8	20.4
Old age	16.5	26.2	Accidents	2.7	1.4	1.4	0.8	0.9
Accidents	2.5	0.3	Other	3.2	8.6	6.4	6.6	6.5
Other	6.0	2.2						
Total	67.0	46.9	Total	64.9	75.6	67.7	55.4	50.5

Table 5.13: (continued)

(7) All age groups

Cause of death	1751–1770		Cause of death	1821–1830				
	S	RM		M	S	U	RM	R
Epidemic infections	8.0	5.9	Epidemic infections	6.3	4.5	4.4	4.2	3.2
Phthisis	6.0	1.4	Phthisis	2.8	7.8	4.6	1.6	1.7
Pneumonia	2.8	2.9	Inflammation fever	0.9	3.8	2.9	1.8	3.1
Fever fits	7.9	2.6	Remittent fever	0.3	1.3	1.6	1.1	1.0
Ague fits	1.0	0.3	Dropsy	0.8	3.3	2.0	0.7	0.9
Dropsy	1.8	0.6	Pine away disease	2.1	1.7	1.1	0.6	0.5
Pine away disease	0.6	0.7	Stroke/violent death	0.1	0.4	0.3	0.3	0.2
Old age	2.5	4.7	Old age	5.3	2.4	3.4	4.7	3.4
Accidents	0.6	0.3	Accidents	1.4	1.5	1.3	0.6	0.8
Other	13.9	10.1	Other	8.4	16.3	11.7	7.9	7.4
Total	45.1	29.5	Total	28.4	43.0	33.3	23.5	22.2

Note: Concerning the total country of Malmöhus in 1751–1770, see footnote 7.
Source: SCB Tabellverket, MS.

Table 5.14: Mortality per 1,000 from different causes of death in different age groups, 1861–1870 to 1911–1914, for Malmö (M), Stockholm (S), urban Sweden (U) and rural Sweden (R)

(1) Age group 0–1

Cause of death	1861–1870		1875–1880	1881–1890	1891–1900			1901–1910	1911–1914			
	M	S	U	U	M	S	U	U	M	S	U	R
Smallpox	1.9	4.8	0.9	–	–	–	–	–	–	–	–	–
Scarlatina	4.1	2.1	3.4	2.0	0.1	0.8	0.6	0.2	0.7	0.1	0.2	0.2
Measles	3.9	2.9	1.6	3.0	0.5	3.7	2.0	1.2	0.4	1.7	1.4	0.9
Diphtheria	3.2	5.3	2.9	2.5	1.1	3.0	1.8	0.7	0.7	0.5	0.5	0.3
Whooping cough	6.7	2.7	4.5	4.1	2.9	4.4	3.8	2.9	2.0	2.4	3.4	3.5
Typhoid fever	3.6	0.3	0.7	–	–	–	–	–	–	–	–	–
Dysentery	–	0.5	0.5	2.8	–	–	6.0	3.8	–	–	–	–
Epidemic infections	23.4	18.7	14.8	14.4	4.8	11.9	14.2	8.8	3.8	4.7	5.5	4.9
Phthisis	2.3	8.3	1.4	1.4	0.8	1.7	1.3	1.0	0.7	1.5	1.1	0.3
Congenital	27.1	38.7	26.5	30.2	31.5	31.7	25.6	28.8	30.6	26.9	29.8	28.1
Digestion	16.5	72.1	66.2	46.4	34.5	59.3	31.6	19.8	28.8	12.9	17.5	8.1
Respiration	29.7	64.9	37.1	31.4	28.4	41.2	27.8	21.6	24.3	17.1	16.0	9.9
Other	46.1	64.3	34.0	17.2	27.2	24.2	17.5	12.0	11.8	16.1	12.1	16.7
Total	145.1	266.9	179.7	141.0	127.0	170.0	118.0	92.0	100.0	79.2	82.0	68.0

Table 5.14: (continued)

(2) Age group 1–5

Cause of death	1861–1870		1875–1880	1881–1890	1891–1900			1901–1910	1911–1914			
	M	S	U	U	M	S	U	U	M	S	U	R
Smallpox	0.5	2.0	–	–	–	–	–	–	–	–	–	–
Scarlatina	9.8	6.7	7.0	4.5	0.7	3.2	1.8	0.6	1.2	0.5	0.5	0.2
Measles	4.1	4.1	1.5	2.1	0.5	3.0	1.6	0.8	–	1.2	0.9	0.5
Diphtheria	5.9	6.7	6.4	5.4	5.7	5.9	4.3	1.5	1.1	0.7	1.0	0.6
Whooping cough	2.3	1.0	1.3	1.3	1.6	1.2	1.0	0.9	0.5	0.5	0.7	0.6
Typhoid fever	2.8	0.1	0.5	0.2	0.1	–	0.1	–	–	–	–	–
Dysentery	–	0.4	0.1	0.2	–	–	0.2	0.2	–	–	–	–
Epidemic infections	25.4	21.0	16.8	13.7	8.6	13.3	9.0	4.0	2.8	2.9	3.1	1.9
Phthisis	2.7	6.3	1.9	1.6	1.2	1.5	1.2	0.8	1.2	0.8	0.6	0.2
Digestion	3.1	9.1	3.8	2.7	1.7	1.7	1.7	1.1	0.9	0.5	0.8	0.6
Respiration	8.5	19.4	6.8	5.6	4.5	6.3	4.8	3.4	2.7	1.9	2.4	1.7
Other	8.0	17.3	8.2	7.5	7.3	8.3	6.6	5.1	3.2	4.1	4.4	3.0
Total	47.7	73.1	37.5	31.1	23.3	31.1	23.3	14.4	10.8	10.2	11.3	7.4

Table 5.14: (continued)

(3) Age group 5–10

Cause of death	1861–1870		1875–1880	1881–1890	1891–1900			1901–1910	1911–1914			
	M	S	U	U	M	S	U	U	M	S	U	R
Smallpox	0.1	0.3	–	–	–	–	–	–	–	–	–	–
Scarlatina	3.1	2.4	2.6	1.3	1.2	0.2	0.7	0.2	0.6	0.1	0.1	0.1
Measles	0.6	0.5	0.3	0.3	0.3	0.1	0.2	0.1	–	0.1	0.1	0.1
Diphtheria	1.2	1.2	2.1	1.6	1.9	1.5	1.4	0.6	0.4	0.5	0.5	0.4
Whooping cough	–	0.1	0.1	–	0.1	–	0.1	–	–	–	–	–
Typhoid fever	2.2	0.7	0.6	0.2	0.1	0.1	0.1	–	–	–	–	–
Dysentery	–	0.2	–	0.1	–	–	0.2	–	–	–	–	–
Epidemic infections	7.2	5.4	5.7	3.5	3.6	1.9	2.7	0.9	1.0	0.7	0.8	0.7
Phthisis	1.8	1.7	1.1	1.0	0.7	0.8	0.7	0.5	0.8	0.3	0.4	0.2
Digestion	0.1	0.5	0.5	0.3	0.9	0.3	0.3	0.2	0.2	0.1	0.2	0.2
Respiration	1.0	1.8	0.8	0.6	0.4	0.3	0.4	0.3	0.3	0.2	0.2	0.3
Other	3.0	5.1	2.7	2.9	2.4	2.3	2.5	2.2	1.1	1.8	1.9	2.2
Total	13.1	14.5	10.8	8.3	8.0	5.6	6.6	4.1	3.4	3.1	3.5	3.6

Table 5.14: (continued)

(4) Age group 10–20

Cause of death	1861–1870		1875–1880	1881–1890	1891–1900			1901–1910	1911–1914			
	M	S	U	U	M	S	U	U	M	S	U	R
Epidemic infections	1.4	1.3	1.3	0.6	0.5	0.4	0.4	0.2	0.4	0.5	0.4	0.5
Phthisis	1.3	1.5	1.6	1.6	1.1	1.3	1.5	1.6	0.6	1.3	1.3	1.2
Respiration	0.2	0.4	0.4	0.3	0.3	0.2	0.2	0.2	0.2	0.1	0.2	0.2
Digestion	0.3	0.2	0.3	0.2	0.3	0.2	0.2	0.2	0.1	0.1	0.2	0.2
Circulation	0.2	0.2	0.4	0.3	0.4	0.4	0.4	0.5	0.6	0.4	0.5	0.4
Nervous system	0.2	0.6	0.5	0.4	0.3	0.7	0.3	0.2	0.3	0.2	0.2	0.2
Accidents	0.2	0.4	0.4	0.3	0.1	0.2	0.3	0.2	0.2	0.1	0.3	0.3
Other	0.9	0.9	0.8	0.8	0.5	0.3	0.6	0.6	0.1	0.7	–	0.5
Total	4.7	5.5	5.7	4.5	3.5	3.7	3.9	3.7	2.5	3.4	3.1	3.5

Table 5.14: (continued)

(5) Age group 20–40*

Cause of death	1861–1870		1875–1880	1881–1890	1891–1900			1901–1910	1911–1914			
	M	S	U	U	M	S	U	U	M	S	U	R
Epidemic infections	1.3	1.6	0.8	0.4	0.5	0.2	0.2	0.1	0.5	0.4	0.3	0.4
Phthisis	2.0	3.9	3.4	3.2	3.1	2.8	2.7	2.7	2.0	2.8	2.8	2.5
Respiration	0.9	1.9	1.1	0.8	0.4	0.7	0.6	0.4	0.4	0.4	0.4	0.4
Digestion	0.3	0.5	0.5	0.4	0.4	0.3	0.3	0.3	0.3	0.3	0.2	0.3
Circulation	0.3	0.4	0.5	0.5	0.5	0.5	0.4	0.5	0.6	0.4	0.5	0.4
Nervous system	0.2	0.6	0.5	0.4	0.3	0.3	0.3	0.2	0.3	0.2	0.2	0.2
Accidents	0.9	0.6	0.5	0.4	0.3	0.4	0.3	0.3	0.3	0.1	0.5	0.4
Other	1.6	3.5	2.2	1.7	0.7	1.5	1.4	1.2	0.8	1.4	0.7	0.1
Total	7.5	13.0	9.5	7.8	6.2	6.7	6.2	5.7	5.2	6.0	5.6	5.7

Table 5.14: (continued)

(6) Age group 40–60*

Cause of death	1861–1870		1875–1880	1881–1890	1891–1900			1901–1910	1911–1914			
	M	S	U	U	M	S	U	U	M	S	U	R
Epidemic infections	1.1	1.3	0.6	0.3	0.5	0.1	0.1	0.1	0.3	0.4	0.5	0.3
Phthisis	3.6	6.2	4.8	4.3	4.1	3.7	3.1	2.6	2.3	2.3	2.1	1.7
Respiration	2.7	4.2	3.4	2.6	1.7	2.4	1.9	1.4	1.3	1.1	1.5	1.1
Digestion	0.6	1.1	1.4	1.1	0.8	0.7	0.7	0.7	0.5	0.7	0.9	0.6
Circulation	0.6	0.9	1.2	1.4	1.7	2.0	1.2	1.8	2.1	1.8	2.3	1.1
Nervous system	0.7	1.4	1.7	1.5	1.3	1.1	1.1	0.9	1.3	0.9	1.0	0.7
Accidents	0.7	0.6	0.6	0.5	0.4	0.5	0.4	0.4	0.7	0.1	0.5	0.4
Other	5.3	6.4	4.6	4.9	3.2	5.5	4.7	4.2	3.3	4.4	4.3	3.5
Total	15.3	22.1	18.3	16.6	13.7	16.0	13.2	12.1	11.8	11.7	13.1	9.4

Table 5.14: (continued)

(7) Age group 60 +*

Cause of death	1861–1870		1875–1880	1881–1890	1891–1990			1901–1910	1911–1914			
	M	S	U	U	M	S	U	U	M	S	U	R
Epidemic infections	1.7	1.7	0.7	0.3	1.4	0.1	0.1	–	0.2	1.3	1.2	0.6
Phthisis	9.6	5.8	7.1	5.5	6.1	4.2	3.5	2.2	3.6	2.0	2.0	1.3
Respiration	15.9	10.9	13.6	11.0	13.9	10.1	10.4	8.0	9.1	7.8	8.0	6.6
Digestion	2.4	3.8	4.5	3.0	2.8	1.8	2.5	1.9	2.0	2.1	2.1	1.5
Circulation	3.2	3.2	3.8	4.7	4.6	9.3	7.4	8.7	13.5	14.0	17.2	7.3
Nervous system	4.6	7.0	5.9	5.9	4.9	6.3	5.7	5.2	4.9	6.5	5.8	5.5
Accidents	1.4	0.4	0.6	0.3	0.7	0.6	0.5	0.5	0.6	0.2	0.8	0.7
Other	17.7	21.7	23.1	22.3	22.2	25.8	22.4	23.5	24.5	20.9	19.7	33.8
Total	56.5	54.5	59.3	53.0	56.6	58.2	52.5	50.0	58.4	54.8	56.8	57.3

Table **5.14:** (continued)

(8) All age groups

Total	1861–1870		1875–1880	1881–1890	1891–1900			1901–1910	1911–1914			
	M	S	U	U	M	S	U	U	M	S	U	R
Epidemic infections	5.2	4.3	3.1	2.4	1.5	1.1	1.5	0.7	0.9	1.0	0.5	0.8
Phthisis	2.7	4.6	3.3	2.9	2.6	2.6	2.3	2.1	1.7	2.1	1.9	1.4
Respiration	4.1	6.6	4.0	3.3	2.7	3.1	2.8	2.1	2.1	1.7	1.7	1.6
Digestion	1.4	3.3	3.3	2.3	1.7	1.7	1.5	1.1	1.3	0.9	0.8	1.6
Circulation	0.8	0.6	0.8	0.9	0.9	1.5	1.3	1.5	1.7	2.0	2.3	1.3
Nervous system	2.3	3.4	2.2	1.9	1.3	1.1	1.6	1.3	1.7	1.0	0.9	1.0
Accidents	0.6	0.5	0.5	0.4	0.3	0.4	0.4	0.3	0.4	0.1	0.5	0.4
Other	4.9	8.1	5.0	4.5	5.0	6.5	4.6	4.6	3.1	4.5	4.3	5.9
Total	22.0	31.4	22.2	18.6	16.0	18.0	16.0	13.7	12.9	13.3	12.9	14.0

* 1861–1870 these age groups comprise those aged 20–35, 35–55 and over 55.

Sources: 1861–1870: *BiSOS* A and K; 1875–1880 to 1911–1914: *BiSOS* K and SOS, Dödsorsaker; S-Berättelse om Allmänna Hälsotillståndet i Stockholm; M-Hälsovårdens berättelse, R-A (ms), and Malmö Stads Årsbok; R-SOS, Dödsoraker.

APPENDIX 5.I

The different mortality series employed in this chapter are taken from a more comprehensive data set which also includes similarly constructed series from a county and town sample. The difficulties in obtaining homogeneous crude and age-specific mortality series, especially for the eighteenth century, have already been mentioned. Another question is the general reliability of the underlying material. For example, the high mortality of the lower ages for Stockholm in the two decades after 1750 is especially striking and consequently, the later decrease may possibly be too large. However, the four county towns investigated show a similar picture. In relation to the cause of death material, reference is made to Fridlizius (1984b; 1988) and Bengtsson (1988). These investigations also provide additional references. For that reason attention is only paid here to some outstanding problems in this connection. In terms of the cause of death material in the Tabellverket between 1749 and 1830, the disease classification was changed in 1774, 1802 and 1812 as well as in 1821. Between 1861 and 1870 a special classification system was in place which was replaced by a more modern scheme in 1874. For this chapter it has therefore been necessary to incorporate some changes in the disease nomenclature.

1. PHTHISIS: During the earlier period this cause of death was registered together with pneumonia (*bröstfeber*). Between 1774 and 1801 phthisis was registered separately, while pneumonia was listed together with pains in the chest (*håll och styng*) which previously had been listed separately. For the years 1778–1782 the quota of phthisis in this disease-complex has been calculated for the different age groups for Sweden as a whole and for Stockholm. This quota has then been used for calculating the mortality from phthisis during the preceding period for the county of Malmöhus (RM) and Stockholm respectively (the figures for the county of Malmöhus for 1778–1782 could not be used). This implies that there were no structural changes in mortality from these diseases during the period. In earlier investigations using aggregate data, pine away disease (*tvinsot*) has been listed together with phthisis for the period 1749–1830 in accordance with Sundbärg (1905). However, on the basis of recent research by Cronberg (1991), there are reasons for separating pine away disease from phthisis. This has been done for the purpose of this analysis, thereby reducing mortality from phthisis in the lowest and highest ages. For the period 1861–1870 it is difficult to understand the very high figures for pine away disease in the lowest age groups. New figures have therefore been calculated which also serve to diminish the crude death rate of phthisis.

2. SMALLPOX: Between 1749 and 1773 this was listed together with measles. In order to separate mortality from the two diseases a similar approach to that of phthisis has been applied.

3. DIPHTHERIA: Although mentioned in the middle of the eighteenth century, this cause of death is not registered at all. However, during the period from 1774 to 1830 croup (*strypsjuka*) and severe septic throat (*clakartad halsfluss*) are registered separately; between 1861–1870 and 1875–1894 severe septic throat is replaced by diphtheria (*difteri*) and for 1895–1910 croup is incorporated with diphtheria. On the basis of the last nomenclature, the cited variants have been listed as diphtheria.

4. SCARLATINA: Like diphtheria, this disease is not registered in the cause of death tables during the earlier period. The reason for this was possibly that scarlatina seems to have appeared only sporadically at this time.

5. TYPHOID FEVER: Until 1875 mortality from typhus (*t. exanthematicus*) and typhoid (*t. abdominalis*) was listed as mortality from *nervfeber* or *röt-fläkfeber* (with small variations in the nomenclature). In 1875, however, a distinction was made between typhus and typhoid fever. How much of the mortality up until 1875 was caused by typhus or typhoid is uncertain. However, the last epidemic of typhus in Sweden happened in 1874–75. In the above mortality series mortality from typhus after 1875 is on the whole non-existent.

References

ATKINS, P. J. (1992), 'White poison?: the social consequences of milk consumption in London, 1850–1939', *Social History of Medicine*, **5** (2), 207–28.

BEAVER, M. W. (1973), 'Population, infant mortality and milk', *Population Studies*, **27**, 243–54.

BENGTSSON, T. (1988), 'Mortality and causes of death in Västanfors Parish, Sweden', in A. Brändström and L.-G. Tedebrand (eds), *Society, Health and Population during the Demographic Transition*, Umeå, 461–94.

BENGTSSON, T. (1990), 'Migration, wages and urbanization in 19th-century Sweden', in A. Hayami, J. de Vries and A. van der Woude (eds), *Urbanization and Population Dynamics in History*, Oxford, 186–204.

BERGMAN, R. (1963), 'De epidemiska sjukdomarna i Sverige och deras Bekämpande', in W. Kock (ed.), *Medicinalväsendet i Sverige 1813–1962*, Stockholm, 339–51.

BIDRAG TILL SVERIGES OFFICIELLA STATISTIK. A. Befolkningsstatistik; K. Hälso—och Sjukvården (1857–1914), Stockholm.

CRONBERG, C. (1991), 'Pulmonary tuberculosis and Swedish tables of causes of death around 1800', unpublished paper, University of Lund.

FOGEL, R. W. (1988), 'Nutrition and the decline in mortality since 1700: some additional preliminary findings', in A. Brändström and L.-G. Tedebrand (eds), *Society, Health and Population during the Demographic Transition*, Umeå, 369–84.

FRIDLIZIUS, G. (1979), 'Sweden', in W. R. Lee (ed.), *European Demography and Economic Growth*, London, 340–405.

FRIDLIZIUS, G. (1981), 'Handel och Sjöfart—förändringens tid', in O. Bjurling (ed.), *Malmö Stads Historia (1820–1870)*, **3**, Malmö, 289–541.

FRIDLIZIUS, G. (1984a), 'Från spannmålstunnor till smördrittlar. Malmö handel och sjöfart 1870–1914', in O. Bjurling (ed.), *Malmö Stads Historia (1870–1914)*, **4**, Malmö, 395–522.

FRIDLIZIUS, G. (1984b), 'The mortality decline in the first phase of the demographic transition: Swedish experiences', in T. Bengtsson, G. Fridlizius and R. Ohlsson (eds), *Pre-industrial Population Change*, Lund, 75–114.

FRIDLIZIUS, G. (1988), 'Sex differential mortality and socio-economic change, Sweden 1750–1910', in A. Brändström and L.-G. Tedebrand (eds), *Society, Health and Population during the Demographic Transition*, Umeå, 237–72.

FRIDLIZIUS, G. (1989), 'The deformation of cohorts: nineteenth-century mortality decline in a generational perspective', *Scandinavian Economic History Review*, **3**, 3–17.

FRIDLIZIUS, G. (1990), 'Agricultural productivity, trade and urban growth during the commercialization phase of the Swedish economic development, 1810–70', in A. Hayami, J. de Vries and A. van der Woude (eds), *Urbanization and Population Dynamics in History*, Oxford, 113–33.

HISTORISK STATISTIK FÖR SVERIGE (1959), **II**, Stockholm.

HÖGBERG, U. (1983), *Svagårens barn*, Stockholm.

HÖJER, A. (1934), 'Spädbarnsdödlighetens avtagande och orsakerna därtill', *Hygienisk revy*, **XXIII** (3), 23–49.

JÖRBERG, L. (1972), *A History of Prices in Sweden 1732–1914*, Lund.

LEE, R. (1988), 'Infant, child and maternal mortality in Western Europe: a critique', in A. Brändström and L.-G. Tedebrand (eds), *Society, Health and Population during the Demographic Transition*, Umeå, 9–22.

PURANEN, B.-I. (1984), *Tuberkulos. En sjukdoms förekomst och dess orsaker, Sverige 1750–1980*, Umeå.

ROSTOW, W. W. (1960), *The Stages of Economic Growth*, Cambridge.

SANDBERG, L. G. and R. H. STECKEL (1988), 'Over-population and malnutrition rediscovered: hard times in 19th-century Sweden', *Explorations in Economic History*, **25**, 1–19.

SCHÖN, L. (1985), *Jordbrukets omvandling och konsumtionens förändringar 1800–1870*, Lund.

SKÖLD, P. (1996), *The Two Faces of Smallpox. A Disease and its Prevention in Eighteenth- and Nineteenth-Century Sweden*, Umeå.

SÖDERBERG, J. (1982), 'Poverty and social structure in Stockholm 1850' (Research Report No. 1 in the project 'Stagnating metropolis'), Stockholm University.

SÖDERBERG, J. (1989), 'Hard times in 19th-century Sweden: a comment', *Explorations in Economic History*, **26**, 477–91.

SUNDBÄRG, G. (1905), 'Dödligheten i lungtuberkulos i Sverige 1751–1830', *Statistisk Tidskrift*, **VI**.

SUNDBÄRG, G. (1909), 'Fortsätta bidrag till en svensk befolkningsstatistik', *Statistik Tidskrift* **X**.

SUNDBÄRG, G. (1913), *Emigrationsutredningen, Betänkande*, Stockholm.

Chapter 6

POPULATION DYNAMICS AND ECONOMIC CHANGE IN TRIESTE AND ITS HINTERLAND, 1850–1914*

MARINA CATTARUZZA

THE POLITICAL AND ECONOMIC CONTEXT

The outbreak of the First World War marked a sudden interruption in the exceptional economic development of the port of Trieste which was never to recur in the history of the town. The increase in shipping tonnage arriving in the port between 1905 and 1913 exceeded that of other major continental ports (Figure 6.1). Between 1912 and 1913, after the opening of the new Franz Joseph port, port traffic increased by 907,000 net tons; only Rotterdam in that year recorded a higher increase (Camera di Commercio, 1914; Babudieri, 1962, pp. 1–8). In 1913, thanks to the record tonnage arriving in the port, Trieste was the fifth most important continental port, just behind Genoa but ahead of Bremen (Camera di Commercio, 1914; Babudieri, 1982, p. 172; see also Table 6.1). In terms of financial revenue, it was the third largest Austrian town and, with a population of 230,000 in 1910, only Vienna and Prague within the Austro-Hungarian Empire had more inhabitants.

The 'first port of the Empire' was a relatively recent construction of the Hapsburgs (Figure 6.2): at the beginning of the eighteenth century Trieste was still a self-administered town with a poor economy, dependent on saltpits, fishing and agriculture, ruled by a traditional municipal and aristocratic system and with less than 4,000 inhabitants (Martini, 1968, p. 165). In 1717, in accordance with mercantilist principles, Charles VI proclaimed the freedom of transit through the Adriatic Sea and in 1719 the port was exempted from customs duty. In 1769 Maria Theresa extended this exemption to the whole town, laying the foundations for its expansion as a commercial centre (Babudieri, 1964; Luzzatto, 1953, pp. 6–11).

Jewish, Greek, Serbian and Armenian immigrants, who were attracted to Trieste by the new economic opportunities, were granted by various statutes relative legal autonomy, full freedom of worship and the right to undertake commercial activities. These ethnic and religious groups, with their own judicial institutions, were called 'nations' (Martini, 1968, pp. 93–125). In a

* This research has been supported by a contribution from the Ministero della Pubblica Instruzione. The author wishes to thank Ellen Ginzburg for her invaluable help with the translation.

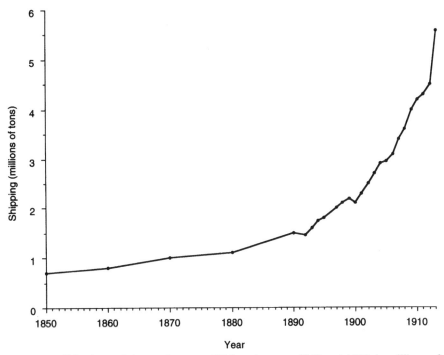

Figure 6.1: Shipping arriving at the port of Trieste between 1850 and 1913, in millions of registered tons. *Source:* Babudieri, 1982, p. 192.

Table 6.1: *Movements of maritime freight in some of the main continental European ports in 1913 (loaded and unloaded freight, in millions of quintals).*

Port	1913	Difference with respect to 1912
Hamburg	14,241,894	+ 674,000
Rotterdam	13,036,174	+ 942,000
Marseilles	10,509,048	+ 827,000
Genoa	7,089,859	− 15,000
Trieste	5,480,074	+ 907,000
Bremen	5,251,267	+ 299,000
Fiume	2,898,734	+ 334,000
Venice	2,338,009	− 227,000

Source: Babudieri, 1982 p. 172.

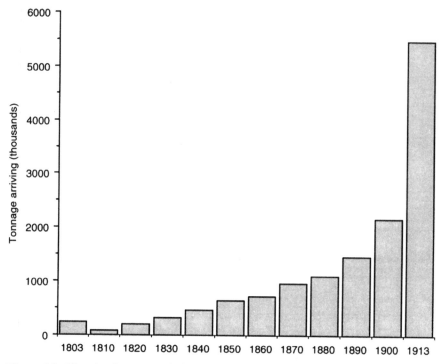

Figure 6.2: The development of the port of Trieste, 1803–1913 (arriving tonnage).
Source: Babudieri, 1982, p. 192.

short period of time a new commercial and cosmopolitan town developed adjacent to, but at the same time in contrast with, the old medieval borough: the 'new Trieste' represented a sort of island, characterized by religious tolerance and economic liberalism, in the semi-feudal and corporative background of the extremely Catholic Hapsburg Empire.

The 'nations' differed in size and in relation to social stratification and economic influence. At the beginning of the nineteenth century, for example, the Armenian 'nation' disappeared almost entirely and was abolished by decree (Martini, 1968, pp. 141–52). From an economic standpoint the Jewish 'nation' was the most powerful; it was very influential in insurance and trade and numbered 1,247 members in 1802 (Zoller, 1924; Ara, 1987). The Greek community specialized in trade with the Middle East which represented the main branch of activity in the free port. In the 1820s some Greek merchant families founded the *Adriatico Banco di Sicurtà* which, for some years, was the most important insurance company in the city (Stefani, 1960; Sapelli, 1984; Martini, 1968, pp. 126–40).

In 1802 there were 2,457 non-Catholics in Trieste, representing a significant 16.5 per cent of the total population of 17,424. According to the 1857 census there were 3,301 Jews, 623 Orthodox Greeks, 396 Protestants and 112 Greek Catholics (Martini, 1968, p. 155). It is likely that there were more, since 'foreign' residents were not recorded according to religion. Nevertheless, by the middle of the nineteenth century the descendants of eighteenth-century 'nations'—which were still recognizable as separate communities—were now a small minority, compared with the 72,298 Italian and Slovenian Catholics who increasingly dominated the town from a religious and ethnic point of view.[1] In 1880 there were 4,640 Jews, 1,861 Orthodox Greeks, 80 Catholic Greeks, 1,598 Protestants and 217 people without a declared religion in Trieste (K. K. Statistische Central-Commission, 1882, pp. 34–35) out of a total population of 144,844 inhabitants.

Further differences were evident on a residential basis: the wealthier part of the Serbian 'nation' was concentrated near the Orthodox church in a strategic position for the docks and warehouses. Even in 1918 an observer noticed that the orthodox Serbian community occupied one of the best locations in the city, centred on the church of Saint Spiridion, with its own Serbian school and ethnic societies (Primorac, 1918, p. 69). The poorer elements of the Jewish community, however, had to remain in the ghetto, even after 1785 when Jews were permitted to settle anywhere (Martini, 1968, p. 120). Despite the specific characteristics of each 'nation', 'newcomers' shared an early bourgeois entrepreneurial mentality and a vague belief in the House of Hapsburg founded on utilitarian and contractualist precepts based on the principle of *allgemeine Wohlfahrt* (general welfare).[2]

In 1755 the *corpo mercantile* was established as the representative organ of trade interests in Trieste. From then onwards the most important merchants were able to exercise broad rights of self-government concerning navigation laws and commercial transactions through the stock exchange (Kandler, 1864, pp. 216–19). The cosmopolitan merchants, organized on a corporate basis, by now had replaced completely the local aristocrats as the recognized urban élite of Trieste.

During the Napoleonic Wars Trieste was occupied twice by French troops and this period, as a whole, was characterized by economic stagnation (Good, 1980, p. 252). The French governor of the Illyric provinces, Marmont, gave the following description of the region in his memoirs: its population amounted to almost two million individuals and was composed of Germans, Illyrians, Italians and Albanians and people from all countries gathered together in Trieste (Marmont, 1857, Vol. III, pp. 341–42). To this extent it represented a 'melting-pot of populations' (Vivante, 1912, p. 22). In the 1830s new economic activities developed: in 1836 a local association of insurers and traders set up a

---

1 *Popolazione* ... (1859), p. 2. At that time there were a further 38,574 foreign inhabitants in Trieste of unknown religion.

2 On the unofficial pact between the commercial élite and the imperial authorities, see Apih (1957, pp. 40–77) and Negrelli (1978, pp. 32–69).

company for steam navigation called the *Società di navigazione a vapore del Lloyd Austriaco*, which was to remain the most important Austrian shipping company until the fall of the empire (Coons, 1982, pp. 49–54). The *Assicurazioni Generali* (1831) and the *Riunione Adriatica di Sicurtà* (1838) were also set up by Jewish and Greek traders and in a short period of time they transformed the town into one of the most important European insurance centres (*Assicurazioni Generali*, 1931; Stefani, 1931, pp. 33–70; Sapelli, 1984).

In the course of the eighteenth century insurance was to become one of the main economic activities of many European ports. In Trieste, however, it became the most important economic activity because of the sharp decline in freight transportation in the 1840s[3] and as a reaction to the persistent inadequacies of the existing credit and financial infrastructure (Sapelli, 1984, p. 825). Local capital in search of investment opportunities was increasingly channelled towards a branch of business which had rapidly overcome the limits and weaknesses of the port itself. Insurance companies based in Trieste initially extended their activity from Austria to the Italian states and Switzerland and later to all European countries (Stefani, 1931, pp. 70–182). Between 1879 and 1882 the *Assicurazioni Generali*, for example, opened agencies in Bombay, Colombo, Shangai, Hong Kong, etc. (Stefani, 1931, p. 182) and even competed with important English insurance companies in overseas markets.

The economic boom of the 1830s resulted in a large population increase, mainly due to in-migration. The population of Trieste, which numbered 31,589 people in 1801, had dropped to 24,633 by 1812 as a result of the French occupation. By 1815 it had increased to approximately 45,000 and in 1840 had jumped to 80,414, which represented an increase of almost 80 per cent. Thereafter the population remained relatively stable: in 1850 there were 82,596 inhabitants in the town (Montanelli, 1905, p. 50). The 1859 census, which registered a total population of 109,707, provides an indication of the spatial origins of the 38,574 'foreigners'. The major area from which in-migrants came was the immediate hinterland of the port; 16,467 'foreigners' were from the *Küstenland* (coastal area) and 5,599 had migrated from Carniola. In-migration increased in the second half of the nineteenth century, with a large number of immigrants coming from the provinces of Lombardy and Venice (9,841 individuals) which were at that time Austrian territories (*Popolazione...*, 1859, p. 6). This movement decreased after the founding of the Kingdom of Italy in 1861. Only in the first decade of the twentieth century did migration from Italy resume again with renewed force.

As far as industrial activity was concerned, it remained more or less unchanged from the eighteenth century to the end of the nineteenth century. It was not until the final abolition of the port's customs privileges in 1891 that a

---

3 On the structural causes for the crisis of the port, see Nereo Salvi (1961, pp. 201–65, especially p. 212).

new kind of industrial development finally emerged. In Trieste up to that time industrial and manufacturing firms to a large extent were connected directly with port and shipping activities; ship-yards, rope-making, wax and bottle factories and artisan-based cooperage predominated. In addition, some small industrial firms had developed which processed raw materials from overseas for re-export, such as tanneries, soap-works, sugar refineries and food-processing factories for making chocolate, liquors, etc. (Babudieri, 1982, pp. 93–102, 134): grain milling was also increasingly important (Matis, 1972, p. 125).

The reforms of the neo-absolutist period after the 1848 Revolution, including the *Grundentlastung* (agrarian reform legislation) and *Gewerbefreiheit* (freedom of trade), represented for the Hapsburg Monarchy an important break with its semi-feudal past and provided the basis for industrial development (Matis, 1973, pp. 29–41; Rudolph, 1983). The Minister of Commerce of the 'Bach Era', Karl Ludwig von Bruck, was one of the most active supporters of this development. As an advocate of economic liberalism he was connected with the commercial circles of Trieste, a co-founder of the Austrian Lloyd and a prominent member of the Society for Surveying the Suez Canal (*Società di studio per il Canale di Suez*) (Treue, 1970, pp. 536–38).

The abolition of domestic customs duties and a vast programme of railway construction (Bachinger, 1973, pp. 284–87) were carried out during the Bruck administration; they represented the first steps towards the economic integration of the Monarchy's territory, as the state finally was forced to respond to social class and interest group pressure (Matis, 1973, pp. 29–41; Good, 1984, 1988). According to Karl von Bruck and the small circle of supporters of economic liberalism, Trieste was to become the focal point for the economic penetration of the Far East by 'Greater Austria' (or *Mitteleuropa*) and also an obvious port for ships travelling to the Near East through the Suez Canal (Treue, 1970, pp. 537–38). However, after the defeat of Austria by the Prussian army at Königgrätz in 1866 the dream of the House of Hapsburg exercising overwhelming influence over the German Confederation was shattered once and for all. German unification was carried out under Prussian aegis (the so-called *kleindeutsche Lösung*), thus destroying the idea of a Central European Empire 'with 70 million inhabitants' which would have necessitated extensive plans to develop the port of Trieste. In 1869 a French company carried out the work for the Suez Canal and the only part of Karl Bruck's vast plan that was ever implemented was the Trieste–Vienna railway line. Trieste, as the main port of Austria within the framework of the pattern of world trade, remained on the outer periphery of a minor sea (Böhme, 1966, p. 152; Treue, 1970, pp. 554–55).

Trieste finally became part of the customs territory of the Hapsburg Monarchy in 1891 (Babudieri, 1982, pp. 145–47). Free ports, such as Buccari, Carlopago, Fiume, Porto Ré, Trieste and Zengg (Matis, 1972, p. 377), were places where unrestricted commercial transactions could take place, but at the same time they were completely isolated territorially from their hinterland. Certainly by the mid-nineteenth century they had undergone a period of crisis throughout Europe as the strengthening of national economic policies, which implied a uniform customs policy, undermined the specific commercial interests of many free ports (Salvi, 1961). At the same time the transport revolution (railway construction, steam navigation, new shipping companies, etc.) and improvements in communications (the telegraph and telephone) had facilitated long-distance transactions, thus striking a hard blow at commercial centres like Trieste which had been developed within the context of a slow, irregular and unreliable system of communication. Moreover, the abolition of the British Navigation Acts and the fact that the English, Spanish and Portuguese colonies in the Americas had obtained their independence also facilitated direct commercial relations between European powers and former colonies, thus making the intermediary role of the free ports even more obsolete (Salvi, 1961; Mathies, 1924).

After its inclusion in the Austrian customs territory Trieste developed as a centre of mixed commercial and industrial activity. Industrial plants were set up with direct government support which, with the abolition of the free port, had decreed a ten-year exemption from taxes for new industries. By 1891 the main Austrian bank for the financing of industrial enterprises, the *Credit-Anstalt für Handel und Gewerbe* (Alberti, 1915, pp. 60–65),[4] had already contributed to the foundation of an oil refinery in Trieste and later participated as a major shareholder in the establishment of a linoleum factory. By the beginning of the twentieth century the ship-building industry and the Austrian Lloyd had also passed under the direct control of the Viennese banks (Weichs-Glon, Freiherr zu, 1912, p. 11; Křížek, 1963, p. 108). In 1895, the *Krainische Industrie-Gesellschaft*, which owned some iron- and steel-works in Styria, developed a modern blast furnace plant on the outskirts of Trieste for the production of pig-iron which was then used as a raw material by the steel-works and rolling-mills in the interior. Between 1891 and 1893 a number of factories were set up in the city for the production of seed oil and two were founded for rice-peeling: a few years later a jute factory was also established (Mastrolonardo, 1921, pp. 29, 231–90). Such industrial sectors, characterized by a low technological level and dependent on raw material imports, were typical of the economic structure of many port-cities in that period.[5]

In summary, placing Trieste within the customs territory of the Monarchy brought about the following changes in its industrial structure. First, it fostered the development of more modern industries (iron-works, a linoleum factory, an oil refinery), based on the traditional practice of working with imported raw

4 For the role of the *Credit-Anstalt für Handel und Gewerbe* in financing Austrian industry, see Eduard März (1968), passim. The *Credit-Anstall* had already been involved in the foundation of the *Banca Commerciale Triestine* in 1858 (März and Socher, 1973, pp. 334–35).

5 For an overview of the economic structure of Hamburg, see Friedrich Jerchow (1984, pp. 46–56); see also Wischermann, chapter 8 below.

materials and reinforcing the clear connection between industrial and commercial activities. Secondly, many of the new industries were promoted by Viennese finance capital through the *Credit-Anstalt für Handel und Gewerbe* and the *Wiener Bankverein* (Rudolph, 1976), which marked the end of the hegemony of indigenous capital (both commercial and insurance) in local economic activities. Thirdly, it reintegrated local industry in the internal market of the Monarchy and this trend was reinforced by the abolition of the customs border dividing Trieste from its hinterland in 1891.

About fifty years after the Bruck administration there was a second (and last) attempt to initiate a process of economic modernization in the Monarchy and to develop an open system of exchange between the agricultural and industrial sectors (especially between the Austrian and Hungarian territories). Within the framework of a vast project for the construction of railways and navigable canals (Matis, 1972; Gerschenkron, 1977) Prime Minister Koerber proposed further improvements in 1901 for the port of Trieste and the creation of a second railway link with the interior. This plan was intended to accomplish the effective economic integration of the various territories (*Länder*) of the Monarchy, to open the country to international trade and to promote a progressive equalization between industrial and agricultural areas by means of an investment programme for the most backward *Länder* (Matis, 1973, pp. 56–59).

Although the plan was approved by Parliament and was supported in industrial, commercial and banking circles, it was only partially implemented and did not succeed in promoting the 'integrated' economic development of the various *Länder* of Cisleithania (the territory of Austria as defined in the Dual Settlement of 1867). On the one hand, the Finance Minister, Böhm-Bawerk, was concerned that state resources might be considerably reduced by unnecessary expenditure: on the other hand, the Koerber plan was boycotted by agrarian interest groups which feared that the new canals and river improvement schemes might favour grain imports from Russia (Gerschenkron, 1977; Good, 1991, p. 233).

In 1904 national conflicts caused the fall of the Koerber administration so that the navigable canals were never built: only the new Franz Joseph port and the second railway link between Trieste and the interior were implemented. Trieste thereby became one of the major development areas in the Monarchy, although Koerber's hopes were not fulfilled since balanced economic growth between the various *Länder* of the Hapsburg Monarchy was not achieved (Matis, 1972, pp. 390, 446). The persistence of traditional protectionist policies prior to 1914 that prioritized prestigious investments and rearmament prevented the implementation of new economic policies (Matis, 1972, p. 390 *et seq.*; Tapiè, 1972).

The persistent weakness of Austrian exports in world markets constituted a major constraint on the expansion of the port of Trieste. In the eighteenth century the Hapsburgs had not succeeded in achieving their aim of supplying international markets with Austrian manufactured products exported through the free port (Luzzatto, 1953, p. 10). In fact Trieste had become increasingly isolated from its hinterland. Even during the most favourable period of the port's activity between 1905 and 1913 raw material imports for local industry and the hinterland constantly exceeded exports, so that Trieste in 1913 was ranked fifth in continental Europe in terms of port traffic but only tenth in terms of the value of freight handled (Table 6.1) (Vivante, 1912, p. 235).

Table 6.2, which shows the value of freight which passed through Trieste in 1913, provides confirmation of an increased degree of integration between the former free port and its hinterland. The bulk of the freight handled in Trieste either originated from or was destined for Central Europe.

In 1911 the *Industrierat*, a consultative body for industry connected with the Ministry of Commerce, summarized as follows the position of Austria in international markets:

We excel only in three sectors, i.e., in industrial products that depend on agriculture such as sugar, lard and wood. The chemical, iron and mechanical industries are the backbone of German exports, accounting for 40 per cent. The iron industry plays a similar or identical role in other big exporting countries. Our industries contribute less than ten per cent to exports...

In this situation, we cannot aspire to being a great exporting power and no supportive measure can help us achieve this status. We export only half of what France does, less than small Belgium and only twice as much as Switzerland. (Büro des Industrierates, 1911)

However, no other economic area in Austria was dependent to such an extent on the decisions of central government as Trieste. The volatile cyclical pattern of port-city development therefore provides an important means of interpreting the history of the Hapsburg Monarchy during its last period, torn between its destiny as a 'Great Power' and the *de facto* impossibility of carrying out this role.[6]

Table 6.2: *The origins of imports and exports handled by the port of Trieste in 1913, in millions of crowns.*

Region	Imports	Exports
Central Europe (by rail)	845	740
The Balkans and Dalmatia (by rail and ship)	101	253
Russia	9	10
The Middle East, Greece, Egypt	185	355

Source: Babudieri, 1962, p. 14.

6 The 'tragic' condition of the Hapsburg Monarchy has been masterfully described by Robert Musil (1952, p. 33).

DEMOGRAPHIC GROWTH AND IN-MIGRATION

The demographic development of Trieste between the middle of the nineteenth century and 1910 to a large extent reflected the overall pattern of economic trends (Table 6.3 and Figure 6.3).[7] Demographic growth was mainly caused by in-migration from the rural hinterland (Helczmanovszki, 1979, p.35),[8] a phenomenon common to many urban centres in the nineteenth century. In comparison with the demographic growth of other Austrian cities which were heavily dependent on in-migration, the urbanization of Trieste, even as late as 1890, remained within moderate limits. According to the 1890 census 73.2 per cent of the population of Linz had been born elsewhere; in Prague the relative proportion was 74.7 per cent, in Vienna 65.2 per cent, in Ljubljaná 75.8 per cent and in Maribor 85.7 per cent. In Trieste, on the other hand, 61 per cent of the resident population came from the town (*Österreichische Statistik*, 1893a, p. IX), and even in 1910 the native element in the port-city's population was still 57 per cent (*Österreichische Statistik*, 1912).

An eminent local demographer, Paolo Luzzato-Fegiz, calculated the relative contribution of in-migration and natural increase to Trieste's population development (Luzzato-Fegiz, 1929, p. 18) (see Table 6.4). There were two phases in the pattern of migration. Up to 1890, when the urban labour market was characterized by a phase of stagnation, in-migration was the result of socio-economic adjustment processes in the agricultural areas of Carniola and

Table 6.3: *The demographic development of Trieste, 1857–1913.*

Year	Total population	Increase (%)
1857	104,707	–
1869	123,098	17.56
1875	126,633	2.87
1880	144,844	14.38
1890	157,466	8.71
1900	178,599	13.42
1910	229,510	28.50
1913	240,834	4.93

Source: Official census returns.

7 The statistical data relating to the demographic growth of Trieste and urban in-migration have been taken from the general censuses of 1857, 1880, 1890, 1900 and 1910 and from the local census of 1875: see *Popolazione* ... (1859); *La popolazione* ... (1878); *Osterreichische Statistik*, **I–II** (1881 and 1882), **XXXII** (1893a and b), **XXXIII** (1894), **LXIII** (1902–1903), **LXIV** (1903), **LXV** (1903–1905), new series, **I** (1914), **II** (1912–13), **III** (1915a and b).
8 The hinterland of Trieste included the county of Gorizia and Gradisca, the Margraviate of Istria and the Land Carniola.

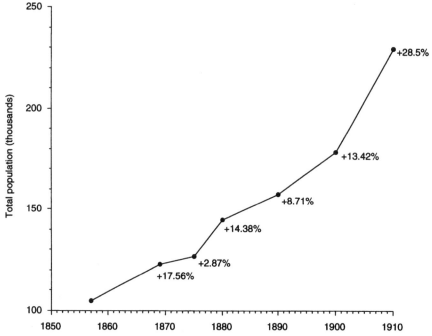

Figure 6.3: The increase in the population of Trieste, 1857–1910. *Sources:* Author's calculations; Comune di Trieste, 1873–1914; Comune di Trieste, 1904–1914. See also Table 6.3.

Table 6.4: *The relative contribution of in-migration and natural increase to Trieste's population growth, 1881–1910.*

Period	Absolute increase	Natural increase	Net in-migration
1881–1890	12,622	4,444	+ 8,178
1891–1900	21,133	4,225	+ 16,908
1901–1910	50,911	14,374	+ 36,537

Source: Luzzato-Fegiz, 1929, p.18.

the County of Gorizia. Until the mid-nineteenth century the Slovenian territories of Carniola and the areas around Gorizia still represented a closed rural economy; the rural peasant communities enjoyed pasturage and timber rights on feudal lands in return for compulsory labour services in accordance with customs sanctioned by centuries-old traditions. In 1848 agrarian reform legislation (the *Grundentlastung* of 7 December) abolished feudal servitude and recognized full private property rights for the peasantry. These measures triggered off a process of rationalization in the agricultural areas of Slovenia. The division of most common lands among the indigenous inhabitants of the villages led to the formation of a network of medium-sized, family-run farms. The flourishing Slovenian co-operative movement was based on these farms and the expanding urban centres created a buoyant demand for their agricultural produce.[9]

However, the collapse of the traditional economic system based on agrarian subsistence and the progressive integration of the Slovenian economy into international markets led to the expulsion from the countryside of the lower strata of rural society. Servants (*Gesinde*), seasonal workers, landless peasants, younger sons and daughters, who were now surplus to the needs of the market economy, were forced to migrate *en masse* (Luzzato-Fegiz, 1929, p. 20; Cattaruzza, 1978, pp. 36–55).Thousands of young peasants between the ages of 14 and 30 emigrated from Carniola and the areas around Gorizia to Trieste and reinforced the relative proportion of individuals in the productive age group (between 14 and 59 years of age) in the town's total population (*Österreichische Statistik*, 1893b, pp. 80–81; 1914, pp. 106–09). They joined other in-migrants in Trieste from the rural hinterland and from Friuli and were frequently employed in port activities and general transportation after the founding of the free port (Apih, 1957, p. 78; *Popolazione*..., 1859, p. 6). By contrast immigrants from the Middle East, from Italy and the German states, including a Jewish element as previously indicated, belonged to the middle-class elements within the city.

Women mostly migrated to Trieste while the men preferred to move to the industrial centres of Lower Austria and Styria (see Table 6.5). In this respect, as an Austrian demographer observed:

Table 6.5: *The place of birth of Trieste residents (men and women), 1890.*

Place of birth	Men	Women
Carinthia	574	1,183
Carniola	3,100	6,092
Areas around Gorizia	7,822	9,640
Istria	4,507	4,714

Source: Census data.

9 For the economic changes that occurred in the hinterland of Trieste, see Marina Cattaruzza (1978, pp. 21–66, especially pp. 28–63).

the most powerful gravitational communities of big urban centres such as Vienna, Trieste and Central Bohemia, housed more women than men. The prevalence of the female sex—employed as household servants—and the widespread and often concomitant aspiration to settle in the big city, are enough to explain this. (*Österreichische Statistik*, 1893a, p. LXXIV)

Starting from 1890 a second phase in the pattern of migration can be detected. With the expansion of the urban labour market and significant industrialization male in-migration became more predominant, thus producing a balanced sex ratio among the younger age groups. By contrast, the labour market for women became stagnant. Domestic service, which represented the main occupation for in-migrant women in Trieste, witnessed only a modest expansion in the numbers employed from 7,219 in 1890 to 7,803 by 1910. Total female employment among industrial workers actually decreased from 8,276 in 1890 to 5,211 in 1900 and to only 3,928 by 1910. For the first time during the period under consideration there was a higher level of male than female net migration into Trieste between 1890 and 1900, with male and female in-migrants exceeding out-migrants by 9,105 and 7,803 respectively (*Österreichische Statistik*, 1902, pp. XXVI–XXVII). By 1910 the preponderance of women in the port-city had decreased: whereas in 1890 there had been 9,815 more women than men in Trieste, by 1910 there were just 4,894 more women. The greatest decrease took place in the number of women in the age group 24–30, an age group particularly sensitive to changing levels of in-migration (*Österreichische Statistik*, 1893b; 1914). By 1910 the balance between in-migrant men and women was as shown in Table 6.6.

Until 1890 Trieste had been roughly speaking a sort of 'passive receptacle' for the agricultural labour surplus; during the second phase between 1890 and 1914 the town actively attracted the neighbouring rural population. The attraction of the urban labour market caused a real 'escape from the land' which led to the gradual deterioration of many farm estates owned by the upper class (Moritsch, 1969, pp. 20–56).

New areas and social groups were now involved in the migratory process, like the peasants and labourers from Istria—one of the most backward *Länder*

Table 6.6: *Gender-specific migration into Trieste, 1910.*

Place of birth	Resident in Trieste	
	Men	*Women*
Carniola	4,553	6,870
Areas around Gorizia	10,407	11,785
Istria	10,215	10,070

Source: Census data.

of the Monarchy—and the peasants of the Friuli lowlands who had been reduced to poverty by competition from American cereal imports. Between 1910 and 1913, when the town underwent its phase of maximum development, there was also strong in-migration from the Kingdom of Italy: in 1915, when Italy entered the war, the Austrian police held a census of the Italian population which revealed about 50,000 Italian subjects living in Trieste.[10]

The data in Table 6.7 show how migration from those areas within the traditional gravitational influence of Trieste gradually gave way to a wave of migration from Istria and from Italy. Most of the people moving to Trieste from abroad were in fact Italians (see also Figure 6.4).

Despite these changes in the pattern of migration, as well as in the national and gender composition of in-migrants, there was no substantial modification to the age structure of the urban population (Table 6.8). The larger percentage of children under 13 years of age in 1910, compared with 1880, was due to a small decrease in the mortality rate, mostly in the age group one to five years, and also to the high birth rate of in-migrants from the countryside who were now present in the town to a greater extent. The youngest age group (0–13), however, remained much smaller in comparison with predominantly rural regions; in Carniola 35 per cent of the population was under 13 years old; in Istria and in the County of Gorizia and Gradisca the figure was about 34 per cent (*Österreichische Statistik*, 1893b; 1914).[11]

Women were employed largely in domestic service and as dressmakers and laundresses. They were registered both as self-employed and as employees or apprentices in small shops. A third area of female employment—which declined, however, after the abolition of free port privileges—consisted in

Table 6.7: *The spatial origins of migrants into Trieste (per 10,000 inhabitants), 1890–1910.*

Year	Carniola	Trieste region	Areas around Gorizia	Istria	From abroad
1890	583	6,095	1,109	585	937
1900	570	5,963	1,040	798	902
1910	498	5,696	967	884	1,170

Source: Census data.

10 Verwaltungsarchiv Vienna, Innenministerium. Präsidiale, 16893, Die Tätigkeit der k.k. Polizeidirektion in Triest im Jahre 1915–16.
11 See also for the age structure of Trieste in 1880, 'Die Ergebnisse der Volkszählung vom 31 December 1880, Die Bevölkerung der im Reichsrate vertretenen Königreiche und Länder', *Österreichische Statistik*, Vol. II, Part I, Vienna, 1882, pp. 128–32.

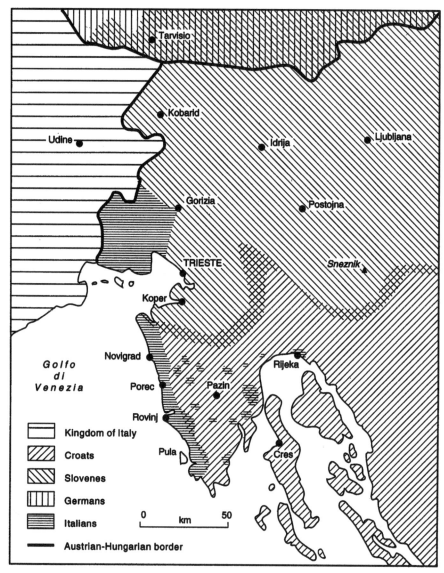

Figure 6.4: National and ethnic composition of the main supply areas of migrants to Trieste. *Source:* Map worked out on the basis of Parovel, 1985, p. 8.

Table 6.8: *The age structure of the population of Trieste, 1880 and 1910.*

Age group (in years)	1880		1910	
	Total	*%*	*Total*	*%*
0–13	35,585	24.5	61,972	27.0
14–23	27,045	18.6	43,148	18.8
24–30	18,379	12.7	31,309	13.6
31–40	22,054	15.2	34,953	15.2
41–50	17,550	12.1	24,647	10.7
51–60	12,903	9.0	17,952	7.9
61–70	7,489	5.2	10,362	4.5
70 +	3,839	2.7	5,167	2.2
Total	144,844	100	229,510	100

Source: Census data.

peeling coffee beans and incense and in sorting and packaging citrus fruits inside port warehouses. A small percentage of women also worked as unskilled labourers in food-processing factories, in printing shops and distilleries (Cattaruzza, 1979, pp. 107–09).

Migrant men were employed in the key sectors of the town's economy such as the port, various building trades (including the construction of docks and railways) and also as common labourers in the ship-yards and in the iron-works (Cattaruzza, 1979, pp. 147–58).[12] The port and the building trades were branches which were characterized by irregular employment, as they were influenced by both climatic and seasonal factors. In-migrants, therefore, were subject to precarious employment conditions, a situation that was aggravated by the refusal of local entrepreneurs to introduce more regular employment schemes. After Lemberg, Trieste had the highest percentage of casually employed labourers (*Taglöhner mit wechselnder Beschäftigung*) among all the towns of the Monarchy: in 1910 they constituted 13 per cent of the employed population, but in the building trades and transport sectors their proportion rose to 20.1 per cent (*Österreichische Statistik*, 1915b). The lack of employment stability for most of the male working class not only retarded and weakened the process of trade union organization, but also caused widespread instability which affected the living conditions, health and survival of large sections of the urban population.

12 For a statistical overview of the main occupational groups within the population of Trieste, see
Österreichische Statistik (1882, pp. 98–107; 1894, pp. 38–93; 1904; 1915a, pp. 2–37, 56–63).

NATURAL POPULATION GROWTH

During the second half of the nineteenth century natural population growth remained within moderate limits.[13] As a matter of fact a very high mortality rate—especially in relation to infants and children—produced a precarious annual balance between births and deaths, in contrast to a significant birth surplus registered for Austria as a whole and for other European states such as Germany and England (Costantini, 1888, p. 36). Up to 1914 Trieste recorded birth and mortality rates which were higher than those of most Austrian and European cities. However, within this context, it is possible to isolate specific cycles which were the result of economic trends and demographic fluctuations. Between 1876 and 1896 the birth rate followed an irregular trend, with peaks of 40.6 per 1,000 inhabitants in 1876 and 1879 and troughs of around 26–27 in 1892 and 1895 (Table 6.9).[14] These fluctuations reflected not only the changing total population of Trieste between different census years, but also the mobility of that part of the population which commuted on a temporary basis to the city. In periods of economic depression and rising unemployment members of this group frequently returned to their place of origin.[15]

Between censuses population growth was estimated according to the average growth of the preceding decade and the figures are therefore somewhat imprecise (see Figure 6.3). Estimates of population growth for the decades 1881–1890 and 1901–1910 are more accurate. Since 1909 the city council made partial estimates of the population between censuses and these provide a more reliable basis for calculating actual population growth.

The absolute number of births in the late-nineteenth century fluctuated considerably: Trieste recorded the highest number of new-born children (5,542) in 1873 and the lowest in 1892 (4,794) (see Table 6.10). Starting from 1899 the number of births showed a rising trend, reaching a peak of 7,287 in 1910 (Comune di Trieste, 1911, p. 17), but declining marginally in the following years up to 1914, although the resident population continued to increase. However, by the outbreak of war Trieste was the town within the Monarchy with the highest birth rate after Innsbruck (Comune di Trieste, 1915, p. 18). The generally downward trend in the birth rate (Shorter, 1977), however, did not completely change the town's position in relation to the other urban areas of the Monarchy. The birth rate in Trieste fell from almost

13 Since the population's growth was deeply influenced by social factors in general, by attitudinal factors, as well as by gender power relations, I am critical of the use of the normal demographic definition 'natural growth'.

14 These statistical data and those following have been calculated—if there are not different indications—on the basis of Comune di Trieste (1876–1914; 1904–1914).

15 Given the present availability of relevant source material, the extent of commuting is not quantifiable. However, some indications can be found in Moritsch (1969, p. 132) and in Cattaruzza (1979, p. 118).

Table 6.9: *Annual crude birth, marriage and death rates per 1,000 in Trieste, 1875–1914.*

	Birth rate (live births)	Marriage rate	Death rate
1875	39.42	9.20	35.27
1876	40.60	n.a.	35.30
1877	37.80	8.19	34.70
1878	35.70	8.10	34.70
1879	40.60	8.65	43.20
1880	33.32	8.12	32.09
1881	30.30	8.17	30.80
1882	38.11	n.a.	28.90
1883	34.89	8.00	29.68 (smallpox epidemic)
1884	32.13	8.37	45.97 (smallpox epidemic)
1885	40.59	8.16	30.84 (smallpox epidemic)
1886	40.08	7.81	32.11 (cholera epidemic)
1887	36.37	8.32	38.24
1888	34.29	8.36	31.66
1889	31.13	7.78	31.66
1890	31.37	7.93	28.82
1891	33.03	7.24	39.41
1892	26.31	n.a.	27.08
1893	32.18	7.30	35.39
1894	33.94	8.04	19.97
1895	27.12	7.71	27.32
1896	29.85	8.23	31.18
1897	32.00	7.92	27.10
1898	32.70	8.74	28.60
1899	34.70	8.73	36.80
1900	30.55	8.39	27.27
1901	31.80	9.21	25.40
1902	33.10	8.54	26.10
1903	32.20	8.81	25.80
1904	33.50	8.46	25.80
1905	31.80	8.45	28.20
1906	33.90	8.97	25.70
1907	31.90	9.00	25.40
1908	32.80	8.56	24.20
1909	32.54	8.15	24.60
1910	32.90	8.10	22.41
1911	29.60	7.54	23.90
1912	29.70	7.71	20.90
1913	28.62	6.92	21.28
1914	26.30	n.a.	19.70

Source: Commune di Trieste, 1873–1914; 1904–1914.

Table 6.10: *Total live births (legitimate and illegitimate) in Trieste and the proportion of illegitimate births per 100 live births, 1873–1913.*

	Total live births	Legitimate	Illegitimate	Proportion of illegitimate births per 100 live births
1873	5,542	4,657	885	15.97
1874	4,595	3,996	599	13.03
1875	4,993	4,181	812	16.26
1876	5,160	4,261	899	17.42
1877	4,822	3,966	856	17.75
1878	4,926	4,020	906	18.39
1879	4,929	4,057	872	17.69
1880	4,827	3,998	829	17.17
1881	n.a.	n.a.	n.a.	n.a.
1882	5,126	4,241	885	17.26
1883	5,107	4,299	808	15.82
1884	5,085	4,281	804	15.81
1885	5,040	4,221	819	16.25
1886	5,307	4,433	874	16.46
1887	5,191	4,299	892	17.18
1888	4,973	4,195	778	15.64
1889	5,156	4,423	733	14.21
1890	4,941	4,237	704	14.24
1891	5,023	4,275	746	14.85
1892	4,794	3,975	819	17.08
1893	4,969	4,228	741	14.91
1894	5,012	4,186	820	16.36
1895	4,986	4,216	770	15.44
1896	5,046	4,218	828	16.40
1897	5,170	4,400	770	14.89
1898	5,159	4,336	823	15.95
1899	5,353	4,535	818	15.28
1900	5,457	4,631	826	15.13
1901	5,648	4,684	964	17.07
1902	5,981	4,996	985	16.47
1903	5,916	4,890	1,026	17.34
1904	6,347	5,276	1,071	16.87
1905	6,093	5,048	1,045	17.15
1906	6,623	5,488	1,135	17.13
1907	6,609	5,427	1,182	17.88
1908	6,934	5,697	1,237	17.83
1909	7,079	n.a.	n.a.	n.a.
1910	7,287	5,975	1,312	18.00
1911	6,785	n.a.	n.a.	n.a.
1912	6,959	5,642	1,317	18.92
1913	6,895	5,553	1,342	19.46

Source: Comune di Trieste, 1873–1914; 1904–1914.

Table 6.11: *The proportion of marriages registered in Trieste where the wife or husband was under 30 years old, 1873–1914 (per cent).*

Year	Wife under 30	Husband under 30
1873	68.14	52.80
1875	71.67	57.68
1880	68.00	53.00
1885	72.28	55.35
1890	70.40	55.00
1895	70.00	55.00
1900	73.00	58.00
1905	75.68	60.50
1910	73.38	59.62
1911	77.86	63.20
1912	78.54	63.80
1913	79.30	62.00
1914	77.29	63.72

Source: Comune di Trieste, 1873–1914; 1904–1914.

35 per 1,000 in 1899 to 28.62 in 1913 (Table 6.9), but in the same year the birth rate for Vienna was 17.67. All the other cities in the Monarchy, including Prague (23.37), Graz (26.7), Budapest (25.67) and Salzburg (21.27), had lower birth rates. The persistently high birth rate in Trieste throughout this period undoubtedly reflected the role of in-migration in urban growth and the age structure of the immigrant population; it was also related to the economic structure of the port, where the ability of male workers to obtain peak wages at a comparatively young age encouraged early marriage. The proportion of marriages in Trieste involving either a wife or husband under 30 also rose perceptibly between 1873 and 1914 (Table 6.11). If only 68 per cent of all wives married under the age of 30 in 1880, by 1913 this proportion had risen to almost 80 per cent, reflecting a noticeable decline in the average age at marriage (Cattaruzza, 1979, pp. 60 ff). A local medical officer, Dr Achille Costantini, commented on the number of new births in 1909:

> The births in 1909 amount to 7,079 (excluding those still-born), which has never happened before ... and it corresponds to 32.90 per 1,000 inhabitants, i.e., a higher figure than that of the main cities of the Monarchy (Vienna 22.1, Graz 28, Ljubljanà 24.9, Prague 26.6, Brünn 26.9, Linz 27.8, Lemberg 32.7, Czernowitz 32.5). Only Innsbruck had a higher rate (41.6). In general, an excessive birth rate is not a sign of welfare, and it anyway contributes to an increasing death rate, especially in a town where child mortality is, as in Trieste, still very high. (Costantini, 1910, p. 2)

Moreover, there are other factors that support the definition of the years 1898–99 as a sort of demographic 'watershed'. A number of important demographic indicators, which had previously been characterized by a certain volatility, now revealed a distinct trend. Both the percentage and absolute number of illegitimate births increased (Table 6.10), while the overall mortality rate fell below 30 per 1,000 (Table 6.9). Adult mortality had already fallen after 1886, the year of the last cholera epidemic. This, in turn, reflected an expansion of the labour market, a greater stability of the immigrant population and a relative improvement in living conditions.

However, as far as infant and child mortality was concerned, Trieste held an anomalous position among other European cities. During the 1870s 50 per cent of the children born in Trieste died before they reached five years of age (Castiglioni, 1877, pp. 13–15) and this contributed to rising overall mortality rates that reached over 40 per 1,000 in 1879 and 1884 (Table 6.9). This figure was very high in comparison with almost all other European cities, apart from Budapest, which suffered extensively from diphtheria and smallpox. In the years that followed child mortality (1–5) decreased considerably, but the proportional contribution of infant deaths (0–1) to total mortality remained relatively high (Table 6.12), despite the fact that the infant mortality rate registered a slight decline by the early-twentieth century (Table 6.13). By 1905 20.8 per cent of legitimate children still died before they were one and 29.2 per cent of illegitimate children failed to survive the first year of life (Costantini, 1906, p. 10). Although illegitimate infant mortality fell from the late 1890s onwards (Table 6.13) it still remained considerably higher than the mortality levels of legitimate offspring. Between 1905 and 1913 registered illegitimate births constituted 18–19 per cent of total births, but the proportion of infant deaths accounted for by illegitimate children fluctuated between 23 and 26 per cent. The significant extent and increasing level of illegitimacy in the port-city of Trieste immediately prior to the First World War (Table 6.10) was a further factor in the persistence of high overall infant mortality rates. The situation was further aggravated by an exceptionally high incidence of still births per 1,000 live births (Table 6.13), at least in comparison with other European countries (del Panta, 1979, p. 228) which tended to increase in the years immediately prior to the outbreak of the First World War.

In comparison with the larger cities of the Hapsburg Monarchy the treatment of illegitimate children in Trieste evinced certain specific characteristics. In particular the custom of sending new-born babies to peasant women in the countryside was almost unknown, as was the practice of raising foster children *(Pflegekinder)* for a small sum. By contrast both customs were quite common in Vienna and Prague.[16] According to the 1890 census most

---

16 See, for a comparison, *Österreichische Statistik* (1905), p. xvii. Diana de Rosa observes that
   Pflegekinder (foster children) were also unusual in the villages around Trieste in the eighteenth
   century: see Triscuzzi and de Rosa (1986, p. 76).

Table 6.12: *Infant (0–1) and child (1–5) deaths as a proportion of total deaths, and illegitimate infant deaths as a proportion of total infant deaths in Trieste, 1877–1914.*

Year	Infant deaths (%)	Child deaths (%)	Illegitimate infant deaths (%)
1877	27.76	20.38	n.a.
1878	29.01	21.66	n.a.
1879	27.42	19.65	n.a.
1880	27.00	21.94	n.a.
1881	24.96	21.58	n.a.
1882	n.a.	n.a.	n.a.
1883	23.75	18.94	20.66
1884	22.00	23.24	20.41
1885	23.12	22.85	21.42
1886	21.50	25.48	18.60
1887	24.50	19.70	23.20
1888	25.90	18.54	20.23
1889	24.80	15.93	20.95
1890	27.20	18.28	24.00
1891	23.00	20.53	20.89
1892	24.00	16.95	13.32
1893	23.70	18.81	15.75
1894	23.40	23.24	14.92
1895	26.50	16.95	16.30
1896	24.70	n.a.	26.10
1897	25.20	14.73	20.35
1898	27.40	13.83	21.80
1899	23.20	14.76	23.85
1900	25.77	14.32	24.12
1901	n.a.	12.42	n.a.
1902	24.00	14.82	24.00
1903	24.00	13.69	21.00
1904	24.57	11.67	24.00
1905	24.28	14.76	23.26
1906	n.a.	11.99	22.71
1907	25.00	12.81	24.00
1908	25.80	10.72	26.00
1909	n.a.	n.a.	n.a.
1910	27.00	13.78	24.67
1911	25.70	11.72	25.00
1912	24.88	11.43	26.24
1913	26.90	10.88	19.00
1914	24.30	12.69	24.06

Source: Comune di Trieste, 1873–1914; 1904–1914.

Table 6.13: *Infant mortality rates and still birth rates (per 1,000 live births) in Trieste, 1873–1914.*

Period	Overall IMR	Legitimate IMR	Illegitimate IMR	Still birth rate
1873–79	256.5	n.a.	n.a.	64.8
1880–84	224.6[a]	198.4[b]	272.9[b]	70.4[a]
1885–89	219.4	204.6	284.9	66.7
1890–94	228.9	225.1	263.7	65.5
1895–99	222.6	207.4	305.8	60.6
1900–04	199.1	182.0	281.2	68.2
1905–09	197.0[c]	181.7[c]	268.7[c]	68.0
1910–14	191.4	172.5[d]	232.9[d]	79.2

[a] excluding 1881.
[b] excluding 1880, 1881, 1882.
[c] excluding 1909.
[d] excluding 1911, 1914.
Source: Calculated from Comune di Trieste, 1873–1914; 1904–1914.

illegitimate children in Trieste were raised by the mother or by both parents, even though they were not married. Women who were listed as economically 'independent' constituted the highest proportion of unmarried mothers: 609 heads of households with children belonged to this category. It was a very heterogeneous social group including landladies, women who sub-let rooms, those who received pensions or subsidies, as well as dressmakers and washerwomen (*Österreichische Statistik*, 1905, pp. 84–85, vi–xxxiii).[17] Women workers constituted the second most important group of unmarried mothers (*Österreichische Statistik*, 1905), although in this case a higher proportion actually lived with men rather than being registered as unmarried heads of households. Other evidence indicates that the custom of men and women living together unofficially or of deferring marriage until after one or more children were born was widespread among the working class. For example, the charitable organization of S. Francesco Regis offered economic assistance to couples who wanted to legalize their relationship. Between 1899 and 1908 1,585 unmarried couples, who had had 2,740 illegitimate children of whom 1,751 were alive and 889 already dead, turned to the organization for assistance. They were largely unskilled workers, servants and female day-labourers (Fabi, 1984, p. 231). From 1910 to 1914 Luzzato-Fegiz (1929, p. 57) calculated the proportion of marriages which involved the legitimization of children: this varied from 18 per cent (1912) to 27 per cent (1914).

17 For the professional composition of 'independents', see *Österreichische Statistik* (1882; 1894; 1905; 1915a).

Up to the outbreak of the First World War the infant mortality rate in Trieste was exceeded only in the most backward areas of the Monarchy, such as Czernowitz and, within Europe, by a number of Prussian port-cities, such as Danzig and Stettin, or by St Petersburg in Russia. The proportion of infant deaths to total deaths in Trieste remained relatively stable throughout the entire period under consideration: in fact both in 1880 and in 1910 it amounted to 27 per cent (Table 6.12). By contrast there was a noticeable fall in the proportion of child deaths (1–5) during the same period. Traditional medical explanations for this high infant mortality rate focused on congenital weaknesses, lung disease and diseases of the digestive tract which, according to doctors and social reformers, were caused by the poor living conditions of the lower classes (Castiglioni, 1877, pp. 20–56; Tedeschi, 1889). However, the 'general causes' emphasized by contemporary doctors are not sufficient in my view to explain a mortality rate similar to that of the preceding 'golden century' of pauperism in one of the richest economic and industrial centres of the nineteenth century (Geremek, 1973; Gutton, 1977, pp. 126–54). In fact alcoholism, poor living conditions, bottle-feeding and over-crowded housing were elements that could be found in all big European cities at the end of the nineteenth century, as the case of Hamburg indicates (Grüttner, 1983; 1984; Evans, 1987) and yet their respective infant mortality rates were lower than in Trieste. In Hamburg, for instance, infant mortality was generally only one-third that of Trieste, with the exception of 1892 when unusually high rates were due to the severe cholera epidemic (Costantini, 1897, p. 158).

Apart from these general explanations for Trieste's high infant mortality rate, which can be interpreted as an inevitable result of rapid urbanization and a lack of necessary urban structures, further factors need to be taken into consideration in this specific case. In particular there was a high level of segregation of the poorer classes: the new immigrants, for example, were concentrated in the sixth district of S. Giacomo and in the suburbs of S. Anna and Servola which were close to industrial areas. These districts, in terms of overall living standards, were markedly worse off than those of the centre where the middle and upper classes lived. S. Giacomo, for instance, had the highest overall mortality, child mortality and death rates from tuberculosis and pneumonia of all the town's districts (Table 6.14).[18] It also registered the highest birth rate within the port-city and suffered from chronic over-crowding. At the beginning of the twentieth century the incidence of tuberculosis and the level of over-crowding, as well as the birth rate of S. Giacomo, increased even further as a result of a peak level of in-migration (Costantini, 1906; Luzzato-Fegiz, 1929). Significantly, disease-specific and overall mortality rates were higher in S. Giacomo than in Cittavecchia where the urban proletariat lived and which was considered—like the *Gängeviertel* of

18 For the living conditions, morbidity and death rates of the district of S. Giacomo, see Vincenzo de Giaxa (1886; 1887) and Achille Costantini (1888; 1897; 1906; 1910).

Table 6.14: *Intra-urban indicators of differential living standards in Trieste, 1878–1905.*

City district	Birth rate per 1,000 inhabitants			Illegitimacy rate per 1,000 births
	1885	1886	1894	1886
Cittavecchia	32.5	37.2	30.3	13.6
Cittanuova	24.2	25.6	18.8	8.7
S. Giacomo	27.3	22.6	36.2	26.5
S. Anna and Servola	43.1	33.6	43.1	23.0

	Average death rate per 1,000 inhabitants		
	1878–1887	1881–1890	1905
Cittavecchia	33.95	32.52	27.8
Cittanuova	19.82	19.94	20.6
S. Giacomo	35.45	33.99	34.4
S. Anna and Servola	34.47	32.48	35.8

	Infant and child death rate (0–5 years) per 1,000		
	1885	1886	1887
Cittavecchia	134.63	145.51	115.3
Cittanuova	112.33	72.30	77.2
S. Giacomo	107.84	169.59	86.6
S. Anna and Servola	111.79	159.55	n.a.

Sources: de Giaxa, 1886; 1887; Costantini, 1888; 1897; 1906.

Hamburg (Grüttner, 1983)—a sort of social sore which ought to be removed. In 1910 Cittavecchia was described as 'a big melting-pot of poverty and filth where one perceives cobwebs and rats' nests, old plaster, used wood, unmade beds and rusty hardware, fresh hide and wet lumber, fried food, rubbish, alcoholism and prostitution' (Benco, 1910, p. 49). Actually Cittavecchia was a centre of prostitution, petty criminality, smuggling and illicit trading (Cattaruzza, 1979, pp. 86–91) and also a place where the 'disquieting' elements of society, gravitating around the port, lived. On the other hand, it was not entirely separated from that part of town where the middle and upper classes resided, so that the area as a whole was not characterized by a complete collapse of living conditions.

Table 6.14 allows us to compare the different standards of living in the middle- and upper-class district of Cittanuova, Cittavecchia as an area where the urban proletariat had settled, as well as S. Giacomo and S. Anna and

Servola where the new in-migrants had clustered. Differential class-specific living conditions, in terms of basic demographic indicators, undoubtedly favoured the persistence of traditional attitudes towards fertility and children, with birth rates noticeably higher in S. Anna and S. Giacomo. In 1877 Doctor Arturo Castiglioni noted that the death of a child among the poorer classes was less important than that of a cow or of a horse (Castiglioni, 1877, p. 56). In order to support this opinion, he gave the following description of a typical funeral:

> When a poor sick child's suffering finally ends, they [the relatives] organize a vigil by the child's bedside to commemorate his departure to heaven. Several litres of wine are drunk, and it usually ends up in a fight with subsequent punches and slaps. (Castiglioni, 1877, pp. 34–35)

However, this description should be interpreted more as an expression of the writer's distress concerning behaviour patterns which were perceived as alien and incomprehensible rather than as evidence of real working-class indifference towards the death of a child. In the years that followed medical reports also recorded a reluctance on the part of mothers to breast-feed their children. Women used to feed them with unsterilized cow's milk which could cause gastro-intestinal diseases and death (Tedeschi, 1889; Timeus, 1903).[19] In 1905 Doctor Tedeschi was alarmed by the widespread custom of bottle-feeding (Timeus, 1906, p. xxxxi). Since the city council was unable to stop the practice, it tried to limit its negative consequences by opening a health centre for babies

Table 6.15: *Infant deaths (0–1) and type of infant feeding in Trieste, 1910–1913.*

Year	Breast-feeding	Wet-nursing	Bottle-feeding	Mixed	None	Unknown	Total
			Type of infant feeding				
1910	580	36	391	109	204	62	1,382
1911	580	32	470	83	188	109	1,462
1912	581	34	349	70	179	65	1,278
1913	596	71	440	68	173	86	1,434
Total	2,337	173	1,650	330	744	322	5,556
%	42.06	3.11	29.69	5.94	13.39	5.79	100.00

Source: *Bollettini di statistica, Riassunti di statistica.*

19 Very accurate figures on the relationship between infant and child mortality and forms of nursing are provided in Pulma and Turpeinen (1987). For the French case, see George D. Sussman (1982), *passim*.

where needy mothers could obtain suitable milk. Municipal statistics starting from 1910 on infant mortality and different forms of infant feeding are instructive in this context (see Table 6.15).[20] Even though breast-feeding was the most widespread form of infant nursing, collectively other forms were predominant: between 1910 and 1913 only 42 per cent of infants whose deaths were recorded had been breast-fed. The relationship between bottle-feeding and death caused by digestive illnesses needs to be emphasized, along with the fact that there were surprisingly few wet-nurses practising in the city. Of the 1,650 infants who were bottle-fed, a total of 615 (or 37.2 per cent) died as a result of digestive illnesses. The disconcerting category of babies for whom no type of infant feeding was recorded related to cases where death had been caused by congenital weaknesses. Contemporary doctors, unable to give a satisfactory explanation for this phenomenon, blamed it on unsanitary housing conditions, insufficient maternal assistance, or other equally vague factors, thinking it was even caused by premature deliveries (de Giaxa, 1886, p. 38). Congenital weakness was the most common cause of death in the first three days of a baby's life. Nonetheless, to this day the reason why hundreds of babies were not fed after birth remains a secret.

According to available criminal statistics there were 59 cases of child murder between 1819 and 1850, only 17 of which ended with a verdict.[21] Moreover, until the mid-nineteenth century babies could be legally and anonymously abandoned at the entrance of the city hospital (Triscuzzi and De Rosa, 1986, pp. 19–62). Trieste would appear to have had a relatively high rate of infanticide, while the custom of abandoning new-born babies was regarded as an acceptable solution in extreme cases among the poorer classes. Both factors might indicate that some babies—the number is difficult to estimate—who died without having been fed were more or less intentionally neglected by their mothers or by both parents. However, the statistics offer no evidence of a significantly higher mortality among illegitimate children who were not fed. The proportion of illegitimate children in this group ranged between 21 and 26 per cent in the years between 1910 and 1913. In other parts of Europe evidence indicates that the victims of maternal negligence were overwhelmingly illegitimate infants. The stronger integration of illegitimate children within the family environment in Trieste might therefore explain the absence of any significant difference in the death rates of legitimate and illegitimate babies when infant feeding practices are taken into consideration.

In rural areas new-born children were so bundled up that they would not disturb their mothers in the fields and were soothed with cloths used as

---

20 These statistical data are also recorded by the *Bollettini di statistica* and by the *Riassunti di statistica*.

21 I am grateful to Ms Carla Triadan of the Archivio di Stato in Trieste for this information. See, for England, Lionel Rose (1986); with regard to infanticide in Italy, see the case studies by Rossella Selmini (1987), Maria Pia Casavini (1983) and V. de Giaxa (1886, p. 38).

dummies soaked in herbal potions or *eau-de-vie* (Verginella, 1985, p. 169). Doctors condemned these practices, since they wanted to be the only ones responsible for the health of the entire population: they criticized traditional medical beliefs (Castiglioni, 1877, pp. 36–54),[22] including the custom of seeking advice from midwives and elderly women, and all other practices which kept people from seeking their professional services. Their monopoly claims were not so much justified by the ability to cure children's diseases as by the positivistic ambitions of medicine at that time.[23]

As a matter of fact, the new sentimental attitude towards children[24] among the working class arrived remarkably late in Trieste in comparison with its earlier adoption by the middle and upper classes.[25] This can perhaps be explained as a function of differential family size and the presence of outsiders in working-class homes. Compared with other cities of the Monarchy, Trieste had the second highest number of people per family unit, with an average of 4.5. Households contained a relatively high proportion of outsiders and of close and more distant relatives (*Österreichische Statistik*, 1905, pp. VI–XXXIII). Trieste also recorded the highest proportion of sub-tenants per household of all Austrian cities, especially among the so-called 'independents' and workers. Over-crowding, which was particularly severe in certain districts of Trieste (Figure 6.5), as well as promiscuity certainly did not favour an intimate relationship between husbands and wives or between parents and children which corresponded with contemporary middle- and upper-class ideals.

On the other hand, as in the majority of port-towns, only a small number of women were employed and they were mostly unmarried women under 30. In 1890, with the exception of domestic servants, the largest number of women (4,998) were employed in the clothing industry, but only 376 of these were married and 2,810 were younger than 20 (*Österreichische Statistik*, 1894, pp. 66–67). In the whole town there were no more than 558 married women who were employed as workers in the industrial sector.

There seems to have been no clear relationship between female industrial employment and infant mortality levels, despite the fact that numerous health

---

22 For the discrepancy between the views of enlightened doctors and adherents of traditional culture in France, see Sussman (1982, pp. 55–56, 94).

23 For the complex relations between doctors and the poorer classes, see Flaviana Zanolla (1981). Also Hunecke noted in his study on abandoned children how breast-feeding, recommended by doctors, remarkably reduced infant mortality. Medical treatment of children's diseases was, on the contrary, mostly ineffective (see McKeown, 1979, *passim*). For the broader social functions of medicine in the nineteenth century, see Panseri (1980).

24 For a general treatment of the subject, see, for instance, Elisabeth Badinter (1980): for criticism of Badinter, see Stephen Wilson (1984).

25 In the middle-class periodical *La Favilla* from the first half of the nineteenth century such family patterns were fully developed. See Giorgio Negrelli (1985, pp. 286–324).

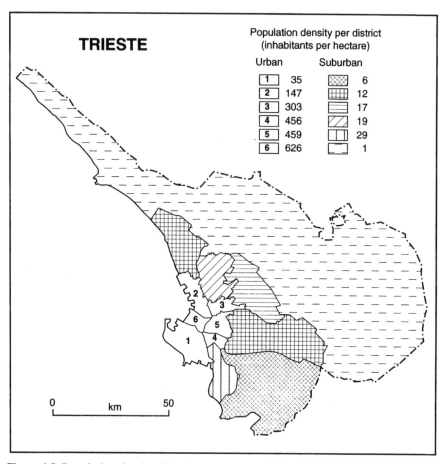

Figure 6.5: Population density (inhabitants per hectare) in Trieste and its suburbs, 1910. *Source:* Census of 1910.

reports supported this idea (Tedeschi, 1889, pp. 6–7; de Giaxa, 1886, p. 37; Timeus, 1906; Castiglioni, 1877).[26] Other contemporary opinions on the low educational level of working-class women regarding healthcare and home economics seem just as ideological, especially if one considers the sanitary conditions prevailing in Trieste under the Hapsburgs. Rather than analysing the situation objectively, these reports were more concerned with reinforcing the contemporary middle- and upper-class point of view that poverty, with all

26 In my opinion Sussman also places too much emphasis on the role of female employment in determining the form of infant-rearing. For a stronger emphasis on cultural factors, see Knodel (1968). For an alternative view, see Lee (1990, pp. 61–62).

its attendant problems, was primarily the individual's fault and that social problems could only be solved by education.[27]

A further element that needs to be taken into consideration was the general sanitary condition of the town. The main problems were the inadequate sewerage system, which was practically the same as it had been in the eighteenth century, and the high level of pollution of the existing wells. A survey carried out in 1886 on a sample of 330 wells produced the following results:

1. the water of most of the wells was not suitable for drinking;
2. the underground water pollution and, therefore, the subsoil pollution of Trieste was remarkably high; cleansing measures were therefore required;
3. the pernicious influence of extremely polluted water and subsoil on the sanitary conditions of the area partially explained the excessive mortality of Trieste and particularly the persistence of infectious diseases in the town (de Giaxa, 1887, pp. 22–23).

Indeed up to the outbreak of the First World War smallpox and cholera had still not completely disappeared, even if after 1886 they were no longer as widespread, and typhus remained quite common, particularly in the summer months (Costantini, 1912). Significantly, even as late as 1887 more than 58 per cent of the houses in Cittavecchia were still not connected to a sewerage system, while most of the town's houses (approximately 3,000) were only provided with cesspools. The suburban districts had no sewers at all, with effluent merely collected on dung hills near the houses and later discharged through open canals (de Giaxa, 1887, p. 149; Costantini, 1888, pp. 179–80). 'Under our houses and squares, along the sea shore and everywhere else, the stench coming from the sewers contaminates us and is the cause of all our disease' claimed the city's medical officer in 1887, noting that no other town as important as Trieste had such deplorable sanitary conditions (Costantini, 1888, p. 179). Even in the following years, with a substantial increase in population, the municipality still proved incapable of providing the town with a sufficient water supply and with a proper sewerage system for the whole urban area.

The official sanitary report for 1905, for example, claimed that the daily water consumption had risen from approximately 20–25 litres per head to 44 litres, but that this was still an inadequately low level. The report further argued that the economic development of the city and in particular rapid population growth had made the situation far more serious than it had been in the early 1880s. The provision of an adequate water supply was viewed as the most important task facing the city. The report concluded that 'It was the new

---

27 For the influence of such principles on children's assistance in Vienna, see Peter Feldbauer (1980, pp. 67–155).

City Council's urgent duty to come to grips with this problem' (Fabi, 1986, p. 224). However, the implementation of a new water supply system was repeatedly delayed because of the prioritization of different projects. In 1909 the report on Trieste's sanitary conditions repeated the earlier arguments and estimated that a proper water supply would save at least 800 lives every year (Fabi, 1986, p. 224).[28]

Employment instability also negatively affected the living conditions of the working classes and their families. In 1877 Arturo Castiglioni noted that in the case of the families of day-labourers, carters and caulkers earnings were frequently limited to a few days a week or to a few months a year, causing 'excessive eating and drinking followed by an absolute shortage of everything' (Castiglioni, 1877, p. 27). Infant- and child-feeding did not correspond to sanitary prescriptions; it was inadequate and often insufficient. Another important factor was how the working-class budget was divided among family members. In a situation where there was widespread temporary employment for men and few jobs for women, it was no wonder that the former imposed their spending habits on the weaker members of the family.[29] Finally, the continuing arrival in Trieste of workers from the agricultural hinterland retarded any significant reduction in child mortality (Nova, 1985, pp. 37 et seq.).

In fact municipal assistance for children was directed to improving the living conditions of school or pre-school children (Fabi, 1984, pp. 225–30; Castiglioni, 1896; Milazzi, 1980). In 1910 970 children attended municipal kindergartens and all primary-school pupils had access to school meals (Timeus, 1910a, pp. 4–5). These forms of assistance were also a sort of investment for the Italian National-Liberal Party which enjoyed an electoral majority in Trieste as they guaranteed the political support of succeeding generations. In 1917 the last representative of the Austrian Empire expressed the following judgement on how Trieste was governed:

> Despite the many epidemics, nothing was done to keep up with the needs of such a rich town as far as housing and urban planning was concerned. The town funds, however, were totally depleted since the Administration preferred superficial measures which had nationalistic and propagandistic aims.[30]

The factors considered here had a differential effect on the various social classes and districts of the town. Admittedly, each factor considered individually was not exceptional, if one considers the urban conditions of the time. Nonetheless, the peculiar structure of the labour market, together with the high level of segregation and the negligence of the city council in the sphere

---

28 See, for an overview, Giulio Timeus, *Studi in relazione al provvedimento d'acqua per la città di Trieste. Dati idrologici, chimici e batteriologici,* Trieste (1910b).

29 The issue of different living standards within the working-class family, particularly between men and women, up to now has been neglected by social and labour historians.

30 "Die politische Verwaltung des Küstenlandes in eineinhalb Kriegsjahre', Trieste, 1916.

of sanitary provision, resulted in an 'explosive mixture' which made Trieste one of the most unhealthy towns of the Hapsburg Monarchy in the pre-1914 period.

References

ALBERTI, M. (1915), *Trieste e la sua fisiologia economica*, Rome.

APIH, E. (1957), *La società triestina nel secolo XVIII*, Turin.

ARA, A. (1987), 'The Jews in Trieste', paper presented at the conference on 'Governments and non-dominant ethnic groups in Europe', Brussels, 8–12 April.

ASSICURAZIONI GENERALI (ed.) (1931), *Il centenario delle Assicurazioni Generali, 1831–1931*, Trieste.

BABUDIERI, F. (1962), 'L'attività marittime dell'emporio di Trieste nel periodo immediatamente precedente e susseguente la prima guerra mondiale', *Annali dell'Istituto Universitario Navale di Napoli*, **XXXI**, Naples, 1–48.

BABUDIERI, F. (1964), 'La nascita dell'emporio commerciale e marittimo di Trieste', *Atti dell'Accademia Nazionale di Marina Mercantile*, Genoa.

BABUDIERI, F. (1982), *Industrie, commerci e navigazione a Trieste e nella Regione Giulia dall'inizio del Settecento al primi anni del Novecento*, Milan.

BACHINGER, K. (1973), 'Das Verkehrswesen', in Alois Brusatti (ed.), *Die wirtschaftliche Entwicklung* (A. Wandruszka and P. Urbanitsch (eds), *Die Habsburger Monarchie 1848–1918*), Vienna, 278–322.

BADINTER, E. (1980), *L'Amour en Plus*, Paris.

BENCO, S. (1910), *Trieste*, Trieste.

BÖHME, H. (1966), *Deutschlands Weg zur Großmacht. Studien zum Verhältnis von Wirtschaft und Staat während der Reichsgründungszeit 1848–1881*, Cologne and Berlin.

BÜRO DES INDUSTRIERATES IM K. K. HANDELSMINISTERIUM (ed.) (1911), *Verhandlungen und Beschlüsse des Industrierates*, **VI**, Punkt 28, Fragen der Industrieförderung, Vienna.

CAMERA DI COMMERCIO E DI INDUSTRIA DI TRIESTE (ed.) (1914), *Relazione per il 1913*, Trieste.

CASAVINI, M. P. (1983), 'Il buan matrimonià. Tre casi di infanticidio nell' Ottocento', *Meinoria, Revista di storia delle donne*, **7**, 27–36.

CASTIGLIONI, A. (1877), *La mortalità a Trieste e le sue cause speciali*, Trieste.

CASTIGLIONI, V. (1896), *Storia delle istituzioni educative per l'infanzia del Comune di Trieste*, Trieste.

CATTARUZZA, M. (1978), 'L'emigrazione di forza-lavoro verso Trieste dalla metà del secolo XIX alla prima guerra mondiale', *Movimento Operaio e Socialista*, New Series, **I**, 21–66.

CATTARUZZA, M. (1979), *La formazione del proletariato urbano. Immigrati operai di mestiere, donne a Trieste dalla metà del secolo XIX alla prima guerra mondiale*, Turin.

COMUNE DI TRIESTE (ed.) (1873–1914), *Bollettini Statistici*, Trieste.

COMUNE DI TRIESTE (ed.) (1876–1914), *Bollettini mensili di statistica*, Trieste.

COMUNE DI TRIESTE (ed.) (1904–1914), *Riassunti di statistica*, Trieste.

COMUNE DI TRIESTE (ed.) (1911), *Riassunti di statistica per l'anno 1910*, Trieste.

COMUNE DI TRIESTE (ed.) (1915), *Riassunti di statistica per l'anno 1914*, Trieste.

COONS, R. E. (1982), *I primi anni del Lloyd Austriaco. Politica di governo a Vienna ed iniziative imprenditoriali a Trieste (1836–1848)*, Udine.

COSTANTINI, A. (1888), *Rapporto sanitario per l'anno 1887*, Trieste.

COSTANTINI, A. (1897), *Rapporto sanitario per il quadriennio 1891–1894*, Trieste.

COSTANTINI, A. (1906), *Riassunto di statistica sanitaria per l'anno 1905*, Trieste.

COSTANTINI, A. (1910), *Riassunto di statistica sanitaria per l'anno 1909*, Trieste.

COSTANTINI, A. (1912), *Il colera a Trieste nel 1911. Considerazioni relative alla profilassi e all'epidemiologia*, Trieste.

de GIAXA, V. (1886), *Rapporto sanitario per l'anno 1885*, Trieste.

de GIAXA, V. (1887), *Rapporto sanitario per l'anno 1886*, Trieste.

del PANTA, L. (1979), 'Italy', in W. R. Lee (ed.), *European Demography and Economic Growth*, London, 196–235.

EVANS, R. J. (1987), *Death in Hamburg. Society and Politics in the Cholera Years 1830–1910*, Oxford.

FABI, L. (1984), *La carità dei ricchi. Povertà e assistenza nella Trieste laica e asburgica del XIX secolo*, Milan.

FABI, L. (1986), 'Salute e malattia', in *Sanità e società Friuli-Venezia-Giulia. Secoli XVI–XX*, Udine, 175–261.

FELDBAUER, P. (1980), *Kinderelend in Wien. Von der Armenpflege zur Jugendfürsorge (17–19 Jahrhundert)*, Vienna.

GEREMEK, B. (1973), 'Il pauperismo nell'età preindustriale (secoli XVI–XVIII)', *Storia d'Italia Einaudi*, V, 1, Turin, 670–98.

GERSCHENKRON, A. (1977), *An Economic Spurt that Failed*, Princeton.

GOOD, D. F. (1980), 'Modern economic growth in the Habsburg monarchy', *East Central Europe'Europe du Centre-Est*, 7, 248–68.

GOOD, D. F. (1984), *The Economic Rise of the Habsburg Empire: 1750–1914*, Berkeley.

GOOD, D. F. (1988), 'The political economy of regional inequalities in the Habsburg Empire', unpublished paper.

GOOD, D. F. (1991), 'Austria-Hungary', in R. Sylla and G. Toniolo (eds), *Patterns of European Industrialization. The Nineteenth Century*, London and New York, 218–47.

GRÜTTNER, M. (1983), 'Soziale Hygiene und soziale Kontrolle. Die Sanierung der Hamburger Gängeviertel 1892–1936', in D. Herzig, D. Langewiesche and A. Sywottek (eds), *Arbeiter in Hamburg. Unterschichten, Arbeiter und Arbeiterbewegung seit dem ausgehenden 18. Jahrhundert*, Hamburg, 359–71.

GRÜTTNER, M. (1984), 'Arbeiterkultur versus Arbeiterbewegungskultur', in Albrecht Lehmann (ed.), *Studien zur Arbeiterkultur*, Münster, 244–82.

GUTTON, J. P. (1977), *La società e i poveri*, Milan.

HELCZMANOVSZKI, H. (1979), 'Austria-Hungary', in W. R. Lee (ed.), *European Demography and Economic Growth*, London, 27–78.

JERCHOW, F. (1984), 'Handel, Schiffahrt und Gewerbe', in Volker Plagemann (ed.), *Industriekultur in Hamburg, Des Deutschen Reiches Tor zur Welt*, Munich, 46–56.

KANDLER, P. (ed.) (1864), *Emporio e Portofranco di Trieste*, Trieste.

K. K. STATISTISCHE CENTRAL-COMMISSION (ed.) (1882), *Die Bevölkerung der im Reichsrate vertretenen Königreiche und Länder nach Religion, Bildungsgrad, Umgangssprache und nach ihren Gebrechen*, I, part II, Vienna.

KNODEL, J. E. (1968), 'Infant mortality and fertility in three Bavarian villages', *Population Studies*, 22 (3), 297–318.

KŘIŽEK, J. (1963), *Die wirtschaftlichen Grundzüge des österreichisch–ungarischen Imperialismus in der Vorkriegszeit (1900–1914)*, Prague.

La popolazione di Trieste nel 1875 (1878), Trieste.

LEE, W. R. (1990), 'Women's work and the family: some demographic implications of gender-specific rural work patterns in nineteenth-century Germany', in Pat Hudson and W. R. Lee (eds), *Women's Work and the Family Economy in Historical Perspective*, Manchester, 50–75.

LUZZATO-FEGIZ, P. (1929), *La popolazione di Trieste*, Trieste.

LUZZATTO, G. (1953), *Il Portofranco di Trieste e la politica mercantilistica austriaca nel '700*, Trieste.

MARMONT, A. F. L., Duc de Ragusse (1857), *Mémoires de 1792 à 1841*, 9 vols, Paris.

MARTINI, L. de A. (1968), *Portofranco e comunità etnico-religiose nella Trieste settecentesca*, Milan.

MÄRZ, E. (1968), *Österreichische Industrie- und Handelspolitik in der Zeit Franz Joseph I*, Vienna.

MÄRZ, E. and K. SOCHER (1973), 'Währung and Banken in Cisleithanien', in A. Brusatti (ed.) *Die Habsburgermonarchie 1848–1918*, Band I, *Die Wirtschaftliche Entwicklung*. Vienna, 323–68.

MASTROLONARDO, G. (ed.) (1921), *Il risorgimento economico della Venezia Giulia*, Milan.

MATHIES, O. (1924), *Hamburgs Reederei 1814–1914*, Hamburg.

MATIS, H. (1972), *Osterreichs Wirtschaft. Konjunkturelle Dynamik und gesellschaftlicher Wandel 1848–1913*, Berlin.

MATIS, H. (1973), 'Leitlinien der österreichischen Wirtschaftspolitik', in Alois Brusatti (ed.), *Die wirtschaftliche Entwicklung* (A. Wandruszka and P. Urbanitsch (eds), *Die Habsburger Monarchie 1848–1918*, I), Vienna, 19–67.

McKEOWN, T. (1979), *The Role of Medicine*, Princeton.

MILAZZI, L. (1980), *Politica scolastica ed irredentismo. I ricreatori comunali a Trieste*, Udine.

MONTANELLI, P. (1905), *Il movimento storico della popolazione di Trieste*, Trieste.

MORITSCH, A. (1969), *Das nahe Triester Hinterland*, Vienna.

MUSIL, R. (1952), *Der Mann ohne Eigenschaften*, Hamburg.

NEGRELLI, G. (1978), *Al di qua del mito. Diritto storico e difesa nazionale nell'autonomismo della Trieste asburgica*, Udine.

NEGRELLI, G. (ed.) (1985), *La Favilla (1836–1846)*, Udine.

NOVA, C. (1985), 'Diversi destini e diverse fortune. Bimbi e lattanti nella Trieste del primo '900', *Qualestoria. Bollettino dell'Istituto regionale per la storia del movimento di liberazione nel Friuli-Venezia Giulia*, 12 (2), 19–47.

Österreichische Statistik (1881), 'Die Ergebnisse der Volkszählung vom 31 December 1880, Die Bevölkerung der im Reichsrate vertretenen Königreiche und Ländern', II, Part I, Vienna.

Österreichische Statistik (1882), 'Ergebnisse der Volkszählung vom 31 December 1880', I, Part III, Vienna.

Österreichische Statistik (1893a), 'Die Ergebnisse der Volkszählung vom 31 December 1890. Die Bevölkerung nach Heimatsberechtigung und Gubürtigkeit', XXXIII, Part II, Vienna.

Österreichische Statistik (1893b), 'Die Ergebnisse der Volkszählung vom 31 December 1890 in den im Reichsrate vertretenen Königreichen und Ländern. Die Bevölkerung nach Grössen-Kategorien der Ortschaften, Stellung zum Wohnungsinhaber, Geschlecht, Alter und Familienstand, Confession, Umgangssprache, Bildungsgrad, Gebrechen', XXXII, Part III, Vienna.

Österreichische Statistik (1894), 'Berufsstatistik nach den Ergebnissen der Volkszählung vom 31 December 1890, Trieste und Gebiet, Görz und Gradisca, Istrien', XXXIII, Part VI, Vienna.

Österreichische Statistik (1902), 'Die Ergebnisse der Volkszählung vom 31 December 1900. Die summarischen Ergebnisse der Volkszählung', LXIII, Part I, Vienna.

Österreichische Statistik (1903), 'Die Ergebnisse der Volkszählung vom 31 December 1900, Haushaltungs- und Familienstatistik in den Großstädten', LXV, Part V, Vienna.

Österreichische Statistik (1905), 'Berufsstatistik nach den Ergebnissen der Volkszählung vom 31 December 1900, Trieste und Gebiet, Görz und Gradisca, Istrien', LXVI, Part VI, Vienna.

Österreichische Statistik (1912), 'Die Ergebnisse der Volkszählung vom 31 December 1910. Die Bevölkerung nach der Gubürtigkeit, Religion und Umgangssprache in Verbindung mit dem Geschlechte, nach dem Bildungsgrade und Familienstande', New Series, I, Part III, Vienna.

Österreichische Statistik (1914), 'Die Ergebnisse der Volkszählung vom 31 December 1910, Die Alters- und Familienstandsgliederung und Aufenthaltsdauer', New Series, I, Part III, Vienna.

Österreichische Statistik (1915a), 'Berufsstatistik nach den Ergebnissen der Volkszählung vom 31 December 1910, Küstenland und Dalmatien', New Series, III, Part VI, Vienna.

Österreichische Statistik (1915b), 'Statistik der Beschäftigungen und Berufe nach den Ergebnissen der Volkszählung vom 31 December 1910, Hauptübersicht und auflösende Bearbeitung', New Series, III, Part I, Vienna.

PANSERI, G. (1980), 'La nascita della polizia medica: l'organizzazione sanitaria nei vari Stati italiani', *Storia d'Italia Einaudi Annali*, III, Turin, 157–96.

PAROVEL, P. (1985), *L'identità cancellata*, Trieste.

Popolazione e bestiame del Litorale secondo la numerazione del 31 ottobre, 1859, Vienna.

PRIMORAC, V. (1918), *Trieste et l'Istrie*, Paris.

PULMA, P. and O. TURPEINEN (1987), *Suomen lastensuojelun Historia*, Helsinki.

ROSE, L. (1986), *Massacre of the Innocents. Infanticide in Great Britain 1800–1939*, London.

RUDOLPH, R. (1976), *Banking and Industrialization in Austria-Hungary*, Cambridge.

RUDOLPH, R. (1983), 'Economic revolution in Austria? The meaning of 1848 in Austrian economic history', in J. Komlos (ed.), *Economic Development in the Habsburg Monarchy in the Nineteenth Century*, Boulder.

SALVI, N. (1961), 'La crisi di transformazione dell'emporio di Trieste in porto di transito (1856–1865)', in Istituto per la Storia del Risorgimento Italiano. Comitato di Trieste e Gorizia (ed.), *La crisi dell'Impero Austriaco dopo Villafranca*, Trieste.

SAPELLI, G. (1984), 'Uomini e capitali nella Trieste dell'Ottocento. La fondazione della Riunione Adriatica di Sicurtà', *Società e Storia*, VII (26), 821–74.

SELMINI, R. (1987), *Profili di uno studio sull'infanticido*, Milan.

SHORTER, E. (1977), 'Emancipazione feminile, controllo delle nascite e fecondità nella storia europea', in M. Barbagli (ed.), *Famiglia e Mutamento Sociale*, Bologne, 317–59.

STEFANI, G. (1931), *Il centenario delle Assicurazioni Generali 1831–1931*, Trieste.

STEFANI, G. (1960), *I greci a Trieste nel Settecento*, Trieste.

SUSSMAN, G. D. (1982), *Selling Mother's Milk. The Wet-Nursing Business in France, 1715–1914*, Chicago and London.

TAPIÈ, V. L. (1972), *Monarchia e popoli del Danubia*, Turin.

TEDESCHI, V. (1889), *L'alimentazione della prima infanzia*, Trieste.

TIMEUS, G. (1903), *Igiene alimentare. Il latte*, Trieste.

TIMEUS, G. (1906), *Il latte fornito alla città di Trieste e i provvedimenti di igiene alimentare infantile*, Trieste.

TIMEUS, G. (1910a), *Sul servizio della refezione scolastica nei giardini d'infanzia del Comune di Trieste*, Trieste.

TIMEUS, G. (1910b), *Studi in relazione al provvedimento d'acqua per la città di Trieste. Dati idrologici, chimici e batteriologici*, Trieste.

TREUE, W. (1970), 'Das österreichisch-mitteldeutsche und das norddeutsche staats- und privat wirtschaftliche Interesse am Bau des Suezkanals', *Vierteljahrschrift für Sozial- und Wirtschaftsgeschichte*, LVII, 534–55.

TRISCUZZI, L. and D. de ROSA (1986), *I bambini di Sua Maestà. Esposti e Orfani nella Trieste del '700*, Milan.

VERGINELLA, M. (1985), 'Strategie familiari nel corso dell'Ottocento a Dolina', unpublished dissertation, University of Trieste.

VIVANTE, A. (1912), *Irredentismo adriatico. Contributo alla discussione sui rapporti austro-italiani*, Florence (2nd ed., Trieste, 1984).

WEICHS-GLON, F. Freiherr zu. (1912), *Österreichische Schiffahrtspolitik*, Vienna.

WILSON, S. (1984), 'The myth of motherhood: the historical view of European child-rearing', *Social History*, 9, 181–98.

ZANOLLA, F. (1981), 'Pediatrie e contadini intorno alla morte di un bambino povero', *Qualestoria. Bollettino dell'Istituto regionale per la storia del movimento di liberazione nel Friuli-Venezia Giulia*, **9** (3), 39–73.

ZOLLER, I. (1924), 'La comunità israelitica di Trieste. Studio di demografia storica', *Metron*, **3–4**, 521–55.

Chapter 7

THE ADMIRALTY CONNECTION: PORT DEVELOPMENT AND DEMOGRAPHIC CHANGE IN PORTSMOUTH, 1650–1900

BARRY STAPLETON

INTRODUCTION

In south-east Hampshire the population centre of Portsmouth is a relatively new settlement.[1] Non-existent in 1086 at the time of the Domesday Book (Stapleton, 1989),[2] it was founded in the late-twelfth century during a prolonged period of medieval population growth. As a new community it was much smaller than its more established neighbouring market towns at Titchfield and Fareham, or even markets such as that at Havant created at about the same time. Even as late as the beginning of the seventeenth century it seems likely that Portsmouth was still only the fourth or fifth largest parochial community in the region. The parishes of Titchfield, Fareham and Hambledon, all holding markets, apparently contained larger numbers than Portsmouth, and Havant was approximately the same size.[3]

During the seventeenth century, however, Portsmouth's population growth, alongside that of its neighbour across the harbour, Gosport, began to dominate that of the south-east Hampshire region. In the sixteenth century Portsmouth had grown at a rate very similar to that of the region as a whole. During the first three-quarters of the seventeenth century, when the region's population grew by 83.5 per cent (from over 10,000 to over 19,000 inhabitants), Portsmouth and Gosport accounted for 64.7 per cent of the total growth. While the two harbour communities were growing rapidly, the evidence from the rest of the region suggests that population growth was slowing down. This divergence between Portsmouth and Gosport and the rest of the region was even more heavily marked in the last quarter of the seventeenth and the first quarter of the eighteenth century. The Bishop of Winchester's Visitation

1 South-east Hampshire is defined as including the city of Portsmouth, the area eastwards to the borders of West Sussex, northwards to Butser Hill, and westwards to the Hamble River. It therefore includes the harbour communities of Emsworth, Fareham, Gosport and Havant including Hayling Island, and the parishes of Bedhampton, Blendworth, Boarhunt, Catherington, Chalton, Clanfield, Droxford, Farlington, Hambledon, Meonstoke, Portchester, Rowner, Soberton, Southwick, Titchfield, Wickham, Widley and Wymering, as well as Waterlooville.

2 See Victoria County History of Hampshire, Vol. 1 for Domesday population of south-east Hampshire, and Barry Stapleton (1989, pp. 84–85).

3 British Library Harleian MS 595, ff239–39. Liber Cleri (communicants list), 1603.

Return of 1725 indicates that the regional population grew by about 24 per cent from over 18,200 to over 22,600 people.[4] However, if Portsea Island and Gosport are excluded from these calculations, the remainder of the region's population appears to have declined by 6 per cent, whereas that of the two harbour communities rose by 56 per cent—eloquent testimony to the increasing importance of the Portsmouth harbour settlements to the whole region. By this time Portsmouth and Gosport constituted 52.7 per cent of the region's population, or 14,500 out of 22,649, thus consolidating the position of 1676 when they contained some 47 per cent of the region's inhabitants. No wonder that Defoe could write in the mid-1720s that Portsmouth was a town 'well-inhabited, thriving, prosperous', with naval docks and yards 'now like a town by themselves' (Defoe, 1962, pp. 136–37).

It is not until three-quarters of a century later, with the first census of 1801, that the region's population can be calculated again. In those cases where the parishes are directly comparable, the region's population, excluding Portsmouth and Gosport, had increased from about 8,650 in 1725 to over 16,400 by 1801, a rise of 90 per cent. When the two naval towns are included, the overall increase was from about 22,650 to over 60,900, a remarkable growth of 169 per cent. Thus it can be seen that the numerical dominance of the Portsmouth harbour communities was strengthened throughout the eighteenth century when, after a period of slow growth or even decline in other parts of the region in the late-seventeenth or early-eighteenth century, the population again began to grow more rapidly (Figure 7.1).

This pattern of population change in the Portsmouth region from the early-sixteenth to the end of the eighteenth century is in many ways a microcosm of the nation's demographic experience. England's population grew in the sixteenth and early-seventeenth centuries, slowed down and probably fell in the late-seventeenth century, only to rise to new heights in the eighteenth century. At the same time, the capital city, London, consistently increased its domination of national population until by the mid-eighteenth century it contained more than one in ten of all English residents (Wrigley and Schofield, 1982, pp. 208–09, 77–88). The population experience of the Portsmouth region has more than an echo of this national pattern, with Portsmouth itself taking an increasing share of total population, rising consistently from 7.5 per cent in 1603 to 22 per cent in 1676, approximately 33 per cent in 1725, and 52.7 per cent by 1801.

THE EARLY DEVELOPMENT OF THE NAVAL DOCKYARD

In two centuries Portsmouth had increased its share of the region's population more than seven-fold to become the dominant community. Defoe had

4 In 1725 no figures were returned for Southwick, Boarhunt, Widley and Wymering, and thus the 1676 figures taken from the Compton Census, William Salt Library, Stafford, MS Salt 33, have been adjusted to take account of these omissions.

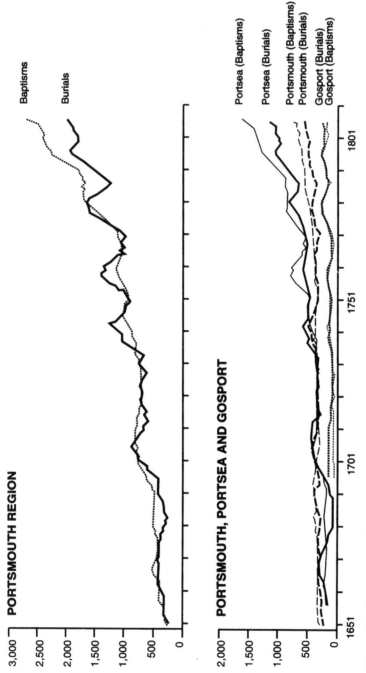

Figure 7.1: Nine-year moving average of baptisms and burials in the Portsmouth region.

perceptively noted the major reason for this growth—the emergence of the naval dockyard into a veritable urban community itself. This expansion would appear to have begun around the mid-seventeenth century. Prior to this Portsmouth was only a centre of slight importance for the Lords of the Admiralty. Whereas expenditure on wages and materials at the Chatham and Woolwich dockyards rose between 1597 and 1617, at Portsmouth it fell. Chatham was clearly dominant with expenditure even at its lowest point reaching nearly £600 in April 1597 when Portsmouth was only allocated just over £3 (Chalklin, 1965). It is not surprising that a decade later, in 1627, Sir George Blundell could describe the town as a 'poor beggarly place, where there is neither money, lodging or meat'.[5] However, the 1630s was a period of some recovery; whereas in 1617 monthly naval expenditure at Portsmouth had represented only 0.2 per cent of the total for the four royal dockyards, by 1636 it had risen to 25 per cent, with over £3,000 being spent monthly on small-scale ship repairs (Gates, 1900b).

This recovery was maintained partly as a result of the Civil War (see Figure 7.2). Portsmouth, after initially declaring for Charles I, fell to the Parliamentary forces and thereafter remained loyal to Parliament. Hence it may be no coincidence that the Cromwellian Commonwealth saw the re-emergence of Portsmouth as a ship-building centre when in 1650 the *Portsmouth* was launched. In the 1650s an average of one ship per year was built (Sparks, 1912) and a request for a substantial increase in the number of men from the 180 currently employed was made by the Dockyard Commissioner.[6] The dockyard was extended by another one-and-a-half acres and a new dry dock was built between 1656 and 1658. No doubt the first Anglo-Dutch War of 1652–53, involving considerable naval activity, was a prime cause of these developments; moreover, war with the Dutch recurred between 1665 and 1667 and Portsmouth's share of naval ship-building increased, with more first- and second-rate warships being built there between 1660 and 1688 than at any other royal dockyard (Coleman, 1953).

The Dutch attack on Chatham in June 1667, capturing the pride of the navy, the *Royal Charles*, and causing considerable panic in London (Latham and Matthews, 1974, pp. 256–72), probably helped to ensure Portsmouth's development (see Figure 7.3) away from the vulnerable Thames yards. The third Anglo-Dutch War between 1672 and 1674 endorsed Portsmouth's growing naval importance and the years 1670 to 1673 have been described as 'the busiest that the Portsmouth yard had ever experienced' (Sparks, 1912, p. 46). Monthly expenditure on labour and materials at Portsmouth rose

5 Cal. S.P. Dom. 1627–1628, 24 April 1627, Sir George Blundell to Buckingham, pp. 148–49.

6 Dockyard employment figures for the years from 1687 to 1711 are derived from British Library Add. MSS 9324 and National Maritime Museum Sen/131. I am greatly indebted to my former colleague Trevor Harris for making his collected statistics available to me. No statistics on dockyard employment are available for the period 1718–1750.

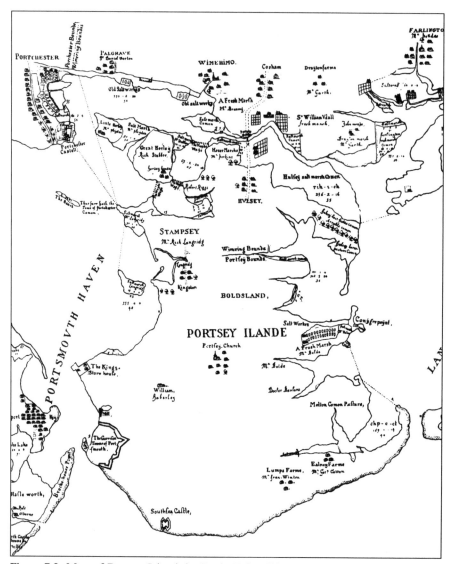

Figure 7.2: Map of Portsea Island, by De la Fabvollière, c. 1665.

dramatically to over £5,000 in 1648–49, £20,000 in 1670 and over £46,000 by 1685 (Gates, 1900b; Sparks, 1912), representing some 30 per cent of total expenditure on the royal dockyards.

It was from 1689, however, that the real growth of Portsmouth can be dated, although the town was already the country's most heavily-fortified community by the mid-1680s (see Figure 7.3; Thomas, 1989, p. 60). The accession of William III brought England and Holland together and shifted the European

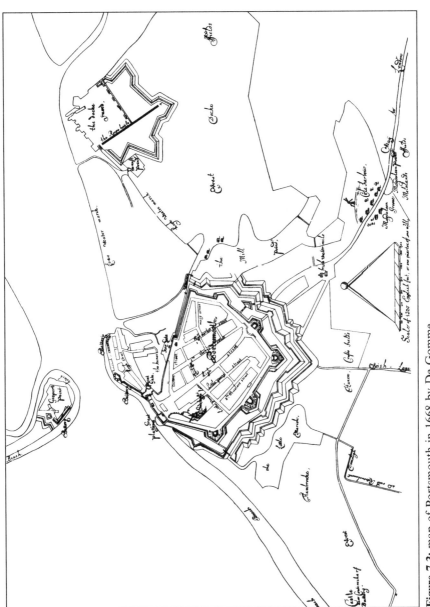

Figure 7.3: map of Portsmouth in 1668 by De Gomme.

military balance, with France becoming the main enemy until 1815. Major building works were commenced in 1689, which saw ten acres reclaimed from the sea and a non-tidal basin, the Great Ship Basin, constructed (Riley, 1985). Simultaneously, the number of dockyard employees dramatically increased, as did baptisms at Portsmouth and Portsea churches. By 1687 there were 294 men employed in the dockyard, but the number had risen to 591 by 1690 and then rose each year to reach 1,271 in 1697 when construction work was completed. Naval preparations for the War of Spanish Succession, which was to last until 1713, maintained buoyant employment levels.[7] The number of employees stood at over 2,000 in 1711—almost a seven-fold increase within a quarter of a century. Despite a significant reduction in the dockyard labour force by 40 per cent following the end of hostilities, employment once again began to rise, reaching 1,741 by 1718 (see Table 7.1).

The emergence of an industrial unit employing up to 2,000 men in the early-eighteenth century is clearly neither part of the Industrial Revolution nor an aspect of proto-industrialization. By 1700 Portsmouth's dockyard labour force was greater than that of the other royal dockyards and it constituted one of the largest industrial plants in England (Christie, 1976, p. 75). The effects of this rapid growth on the town were economically and demographically dramatic. As early as 1665 complaints of over-crowding were being heard as all the land

Table 7.1: *Naval dockyard employment in Portsmouth, 1687–1718.*

Year	No. employed	Year	No. employed
1687	294	1703	1,392
1688	327	1704	1,460
1689	385	1705	1,610
1690	591	1706	1,652
1691	665	1707	1,863
1692	662	1708	1,846
1693	711	1709	1,869
1694	846	1710	1,953
1695	870	1711	2,008
1696	1,126	1712	1,951
1697	1,271	1713	1,208
1698	910	1714	1,163
1699	1,018	1715	1,160
1700	1,065	1716	1,416
1701	1,356	1717	1,646
1702	1,442	1718	1,741

Sources: British Library Add. MSS 9324 and National Maritime Museum Sen/131.

7 B. L. Add. MSS 9324 and National Maritime Museum Sen/131.

inside the fortified town walls was effectively being used, although not solely for housing purposes. Thomas Middleton, the resident Navy Commissioner, wrote in August 1655 about his fears should the plague, which had broken out in the spring of that year in London, appear 'amongst so crowded and miserably poor a population'. His misgivings were justified: over-crowding and poverty undoubtedly contributed to the high death rate during the subsequent plague outbreak in 1665–66 (Figure 7.4).[8]

As the town filled up, further expansion could only take place outside the walls. However, any such development encountered military objections, since a clear arc of fire was required by the town's defenders. Thus, the obvious place for new building construction was to the north, outside the expanding

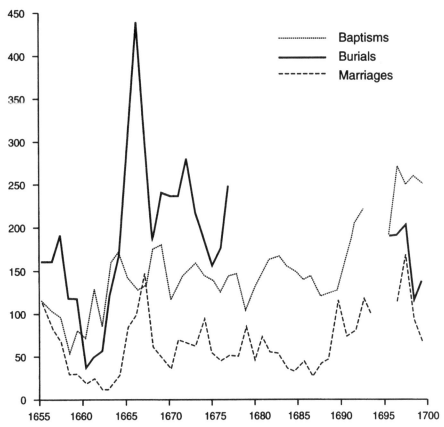

Figure 7.4: Annual registrations of baptisms, burials and marriages at St Thomas's parish, Portsmouth, 1655–1700.

8 Chapman (1974, p. 175), and Cal. S.P. Dom. 1665–66, p. 32.

dockyard. Here, inland and to the east of the dockyard, a new community was beginning to develop on Portsmouth Common. The Anglican parish registers of St Mary's parish Portsea, which covered most of Portsea Island outside the town walls, recorded a spectacular growth in the number of baptisms from 1695 onwards. A record of Portsea baptisms first survives for the ten years from 1654 to 1663 when they averaged 20.7 per annum; the same figure was recorded between 1675 and 1684. For the following ten years, 1685–1694, they rose marginally to an average of 22.0 per annum, suggesting a relatively stable population in Portsea. Thereafter, annual baptisms increased rapidly from an average of 71.3 between 1695 and 1704 to 186.9 between 1705 and 1714[9] (see Figure 7.5).

These figures clearly echoed the rising employment levels in the dockyard during the War of Spanish Succession and the growing number of houses constructed on Portsmouth Common. The surviving lists of those rated for poor relief show that 65 houses were expected to contribute in 1700. By 1703

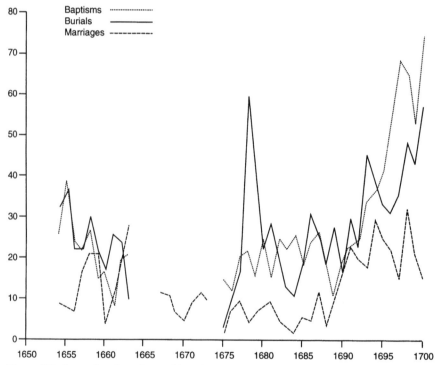

Figure 7.5: Annual registrations of baptisms, burials and marriages at St Mary's parish, Portsea, 1654–1700.

9 PCRO CHU3/1A/1–14, Portsea Parish Registers.

the figure had risen to over 100 and in 1706 it stood at 223; by 1719 it had reached 372, almost a six-fold increase in 20 years (Cramer, 1985a). Even so, house-building lagged behind the more than eight-fold rise in baptisms as the map of Portsmouth and its common in 1716 indicates (see Figure 7.6).

These war-related developments in the first quarter of the eighteenth century were aptly described by Daniel Defoe when visiting Portsmouth in 1724:

> Since the encrease of business at this place, by the long continuance of the war, the confluence of people has been so great, and the town not admitting any enlargement for buildings, that a kind of a suburb, or rather new town has been built on the healthy ground adjoining to the town, which is so well built, and seems to encrease so fast, that in time it threatens to outdo for numbers of inhabitants, and beauty of buildings, even the town itself. (Defoe, 1962, vol. I, pp. 138–39)

An assiduous observer, Defoe also commented separately on the growth of the dockyard itself:

> These docks and yards are now like a town by themselves, and are a kind of marine corporation, or a government of their own kind within themselves; there being particular large rows of dwellings built at the publick charge, within the new works, for all the principal officers of the place; ... the tradesmen likewise have houses here, and many of the labourers are allow'd to live in the bounds as they can get lodging. (Defoe, 1962, vol. I, p. 137)

In January 1725 Stephen Martin-Leake, a clerk in the navy pay office, on a visit during the course of his duties described Portsmouth as having 'considerable suburbs'; the Point was 'very populous and thriving being the Wapping of Portsmouth' and the emergent Portsea, built on Portsmouth Common, consisted of 'very large suburbs extending to the dock'. Portsmouth Town itself was not inconsiderable, containing a 'large and commodious cooperage for use of the Navy, and handsome new barracks of brick' (Markham, 1895, p. 206). This may have been a reference to Colewort Barracks, the first built in the town and used by the military since 1694 for soldiers who were required to man the defences of Portsmouth. According to Martin-Leake, 'The garrison in war is usually two regiments of foot, but in peace eight companies of invalids, making 400 men' (Markham, 1895, p. 209). Such a peacetime complement would have affected the demography of the town, but the two regiments in wartime would have had an impact up to six times greater since in the early-eighteenth century a regiment consisted of eleven companies, each of 113 men, making nearly 1,250 in total (Barnett, 1974). Thus two regiments constituted approximately 2,500 men, so that the number of military personnel present in wartime was even greater than the dockyard labour force. Naturally, sailors who may have been in port should be added to these numbers.

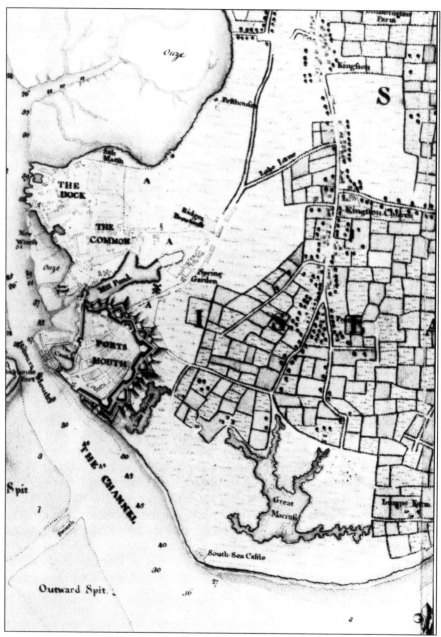

Figure 7.6: Map of Portsmouth and its common, 1716.

SEABORNE TRADE AND THE GROWTH OF SERVICE INDUSTRIES

Defoe commented that Portsmouth:

> hath been greatly enrich'd of late by the fleet's having so often and so long lain
> there, as well as large fleets of merchantmen, as the whole navy during the late
> war; besides the constant fitting out of men here, and the often paying them at
> Portsmouth, has made a great confluence of people thither on their private
> business, with other things which the attendance of those fleets hath requir'd:
> These things have not only been a great advantage to the town, but has really
> made the whole place rich ... (Defoe, 1962, p. 138)

Apart from the obvious benefits to Portsmouth of its defence connections,
Defoe was commenting on two important economic consequences of the
emergence of Portsmouth as the premier naval dockyard: first, the development of seaborne trade; and, secondly, the growth of service industries. With
thousands of soldiers, sailors and dockyard workers concentrated into the
south-western corner of Portsea Island, it is hardly surprising that 'a great
confluence of people ... on private business' could be found. How developed
seaborne trade was at Portsmouth remains somewhat conjectural, but in the
late-seventeenth and early-eighteenth centuries Portsmouth had connections
with the East India Company, a company agent having been established there
along with repair facilities for its ships (Thomas, 1985). Even so, Portsmouth's
overseas trading activity appears to have been limited; according to the
customs report of 1676, 'Very few or no merchants live there' and trade was
described as 'inconsiderable'.[10] Portsmouth was also excluded from those ports
authorized to grant passes allowing trading from the harbour to merchants'
vessels (Sparks, 1912). However, the growth of the dockyard and related
military and naval activity must have caused some growth in commercial trade
and it is noticeable that customs revenue from Portsmouth rose from
approximately £3,900 in 1710 to £11,600 in 1760 and to £79,000 in 1800.[11]
Even allowing for changes in customs valuations, there can be little doubt that
Portsmouth's imports grew considerably in the eighteenth century. Its coastal
shipping activities also grew. Despite apparent stability up to 1730, by 1751
there had been a 64 per cent rise in the port's tonnage from 720 to 1,179 tons.[12]
The inward trade, not surprisingly, consisted primarily of coal, tobacco, timber
and agricultural produce, whereas outward cargoes included salt from the
Salterns located at Langstone Harbour on the eastern edge of Portsea Island
and wheaten flour (Willan, 1967, pp. 154–55). Inevitably, however, the
Admiralty was concerned that the commercial development of Portsmouth
harbour was not too extensive and did not jeopardize its primary naval
function.

10 Cal. S.P. Dom. 1676–77, p. 200, quoted in Thomas (1985, p. 12).
11 B. L. Add. MSS 8133a, f128 quoted in Thomas (1985, p. 13).
12 B. L. Add MSS 11,255 tabulated in Willan (1967, pp. 220–21).

The growth of services for the 'fitting out of men' in Portsmouth was reflected in the occupational structure of the town which, apart from the ship-building trades, was dominated by those involved in supplying food and drink and those providing clothing and footwear. The latter had clear links with the fitting out of naval personnel; tailoring in particular was a high-profile activity which developed in response to the demand for uniforms for the armed forces (Jackson, 1974). Bakers, brewers and maltsters were prominent in food-processing and retailing, but they were by no means as prominent as beer-sellers at the beginning of the eighteenth century, although many of these retailers carried out this activity as a secondary occupation. In the following decades many of these dual occupations were to disappear as the growing population created a market demand which could sustain larger-scale inn-keeping. By 1715 there were already 47 public houses, 17 brandy shops and 3 coffee houses in Portsmouth, a further 30 inns, 7 brandy shops and 3 coffee houses at Portsmouth Point, while Portsmouth Common (with Kingston) had 46 more inns and 8 brandy shops, giving a total of over 120 inns, 22 brandy shops and 6 coffee houses.[13]

THE EXPANSION OF THE NAVAL DOCKYARD AND ITS CONSEQUENCES

It is clear that Portsmouth had developed sufficiently for a substantial underlying market economy to exist independently of war and naval demands, although in peacetime demand was noticeably lower. Even so, in the eighteenth century it was dockyard expansion which led to greater economic prosperity in Portsmouth. Additionally, the growth of the British Empire gave rise to a considerable increase in merchant shipping which needed protection around the world and increasingly meant that the Navy had to be permanently sea-worthy and operative. Further dockyard extensions occurred in the 1720s, 1770s and in 1790, until the yard covered an area of 82 acres (Morgan, 1947, pp. 414–16; 1948). From the 1760s to the 1790s there was an almost continuous building programme within the dockyard of docks, ships, houses, stores and shops, as well as a church and Naval Academy (Kitson, 1947).

From 1750 the effect of these developments on the dockyard labour force can be calculated from an unbroken series of employment statistics which survive until 1832 (Table 7.2).[14] Workers employed in 1750 numbered around 1,600, falling to 1,350 in 1753–54. Thereafter there was a generally upward trend in dockyard employment levels. Expansion in this area was inevitably fuelled by wartime requirements, as during the war of American Independence and the war against France. Although numbers declined to under 2,400 in 1802, they peaked at 3,878 in 1814. The end of the Napoleonic Wars in 1815

13 PCRO S3/B/189 a–h.
14 National Maritime Museum ADM/B and ADM/BP, from information provided by Dr Trevor Harris.

Table 7.2: *Naval dockyard employment in Portsmouth, 1750–1841.**

Year	No. employed	Year	No. employed	Year	No. employed
1750	1,607	1778	2,106	1806	2,511
1751	1,596	1779	2,280	1807	2,596
1752	1,547	1780	2,371	1808	n.a.
1753	1,342	1781	2,405	1809	3,060
1754	1,351	1782	2,385	1810	3,201
1755	1,587	1783	2,351	1811	3,290
1756	2,007	1784	2,300	1812	3,549
1757	2,026	1785	2,196	1813	5,623
1758	2,149	1786	2,130	1814	3,878
1759	2,099	1787	2,129	1815	3,658
1760	2,021	1788	2,101	1816	3,413
1761	1,951	1789	2,084	1817	3,188
1762	1,982	1790	2,058	1818	3,241
1763	1,704	1791	2,203	1819	3,219
1764	1,659	1792	2,170	1820	3,208
1765	1,820	1793	2,222	1821	n.a.
1766	1,854	1794	2,334	1822	2,946
1767	1,874	1795	2,717	1823	2,464
1768	1,793	1796	2,697	1824	2,392
1769	1,782	1797	1,908	1825	2,414
1770	1,801	1798	2,811	1826	2,419
1771	2,185	1799	2,798	1827	2,371
1772	2,228	1800	2,908	1828	2,218
1773	2,162	1801	2,995	1829	2,158
1774	2,174	1802	2,396	1830	2,103
1775	2,056	1803	2,431	1831	2,041
1776	2,028	1804	2,322	1832	1,961
1777	1,949	1805	2,428	1841	2,227

* In addition to the workforce in the dockyard, there could be other men employed on the reserve fleet anchored in the harbour. For instance in 1774 an additional 685 were so engaged (Horne, 1965, p. 24; Riley, 1976, p.11).
Sources: National Maritime Museum ADM/B, ADM/BP.

saw employment fall again, declining steadily back to 2,000 men by the early 1830s, a reduction of nearly 50 per cent which inevitably had serious effects on the local economy.

The workforce in the yard fluctuated not only because of the onset of war and peace, but also according to developments in the yard itself. Of the 2,198 men employed in January 1775, a significant proportion were shipwrights, sawyers and spinners employed in the Ropeyard (Table 7.3). Another 685 men

Table 7.3: *The occupational composition of the dockyard labour force at Portsmouth, 1775–1784.*

Occupation	1775	1784
Shipwrights	861	790
Sawyers	134	134
Spinners	115	117
Smiths	85	76
House carpenters	82	88
Caulkers	75	103
Scavelmen	67	80
Riggers	55	140
Bricklayers	51	17
Sailmakers	20	52
Riggers' labourers	18	110
Hatchellers	18	29
Joiners	64	69

Sources: Horne, 1965; British Library, Add. MSS 41363, Martin Papers, cited in Geddes, 1970.

were working on the reserve fleet anchored in the harbour, making a grand total of 2,885 (Horne, 1965, p. 71; Riley, 1985). Ten years later, in 1784, with the dockyard labour force having risen to 3,000 (including men working on the reserve fleet), there were fewer shipwrights and bricklayers, but there had been a substantial expansion in the number of riggers and riggers' labourers, as well as caulkers employed at the yard.[15] It would seem that in 1774 much more building work was being carried out both on ships and on the dockyard infrastructure. By 1784 both these activities had been reduced in scale, whereas ship-refitting and repairs, which needed more riggers and caulkers as opposed to shipwrights, had clearly been expanded.

The further importance of the dockyard was demonstrated in 1770 when the fortification of Portsea, similar to that of Portsmouth, was begun, although it was not completed until 1809 (Masters, 1968, p. 9). Portsea also witnessed an almost four-fold increase in the number of listed properties between 1725 and 1775 (Figure 7.7), at least on the basis of the extant poor rate books for Portsmouth and contemporary cartographical evidence. By the outbreak of war in 1793 the number of listed properties in the town of Portsea had risen to over 2,000 and by 1816 to nearly 2,500.[16] By this time, however, growth in the rest of Portsea parish was outstripping that of Portsea town. In the 1780s Portsea parish outside the town had just over 700 rated properties. By the

15 B. L. Add. MSS 41363, Martin Papers, quoted in Geddes (1970, p. 18).
16 PCRO 81A/3/21/2 and Portsea Parish Poor Rate Books 1815/16 (B and F), quoted in Cramer (1985a, pp. 56–58 and 126).

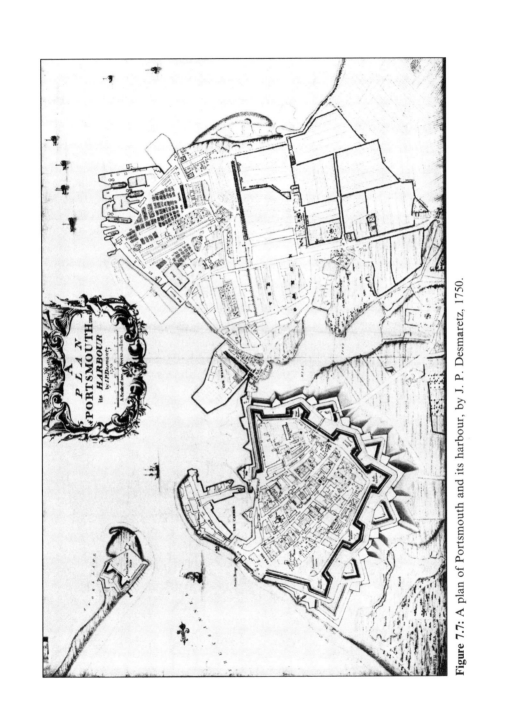

Figure 7.7: A plan of Portsmouth and its harbour, by J. P. Desmaretz, 1750.

1790s this figure had risen to over 1,000, but in the first 15 years of the nineteenth century expansion accelerated to over 3,000, an increase of more than 200 per cent.

Not surprisingly, these increases in employment and house-building were reflected in the level of baptisms recorded in the Portsmouth and Portsea parish registers (Figures 7.8, 7.9 and 7.10). After the peak of baptisms reached in the later years of the War of Spanish Succession, there followed a decline which lasted until the late 1730s. Once again war, in the form of the Austrian Succession (1740–1748), appears to have enhanced Portsmouth's population: both Portsmouth's and Portsea's baptisms peaked in 1747. From the mid-eighteenth century onwards the daughter town was to constantly record more baptisms than its parent settlement. Inevitably the walled town of Portsmouth was nearing its limits of growth as the 'use of the small remaining amount of vacant land within the town provided sites for several hundred more houses' (Chalklin, 1974, p. 122) probably built on gardens and by creating crowded courts. Any additional growth would have to take place outside the town and away from its fortifications, hence the more rapid growth of Portsea (see Figures 7.8, 7.9 and 7.10).

Even so, both communities recorded increases in baptisms from 1756 when the Seven Years' War began and reductions after the war ended. In the five-year period from 1751 to 1755 Portsmouth averaged 190 baptisms per annum and Portsea 251. In the last five years of the decade, all war years, the respective

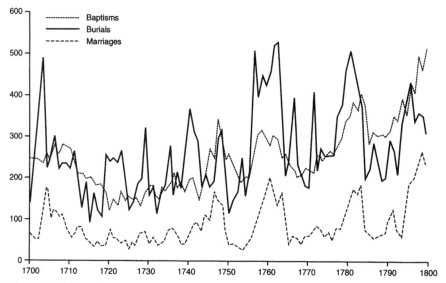

Figure 7.8: Annual registrations of baptisms, burials and marriages at St Thomas's parish, Portsmouth, 1700–1800.

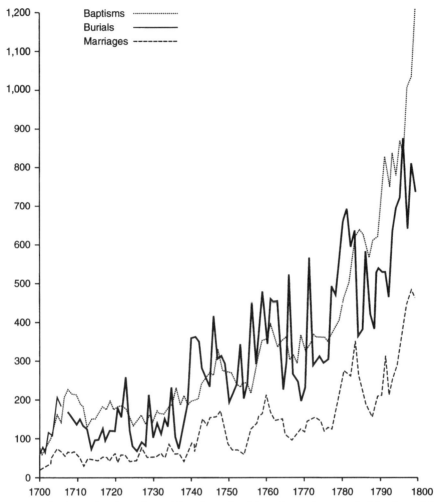

Figure 7.9: Annual registrations of baptisms, burials and marriages at St Mary's parish, Portsea, 1700–1800.

totals were 262 and 326, representing increases of 25 and 30 per cent respectively. In the five years immediately following the end of the war the annual totals were 210 and 330: Portsmouth's numbers fell, while Portsea's growth was maintained. From this time on the general trend of Portsea's baptisms was constantly upwards, with the largest increases occurring during the French wars; by 1800 over 1,000 baptisms were registered annually. Baptisms in Portsmouth also rose in the 1790s reaching an average of nearly

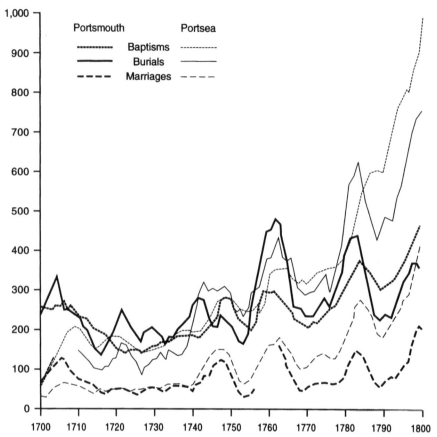

Figure 7.10: Five-year moving average of registrations of baptisms, burials and marriages at St Thomas's parish, Portsmouth and at St Mary's parish, Portsea, 1700–1800.

500 in the last few years of the century, but this was followed by a fall to an average of not much over 300 in the first decade of the nineteenth century, whereas Portsea's growth continued. Bearing in mind the growth of non-conformity in the late-eighteenth and early-nineteenth century, these figures clearly understate the extent of population development.

The parish registers of Portsmouth Town only recorded a limited number of registered non-conformist baptisms, but the presence of the Baptist and Congregational chapels in Portsea meant that the parish's total was supplemented by approximately 200 additional annual baptisms by the end of the eighteenth century.[17] From the 1750s Portsea appears to have achieved

17 Baptist records are at the PRO RG4 1806 and Congregationalists at PCRO, CHU 91/2.

self-sustaining demographic growth. There seems little doubt that this was largely due to the expanding dockyard as the naval authorities continued to actively oppose the development of commercial shipping. As late as 1851 the Board of Ordnance refused Portsmouth Corporation permission to establish a commercial port at the Mill Pond located north of the town between it and the dockyard (Gates, 1928).

Perhaps the Admiralty's opposition to commercial port development sprang not only from fear of interference with the passage of naval ships, but also from the increasing self-sufficiency of the dockyard and its consequent limited need for imported supplies. The range of occupations undertaken in the dockyard indicates its breadth of manufacturing including, for example, sailmakers, mastmakers and ropemakers. The existence of metal-, saw- and block-mills were the most obvious manifestations of the dockyard's own manufacturing activities. In addition, the military and naval authorities had developed their own facilities for provisioning the armed forces. In the town a great brewery had been established and in 1774 the Reverend William Gilpin referred to 'The bakery, salting-houses, and other victualling offices' which, he said, 'would appear enormous if we had not a counterpart in the many floating castles and towns lying ready in the harbour to receive their contents...' (Gilpin, 1804; Hoad, 1972, p. 21). Naval bakehouses were operated to provide the Navy with biscuits, and the Crown had bought in 1714 the one tide-mill in Portsmouth, Kings Mill, to supply the bakeries with flour (Riley, 1976). This considerable level of self-sufficiency reduced the opportunities for Portsmouth manufacturers to supply the Navy and, since much of the victualling was transferred to the Royal Clarence Victualling Yard at Gosport, this also failed to offer employment to the local population. Nevertheless, by the beginning of the nineteenth century an industrial complex as large as the dockyard must have been of considerable value to the local economy, particularly since self-sufficiency could never be total. In 1800, for example, 39,300 cwt of biscuits, 26,400 cwt of beef, 3,000 bushels of salt and 14,300 quarters of malt were purchased, almost certainly in part from the stocks of local suppliers (Thomas, 1961, pp. 52–54).

Whether those local suppliers lived in Portsmouth rather than Portsea is conjectural. It seems likely that those established in Portsmouth before the later growth of Portsea would have been advantageously placed to supply whatever the dockyard required. This view is strengthened by the fact that the overwhelming number of references to Portsea occupations in the eighteenth century concern those employed in the dockyard itself. Portsea was the town where the dockyard workers lived, particularly shipwrights, but also sawyers, blockmakers and mastmakers, caulkers, sailmakers, riggers and ropemakers. The town, therefore, had a high degree of specialization in dockyard work.

One eighteenth-century observer, however, did suggest that Portsmouth was developing in an entirely new direction. Dr Richard Pococke stated in 1754 that 'The town of late has been resorted to for batheing and drinking the sea water, and they have made a very handsome bathing-house of wood, at a great expense...' (Cartwright, 1889, p. 115). Other references to such a development are few, although an anonymous writer in 1807 commented that 'On the beach at Portsmouth are bathing machines; but the bathing is very uncomfortable owing to the quantity of sea-weed in which one gets entangled' (Anon, 1809; Hoad, 1973, p. 10). These developments were probably for the residents of Portsmouth and Portsea (Cramer, 1985a): not until after the Napoleonic Wars, with the building of a pump room and baths near the sea front in 1816, was a conscious attempt made to attract visitors to a holiday resort. Permission for the pump room's erection close to the seaward end of the town's fortifications was granted by the Board of Ordnance, but it was conditional on its easy removal should it interfere with the arc of fire of the artillery batteries (Gates, 1928, p. 5). The military authorities also controlled Southsea Common along the whole seafront west of Southsea Castle and their influence on the potential development of a resort was considerable.

DEMOGRAPHIC DEVELOPMENTS IN THE NINETEENTH CENTURY AND THEIR CONSEQUENCES

In the nineteenth century it becomes possible through the availability of census data to ascertain the demographic characteristics and occupational structure of the two communities with greater certainty. In this context, the 1851 census is perhaps the most useful, since it provides figures for Portsea Island in which both Portsmouth and Portsea towns are separately identified from the growing sub-districts outside them (Kingston in the north-east and Landport, including Southsea, in the south-east of the island). Moreover, the number of people in these sub-districts of Portsea parish are estimated back to 1801, whereas in reality they are only separately distinguishable in the census returns from 1841 (Census of Great Britain, 1851; Census of England and Wales, 1861–1891). The census figures show that the rapid population growth demonstrated by the baptism registrations in the last decade of the eighteenth century continued in the first half of the nineteenth. The population of the island, excluding the northern periphery which lay in Wymering parish, more than doubled from 33,226 in 1801 to 72,126 in 1851, in parallel with that of the nation as a whole, and its share of south-east Hampshire's population further increased from 52.7 to 61.1 per cent.

The increase was uneven both chronologically and spatially (Table 7.4), with substantial population growth recorded in the first and last decades of the half century. In the first decade population increased by over 25 per cent, with Portsea and its two expanding suburbs of Kingston and Landport growing by 32 per cent: Portsmouth Town, by contrast, actually declined. This overall growth rate was undoubtedly related to the expanding dockyard activity during the Napoleonic Wars, although the contemporaneous decline in Portsmouth's population is more difficult to explain. It could be that a

Table 7.4: *Census population totals and intercensal changes, Portsmouth Borough, 1801–1891.*

Portsmouth Borough	*1801*	*1811*	*1821*	*1831*	*1841*	*1851*	*1861*	*1871*	*1881*	*1891*
Portsmouth Town	7,839	7,103 (−9.4%)	7,269 (+2.3%)	8,083 (+11.2%)	7,135 (−11.7%)	8,218 (+15.2%)	10,346 (+25.9%)	11,169 (+8.0%)	7,591 (−32.0%)	7,661 (+0.9%)
Portsea Town	8,348	11,004 (+32%)	12,622 (+14.7%)	13,919 (+10.3%)	14,177 (+1.8%)	16,383 (+15.5%)	19,967 (+21.9%)	18,430 (−7.7%)	17,183 (−6.8%)	14,730 (−14.3%)
Landport (including Southsea)	10,130	13,353 (+32%)	15,315 (+14.7%)	16,888 (+10.3%)	17,139 (+1.5%)	26,742 (+56.0%)	41,426 (+54.9%)	55,455 (+33.9%)	64,721 (+16.7%)	80,306 (+24.1%)
Kingston	6,909	9,107 (+32%)	10,442 (+14.7%)	11,449 (+10.1%)	12,105 (+5.3%)	17,626 (+45.6%)	23,089 (+31.0%)	28,541 (+23.6%)	39,127 (+37.1%)	56,581 (+44.6%)
Total	33,226	40,567 (+21.1%)	45,648 (+12.5%)	50,389 (+10.4%)	50,556 (+0.3%)	68,969 (+36.4%)	94,828 (+37.5%)	113,595 (+19.8%)	128,622 (+13.2%)	159,278 (+23.8%)

Note: Percentages in brackets are the intercensal changes in population.
Source: Censuses of Great Britain, 1851 and of England and Wales, 1861–1891.

number of the less well-off inhabitants moved out as rates and rents rose to unaffordable levels, whereas other families may have moved to better properties in the expanding suburbs. Alternatively, assuming that the first two censuses are fairly accurate, there were nearly 50 fewer occupied houses in 1811 than in 1801; perhaps some older properties had become uninhabitable or been demolished without having been replaced.

In each decade from 1811 to 1841, unlike other major urban centres of England, Portsmouth's growth rate progressively declined, with Portsea, Kingston and Landport registering almost parallel trends. From 1811 to 1821 they grew at just under 15 per cent; from 1821 to 1831 they increased by 10 per cent or so; from 1831 to 1841 Portsea and Landport grew by less than 2 per cent and Kingston by just over 5 per cent. It seems probable that the decline in dockyard employment from a peak of approaching 4,000 in 1814 to less than 2,000 by 1832 influenced this declining growth rate, particularly given the fact that by 1841 well over half (58 per cent) of Portsmouth's industrially-occupied male labour force were dockyard workers (Cramer, 1985b, p. 43; Census of Great Britain, 1851; Riley, 1976, p. 9). Total weekly dockyard wages fell from £6,000 to £3,000 and those still employed had their wages reduced (Gates, 1900a, p. 606). Similarly, between 1810 and 1813 there had been 19,200 naval and marine personnel in Portsmouth; between 1816 and 1830 their number had declined by 80 per cent to 3,800 (Thomas, 1961, p. 85). However, in the 1840s unequivocal growth was once again experienced: the overall intercensal increase (1841–1851) on the island was 36 per cent, but there were exceptionally large increments in Landport, including the emergent Southsea, of over 56 per cent, as well as in Kingston of 45.6 per cent. Portsea was still growing, but by only 15 per cent, and in the case of Portsmouth the increase only marginally restored the losses of the previous decade. It would seem that both the fortified towns were beginning to reach the limits of expansion within their walls. Portsmouth, apparently, had done so in the eighteenth century, growing by under 5 per cent between 1801 and 1851 and, despite a later boost resulting from the presence of military personnel, the town ended the century with a smaller population than it had at the beginning. Portsea, the fortifications of which were completed only in 1809, had grown to its intramural limits by the mid-nineteenth century and had almost doubled its population in 50 years so that it was now twice the size of its parent community (see Figure 7.11).

However, it was in the developing suburban sub-districts of Kingston and Landport that the most dramatic population increases were experienced. Between 1801 and 1851 the former had an estimated increase of 155 per cent and the latter of 164 per cent. Landport was almost certainly larger than either of the towns as early as 1801 and Kingston became so by 1851 by which time Landport and Southsea had a greater population than both towns combined. Landport's spectacular growth in the 1840s can be ascribed to two major causes. First, the development of larger steam-powered ships necessitated an extension of the dockyard; a seven-acre steam basin was built between 1843

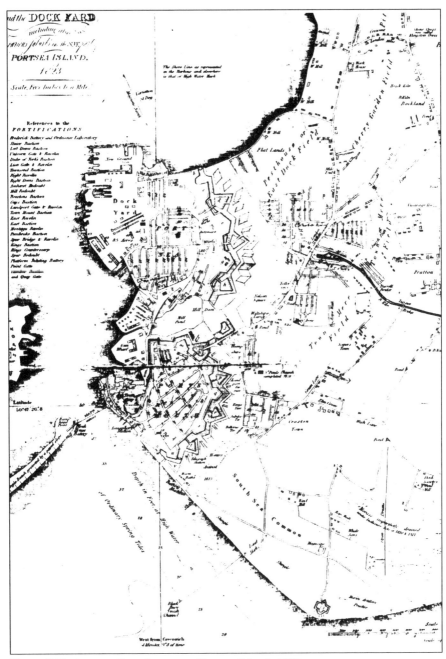

Figure 7.11: A map of south-western Portsea Island, 1823.

and 1848 and a 600 feet-long steam factory was opened the following year
(Riley, 1985, pp. 15–21). Not surprisingly, the size of the dockyard labour force
increased, reaching nearly 3,000 in 1851 when it employed some 63 per cent of
male industrial workers in Portsmouth. Secondly, came the continuing
development of Southsea as a residential suburb and its beginnings as a
seaside resort. In the early-nineteenth century Landport was already
developing east of Portsea and what was to become known as Southsea was
emerging east of Portsmouth in a small area known as Croxton Town (Figures
7.11 and 7.12) with housing for artisans, most probably dockyard workers in
the French wars. However, on the western extremity of this development,
Regency terraces were being built with views overlooking the open pasture in
front of Portsmouth's fortifications and with much higher rateable values.
They were completed by 1827 and became the residences of Portsmouth's rising
middle class, with more than one-third of them occupied by the nobility and
gentry. To the east of Croxton Town new villas built in their own spacious
grounds were also beginning to appear. The middle-class residents included
many of the senior naval and military personnel, some having migrated from
the crowded old town of Portsmouth to the open environment on the western
and eastern peripheries of Croxton Town. It was only after 1830, however, that
the more rapid expansion of Southsea, as it was now known, occurred (see
Figure 7.12).

To the north-east, expansion meant that by the 1840s Southsea had grown to
merge with Landport. To the south-east, expansion reached the seafront by the
1850s, with new villas extending along the northern edge of Southsea Common
which had been drained of much of its marshy area in 1823 and completely
levelled 20 years later. What was significant about this two-directional
development was that, unlike the old town of Portsmouth, distinct social
stratification emerged. The northern sector possessed many of the characteristics of Landport. It was overwhelmingly artisan in nature, housing many
dockyard workers or those employed in support services for the yard. In terms
of housing density and its lack of open space, it was, like Landport, very much
a working-class residential area. Conversely, the southern sector contained
development of an entirely different nature; spacious houses in their own
grounds scattered thinly over the district clearly confirmed its middle-class
standing (Figure 7.13) (Riley, 1972, pp. 3–9). Simultaneously, the Regency
terraces overlooking Portsmouth's fortifications had become less attractive to
the middle class who had largely moved out to the spacious environment of
East Southsea. By the 1840s, these terraces contained 30 lodging-houses, nearly
four-fifths of the total existing in 1847, and provided the first indication that
Southsea was becoming an attraction for seaside visitors (Riley, 1972, p. 11).
Thus it was not until the second half of the nineteenth century that tourism
developed along the seafront at Southsea which, until then, had expanded as a
middle-class residential suburb of Portsmouth providing spacious housing for
military and naval personnel and those profiting from supplying them.

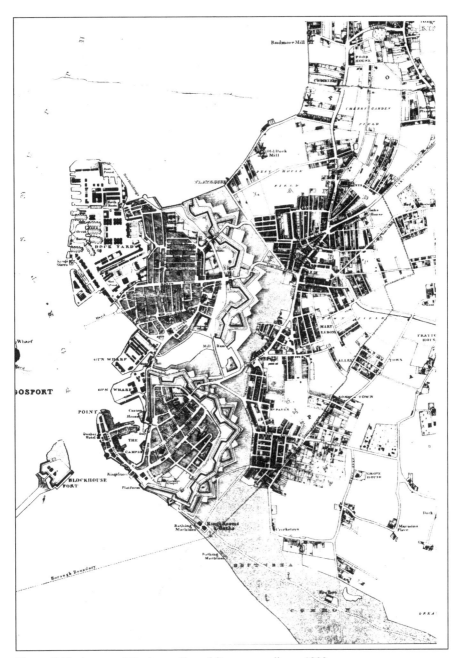

Figure 7.12: A map of Portsmouth and its surroundings, 1833.

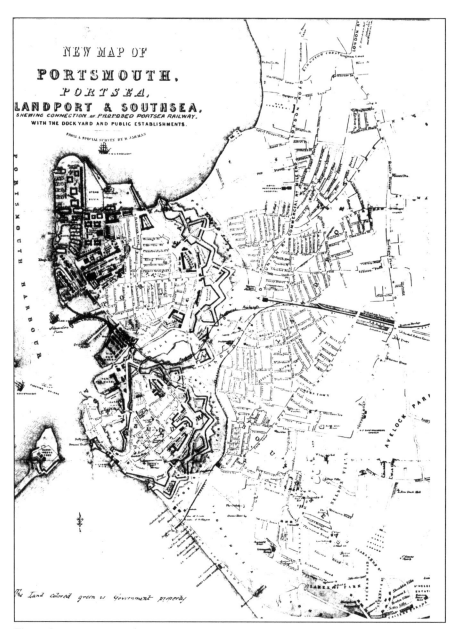

Figure 7.13: New map of Portsmouth, Portsea, Landport and Southsea, by R. Jarman, 1853.

The overall scale of development can be estimated from the figures of inhabited houses provided in the decennial censuses. Whereas Portsmouth Town had almost exactly the same number of houses in 1851 as in 1811, this was some 54 (4.5 per cent) fewer than in 1841. Portsmouth, within its ramparts, had no space to grow and the 1840s saw some inhabitants leave the town to settle in Southsea. Portsea parish, meanwhile, saw its occupied housing grow from 4,393 in 1801 to 5,768 in 1811, 7,527 in 1821 and to 8,215 in 1831, an increase of 87 per cent, while its population grew by two-thirds. From 1841 to 1851 it is possible to separate Portsea Town's housing figures from those for the rest of the parish and it is noticeable that Portsea's housing stock, unlike its population, had begun to decline. In 1841 Portsea possessed 2,969 houses, whereas in 1851 this had shrunk to 2,820—a loss of over 5 per cent. These figures indicate that while Portsea's population had increased by some 2,200 people in the 1840s, thereby considerably exacerbating over-crowding, some of the better-off had migrated to the developing and more spacious suburb of Southsea, as well as to Landport and Kingston.

The 1850s saw the problem of Portsea's over-crowding worsen; while the housing stock remained much the same, the population increased by over 3,500, or by nearly 22 per cent. For the next 30 years, however, both the number of houses and the population steadily declined. Total houses fell from 2,831 to 2,611, while population shrank from nearly 20,000 to under 15,000. Thus Portsea's houses, which contained an average household of 7.5 persons in 1861, were less crowded by 1891, with an average of 5.5 persons.

The town of Portsmouth also registered a decline in both the number of houses and people in the second half of the nineteenth century. Between 1851 and 1891 the housing stock declined by 149 (14.4 per cent) and simultaneously the population, after initially rising to over 11,000 in 1871, fell to 7,661 by 1891. These fluctuations were heavily influenced by the presence or absence of service personnel. For example, in 1871 five naval ships were in port containing nearly 2,300 men, but only two ships with under 500 men were enumerated in 1881. Consequently, whereas total personnel in ships and barracks in 1871 numbered nearly 5,000, there were less than 2,000 in 1881. Thus most, although not all, of the population decline of over 3,500 between 1871 and 1881 can be attributed to the movement of service personnel, as could the growth of population between 1851 and 1861.

That other factors also affected the demographic development of Portsea and Portsmouth, however, is amply demonstrated in the 1871 census where it was noted that there had been:

a gradual removal of residents from the business centres of Portsea and Portsmouth to the modern suburbs outside the walls. Landport, one of these suburban parts, possesses the attractions of a large open common and a long stretch of sea-beach ... Another cause of the increase of population is the growing reputation of Southsea as a watering-place, and the consequent great demand for houses of a superior description. (See Figure 7.13)

Nevertheless, the census officials were not unaware of the demographic consequences of the services, for the entry also stated that the 'naval and military (and consequently to some extent the civilian) population is liable to great fluctuation'. Furthermore, the important effect of the dockyard on the island's population was recognized since the note continued 'Government works now in progress (the principal of which is the extension of the dockyard) employ several thousand men, a large proportion of whom live outside the town' (Census of England and Wales, 1871, p. 77). This latter comment was essentially a repetition of a similar one made in the previous census of 1861 when the increase in population on Portsea Island was 'attributed mainly to the government works in progress; the number of labourers and artizans employed in H. M. Dockyard, as well as the military force in the garrison, is much larger than in 1851' (Census of England and Wales, 1861, p. 254).

It is the housing figures of the 'modern suburbs' which indicate clearly where urban growth in the 1840s was taking place. Kingston in 1841 had a stock of 2,539 houses, but in 1851 this had expanded to 3,597, including 58 under construction, an increase of nearly 42 per cent. Landport, which included Southsea, had an even more phenomenal growth with the number of houses increasing by 55 per cent from 3,911 to 6,064 (including 107 under construction). The scale of housing development substantially benefited both employers and employees in the building industry which registered an increase of 82 per cent in its workforce between 1841 and 1851. The number of enumerated builders rose from 34 to 57 and of identifiable building workers from 398 to 729.[18]

These increases heralded a half-century of Victorian expansion in the two suburbs. Whereas in the 1840s and 1850s some 3,000 new homes were constructed, the 1860s and 1870s each saw the figure rise to about 4,000 before the astonishing boom of the 1880s when almost 7,500 houses were built. Until 1871 approximately two-thirds of this growth in housing stock took place in Landport, mostly in the Southsea part of the suburb, following the release of land by local landowners (Riley and Chapman, 1989, p. 80). In the 1870s, however, slightly more than half the new houses were constructed in Kingston which witnessed a doubling in its newly-built housing to nearly 6,000 in the 1880s (Figure 7.14). This growth was reflected in the rising number of employed building workers which had risen to over 1,600 by 1881 (Census of England and Wales, 1881). By then the number of carpenters and joiners had increased to over 1,400 and, since the Navy was rapidly becoming an ironclad one, most of these men must have been employed in the building sector.

18 Carpenters have been excluded from the number of building workers since it is not known what proportion of them worked in the dockyard. There were 517 enumerated in 1841 and 704 in 1851.

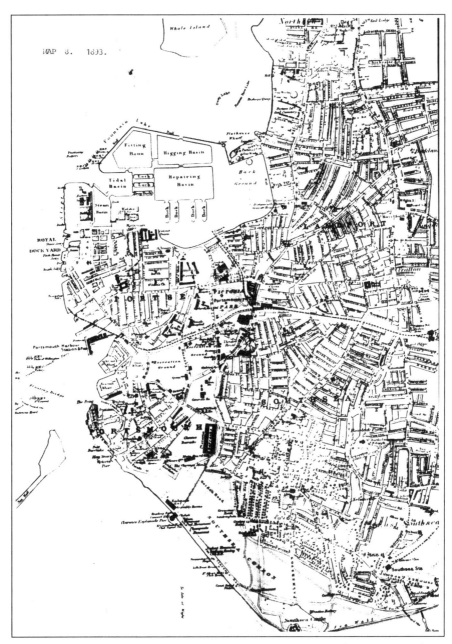

Figure 7.14: Ordnance Survey map of Portsmouth, Portsea, Landport and Southsea, 1893–1896.

The other employment area to benefit from Southsea's growth was domestic service. In 1841 some 2,750 individuals, mostly women, were employed as domestic servants; by 1851 this figure had risen to over 4,000. One factor which contributed to this increase in female employment was the curiously imbalanced sex ratio of the population on Portsea Island. Between 1801 and 1841 there were never fewer than 3,500 more females than males and a peak of over 6,500 surplus females was reached in 1831, when they represented 13 per cent of the total population (Tables 7.5 and 7.6; Census of Great Britain, 1851). The next three censuses show a gradual reduction in this unbalanced sex ratio until 1861 when it had almost completely disappeared. However, by 1891 the number of surplus females had risen once more to over 6,000. The expansion of Southsea and the demand for increasing numbers of domestic servants clearly does not provide a complete explanation for fluctuations in the sex ratio. An examination of marital status and age structure reveals some interesting differences. Despite the general surplus of females, the censuses show that among single people aged 20 and over there were always considerably more males than females, fluctuating between a low of almost 2,000 in 1891 and a peak of over 6,300 in 1871. Clearly, then, it was among the married and the widowed that females predominated. In fact the number of surplus married females rose steadily from over 1,700 in 1851 to more than 4,600 in 1901, while there were rarely fewer than 2,000 surplus widows and as many as 4,700 in 1891. However, when the distribution of males and females in the most fertile age groups between 15 and 34 is examined, Portsmouth and Portsea always had a surplus of young men, with Landport (including Southsea) and Kingston—the expanding suburbs—exhibiting a surplus of resident females. The former two districts contained most of the army barracks and naval ships and this provides an explanation for the fluctuating surplus of young men.

However, most ports with commercial shipping and fishing as important sectors of employment tended by their very nature to report surpluses of females in their census returns. In addition, since many soldiers and naval seamen married locally, Portsmouth had a problem of one-parent families when husbands either put to sea or were posted away. This frequently meant that the income received by their wives was spasmodic or non-existent: some husbands never returned, having been killed or lost overseas. It would seem that the majority of absent soldiers and seamen were resident in Kingston and Landport and hence the suburbs' surplus of married women was directly related to the military and naval presence. The imbalanced marital structure of the island's population, in turn, created a volatile situation with attendant social problems. The loss of a Portsmouth-based ship, such as the *Birkenhead*, which went down in 1852 with the loss of 436 lives, only served to aggravate the situation, producing an increase in the number of widows for whom the Admiralty made no provision (Riley and Chapman, 1989, p. 77). In any case, sailors and soldiers were among the low paid of the nineteenth century and their wages were frequently inadequate to maintain families. Dockyard

Table 7.5: *Population distribution by sex, 1801–1901.*

		1801	1811	1821	1831	1841	1851	1861	1871	1881	1891	1901
Portsmouth Town	M	3,148	2,887	2,881	3,347	4,800	5,784	6,405	7,425	4,580	5,184	91,069
	F	4,691	4,216	4,388	4,736	4,093	4,113	3,941	3,744	3,011	2,477	97,064
Portsea	M	3,798	6,041	6,793	6,026	6,725	9,574	12,000	11,226	10,306	8,699	
	F	4,550	5,983	6,924	7,893	8,043	8,161	7,967	7,204	6,877	6,031	
Landport, incl. Southsea	M	4,618	6,104	6,927	7,326	7,520	11,904	19,005	25,357	28,798	35,493	
	F	5,512	7,249	8,388	9,562	9,707	14,894	22,421	30,098	35,329	44,813	
Kingston	M	3,280	4,344	4,919	5,203	5,546	8,223	10,915	14,573	18,739	27,178	
	F	3,629	4,773	5,523	6,296	6,524	9,473	14,174	14,968	20,388	29,403	
Total	M	14,844	19,366	21,520	21,902	24,591	35,485	48,325	57,581	62,423	76,554	91,069
	F	18,382	22,221	25,223	28,487	28,467	36,641	48,503	56,014	65,605	82,724	97,064

Table 7.6: *Population distribution by sex ratios (females per 100 males), 1801–1901.*

	1801	1811	1821	1831	1841	1851	1861	1871	1881	1891	1901
Portsmouth Town	149	146	152	141	85	71	62	50	66	48	
Portsea	120	99	102	131	120	85	66	64	67	69	
Landport incl. Southsea	119	119	121	131	129	125	118	119	123	127	
Kingston	111	110	112	121	119	119	130	110	109	108	
Total	124	121	123	130	116	103	100	97	105	108	107

workers were also among the ranks of the lower-income earners and their wages seldom matched those of workers employed in commercial shipyards (Holland, 1971, pp. 56–57).

Consequently, many wives living in Portsea, Kingston and Landport were forced to find some form of employment. Those with children to support often needed to work from home, and the development of the clothing trades in nineteenth-century Portsmouth was specifically geared to their needs. Since free uniforms were still not issued to naval and military personnel even by the 1850s, the tailoring trade, which was already important in the eighteenth century, continued to flourish. Dockyard self-sufficiency had not developed to the exclusion of all Portsmouth manufacturing, although this was largely the case in relation to shipbuilding, metalworking and engineering (Riley and Chapman, 1989, p. 77). However, the majority of tailors were male—80 per cent of those over 19 years of age in 1841 and 90 per cent in 1851—and the majority of women, over 1,100 in 1841 and more than 2,800 in 1851, were employed as dressmakers, seamstresses and staymakers. Even allowing for some possible under-enumeration in 1841, the increase of over 150 per cent within a ten-year period was impressive. Dressmaking was an activity to be found in all large towns in nineteenth-century England and it was only slightly over-represented in Portsmouth. Seamstresses, however, were more than five times and staymakers over fifteen times more numerous in Portsmouth than in the country as a whole. Clearly some form of industrial concentration had taken place. Most of the seamstresses appear to have been involved in shirtmaking and advertisements were placed in local papers by Landport agents for women to work at home: one advertisement alone in 1846 was for '600 white shirtmakers' (Riley, 1976, p. 15). This provides clear evidence for the expansion of the 'putting-out' or domestic system in mid-nineteenth-century Portsmouth and the rapid growth of the clothing industries. However, a greater proportional expansion occurred in staymaking, with a rise of 168 per cent in its labour force in the 1840s making Portsmouth England's most important centre for the corset industry. Plymouth, also a town with dockyard employees and sailors' wives, had a similar concentration of corset manufacture, suggesting again that the availability of cheap female labour was a critical factor. The origins of the industry in Portsmouth, however, are not clear: there were two staymakers in the town in the late-1790s and six are recorded for the eighteenth century as a whole (Christie, 1976, p. 17). In 1831 there were 19 male staymakers listed in Portsmouth and its suburbs, including Gosport and Alverstoke: by 1841 there were 53 males aged over 19, representing 26 per cent of total staymakers. On this basis, approximately 60 women were employed as domestic workers in 1831, probably supplying their products to the local officers' wives and the rising middle class. By 1841, however, with 233 women employed and staymaking expanding, the market had ceased to be a local one and this was reflected by the establishment of warehouses by those organizing the domestic system to complement a workforce that by 1851 had reached over 500 (Riley, 1981, pp. 241–48).

Clearly, Portsmouth entrepreneurs expanded 'domestic activities' both in the service sector and in industry to take advantage of the available surplus of cheap female labour. The employment problem for surplus females was also resolved in a further manner. In 1841 over 1,800 women were stated to be of independent means, compared with only 421 men. In 1851 the numbers were below 600 and 100, respectively, perhaps reflecting some re-classification process. Although more women were widowed than men, the presence of some 1,800 women of independent means in 1841 calls for an explanation, particularly since their numbers were greater than those employed in both the clothing industries and domestic service. The only satisfactory explanation would seem to be that many of these women belonged to a 'profession' for which Portsmouth had long been known. In 1795 one visitor, G. Pinckard, less than captivated by the charms of the town, felt it necessary to state that:

... hordes of profligate females are seen reeling in drunkenness, or plying upon the streets in open day with a broad immodesty...

To form to yourself an idea of these tender, languishing nymphs, these lovely, *fighting ornaments* of the fair sex, imagine a something of more than Amazonian stature having a crimson countenance, emblazoned with all the effrontery of Cyprian confidence and broad Bacchanalian folly; give to her bold countenance the warlike features of two wounded cheeks, a tumid nose, scarred and battered brows, and a pair of blackened eyes, with balls of red; then add to her sides a pair of brawny arms, fit to encounter a Colossus, and set her upon two ankles like the fixed supporters of a gate. Afterwards, by way of apparel, put upon her a loose flying cape, a man's black hat, a torn neckerchief, stone rings on her fingers, and a dirty white, or tawdry flowered gown, with short apron, and a pink petticoat; and thus will you have something very like the figure of a '*Portsmouth Poll*'.

Callous to every sense of shame, these daring objects reel about the street, lie in wait at the corners, or, like the devouring Kite, hover over every landing place, eager to pounce upon their prey; and each unhappy tar, who has the misfortune to fall under their talons has no hope of escape until plucked of every feather ... and thus poor Jack, with pockets full of prize money, or rich with the wages of a long and dangerous cruise, is, instantly, dragged (though, it must be confessed, not always against his consent) to a bagnio, or some filthy pot-house, where he is kept drinking, smoking, singing, dancing, swearing, and rioting, amidst one continual scene of debauchery, all day and all night, and all night and all day, until his every farthing is gone. He is then left to sleep until he is sober, and awakes to return, pennyless, to his ship, with much cause to think himself fortunate if an empty purse be the worst consequence of his long wished-for ramble ashore. (Gates, 1900b, pp. 487–88)

This colourful, if not lurid, description of the prostitutes of Portsmouth suggests that at least in wartime they existed in large numbers and it seems more than likely that many of the 1,800 women described as 'of independent means' in the 1841 census would have been members of the 'oldest profession'. Even in peacetime in the nineteenth century it was stated that large numbers of prostitutes frequented Portsmouth, some 1,355 being registered in 1865 (Hopgood, 1872; Christie, 1976, p. 230).

The existence of such large numbers of prostitutes is explained not only by the need of many women without husbands to seek financial support, but also by the presence of large numbers of single young men with no counter-balancing proportion of single young women. It seems likely that these prostitutes acted as a damper on the potentially explosive mix of the sexes on Portsea Island since illegitimacy rates did not rise, despite the imbalanced sex ratio. Illegitimate births actually fell from just over four per cent of registered births in 1861 to just over three per cent from 1871 to 1901, a rate that was lower than for the rest of Hampshire.[19]

Given that the island's population growth rate was above the national average, it is reasonable to expect that births generally would have been at a higher level and that consequently the proportion of children under 15 would have been greater than in England as a whole. This should have been reinforced by the fact that the island's population growth was fuelled by in-migration, with the proportion of residents born outside the county rising from 42 per cent in 1851 to 50 per cent by 1871. Since most migration was short-distance, the inclusion of migrants from the rest of Hampshire would imply considerably higher real levels of migration into Portsmouth. As the majority of migrants were young people in the child-bearing age groups (Stapleton, 1988), high birth rates should have been recorded in the second half of the nineteenth century. Yet, while the under 15 age group formed over 36 per cent of the nation's population between 1851 and 1871 (Wrigley and Schofield, 1982, p. 529), in Portsea Island from 1841 to 1881 children only formed between 32 and just over 34 per cent of the total population. The explanation

19 24th, 34th, 44th, 54th and 64th Annual Reports of the Registrar General of Births, Deaths and Marriages in England (1861, 1871, 1881, 1891, 1901).

for such a relatively small child population lay in the presence of numerous military and naval personnel who distorted the island's age structure. In 1851 the fleet was in port; sailors then numbered over 3,500 and the garrison had been expanded to over 2,650 soldiers and 880 marines in response to a perceived threat from France. Since most of the servicemen were based in the town of Portsmouth or in Portsea, it was in these two districts that numbers of children were at their lowest. In Portsmouth Town, which had a disproportionate number of service personnel, children constituted only between 22 and 25 per cent of the total population between 1851 and 1881, and in Portsea between 24.5 and 27 per cent. Clearly, the dockyard's growth made it a paramount factor in the affairs of both the Town and Portsea from the late-seventeenth to the late-nineteenth century. Although there was an underlying local economy of traders, small-scale manufacturing, clothing production, building, domestic service and transport, it can be seen that much of the development was either directly or indirectly due to the expansion or otherwise of the dockyard.

In comparison with Portsmouth Town and Portsea, the suburbs of Kingston and Landport contained no barracks and registered the large child population that would normally be expected in rapidly growing communities. During the period from 1851 to 1881 children under 15 years formed between 35.4 and 37.3 per cent of Landport's population, while in Kingston the proportion rose from 37 to 39.4 per cent, almost matching the nation's largest ever recorded cohort of under-15-year-olds in 1826 (Wrigley and Schofield, 1982). Conversely, Portsmouth Town and Portsea had considerably larger proportions of their populations in the working age group 15–60; in 1881 this group constituted approximately three-quarters of the total population in the town and even more in Portsea. Kingston and Landport, with much larger ratios of dependent children, had only between 53 and 57 per cent of their populations in the working age groups. The elderly, namely those over 60 years of age, constituted between 4 and 8 per cent of the total population in the four districts; the lowest proportion being in Portsmouth Town and the highest in Kingston, which accordingly had the highest overall dependency ratio.

CONCLUSION

With Portsea Island by 1901 containing nearly three-quarters of the region's population, its importance cannot be doubted. If Gosport and Alverstoke are added to the island's total, then nearly 84 per cent of the regional population was provided by the two harbour communities. Growth elsewhere, as in Fareham, the third-largest community in the region with over 8,000 people, as well as in Wymering and Farlington, was equally likely to have resulted from the increasing influence of Portsmouth. In the two-and-a-half centuries from 1650 to 1890 Portsmouth had grown more than forty-fold. No community could have expanded at such a pace without attendant problems of over-crowding, sanitation, water-supply, drainage, vice and poverty. Portsmouth was no exception, as the description of crowded Messum's Court in Old Portsmouth demonstrated:

> below sea-level, and therefore very damp ... reached through a tunnel only two feet wide. Here 116 people lived, some of them in cellars, with one privy between them and one standpipe which supplied water for perhaps ten minutes a day. Through the court ran a large open drain as well as an open midden and when this was emptied the contents would remain for three days on the surface opposite the exit, suffocating the whole area with its stench. (Rawlinson, 1850; Stanford and Patterson, 1974)

Over-crowding in life was paralleled in Portsmouth by over-crowding in death. A local doctor, Henry Slight, commented in 1850 on the burial grounds in both Portsmouth and Portsea. St Mary's churchyard, Portsea, was 'full even to repletion' and of St Thomas's, Portsmouth he noted 'if the walls were to give way, the bodies would fall into the street ... The gasses of putrefaction ... readily escape, poisoning the atmosphere and dealing death and disease in all directions' (Slight, 1850; Phillips, 1974, p. 7).[20]

Slight was commenting in the wake of Portsmouth's only major epidemic of the first half of the nineteenth century, namely the cholera outbreak of 1848. However, the average annual death rate in Portsmouth in the 1840s, prior to the cholera outbreak, was over 25 per 1,000 and since the recently formed national Board of Health was empowered, on request, to investigate any area where mortality exceeded 23 per 1,000 an inquiry began in December 1848 following a request from local residents. Robert Rawlinson, Superintendent Inspector of the General Board of Health, heard the evidence and reported in 1850. His major findings concerned the 'ill-paved and unclean streets, imperfect privy accommodation, crowded courts and houses with large exposed middens and cesspools'. Disease was 'traced to the undrained and crowded districts, to deficient ventilation, to the absence of a full water supply, and of sewers and drains generally'.[21] Rawlinson also commented on the lack of adequate powers for local government and the detrimental effect of the fortifications of Portsmouth and Portsea in interfering with natural drainage. These were both factors which were clearly not unconnected with the restrictive naval and military presence in Portsmouth.

Finally, what may well have been the best solution for Portsmouth's economic and social problems would have been the ability to develop its economy on a broader base, less dependent on the dockyard. There is little doubt that the borough authorities were conscious of this need, attempting to encourage commercial trade in the harbour. The Admiralty, however, was opposed to such developments, so much so that the authorities explored the

20 PCRO 11A/22/13 Henry Slight's report (1850), quoted in Rosemary Phillips (1974, p. 7).
21 For the cholera outbreak and Rawlinson's report, see M. Hallett (1971).

possibilities of locating commercial docks on the eastern side of Portsea Island in Langstone Harbour, away from the town and the dockyard.[22] The costs of this proposal, which included a ship canal from west of Southsea Castle to Langstone Harbour, were to be £2 million, an astonishing sum for the town in the 1840s. There were also clear disadvantages to this scheme, including the inadequate entrance to Langstone Harbour, which necessitated the construction of a canal, and the limited deep-water anchorage. Hence, it was perhaps no surprise that the borough once again in 1851 approached the Board of Ordnance to see if the naval authorities would allow the development of the Mill Pond as a commercial dock. Once again permission was refused. It could be argued that the rapid growth in ship size in the second half of the nineteenth century made this a sensible decision from the point of view of the city's future expansion.

Yet it ensured that Portsmouth grew on a narrow economic base, substantially dependent, whether directly or indirectly, upon employment provided by the Navy and the dockyard (Mason, 1989, p. 167). This was a factor noted in *White's Directory* in 1878 when it was stated that the 'borough derives considerable support from its extensive dockyard and naval and military establishments, but these have prevented it from rising to that commercial importance to which it would have risen if the government would have allowed the construction of large Commercial Docks'.[23] Had the government done so, it can hardly be doubted that the region's population in general, and Portsea Island's in particular, would have seen even more phenomenal growth in the nineteenth century. But the truth was that in distant London the pervasive Admiralty connection maintained power over Portsmouth's port development and thereby also over its demographic growth.

References

ANON (1809), *Journal of a Tour to the Western Counties of England Performed in 1807*.
BARNETT, C. (1974), *Britain and Her Army 1509–1970*, London.
CARTWRIGHT, J. J. (ed.) (1889), *Travels Through England of Dr. Richard Pococke* (Camden Society, **II**), London.
CENSUS OF GREAT BRITAIN (1851), Vol. I.
CENSUS OF ENGLAND AND WALES (1861), Vol. II.
CENSUS OF ENGLAND AND WALES (1871), Vol. II.
CENSUS OF ENGLAND AND WALES (1881), Vol. III.
CENSUS OF ENGLAND AND WALES (1891), Vol. III.
CHALKLIN, C. W. (1965), *Seventeenth-Century Kent*, London.
CHALKLIN, C. W. (1974), *The Provincial Towns of Georgian England*, London.

22 PCRO P3 30 November 1844, Plans and Sections of Spithead and Langstone Docks and Ship Canal. I am grateful to Dr Patricia Haskell for this reference. An earlier scheme in 1837 had proved similarly abortive; see Gates (1928, p. 18).
23 *White's Directory*, 1878, quoted in Riley (1976).

CHAPMAN, J. (1974), 'The geographical evolution of Portsmouth', in J. B. Bradbeer (ed.), *Portsmouth Geographical Essays*, Portsmouth.

CHRISTIE, P. (1976), 'Occupations in Portsmouth 1550–1850', unpublished MPhil thesis, Portsmouth Polytechnic.

COLEMAN, D. C. (1953), 'Naval dockyards under the later Stuarts', *Economic History Review*, 2nd Series, **VI**, 2, 134–55.

CRAMER, J. (1985a), 'The origins and growth of the town of Portsea to 1816', unpublished MPhil thesis, Portsmouth Polytechnic.

CRAMER, J. (1985b), *The Book of Portsmouth*, Buckingham.

DEFOE, D. (1962), *A Tour Through the Whole Island of Great Britain*, London (Everyman edition).

GATES, W. G. (1900a), *Illustrated History of Portsmouth*, Portsmouth.

GATES, W. G. (1900b), *History of Portsmouth*, Portsmouth.

GATES, W. G. (ed.) (1928), *Records of the Corporation 1835–1927*, Portsmouth.

GEDDES, A. (1970), 'Portsmouth during the Great French Wars 1770–1860' (The Portsmouth Papers, No. 9), Portsmouth.

GILPIN, W. (1804), *Observations on the Coasts of Hampshire, Sussex and Kent in 1774*.

HALLETT, M. (1971), 'Portsmouth's water supply 1800–1860' (The Portsmouth Papers, No. 12), Portsmouth.

HOAD, M. J. (1972), 'Portsmouth—as others have seen it. Part I, 1540–1790' (The Portsmouth Papers, No. 15), Portsmouth.

HOAD, M. J. (1973), 'Portsmouth—as others have seen it. Part II, 1790–1900' (The Portsmouth Papers, No. 20), Portsmouth.

HOLLAND, A. J. (1971), *Ships of British Oak. The Rise and Decline of Wooden Shipbuilding in Hampshire*, Newton Abbot.

HOPGOOD, P. D. (1872), 'The workings of the Contagious Diseases Act in Portsmouth', *The Portsmouth Times and Hampshire Telegraph*, 30 March.

HORNE, R. S. (1965), 'H. M. dockyard at Portsmouth: a chronology', mimeo.

JACKSON, R. (1974), 'The development of manufacturing in Portsmouth', in J. B. Bradbeer (ed.), *Portsmouth Geographical Essays*, Portsmouth.

KITSON, Sir H. (1947), 'The early history of Portsmouth dockyard', *Mariners' Mirror*, **33**, 256–65.

LATHAM, R. C. and W. MATTHEWS (eds) (1974), *The Diary of Samuel Pepys*, 9 vols, London (1667).

MARKHAM, C. R. (ed.) (1895), *Life of Captain Stephen Martin, 1666–1740* (Navy Records Society), London.

MASON, H. (1989), 'The twentieth-century economy', in B. Stapleton and J. H. Thomas (eds), *The Portsmouth Region*, Gloucester, 167–78.

MASTERS, B. R. (1968), *Portsmouth Through the Centuries*, Portsmouth.

MORGAN, L. V. (1947), 'An historical review of Portsmouth dockyard', *Engineering*, **164**, 414–16.

MORGAN, L. V. (1948), 'An historical review of Portsmouth dockyard in relation to our naval policy', *Transactions of the Institution of Naval Architects*, **90**, 18–32.

PHILLIPS, R. (1974), 'Burial administration in Portsmouth and Portsea 1820–1900', unpublished Portsmouth Local History Dissertation, Portsmouth.

RAWLINSON, R. (1850), *Report to the General Board of Health on the Sewage, Drainage and Water Supply of Portsmouth*, Portsmouth.

RILEY, R. C. (1972), 'The growth of Southsea as a naval satellite and Victorian resort' (The Portsmouth Papers, No. 16), Portsmouth.

RILEY, R. C. (1976), 'The industries of Portsmouth in the nineteenth century' (The Portsmouth Papers, No. 25), Portsmouth.

RILEY, R. C. (1981), 'The Portsmouth corset industry in the nineteenth century', in J. Webb, N. Yates and S. Peacock (eds), *Hampshire Studies*, Portsmouth, 241–48.

RILEY, R. C. (1985), 'The evolution of the docks and industrial buildings in Portsmouth dockyard, 1698–1914' (The Portsmouth Papers, No. 44), Portsmouth.

RILEY, R. C. and J. CHAPMAN (1989), 'The nineteenth century', in B. Stapleton and J. H. Thomas (eds), *The Portsmouth Region*, Gloucester, 72–82.

SLIGHT, H. (1850), 'Intramural interments, medical statistical and historical evidence ... on the cemeteries of Portsmouth', PRCO 11A/22/13.

SPARKS, H. J. (1912), *A Naval History of Portsmouth*, Portsmouth.

STANFORD, J. and A. T. PATTERSON (1974), 'The condition of the children of the poor in mid-Victorian Portsmouth' (The Portsmouth Papers, No. 21), Portsmouth.

STAPLETON, B. (1988), 'Migration in southern England', *Southern History*, **X**, 47–93.

STAPLETON, B. (1989), 'The population of the Portsmouth region', in B. Stapleton and J. H. Thomas (eds), *The Portsmouth Region*, Gloucester, 83–120.

THOMAS, F. N. G. (1961), 'Portsmouth and Gosport: a study in the historical geography of a naval port', unpublished MSc thesis, London University.

THOMAS, J. H. (1985), 'The seaborne trade of Portsmouth, 1650–1800' (The Portsmouth Papers, No. 40), Portsmouth.

THOMAS, J. H. (1989), 'From civil war to Waterloo', in B. Stapleton and J. H. Thomas (eds), *The Portsmouth Region*, Gloucester, 59–71.

WILLAN, T. S. (1967), *The English Coasting Trade 1600–1750*, Manchester.

WRIGLEY, E. A. and R. S. SCHOFIELD (1982), *The Population History of England 1547–1871. A Reconstruction*, London.

Chapter 8

THE PORT-CITY LEGACY: URBAN DEMOGRAPHIC CHANGE IN THE HANSESTADT BREMEN, 1815–1910*

ROBERT LEE and PETER MARSCHALCK

INTRODUCTION

It is commonly assumed that the accelerated expansion of urbanization in Western Europe in the nineteenth century was primarily a result of large-scale industrialization. This was clearly the case in relation to areas dominated by coal mining and iron and steel production, such as the towns in the Ruhr valley, in northern France, as well as in the West Midlands in England. However, other urban communities, for example port-cities and commercial and service centres, frequently registered population growth on the basis of pre-industrial employment structures and only later underwent industrialization. In particular, with increasing functional specialization within the urban hierarchy of individual European nation-states in the course of the nineteenth century, many port-cities became disproportionately dominated by shipping, commerce and maritime-related activities. They frequently failed to develop a strong and widely-based manufacturing industry and tended to concentrate on the processing or refining of imported raw materials, or acted as centres for a variety of commercial activities from warehousing to trade, banking and insurance. Although individual port-cities, such as Genoa and Glasgow (Felloni, chapter 3, above; Gibb, 1983; Cage, 1987), were able to shift their sectoral emphasis in the course of the nineteenth century, with a perceptible diversification in their employment structures, the emergence of industrial ports is essentially a more recent phenomenon. As a result the development of most port-city economies led to the persistence of pre-industrial employment structures aggravated by an increased demand for poorly-paid, casual labour.

The purpose of this chapter is to analyse the dynamics of demographic change in Bremen in the nineteenth century. In this context Bremen was typical of many European port-cities: for most of the period under consideration it remained disproportionately dependent on trade and commerce, as well as traditional, small-scale handicraft production. It was only after the completion of key infrastructural improvements in railway communications and port

* Research for this paper was funded by Stiftung Volkswagenwerk, Hanover and The Wellcome Trust, London. The authors are grateful for their support.

facilities that large-scale industrial development took place in the last two decades of the nineteenth century. The chapter will therefore examine the demographic implications of urbanization within an essentially pre-industrial framework. It will attempt to assess the interrelationship between the specific pattern of economic development in Bremen and contemporary trends in fertility, mortality and in-migration. In particular it will seek to show how mortality trends and the pattern of in-migration continued to reflect the persistence of pre-industrial employment structures, while significant changes in fertility preceded the development of large-scale industrialization.

ECONOMIC DEVELOPMENT AND EMPLOYMENT STRUCTURE

In terms of the overall structure of employment, occupational data for 1862 and 1905 reveal a marked degree of continuity (Table 8.1). As expected, agricultural employment was insignificant (ranging between 1.5 and 2.2 per cent) and there is little evidence of any substantial increase in employment in the public sector, as was the case in other German states (Cullity, 1967; Henning, 1984). Trade and commerce accounted for approximately one-third of all available jobs: in contrast to the situation in other types of towns and cities, the relative and continuing importance of trade and commerce was a clear reflection of Bremen's role as one of Germany's premier port-cities. The comparative role of this sector in other cities was often marginal: in Barmen (Rhineland) in 1867 trade and commerce accounted for 8 per cent of employment; in Esslingen (Württemberg) in 1868 for 5.8 per cent; and in Lüdenscheid (Rhineland) in 1907 for 10.4 per cent (Köllmann, 1974b, p. 45; Schraut, 1989, p. 33; Herbig, 1977, p. 60). Bremen in the first half of the nineteenth century already functioned as an emigrant port, but concentrated primarily on the import of an extensive range of staple goods, particularly

Table 8.1: *The development of male and female employment in Bremen, 1862 and 1905.*

| | Percentage of all male and female employment, respectively | | | |
| | 1862 | | 1905 | |
Economic sector	Male	Female	Male	Female
Agriculture	2.1	2.4	2.0	2.0
Industry and crafts	46.4	27.1	46.6	24.9
Trade and commerce	34.0	8.4	35.3	19.4
Domestic service	3.2	43.0	0.2	29.1
Public employment	8.6	3.2	9.4	4.6
Unspecified	5.5	13.8	6.4	19.7

Sources: *Zur Statistik des Bremischen Staats*, 1862, p. 25; *Volkszählung vom 1. Dezember 1905 im Bremischen Staate*, 1909, p. 105.

tobacco, sugar, animal skins and French wines. From the 1850s onwards cotton imports became a key component in Bremen's trading and shipping activities.

By the early 1860s industry had become the largest source of employment in Bremen. In 1816 craft production accounted for approximately 38 per cent of available jobs in the port-city; by 1862 this proportion had risen to more than 46 per cent and it remained at this level until the early-twentieth century. However the nature of industrial employment changed significantly during the period under consideration (Table 8.2). At the beginning of the nineteenth century industrial employment was primarily in food production and clothing manufacture, and small-scale craft production was predominant. The industrial development of Bremen began in the mid-seventeenth century with the processing of tobacco and sugar-refining, as well as soap manufacture—all of which were closely dependent on the city's trading activities. As far as the political élite of the city was concerned trade and commerce continued to determine economic development and daily life, as the debates concerning the creation of port facilities in Bremerhaven (1827) and the establishment of the Customs Union (*Zollverein*) reveal (Schwarzwälder, 1976, pp. 121–33). Even by the late 1840s mechanized production remained an exception and was only to be found in glass manufacture and certain aspects of textile production (in particular linen and cotton weaving). Although Bremen had a machine factory and an iron foundry, the level of employment in this sector by 1847 remained insignificant.

In comparison with the early-nineteenth century, data for 1847 reveal a notable reduction in food production and, to a lesser extent, in clothing manufacture and distribution, but a rise in employment opportunities in

Table 8.2: *Industrial employment structure in Bremen, 1816–1905 (per cent).*

Sector	1816	1847	1862	1905
Food production	21.2	8.6	8.7	7.5
Clothing	36.8	29.3	37.5	16.0
Building and ship construction	16.7	26.1	22.1	20.5
Craft production	18.2	9.6	11.0	10.1[a]
Machine construction	–	0.4	2.5	24.6
Tobacco and cigar manufacture	3.1	20.6	14.5	3.8
Miscellaneous	3.9	5.2	3.5	17.6
Total industrial labour force	1,737	4,517	13,596	29,737

Sources: Schäfer, 1957, pp. 172–233; *Zur Statistik des Bremischen Staats*, 1862, p. 25; *Volkszählung vom 1. Dezember 1905 im Bremischen Staate*, 1909, p. 105.

Note: 1816–1862 employers and employees, 1905 only employees.

[a] 1905: craft production = wood products.

building and ship construction and, more specifically, in tobacco and cigar manufacturing. From the 1820s onwards the tobacco industry and cigar manufacturing became typical industries for Bremen and by 1850 this sector offered more employment opportunities than any other branch of industry. At its peak in 1852 approximately 10,000 people were involved, either directly or indirectly, in cigar production (Burgdorf, 1984, p. 46). However, the predominance of this sector was a temporary phenomenon, as Bremen manufacturers increasingly relocated production within the territory of the *Zollverein*, primarily to avoid the imposition of restrictive tariffs. By 1877 cigar manufacturing had virtually disappeared from the city and the return to protectionism in 1879 further undermined Bremen's trading relations with the *Reich* (Henderson, 1984, p. 332).

By the late-nineteenth and early-twentieth centuries fundamental changes had taken place in the structure of industrial employment. The belated modernization of industrial production in Bremen was reflected in the development of extensive employment opportunities in machine construction and metalworking, which by 1905 accounted for almost one-quarter of all industrial employment. In comparison, clothing manufacture, tobacco and cigar production, as well as craft-based production had declined in relative importance (Table 8.2).

The gender-specific employment profile of the period between 1862 and 1905 was characterized by a noticeable decline in the extent of female domestic service and a more than two-fold increase in female employment in trade and commerce (from 8.4 to 19.4 per cent of all female workers). With respect to industrial employment during the same period, the proportion of women employed in clothing manufacture and distribution fell from 66.2 per cent to 40.7 per cent and the decline in tobacco manufacturing was reflected in an even greater fall in female employment from 30.8 per cent to 5.5 per cent. By 1905 a significant number of women were employed in a more modern industrial sector, namely jute spinning, which accounted for 30 per cent of all female workers in Bremen.

The available occupational data for Bremen therefore reflect the relatively late transformation of the port-city's economic and employment structures. Trade and commerce remained disproportionately important and it was only in the latter decades of the nineteenth century that small-scale handicraft production was finally displaced by the emergence of more modern industries, in particular metalworking and machine construction.

POPULATION GROWTH AND MIGRATION

In 1812 Bremen's total population was slightly above 35,000; by 1849 this had risen to over 53,000, an overall increase of 50 per cent (Schäfer, 1957). In comparison with industrializing towns in the Rhineland this rate of population growth was relatively modest: the increase in total population in Barmen was

170 per cent (1809–1858), in Lüdenscheid nearly 90 per cent (1817–1840), and in Krefeld 70 per cent (1823–1840) (Köllmann, 1960, 1974a, p. 187; Matzerath, 1985, p. 78). Moreover, the average annual growth rates of Bremen's population lay well below those of other European port-cities, such as Cardiff and Malmö during the same period (see Lee and Lawton, chapter 1, above). The later decades of the nineteenth century, however, were characterized by higher annual population growth rates, ranging from 1.7 per cent to 2.6 per cent within the period 1849 to 1895, whereas in the decade 1895–1905 Bremen grew at an unprecedented rate of 4 per cent per annum (Table 8.3).

Like many other European cities Bremen's population development depended to a large degree on in-migration. During the first half of the nineteenth century net in-migration was a more important factor in the city's demographic growth than natural population increase. In the 1850s and the 1860s, however, both factors made an approximately equal contribution. Until the 1880s the persistence of pre-industrial employment structures, the continued dominance of small-scale craft production, and the relatively late abolition of guild controls in 1862 to a large degree determined the nature and composition of the city's in-migration. As a result, a pre-industrial migration structure was evident throughout this period of significant urban growth. A high proportion of in-migrants were either craftsmen (*Handwerker*) or domestic servants (*Dienstboten*) who came from the surrounding rural areas or the cities and towns of central and northern Germany. For example, in the early 1830s approximately two-thirds of in-migrant domestic servants came from the adjacent territories of Hanover and Oldenburg and evidence from the 1850s indicates that a large number of in-migrant journeymen still came from these two territories, although long-distance migrants were now relatively more common (Marschalck, 1988).

The abolition of immigration barriers and controls in 1862, together with the

Table 8.3: *Population of Bremen, 1812–1905.*

	Total population	Total increase	% growth per year	Natural growth	Net in-migration
1812	35,370	–	–	–	–
1823	39,581	4,211	1.0	1,184	3,027
1849	53,365	13,784	1.1	5,827	7,975
1862	66,648	13,283	1.7	6,556	6,727
1871	80,779	14,131	2.2	6,299	7,832
1885	115,901	35,122	2.6	21,103	14,019
1895	137,972	22,071	1.8	13,316	8,755
1905	204,329	66,357	4.0	22,516	43,841

Source: Matti, 1979, p. 69 *et seq.*; population figures relate in each case to January 1.

lifting of traditional guild restrictions, had an important influence on the structure of in-migration into Bremen. In the short run, however, it led to a rising level of in-migration by journeymen and craftsmen, some of whom sought employment in handicraft production and traditional trades, whereas the majority could only be accommodated in unskilled work. Although the proportion of non-native inhabitants in Bremen's total population was already high by the mid-nineteenth century, it grew substantially from about 36 per cent in 1862 to more than 46 per cent by 1905. Despite this upward trend, however, in-migrants in many other industrial cities in Germany constituted a far higher proportion of total population, as was the case in 1907 in Gelsenkirchen (61.4 per cent) and Bochum (63.5 per cent), as well as in other Prussian commercial and service centres (Köllmann, 1974a, p. 171; Laux, 1989, p. 136). Despite the increasing role of natural population growth in Bremen's demographic development, the late-nineteenth and early-twentieth centuries witnessed a marked expansion in the level of net in-migration: between 1895 and 1905 it contributed two-thirds of the city's population increase. This further growth in net in-migration was a reflection of the delayed onset of industrial development in Bremen, particularly in the metalworking and machine construction sectors which attracted increasing numbers of workers from eastern regions of Germany during this period.

By 1905 male and female in-migrants represented 61 and 54 per cent of Bremen's total workforce. At the same time there had been a perceptible increase in long-distance migration and in-migrants were now firmly located both in industrial employment and in trade and commerce. In contrast to the situation in the first half of the nineteenth century, in-migrants were now employed in machine construction, metalworking and ship-building, as well as in more traditional sectors such as clothing manufacture, cleaning and food production. Although in-migrant women had fewer opportunities than the native-born in Bremen's formal labour markets, it is important to note that the more modern jute-spinning industry recruited almost half of its female work force from Galicia in Austria-Hungary (Ellerkamp, 1983, 1991). By the early twentieth century domestic service was no longer as important a source of female employment: in 1905 it accounted for just under 30 per cent of all female workers in comparison with 43 per cent in 1862. It also remained largely a preserve of in-migrant women from the surrounding rural areas.

THE SIGNIFICANCE OF LATE INDUSTRIALIZATION FOR MORTALITY TRENDS

Because of their transport links port-cities were frequently prone to an increased risk of exposure, particularly from infectious diseases, which contributed to high levels of mortality. The continuing importance of commerce and trade led to a proliferation of unskilled or casual employment, often associated with residential over-crowding, poor quality housing and relatively high death rates. Although not all port-cities conformed to the law of urban natural decrease (de Vries, 1984), many continued to register high levels of mortality well into the nineteenth century. This was certainly the case, for example, in Bordeaux, Toulouse, Glasgow and Liverpool (Guillaume, 1969; Agulhon, 1980; Cage, 1987; Lawton, chapter 4, above).

In the case of Bremen, however, the crude death rate as early as 1825 was already under 30 per 1,000 (Table 8.4) and for each decade within the period 1830 to 1909 a surplus of births was registered. However, the crude mortality rate underwent a noticeable increase, specifically in the 1860s and the 1870s when infant mortality rates also rose. To a large extent this rise in overall mortality as well as in infant mortality can be attributed to higher levels of in-migration following the abolition of immigration barriers and the extensive influx of migrant workers into a port-city still dominated by pre-industrial employment structures. The unpredictability of unskilled casual employment in this context contributed to the persistence of high infant mortality (Spree, 1995, p. 16).

This point is reinforced by an examination of the changing pattern of the differential mortality of the in-migrant and native-born population of Bremen in the period 1862–1905. In specific sectors of Bremen's port economy in the early 1860s the crude death rates of in-migrants were significantly higher than equivalent rates for the native-born. A great deal of dock work and port-related employment was particularly dangerous and the accident rate, particularly in winter, was often high, contributing to excess male mortality in the age groups 25–30 and above. Employment in trade and commerce involved a high proportion of unskilled labourers, particularly in transport-related activities, and during the 1860s the crude death rate for in-migrants employed in this sector of Bremen's economy was 15.7 per 1,000, in comparison with a figure of 12.6 per 1,000 for native-born workers. Similarly,

Table 8.4: *Mortality trends and crude birth rates in Bremen, 1830–1909 (per 1,000).*

	Crude death rate	Infant mortality rate	Crude birth rate
1830–1839	23.9	177	27.8
1840–1849	21.7	170	29.1
1850–1859	19.5	184	30.2
1860–1869	24.2	208	33.5
1870–1879	23.8	203	39.7
1880–1889	20.1	203	31.4
1890–1899	17.2	192	29.7
1900–1909	16.5	178	30.7

Sources: Böhmert, 1926, p. 42; Matti, 1979, pp. 69–70.

age-specific mortality data from the early 1870s provide clear confirmation of a noticeably higher crude death rate among in-migrant males in the age group 24–32 in comparison with the native-born.

A further insight into the differential health hazards encountered by the native-born and in-migrant elements of Bremen's population can be obtained by an analysis of disease-specific mortality trends. On the basis of the available census data and the civil death registers for the early 1860s and 1870s, disease-specific mortality rates were calculated for 1862 and 1871. Despite the increasing acceptance by the medical profession and the Bremen authorities of the need to adopt an aetiological classification of disease, a symptom-based classification remained predominant during this period (Leidinger, Lee and Marschalck, 1997), thereby facilitating a direct comparison of the two data sets. The analysis focused on individual causes of death which arguably reflected the differential impact of contemporary economic and labour market conditions on the two population groups.

The available evidence (Table 8.5) reveals a perceptible deterioration in general health conditions, as far as the selected individual causes of death are concerned. It is interesting to note, however, that in terms of mortality from liver disease and alcoholism there were no appreciable differences between the native-born and in-migrants. Indeed in-migrant men registered a slightly lower mortality rate than their indigenous counterparts, although the reverse was the case in relation to women in 1871. It would therefore appear that neither in-migrant males nor females had extensive recourse to excessive alcohol

Disease 8.5: *Disease-specific mortality rates in Bremen, 1862 and 1871 (per 1,000).*

	Native-born		In-migrants	
Cause of death	*Male*	*Female*	*Male*	*Female*
1862				
Liver disease and alcoholism	0.31	0.27	0.23	0.21
Lung diseases	4.53	4.33	4.41	3.57
Infectious diseases	4.67	3.16	1.87	0.91
Violence/accidents	1.09	0.19	3.38	0.32
1871				
Liver disease and alcoholism	0.34	0.14	0.28	0.23
Lung diseases	6.60	5.78	6.80	4.80
Infectious diseases	4.82	4.21	3.84	2.24
Violence/accidents	1.35	0.23	3.03	0.35

Note: Lung diseases include tuberculosis and inflammation of the lung; infectious diseases include deaths from measles, scarlet fever, diphtheria, smallpox, abdominal typhus, etc.
Source: Civil Death Registers of the City of Bremen, 1861–1863 and 1870–1872.

consumption that might otherwise have been expected in a new and somewhat insecure environment (Fridlizius, 1988; chapter 5, above). In contrast, both in 1862 and 1871, mortality rates for in-migrants from violent causes of death and accidents were significantly higher than for the native-born; this was particularly the case for male in-migrants, although in-migrant women were also disadvantaged in this respect. The high frequency of deaths from violence and accidents, especially among in-migrant males, provides further confirmation of their disproportionate involvement in more dangerous, casual and unskilled forms of employment during this period and would seem to indicate a more limited integration within Bremen's established economic and social structures.

By the late-nineteenth and early-twentieth centuries the adverse mortality profile of most in-migrant age groups had been reversed and their crude death rates were now lower than the equivalent native-born population. Indeed, among economically active men in the age groups 15–50, who were disproportionately involved in the migration process, mortality rates for in-migrants were significantly lower by 1905 (Table 8.6).

The calculation of life tables for both the in-migrant and native-born components of Bremen's population in 1905 confirms the reversal in relative life expectancy of the two groups. In-migrant males now enjoyed appreciable advantages at ages 15, 20 and 25, in comparison with their native-born counterparts. Slightly higher life expectancies were also registered for in-migrant males at ages 30, 35, 40 and 45. Although the life expectancy of in-migrant females in 1905 was generally higher than that of the native-born population throughout the whole age range 0–80, the differences were not generally as great in comparison with the advantages enjoyed by in-migrant males.

The long-term trends in mortality in nineteenth-century Bremen can be attributed to two factors. First, up until the mid-1860s both the scale and nature of in-migration were shaped by the persistence of an essentially pre-industrial local economy and rigorous official control mechanisms with regard to immigration and settlement. As a result a great deal of in-migration by domestic servants and journeymen/craftsmen was by definition short term. Urban growth in Bremen during the first half of the nineteenth century, as was the case in other German cities undergoing rapid expansion and industrialization, was inevitably accompanied by a significant increase in mortality levels. However, because of the specific nature of its local economy the scale of the urban penalty was far less significant than in most other industrial conurbations or port-cities. As noted above, the increased level of in-migration which resulted from the lifting of immigration and guild controls in 1862 was followed by a noticeable rise in overall mortality. Secondly, although the decline in mortality in the latter decades of the nineteenth century was influenced by a variety of factors, including sanitary reforms and improved living standards among the urban working class (Vögele, 1993; Orsagh, 1969),

Table 8.6: *Life expectancy (in years) at different ages in the city of Bremen, 1905.*

	Native-born population		In-migrant population	
Age	*Male*	*Female*	*Male*	*Female*
0	45.87	51.07	43.27	48.74
1	54.66	58.05	54.96	59.23
5	54.26	58.07	55.57	59.77
10	50.39	54.49	51.62	56.19
15	45.95	50.32	47.51	52.05
20	41.80	46.24	43.23	47.67
25	37.93	42.48	39.04	43.52
30	34.16	38.43	34.90	39.49
35	30.46	34.36	30.80	35.52
40	26.50	30.37	26.84	31.50
45	22.92	26.26	23.17	27.47
50	19.79	22.60	19.59	23.42
60	13.41	15.39	13.63	16.18
70	8.39	9.61	8.68	10.36
80	3.96	6.32	4.76	7.00

Sources: Death Registers for the City of Bremen, 1904–1906; 7,633 cases reported; Census data for the City of Bremen, 1905.

Note: Although the in-migrant population amounted to about 46 per cent of total population the age structures of both native and in-migrant populations differed markedly: the ratio of population aged 0–15 to total population was 48.5 per cent in the native population and only 10 per cent in the in-migrant population. Life expectancy for in-migrants at age 0 therefore might not be correct.

the registered improvements in the mortality profiles of both male and female in-migrants also reflected an important change in Bremen's employment structure and in the migration process itself. The late-nineteenth century witnessed the onset of significant industrialization in Bremen, particularly in relation to the development of the metalworking and machine-construction industries. In addition the completion of extensive infrastructural facilities by the late 1880s, including a new railway terminal and important extensions to the port complex, led to a reduced demand for temporary and largely unskilled construction and building workers. Such changes in local employment conditions in the late-nineteenth and early-twentieth centuries meant that in-migrants were no longer disadvantaged by environmental and working conditions. Indeed, by the end of the period under consideration the opportunities afforded by industrial employment seem to have contributed to the higher life expectancy of both male and female in-migrants in comparison with the native-born population and thereby facilitated the downward trend in mortality.

URBANIZATION, LATE INDUSTRIALIZATION AND REPRODUCTIVE BEHAVIOUR

According to Laux (1983, 1989, pp. 138–40) the significance of city function can often be detected in relation to nuptiality and fertility. The sex ratio of the unmarried adult population and the mean age at first marriage for men were the main factors determining the proportion married in late-nineteenth-century Germany (Knodel and Maynes, 1976). Accordingly, nuptiality in many nineteenth-century port-cities was often constrained by unbalanced sex ratios which were in turn a result of gender-specific migration streams, the specific nature of local labour markets and differentiated employment opportunities. In addition, limited opportunities for female work, particularly in certain types of port, tended to reduce marriage opportunities and to limit nuptiality rates. Similarly, average age at first marriage in some port cities such as Glasgow or Toulon was relatively high (Cage, 1987; Agulhon, 1980), despite the absence of institutional or legal constraints on marriage that still applied in various European regions and cities in the first half of the nineteenth century (Lynch, 1991). A high mean age at first marriage for men, in turn, depressed nuptiality, particularly in cities where population growth was dependent to a large degree on in-migration, which was inevitably accompanied by a high proportion of unmarried young women (Laux, 1989, p. 138). Furthermore, in Prussian cities dominated by commercial and service activities both social stratification and income structure were highly differentiated, which also contributed directly to a lower marriage frequency and to a late mean age at first marriage (Laux, 1989).

At the same time the social structure and economic function of different types of cities played a major role in determining both the level and trend in overall fertility. Many nineteenth-century port-cities were characterized by high birth rates and high overall fertility, primarily as a result of their specific labour markets and contemporary employment opportunities, as well as the scale and composition of in-migration. While many workers in the nineteenth century tended to reach their maximum earning power at a comparatively early stage in the employment cycle (Schomerus, 1981), this was specifically the case in relation to unskilled labour. The predominance of casual and unskilled work in port-cities therefore encouraged a high birth rate by truncating the earnings curve for male workers, thereby providing little, if any, justification for a deferred start to family formation. In addition, the limited opportunities for female employment, at least within the formal structures of port-city economies, sustained high fertility rates and contributed to a comparatively late onset of the secular fertility transition (Woods, 1984, 1987). Haines (1979, 1989) has also shown that many larger commercial ports had a dispropor-tionate number of occupations (such as riveters and ship-platers, as well as general labourers) which consistently registered high marital fertility rates. The persistence of high rates of infant mortality in many port-cities and significant levels of in-migration by young men and women (see chapter 1, above), continued to encourage this tendency towards high birth rates into the early-twentieth century. Indeed for certain localities in late-nineteenth century Germany there was a strong correlation between infant mortality and the birth rate (Vögele, 1994, p. 410).

Throughout the first half of the nineteenth century the crude birth rate as well as marital fertility in Bremen remained relatively stable. The number of children per marriage showed virtually no variation over time. However, on the one hand social class became increasingly an important determinant of completed family size. Upper-class families, whether resident in Bremen itself or in rural areas adjacent to the city, had a perceptively higher overall fertility than lower-class families. On the other hand, in-migrant families had a distinctly lower fertility than the native-born urban population (Table 8.7).

These differences in fertility to a large extent reflect the significance of Bremen's contemporary economic and employment structures and the city's continuing concentration on trade and commerce, as well as handicraft-based production. Upper-class men, such as merchants, ship-owners and ship agents, frequently married at a relatively late age during this period, but invariably selected appreciably younger brides with the effect that completed family size was generally greater than in lower-class families. Equally, in terms of average age at first marriage in the period 1820–1875, the native-born population continued to enjoy a comparative advantage. Whereas native-born men and women from the city of Bremen married on average at the age of 28.4 and 24.5 respectively, the equivalent ages for in-migrants stood at 29.0 and 26.6. In this case, although in-migrant males also married at a

Table 8.7: *Completed family size in Bremen, 1820–1875.*

Marriage cohort	Upper class	Lower class	Overall pop.
City of Bremen			
1820–1824	4.2	4.3	4.3
1835–1839	4.9	4.3	4.4
1850–1854	5.0	4.6	4.7
Native-born			4.6
In-migrants			4.3
Bremen villages			
1820–1824	6.2	4.8	5.1
1835–1839	5.5	4.8	5.0
1850–1854	4.0	5.5	5.0
Native-born			5.0
In-migrants			5.0

Source: Marschalck, 1994, pp. 161, 163.

comparatively late age, their brides tended to be noticeably older than the brides of native-born men. The persistence of pre-industrial employment structures in Bremen and their relative expansion during the first half of the nineteenth century limited the opportunities open to in-migrants for permanent settlement and successful upward social mobility. Family formation was therefore delayed and completed family size was invariably smaller than in the case of the native-born population. To this extent, the specific economic characteristics of Bremen had a direct influence on fertility trends during this period.

The application of a partial family reconstitution analysis based on the civil birth and marriage registers of Bremen also highlights other important aspects of fertility trends in the first half of the nineteenth century. In the first instance it is evident that the most frequent completed family size in all three marriage cohorts was between three and four children. In the case of the marriage cohort 1820–1824 over 57 per cent of the couples had up to four children; for the later marriage cohorts (1835–1839, 1850–1854) the respective figure in both cases was 53 per cent (Table 8.8).

The predominance of relatively small families even during a period of significant urban growth reflected not only the persistence of low fertility levels, at least in comparison with rural communities, but also an increasing practice of family limitation in the urban population. Birth interval evidence reveals a clear tendency towards a deliberate concentration of births within a more restricted period of family life. For couples with a completed family size of no more than three children, the marriage cohort of 1820–1824 already provides evidence of extended birth intervals. In such families the average interval between the first and second births was nearly three years, and between the second and third births it exceeded 40 months (Table 8.9).

A significant differentiation in relation to both social class and place of birth is reflected in generally higher average birth intervals among lower-class than upper-class families and this was equally true in relation to in-migrants in comparison with the native-born (at least as far as the interval between the first and the second births was concerned). In general, couples who ultimately had

Table 8.8: *Marriages classified by number of births in the city of Bremen, 1820–1875.*

Marriage cohort	Families by number of births as a percentage of all marriages					
	0	*1–2*	*3–4*	*5–6*	*7–8*	*9+*
1820–1824	8.0	20.5	28.6	18.7	13.4	10.7
1835–1839	11.9	14.7	26.6	22.0	17.4	7.3
1850–1854	3.6	19.8	29.7	24.3	13.5	9.0

Source: as Table 8.7.

Table 8.9: *Birth intervals in families of different size (in months).*

	Cohorts	Up to 3 children		More than 3 children		Total marital fertility
		1/2	2/3	1/2	2/3	
All territories	all	35.9	40.8	26.2	28.8	4.55
Upper class	all	32.3	38.4	25.3	27.4	4.72
Lower class	all	37.5	42.0	26.5	29.4	4.48
Native-born	all	33.8	42.4	26.4	29.5	4.71
In-migrants	all	39.8	38.1	25.5	27.8	4.20
Rural population	all	35.2	42.1	28.2	30.9	5.04
Urban population	all	36.9	41.7	25.5	26.9	4.46
Total population	1820–1824	36.6	43.9	25.4	28.0	4.63
	1835–1839	33.5	37.6	26.9	28.2	4.53
	1850–1854	37.7	42.2	25.9	29.9	4.50

Note: The intervals given are those between the first and second and between the second and third births respectively; about 40 per cent of the families belonged to the group with up to three children; data refer to married couples primarily in the city of Bremen, but also include families resident in the township of Vegesack and in rural areas of Bremen.
Source: Marschalck, 1994, p. 168.

no more than three children registered longer birth intervals than larger families. Given the noticeable differences in birth intervals between small and large families for all three marriage cohorts, it is reasonable to assume that many urban couples practised birth spacing as a means of family limitation.

Although comparable fertility data for other German cities are not available, the evidence from Bremen would seem to suggest that it did not conform to the stereotypical image of a port-city. Average age at first marriage was certainly high, but urban expansion in the first half of the nineteenth century was not accompanied by any significant increase in either marriage or birth rates. To this extent in-migration did not necessarily lead to higher urban fertility levels. In fact, despite the comparatively late industrialization of Bremen, reproductive behaviour reflected the early adoption of family limitation.

The increased influx of migrants in the 1860s and 1870s undoubtedly contributed to a rise in the city's birth rate; during the latter decade the birth rate stood at over 40 per 1,000. However, it is important to note that this was a temporary phenomenon. The fertility decline in Germany from the early 1870s onwards evinced substantial differences, particularly with respect to the timing and rates of the secular fall in fertility. In the case of Bremen the onset of the late-nineteenth-century fertility decline was particularly rapid: from a base line of peak fertility in 1870–1874, a fall of about 13 per cent was recorded within a decade. By 1905–1909 general fertility had decreased by approximately 34 per cent. In comparison with Hamburg, the decline in marital fertility (I_g) between 1871 and 1890 was far more extensive, although by 1910 both port-cities registered relatively similar levels (Table 8.10) (Knodel, 1974, p. 286).

It would seem reasonable, therefore, to conclude that there were certain similarities in the registered fertility trends in Bremen between the first and second halves of the nineteenth century. An intrinsic urban reproductive behaviour pattern was already evident before the onset of industrialization, with family limitation practised by both in-migrants and the native-born. The later secular decline in fertility, which coincided with significant changes in Bremen's employment structures, represented an extension of earlier behavioural patterns. The decline both in general fertility and in marital fertility was more rapid and more extensive in Bremen than in the comparable port-city of Hamburg. Because of the rapid changes in the city's economic environment and local labour markets, the increased opportunities for upward social mobility reinforced the rationality of family limitation and fertility control.

Table 8.10: *Fertility indicators in Bremen, 1830–1909.*

Period	Marriage rate per 1,000	Birth rate[a] per 1,000	General fertility rate[b]
1830–1834	8.0	30.3	
1835–1839	8.6	31.5	
1840–1844	8.2	31.8	
1845–1849	8.2	32.7	
1850–1854	8.4	33.1	
1855–1859	7.7	31.5	
1860–1864	8.9	33.0	
1865–1869[c]	10.1	36.7	281.3
1870–1874	10.8	40.1	288.2
1875–1879	9.2	41.7	286.8
1880–1884	7.7	35.9	250.4
1885–1889	7.8	31.7	226.2
1890–1894	8.9	32.0	226.8
1895–1899	9.2	31.9	217.6
1900–1904	9.6	32.2	208.2
1905–1909	9.5	29.9	188.8

[a] including still births.
[b] live births per 1,000 married women between 16 and 50 years of age.
[c] 1867–1869.
Source: Matti, 1979, pp.78–79; Böhmert, 1907, p. 53; 1926, p. 16.

CONCLUSION

This chapter has sought to examine the dynamics of demographic change in Bremen in the nineteenth century. Like many other Western European port-cities, Bremen's local economy remained dominated for much of the period under consideration by trading and commercial interests. Although industry was also an important source of employment, it was structured along traditional, pre-industrial lines with a continuing emphasis on small-scale, handicraft production. Even by the 1860s the extent of mechanization remained very limited and it was only in the latter decades of the nineteenth century, with the development of metalworking, machine construction and ship-building, that more modern industries finally emerged.

It is only against this background of changing employment opportunities that the demographic dynamics of Bremen in the nineteenth century can be fully understood. The persistence of traditional employment structures and their continued expansion well into the nineteenth century to a large extent determined the scale and composition of the city's in-migrant streams, which remained essentially pre-industrial in nature. The abolition of immigration barriers and controls in the early 1860s also fuelled the proliferation of poorly paid, unskilled, casual labour. It was only with the belated onset of industrialization in the late-nineteenth and early-twentieth centuries that changes in migration patterns, as well as in mortality and fertility trends, became evident.

Within the framework of Bremen's pre-industrial employment structure in-migrants were particularly disadvantaged, as age-specific mortality data for the central decades of the nineteenth century confirmed. This situation was ultimately transformed by the development of modern industries within Bremen's local economy, so that by the early-twentieth century both male and female in-migrants benefited from a higher life expectancy than the native-born population.

The continuing prioritization throughout most of the nineteenth century of trade and commerce, together with small-scale handicraft production, was accompanied by an early recourse to fertility control and family limitation. This reflected both the exigencies of an urban life-style at a time of pre-industrial population growth, as well as an awareness, particularly by more skilled in-migrants, of the need to adapt reproductive behaviour in order to maximize the opportunities for upward social mobility. The sectoral changes in employment opportunities in Bremen in the late-nineteenth century also had a direct impact on fertility and ultimately reinforced the trend towards family limitation.

This analysis has been based on a broad selection of archival data, including the civil marriage, birth and death registers for Bremen, documents relating to in-migration and the acquisition of citizenship, as well as the published census data for 1862, 1871, 1885, 1895 and 1905. Extensive use has been made of these source materials in order to generate disaggregated indicators of both mortality and fertility trends. A more wide-ranging use of similar source materials for other German cities may well offer a sufficiently robust basis for exploring some of the outstanding issues relating to urban demographic change in the nineteenth century and the impact of industrialization on different city types.

References

AGULHON, M. (ed.) (1980), *Histoire de Toulouse*, Toulouse.

BÖHMERT, W. (1907), 'Bevölkerungsstatistik', in H. Tjaden (ed.), *Bremen in hygienischer Beziehung*, Bremen.

BÖHMERT, W. (1926), '100 Jahre Geburtenstatistik in Bremen', *Mitteilungen des Statistischen Landesamts Bremen*, No. 3.

BURGDORF, D. (1984), *Blauer Dunst und rote Fahnen*, Bremen.

CAGE, R. A. (1987), 'Population and employment characteristics', in R. A. Cage (ed.), *The Working Class in Glasgow 1750–1914*, London, Sydney, Wolfeboro, 1–28.

CULLITY, P. (1967), 'The growth of governmental employment in Germany 1882–1950', *Zeitschrift für die gesamte Staatswissenschaft*, **123**, 201–17.

de VRIES, J. (1984), *European Urbanization 1500–1800*, London.

ELLERKAMP, M. (1983), 'Unendliche Arbeit. Frauen in der "Jutespinnerei und -weberei Bremen", 1888–1914,' in K. Hausen (ed.), *Frauen suchen ihre Geschichte. Historische Studien zum 19. und 20. Jahrhundert*, Munich, 128–43.

ELLERKAMP, M. (1991), *Industriearbeit, Krankheit und Geschlecht. Zu den sozialen Kosten der Industrialisierung: Bremen Texilarbeiterinnen 1870–1914*, Göttingen.

FRIDLIZIUS, G. (1988), 'Sex differential mortality and socio-economic change, Sweden 1750–1910', in A. Brändström and L.-G. Tedebrand (eds), *Society, Health and Population during the Demographic Transition*, Umeå, 237–72.

GIBB, A. (1983), *Glasgow: The Making of a City*, Beckenham.

GUILLAUME, P. (1969), 'La societé et la vie quotidienne', in L. Desgraves and P. Dupeux (eds), *Bordeaux au XIXᵉ siècle*, Bordeaux, 239–66.

HAINES, M. R. (1979), *Fertility and Occupation: Population Patterns in Industrialization*, New York, London.

HAINES, M. R. (1989), 'Class differentials during fertility decline: England and Wales revisited', *Population Studies*, **43**, 305–24.

HENDERSON, W. O. (1984), *The Zollverein* (3rd enlarged edition), London.

HENNING, H. (1984), *Die deutsche Beamtenschaft im 19. Jahrhundert*, Stuttgart.

HERBIG, W. (1977), *Wirtschaft und Bevölkerung der Stadt Lüdenscheid im 19. Jahrhundert*, Dortmund.

KNODEL, J. E. (1974), *The Decline of Fertility in Germany, 1871–1939*, Princeton.

KNODEL, J. E. and M. J. MAYNES (1976), 'Urban and rural marriage patterns in imperial Germany', *Journal of Family History*, **1**, 129–68.

KÖLLMANN, W. (1960), *Sozialgeschichte der Stadt Barmen im 19. Jahrhundert*, Tübingen.

KÖLLMANN, W. (1974a), 'Binnenwanderung und Bevölkerungsstrukturen der Ruhrgebietsgroßstädte im Jahre 1907', in W. Köllmann (ed.), *Bevölkerung in der industriellen Revolution*, Göttingen, 171–86.

KÖLLMANN, W. (1974b), 'Die Bevölkerung der Industriegroßstadt Barmen vor und während der Industrialisierungsperiode', in W. Köllmann (ed.), *Bevölkerung in der industriellen Revolution*, Göttingen, 186–207.

LAUX, H.-D. (1983), 'Structural and regional differences of natural population growth in German cities, 1880–1905', *Erdkunde*, **37**, 22–33.

LAUX, H.-D. (1989), 'The components of population growth in Prussian cities, 1875–1905 and their influence on urban population structure', in R. Lawton and R. Lee (eds), *Urban Population Development in Western Europe from the Late-Eighteenth to the Early-Twentieth Century*, Liverpool, 120–48.

LEIDINGER, B., W. R. LEE and P. MARSCHALCK (1997), 'Enforced Convergence: political change and cause of death registration in the Hansestadt Bremen, 1860–1914', *Continuity and Change*, **12** (2), 221–46.

LYNCH, K. A. (1991), 'The European marriage pattern in the cities: variations on a theme by Hajnal', *Journal of Family History*, **16**, 79–96.

MARSCHALCK, P. (1988), 'Der Erwerb des bremischen Bürgerrechts und die Zuwanderung nach Bremen um die Mitte des 19. Jahrhunderts', *Bremisches Jahrbuch*, **66**, 295–305.

MARSCHALCK, P. (1994), 'Städtische Bevölkerungsstrukturen vor der Industrialisierung', in H.-G. Haupt and P. Marschalck (eds), *Städtische Bevölkerungsentwicklung in Deutschland im 19. Jahrhundert*, St. Katharinen, 143–72.

MATTI, W. (1979), *Die Bevölkerungsentwicklung Bremens seit 1700* (Statistische Mitteilungen des Statistischen Landesamts Bremen, Heft 45), Bremen.

MATZERATH, H. (1985), *Urbanisierung in Preußen 1815–1914*, Stuttgart.

ORSAGH, T. J. (1969), 'Löhne in Deutschland 1871–1913. Neue Literatur und weitere Ergebnisse', *Zeitschrift für die gesamte Staatswissenschaft*, **125**, 476–83.

SCHÄFER, H.-L. (1957), *Bremens Bevölkerung in der ersten Hälfte des neunzehnten Jahrhunderts*, Bremen.

SCHOMERUS, H. (1981), 'The family life-cycle. A study of factory workers in nineteenth-century Württemberg', in R. J. Evans and W. R. Lee (eds), *The German Family*, London, 175–93.

SCHRAUT, S. (1989), *Sozialer Wandel im Industrialisierungsprozeß – Esslingen 1800–1870*, Esslingen.

SCHWARZWÄLDER, H. (1976), *Geschichte der Freien Hansestadt Bremen*, vol. 2, Bremen.

SPREE, R. (1995), 'On infant mortality change in Germany since the early 19th century', *Münchener Wirtschaftswissenschaftliche Beiträge*, **No. 95**.

VÖGELE, J. P. (1993), 'Sanitäre Reformen und der Sterblichkeitsrückgang in deutschen Städten, 1877–1913', *Vierteljahrschrift für Sozial und Wirtschaftsgeschichte*, **80** (3), 345–65.

VÖGELE, J. P. (1994), 'Urban infant mortality in imperial Germany', *Social History of Medicine*, **7**, 401–25.

Volkszählung vom 1. Dezember 1905 im Bremischen Staate (1909), Bremen.

WOODS, R. I. (1984), 'Social class variations in the decline of fertility in late-nineteenth-century London', *Geografisker Annaler*, Series B, **66**, 29–38.

WOODS, R. I. (1987), 'Approaches to the fertility transition in Victorian England', *Population Studies*, **41**, 283–311.

Zur Statistik des Bremischen Staats (1862), Bremen.

Chapter 9

CHANGES IN POPULATION DEVELOPMENT, URBAN STRUCTURES AND LIVING CONDITIONS IN NINETEENTH-CENTURY HAMBURG

CLEMENS WISCHERMANN

INTRODUCTION

The former 'free imperial city of Hamburg' (since 1806 'the free Hansa city') was situated with its northern boundaries about 15 miles from the mouth of the Elbe. Ever since the foundation of Hamburg the harbour has played an important economic role in determining urban location. Nevertheless, the area of the old town (the Altstadt and the Neustadt), which was fortified until the Napoleonic Wars, did not show any distinct functional or social differentiation until well into the second half of the nineteenth century.

INNER-URBAN CHANGES IN POPULATION GROWTH AND STRUCTURE

The pre-industrial town naturally did not lack a structural framework nor elements of planning, especially with respect to the construction of streets, public buildings and churches. Its inner-urban structure was based primarily on concepts of urban political power and incorporated certain values and social positions. The decisions affecting economic location were of secondary importance, although there was a natural preponderance for urban economic life to be based in the harbour area of Hamburg. However, Hamburg's development was not accompanied by a clear separation between housing and working areas which is considered to be the most important spatial characteristic of the process of urbanization and industrialization. Pre-industrial Hamburg witnessed its first important changes only after the devastating fire of 1842 which destroyed sections of the Altstadt (Faulwasser, 1892). But it was not until the 1860s that industrialization and urban growth in Hamburg finally disturbed the once picturesque Alt-Hamburg. During a period of rapid economic and social change new inner-urban structures typical of an industrial city replaced the former concepts of urban organization.

The turning point from an earlier process of slow city growth to rapid urbanization in Hamburg in the second half of the nineteenth century came in the 1860s. The demographic signal for this change was a migration surplus which amounted to about 25,000 people in the decade between 1855 and 1865 and escalated substantially in the following decade to nearly 60,000 individuals. However, this period also coincided with many political reforms which altered the constitution, the acquisition of citizenship, restrictions on marriage and freedom of movement and of trade (Seelig, 1907). The external sign heralding the disappearance of numerous restrictions on social and regional mobility was the abolition of the *Thorsperre* (the barrier at the city gates during the night) which until then had strictly separated the town from its outskirts.[1]

Far into the late-nineteenth century the Altstadt and the Neustadt (subsequently referred to as the city centre) constituted the legal municipal area. St Georg and St Pauli were called *Vorstädte* (suburbs) and were situated between the city and its nearest 15 rural communities which were called *Vororte*. Because of their 'city-like way of housing' they were administered by the town authorities from 1871 onwards, but the legislative act of 22 June 1894 finally led to their formal incorporation and the abolition of their special status. The town area was thereby increased from 5.6 to 77 square kilometres. With the area within its former fortification boundaries, as well as the suburbs of St Georg and St Pauli, Hamburg in 1867 contained 220,000 inhabitants. By 1913 the number had risen to nearly one million inhabitants, including the population of outlying rural communities.

In general, statistical data on suburban and contiguous rural settlements are only available after their incorporation by the town administration (Matzerath, 1978, pp. 78, 88). Hamburg, however, since its reorganization in 1871, formally included the *Vororte* and was divided into 21 and, after 1894, into 24 wards with relatively constant boundaries. Among those pre-war German towns which had established their own statistical bureaux, Hamburg was in a unique position of having rich statistical data for the city's region as a whole which registered further urban growth in the decades after 1870 (Statistik des Hamburgischen Staats, 1867–1919). By the early-twentieth century expansion once again had reached the limits of the official city area, without, however, overflowing and spreading any further (see Figures 9.1 and 9.2).

As late as the middle of the nineteenth century the Altstadt and the Neustadt were the only parts of the city state of Hamburg with a clear urban character. It is generally thought that the high population density of modern towns is a result of industrialization. However, this view ignores the fact that many of the fortified towns of continental Europe had a tradition of multi-storey living since the seventeenth century and thus entered the phase of industrialization with a heavier concentration of inhabitants than is generally assumed (Sutcliffe, 1974, pp. 1–18). The example of Hamburg reveals that the high population density of the central city area in the 1870s was not exceeded in the following decades, even in the new suburbs.

---

1 Until 31 December 1860 the town gates were closed during the night and could only be passed by paying a toll. See, in general, Teuteberg and Wischermann (1992, p. 241).

Figure 9.1: Hamburg in 1874. *Source:* Staatsarchiv Hamburg, Special Map.

Even as late as 1850 the urban outskirts still consisted of farmland managed
by farmers, urban landowners and tenants of the city state. The villas along the
few streets connecting the town with its surrounding villages were only to be
found in the immediate vicinity of the central city area. Although the
Thorsperre was abolished and other restrictions on mobility between the
central town and the *Vororte* were revoked in the 1860s, the spatial expansion
of the town initially progressed slowly. Only the predominantly working-class
quarters near the River Elbe registered a high rate of housing construction: in
the more distant sections of the town increased building activity did not occur

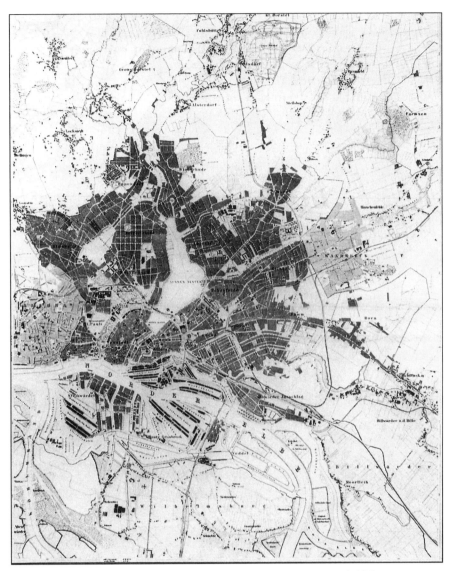

Figure 9.2: Hamburg in 1909. *Source:* Staatsarchiv Hamburg, Special Map.

until the 1880s. This was initiated by the expansion of the harbour and the process of urban renewal in the central city area. In 1883 the harbour entered a new phase of expansion because Hamburg became part of the German Customs Union, although a new free port in the south of the central city area remained excluded from the *Zollverein* (see Figure 9.3) (Ollenschläger, 1940). Hamburg's incorporation within the Customs Union can be seen as a decisive, perhaps even as the most important, landmark in the long history of its industrial development. The change in policy towards protective trade barriers in the German Empire in the late 1870s had brought serious consequences. Hamburg, still excluded from the *Zollverein* after 1871, was virtually foreign territory in customs terms and was cut off from its natural hinterland by the imposition of protective tariffs. Consequently, economic development advanced at a much slower rate. Only after its incorporation within the Customs Union did Hamburg experience a steady economic boom from the early 1880s onwards. The increase in trade, shipping and industry generally helped to

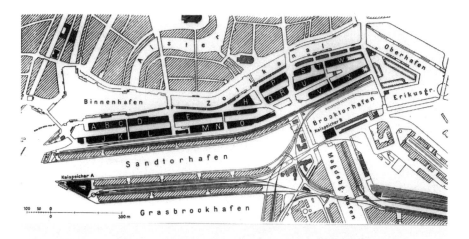

Figure 9.3: The municipal free port area of Hamburg. *Source:* Architekten- und Ingenieur-Verein zu Hamburg (ed.), 1914, pp. 77, 81.

consolidate Hamburg's commercial and fiscal power to a considerable extent (Hietala, 1987, p. 97). This led to an expansion in job opportunities and consequently to an increase in population.

The classification of employed people according to the occupational census returns of the late-nineteenth century reveals the extent and nature of economic development in Hamburg. The figures for the whole of the city state area are more representative in this context than those given for the official city area, because the *Vororte* were not incorporated in the overall figures for 1882 (Table 9.1). By the late-nineteenth century the structural changes in Hamburg's economy had further strengthened the role of the tertiary sector which in any case, in comparison with other German cities, had traditionally been well developed. Besides the increase in trade and commerce, Hamburg's expansion was determined largely by the development of service enterprises in both the private and public sectors. By the late-nineteenth century Hamburg had become the hub of urban commercial enterprise throughout Germany, as well as the most important economic centre in the North German area, attracting job-seekers from all parts of the surrounding territories. In many respects it was a port-city 'run for business' (Howe, 1913, p. 19).

Table 9.1: *Persons employed in the State of Hamburg classified according to economic sector on the basis of the occupational censuses of 1882, 1895 and 1907.**

Economic sector	1882		1895		1907	
	Numbers	*%*	*Numbers*	*%*	*Numbers*	*%*
A. Agriculture	9,473	4.9	10,841	3.7	11,876	2.7
B. Industry	83,278	42.6	114,652	38.6	164,952	38.0
C. Trade and commerce	59,942	30.7	104,642	35.2	162,543	37.4
D. Domestic service and irregular paid work	12,266	6.3	13,111	4.4	16,051	3.7
E. Civil service and so-called free professions	11,895	6.0	21,501	7.2	30,463	7.0
F. Unemployed and pensioners	18,552	9.5	32,295	10.9	48,790	11.2
Total A–F	195,406	100	297,042	100	434,675	100

* Excluding domestic servants registered in the household of employers, relatives supporting households and part-time employees.
Source: *Statistisches Handbuch für den Hamburgischen Staat*, 1921, p. 34; *Statistik des Deutschen Reichs*, 1884, p. 24 et seq.; 1897, p. 392; 1910, pp. 342–50.

Figure 9.4: The urban area of Hamburg in the late nineteenth century by administrative district.

The incorporation of Hamburg within the German Customs Union produced a somewhat ambiguous reaction within its own community. The increase in population and economic viability was balanced by an enormous rise in living and housing costs: it also precipitated a rapid increase in the city's industrial working-class population. These developments were viewed with increasing concern by certain people within Hamburg's traditional upper class. They anticipated great changes in the composition of the city's population and feared an increase in social tension. However, initially these structural changes in the economic and social life of the city tended to generate an enormous increase in demand for services offered by Hamburg's city and state administration, whose sphere of influence had so far been relatively constrained politically and had not extended to such problems as traffic administration and housing regulations.

The southern part of the Altstadt, which had to be cleared because of the establishment of a free port (*Freihafengebiet*), became the most serious problem for communal politicians following incorporation within the Customs Union (Figure 9.4). About 24,000 people were forced to vacate their quarters, which were subsequently demolished (Architekten- und Ingenieur-Verein zu Hamburg 1914; Teuteberg, 1972; Grüttner, 1984). Caring for the homeless and providing for their accommodation needs were tasks which were not yet part of the responsibilities of the State of Hamburg, but were simply left to the mercy of the private housing market. Half a century after the fire of 1842, the disastrous cholera epidemic of 1892 with more than 8,000 deaths (Evans, 1987) resulted in the complete reorganization of the town centre.[2] The threat of epidemics, which came predominantly from the oldest quarters of the town, initiated the greatest housing clearance programme in Germany before the First World War. More than 20,000 people had to be resettled, mainly in the peripheral districts of Hamburg, with the rebuilt areas being taken over by commercial enterprises. The concentration of commercial activity, broadly defined, in the Altstadt and south of the Elbe between 1880 and 1910 is reflected in Figures 9.5 and 9.6. In 1867, of Hamburg's population (within the boundaries of 1894) 59 per cent still lived in the central town area; 24 per cent lived in the so-called *Vorstädte* (St Georg and St Pauli) and only 17 per cent in the much larger areas of the *Vororte*. By 1910 the relative distribution of population had been reversed: 70 per cent lived in the *Vororte*, 19 per cent in the two *Vorstädte* and only 11 per cent in the central town area. Thus, between 1871 and 1910 the town centre lost over one-third of its total population.

Between 1871 and 1910 the city centre in general witnessed a noticeable fall in population which was particularly evident in the Altstadt-Nord and the Altstadt-Süd. On the other hand, most of the *Vororte* recorded a significant increase in population. By 1910 Eilbeck had 54,000 inhabitants, Eppendorf 73,000, Barmbeck 93,000 and Eimsbüttel 116,000 (compared with only 3,000 in 1871). Hamburg, like many other German cities with an original fortress function, had already developed a pattern of multi-storey living at a comparatively early date and by the 1870s this had produced a particularly high population density in the inner-city areas (Figure 9.7). However, the absolute loss of population from the central urban core during the late-nineteenth and early-twentieth centuries and extensive construction and settlement in the *Vororte* altered the earlier concentric pattern of population density. By 1910, although the Neustadt-Süd recorded the highest population density (Figure 9.8) as a function of the continued absence of commercial

---

2 Concerning the details of the cholera epidemic and contemporary sanitary conditions, see Staatsarchiv Hamburg, Rep. Nr. 353–1; Senats- und Bürgerschaftskommission für die Verbesserung der Wohnungsverhältnisse (1894–1927). A summary of the parliamentary debates on housing policies is given by Dorothea Berger-Thimme (1976, pp. 155–75). See also Evans (1987) and Grüttner (1983).

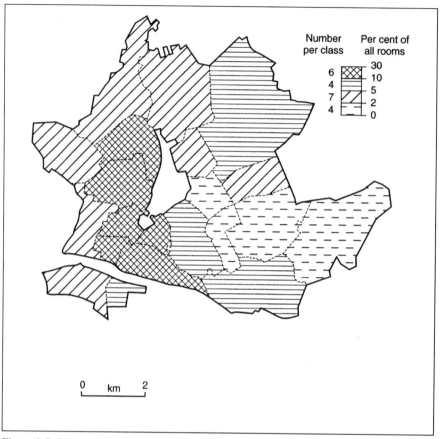

Figure 9.5: Intra-urban distribution of commercial space in Hamburg, 1880 (in per cent of all rooms). Note: in this, as well as in subsequent figures, the number per class refers to the number of city wards in each classified category.

activity in this area, the working-class district of St Georg-Süd and the suburb of Eimsbüttel were now in the same category.

The development of Hamburg's population (see Figures 9.9 and 9.10) shows explicitly the changing structure of the town centre. German contemporaries referred to this phenomenon of urbanization as 'city-building' (Schott, 1907), a term which meant the transformation of a metropolitan area into a commercial and financial centre following the pattern of London, Paris and New York. The industrial establishments, on the other hand, were situated in the area of the free port south of the Elbe.

Numerous new dwellings in the *Vororte* replaced the loss of residential housing in the city centre. As late as the 1870s the single-family house was the dominant type of housing in the rural *Vororte* of Hamburg; not, however, in

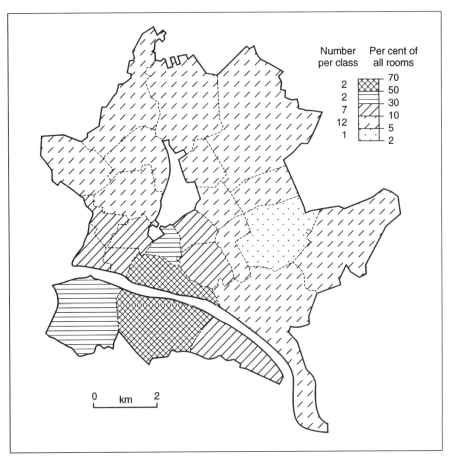

Figure 9.6: Intra-urban distribution of commercial space in Hamburg, 1910 (in per cent of all rooms).

the sense of suburban middle-class settlements of the twentieth century, but as a mixture of agricultural farms, urban villas and old villages (Figure 9.11). With the culmination of the process of urban expansion by 1910 the single-family house had virtually disappeared (Figure 9.12). The town centre, on the other hand, including the surrounding quarters on both sides of the Alster, were dominated by tenement blocks (*Mietskasernen*), many over four storeys (Figures 9.13 and 9.14), which had become the characteristic form of residential housing in Hamburg, as in many other German cities (Asmus, 1982; Teuteberg and Wischermann, 1992, p. 247). During the second half of the nineteenth century city growth and the displacement of inner-urban population, increasing industrialization, as well as selective town-planning measures, had erased the contours of pre-industrial Hamburg. The period of rapid

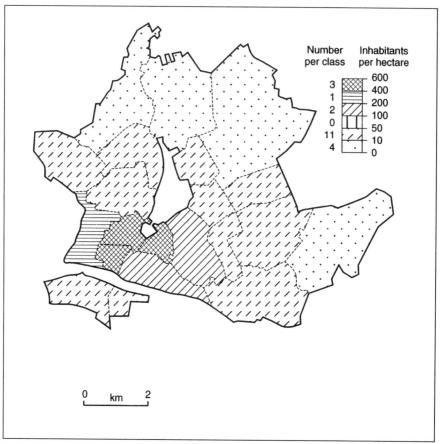

Figure 9.7: The population density of Hamburg in 1871 (inhabitants per hectare excluding areas of water).

urbanization witnessed the emergence of the outlines of a modern metropolis with attendant changes in living and housing conditions.

The following sections will focus on a number of critical aspects of Hamburg's development during this period and explore the impact of rapid urbanization within the port-city on social differentiation, spatial segregation, housing and working conditions.

SOCIAL STATUS AND SOCIAL DIFFERENTIATION

A relatively constant basic structure characterized the extent of social differentiation in Hamburg's districts at the beginning of the period of rapid urbanization. This structure was influenced by the specific location of Hamburg's harbour, as well as by certain topographical qualities of the land

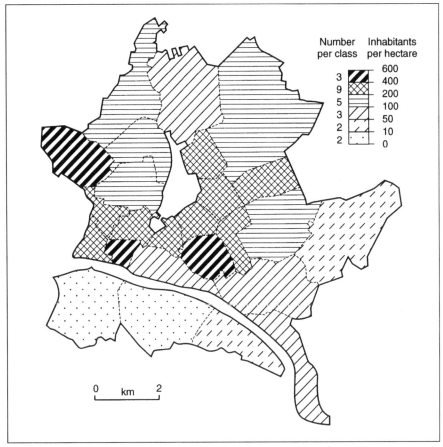

Figure 9.8: The population density of Hamburg in 1910 (inhabitants per hectare excluding areas of water).

surrounding the Aussenalster, an inner-city lake, which took on its present form after the great fire of 1842. Neighbourhood areas of the highest social rank developed on both sides of the Aussenalster and the social position of these upper-class districts remained unchallenged until the late-nineteenth century, despite the slow but permanent decline of Hamburg's city centre. However, the inner-city area, as well as the neighbouring *Vorstädte*, were left behind increasingly in terms of social rank by the emergence of new suburbs which improved rapidly their standing within the neighbourhood hierarchy from the 1890s onwards.

The districts of Veddel and the Billwärder Ausschlag in the extreme southeast of the urban area and the Neustadt-Süd quarter in the city centre represented the lower end of the social scale. These were the residential districts

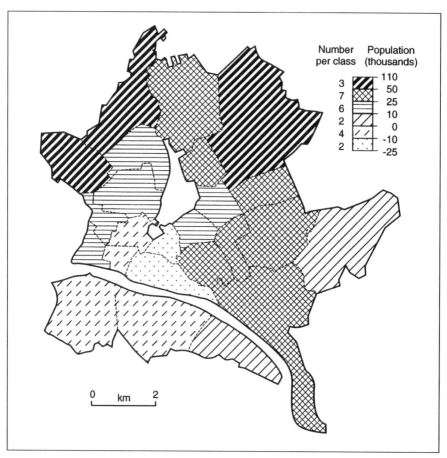

Figure 9.9: Gains and losses of population within the urban area of Hamburg between 1871 and 1910 (absolute figures, in thousands within the borders of 1894).

of the working class, with the lowest income levels and the highest rates of population fluctuation and inner-urban mobility. By 1885 the Billwärder Ausschlag already had a comparatively high population density in terms of its built-up area (Figure 9.15). Both districts reflected the concentration of lower-class housing in two specific types of location which were typical for larger German cities during this period: either in a remnant of the inner city, with very old and run-down buildings and blocks of flats; or as a function of the need to escape high city-centre rents in parts of the urban fringeland that were unattractive and poorly developed, but cheap and situated fairly close to the employment opportunities of the harbour.

Income tax per capita is one of the most useful and commonly used indicators in measuring relative social status. Figures 9.16 and 9.17 show fairly

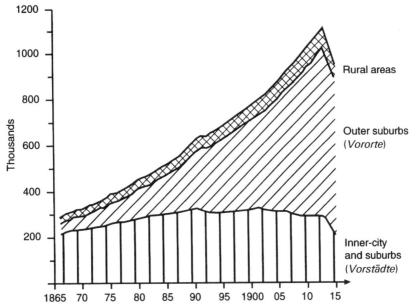

Figure 9.10: The demographic development of the State and City of Hamburg, 1866–1915 (in thousands). Note: *Vororte* = nearest 15 rural communities. *Source:* Figures according to *Statistisches Handbuch für den Hamburgischen Staat*, Ausgabe, 1920, Hamburg, 1921, p. 12.

well the differences revealed by this indicator in the spatial and social framework of Hamburg in the late-nineteenth and early-twentieth centuries. Between 1881 (the first year in which Hamburg's statistical bureau investigated its taxpayers according to their residential location) and 1910 the average taxed income increased from 548 to 872 Marks per capita.[3] In general, all areas of the city benefited from an improvement in income levels, although this is not adequately reflected in the figures due to cartographical reasons. Even in the Billwärder Ausschlag and Barmbeck, which were the districts with the lowest average income per capita in 1881, income had doubled to 450 and 500 Marks respectively by 1910. But in comparing various neighbourhoods it is much more important to note that although many wards were characterized by average income levels there existed a few very exclusive, upper-class districts which showed a further degree of strong social differentiation among themselves (not only in terms of income). These upper-class districts paid several times more tax per capita than even the middle-class wards. During the late-nineteenth century the exclusive social position of the richest quarters remained virtually unchanged. In fact average taxable income increased most

3 The *Statistik des Hamburgischen Staats* is the source for all statistics and figures; in this context it was not possible to cite in detail the sources used. See Wischermann (1983a).

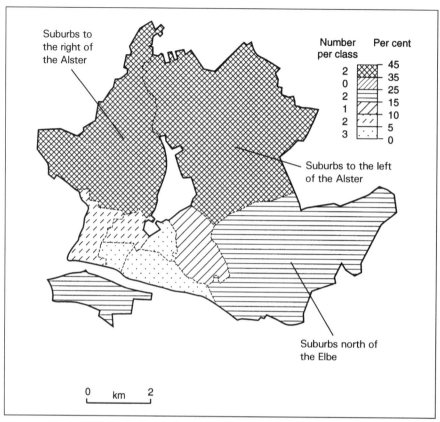

Figure 9.11: Share of single-family houses in Hamburg in 1875 (in per cent of all housing units).

rapidly in the poorer quarters—here average income doubled compared with an improvement of about 50 per cent in the rich quarters—but the absolute income disparity between the wards, which amounted to a maximum of 2,200 Marks in 1881, had increased further to 3,500 Marks by 1910. The social status of Hamburg's wards was therefore characterized by disparities that were almost a direct reflection of the social differentiation between the lowest strata of the working class and the upper class.[4]

URBAN MOBILITY AND SPATIAL SEGREGATION

Hamburg has always been a commercial city which owed most of its growth in population to in-migration from the surrounding rural regions of

4 A detailed comparison of the housing conditions of the lower and middle classes in Hamburg is provided by Wischermann (1983b).

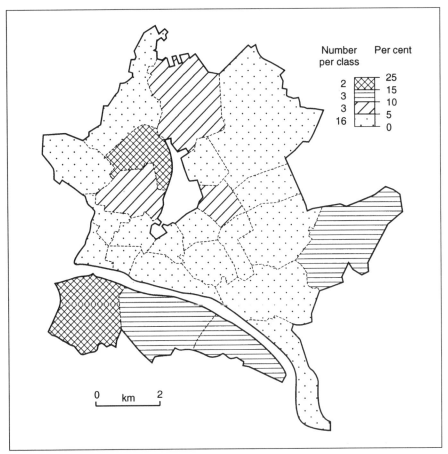

Figure 9.12: Share of single-family houses in Hamburg in 1910 (in per cent of all housing units).

Schleswig-Holstein and Hanover. After the middle of the nineteenth century, however, a remarkable change occurred and Hamburg, like parts of the Ruhr (Köllmann, Hoffmann and Maul, 1990), was increasingly flooded by a stream of in-migrants from the eastern provinces of Prussia (Reincke, 1951). In Prussia, in general, 54 per cent of the total increase in urban population in the last quarter of the nineteenth century was the result of net in-migration, whereas only 31 per cent was attributable to natural increase and approximately 14 per cent to the incorporation of adjacent communities (Laux, 1989, p. 135). But in Hamburg—as in the case of certain major cities in Switzerland and France, as well as German towns dominated by tertiary sector activities—population gains due to in-migration were even more important, contributing up to 60 per cent of the increase in total population between 1871 and 1910

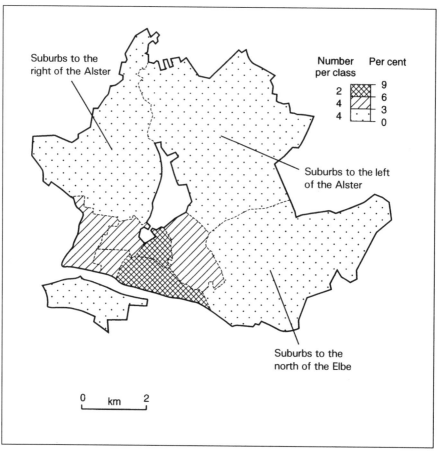

Figure 9.13: Dwellings with four or more storeys in Hamburg in 1875 (in per cent of all housing units).

(Table 9.2) (*Statistisches Handbuch für den Hamburgischen Staat*, 1891, p. 62; 1921, p. 72).

With the abolition of the *Thorsperre* and the emergence of new opportunities regarding regional and social mobility from the 1860s onwards there was not only increased migration into Hamburg, but simultaneously a movement of population from the old town into adjacent new suburbs. In 1871 95.3 per cent of all Hamburg's inhabitants living in the inner districts (including St Pauli and St Georg) had been born in these areas of the city: the *Vororte* revealed the opposite picture, with only 18.3 per cent of the population in the suburbs having been born in the ward where they then resided (Figure 9.18). The majority of the suburban population, by inference, had come from the inner-urban areas of the city. This degree of variation, produced by the cross-

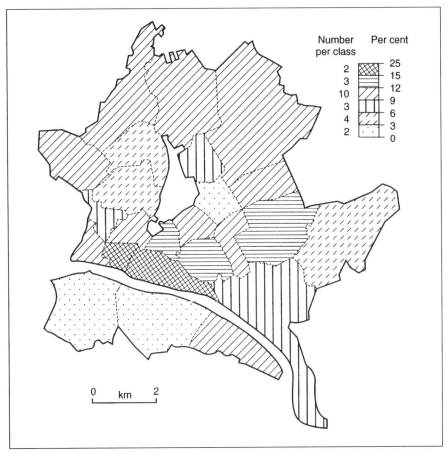

Figure 9.14: Dwellings with four or more storeys in Hamburg in 1910 (in per cent of all housing units).

tabulation of birthplace and residence by ward, characterized the situation in Hamburg at the beginning of the main period of suburban settlement. But even by 1871 only 57.3 per cent of Hamburg's population had been born in the city. Moreover in the following decades this proportion hardly changed: even in the period of greatest in-migration, about half of the population were natives of Hamburg.

Throughout the second half of the nineteenth century the differences in in-migration rates by city district were rather small. The in-migration data for 1900, for example, reveal a typical pattern in relation to the spatial distribution of persons born outside Hamburg (see Figure 9.19) with only a slight degree of variation between the different urban districts. At first glance there seems to be an east–west gradient within Hamburg, but this phenomenon is explained by

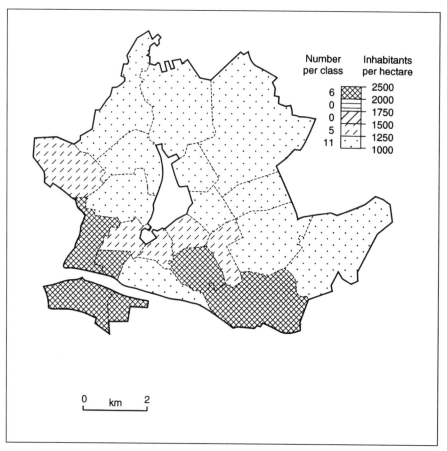

Figure 9.15: Population density of Hamburg's built-up area in 1885 (inhabitants per hectare).

the suburb of Altona which was independently administered. If Altona had been included in the analysis the proportion of in-migrants at ward level would have been far more uniform. All these indicators seem to suggest that urbanization in Hamburg was characterized by two simultaneous, but countervailing, migration movements: movement out of the crowded central city into the adjacent suburbs; and migration into the general urban area from outside. This particular process of urbanization was reinforced by town planning measures, especially the expansion of the port, the establishment of a free port area and the slum clearance programme for the central town district. As a result, spatial segregation of the native population from the new residents was avoided.

Moreover, even in terms of the differentiation of in-migrants according to

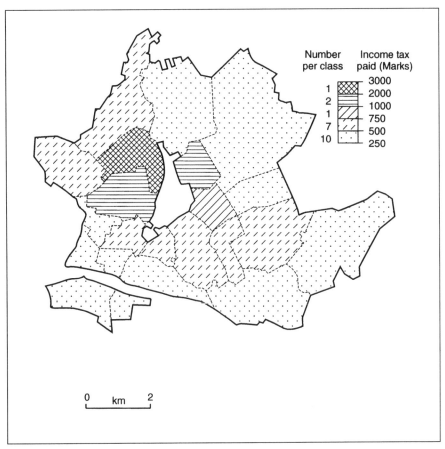

Figure 9.16: Income tax per capita paid by the population of Hamburg in 1881 (in Marks).

place of origin, Hamburg revealed no marked spatial segregation. This phenomenon is particularly astonishing because most of the in-migrants came from rural regions and thus, presumably, would have attempted to settle in residential neighbourhoods with people of similar origin. According to available research on migration into German cities (Kamphoefner, 1983; Schüren, 1989) it is apparent that there was a far lower level of segregation in comparison with the pattern of urban in-migration in North America. Even in such a town as Oberhausen, dominated by heavy industry and characterized by high rates of population growth as a result of extensive in-migration, the trend towards increased social segregation was a relatively late phenomenon (Reif, 1986). This indicates a much easier process of urban adaptation in German cities where in-migrants were not confined solely to the bottom rungs of the

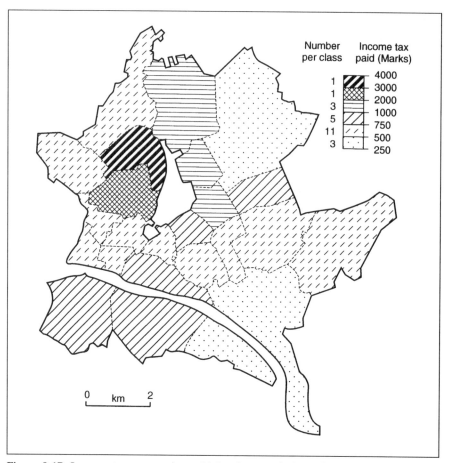

Figure 9.17: Income tax per capita paid by the population of Hamburg in 1910 (in Marks).

social hierarchy, although, as in the case of the port-city of Bremen, they tended to marry at a later age than the indigenous population (Marschalck, 1994, p. 162; see above, Lee and Marschalck, chapter 8). The traditional negative view of urban migration in the nineteenth century was often based on an animosity towards city-life and uncritical generalizations derived from individual misfortunes; it was seldom supported by sound empirical data. Rural–urban migration inevitably involved profound social and economic changes and, selectively, substantial individual hardship, but it by no means resulted in general pauperization.

If there were no recognizable connections between the character of individual urban districts in Hamburg and the settlement pattern of in-migrants, one question must still be raised: why did contemporaries often note

Table 9.2: *The components of population growth in Hamburg, 1871–1910.*

Period[a]	Total population growth[b]	Natural increase (surplus of births over deaths)		In-migration gains	
		Total	% of population growth	Total	% of population growth
1871–1875	49,268	14,021	28.5	35,247	71.5
1875–1880	61,680	26,080	42.3	35,600	57.7
1880–1885	61,300	24,755	40.4	36,545	59.6
1885–1890	97,833	24,841	25.4	72,992	74.6
1890–1895	56,292	33,933	60.3	22,359	39.7
1895–1900	80,186	47,685	59.5	32,501	40.5
1900–1905	97,055	38,289	39.5	58,766	60.5
1905–1910	128,242	43,288	33.8	84,954	66.2
1871–1910	631,856	252,892	40.0	378,964	60.0

[a] The period between consecutive population censuses held at the beginning of December.

[b] 1871–1893 the City (with harbour), suburbs and adjacent regions; from 1894 the area according to the law of 22 June 1894.

Source: *Statistisches Handbuch für den Hamburgischen Staat*, first edition, Hamburg, 1874, p. 23; second edition, Hamburg, 1880, p. 37; third edition, Hamburg, 1885, p. 38; fourth edition, Hamburg, 1891, pp. 41, 62, 64; 1920 edition, Hamburg, 1921, pp. 35, 48, 60, 72.

that migrants, especially the unskilled and the poorest, favoured the central part of the town as a residential quarter? The answer to this can partly be found in the structure of German internal migration which consisted mainly of individual in-migrants attracted primarily by urban job opportunities (Reulecke, 1985, p.11; Langewiesche and Lenger, 1987, pp. 93–94; Jackson, 1995). In addition, changing family structures and new opportunities for industrial employment set free many young people of working age from their families and this group, in particular, tended to look for cheap rooms and lodgings near to their work-place. This demand for lodgings was satisfied predominantly in the central city area and near the harbour where job-seekers rented a room, or sometimes only a bed, from an unknown family (see Figure 9.20).[5] It was not until the end of the nineteenth century that the inner-urban segregation of sub-tenants reached its peak. The growing exodus of population

5 In general, the typical Hamburg sub-tenant was male, unmarried, 25 to 30 years old and born outside the port-city. Thus he corresponded perfectly with the characteristics of the 'lone migrant' in Germany in the nineteenth century as outlined by Langewiesche in his research (see Langewiesche, 1977, especially p. 25 *et seq.*).

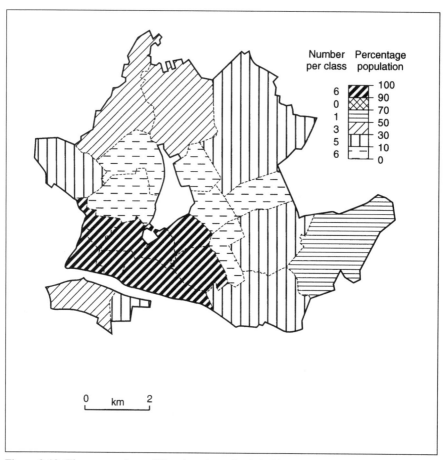

Figure 9.18: The proportion of Hamburg's native inhabitants still living in their ward of birth in 1871 (per cent of the Hamburg-born population).

and households from the central districts, slum clearances in the oldest wards and laws forbidding sub-letting in the newly-built areas increasingly restricted housing opportunities for new arrivals in the central city area and heightened the pressure on the remaining households to release any available accommodation (Figure 9.21).

THE DEVELOPMENT OF HOUSING AND WORKING CONDITIONS

Long before the middle of the nineteenth century the pre-industrial household and work unit—*das ganze Haus*, or whole house (Brunner, 1956; Derks, 1996)—had shown signs of disintegrating. Nevertheless, both the residential and work unit had remained more or less small-scale and familiar even in the

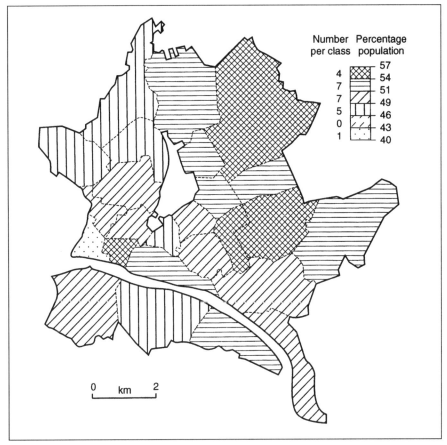

Figure 9.19: Percentage of ward population born in Hamburg in 1900 (per cent of the whole population).

towns. At the onset of rapid urbanization in Germany numerous tasks were still done in the immediate spatial confines of the household. These were performed not by homeworkers compelled by poverty to use their dwelling as a workshop but rather by craftsmen and retail merchants with shops in the immediate proximity, often under the same roof as their family residence.

By the end of the eighteenth century the first signs of a separation between the home and workplace could be noticed among the lower classes. The debate on the establishment of the *Thorsperre* in 1798 had involved a discussion on the need to guarantee daily entry into the city in the early morning for those craftsmen, day-labourers and workers who lived in the suburbs. At the start of the nineteenth century the first factories were founded outside the boundaries of the old town. However, for ordinary craftsmen traditional living conditions

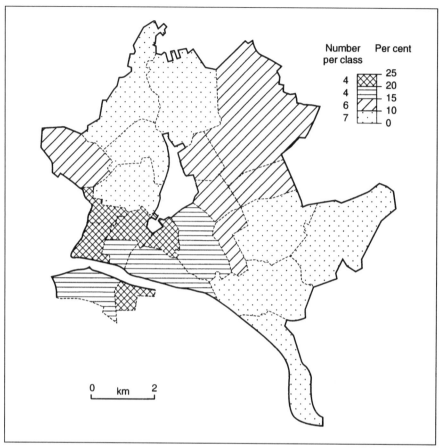

Figure 9.20: Households with lodgers and boarders in the urban area of Hamburg in 1880 (per cent of all households).

and housing structures hardly changed: in contrast to unskilled labourers they continued to possess relative freedom in their choice of housing and enjoyed access to a variety of living quarters (Nahrstedt, 1972).

The more the town expanded in terms of total population and geographical area, the greater became the resulting problem of spatial distance between the place of residence and employment location, especially for dockers and other port workers. Within the original city area every destination could be reached on foot within 20 minutes. By 1890 Heidmann (1891, p. 7) estimated that every morning and evening nearly 50,000 workers 'set out on a voyage' lasting between one and one-and-a-half hours in order to travel between their place of residence and their workplaces on the docks, in the different harbours, and the industrial factories of the free port. The principal axis of inner-urban traffic ran

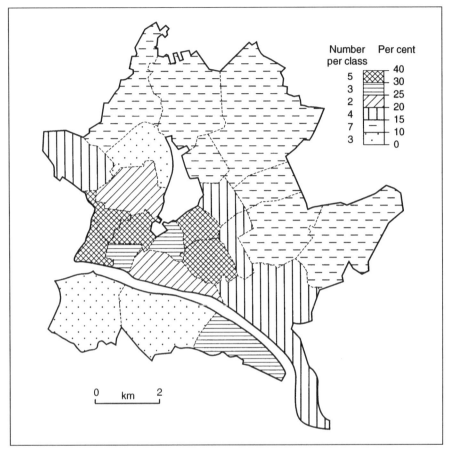

Figure 9.21: Households with lodgers and boarders in the urban area of Hamburg in 1910 (per cent of all households).

concentrically from the suburbs to the working places of the central city and the harbour.

Despite the increasing differentiation in housing styles and in the social structure of individual districts, all quarters showed an extensive separation of work-site and residential dwelling by the end of the nineteenth century (Figure 9.22). Because of the enormous spatial expansion of the port-town, Hamburg's rush hour reached extraordinary proportions compared with other German cities. In 1910 70 per cent of all employees (about 310,000 individuals) took part in the daily migration between home and workplace. The average distance covered two or four times a day was estimated to be two miles in each direction; the maximum distance travelled within the urban area was approximately six miles (ten kilometres).

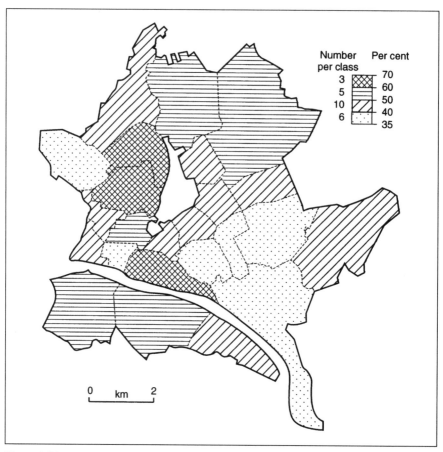

Figure 9.22: Percentage of total working population with place of work in the ward of residence, Hamburg, 1900.

Today the time spent commuting to and from work is known to increase with city size, and the generally accepted threshold limit for commuting evinces a similar pattern. Until the emergence of public and private transportation systems, the loss of time in commuting was determined by the spatial extent of the inner-urban area and was limited by the distance that could be covered on foot. Only an efficient and cheap transportation system could help to extend these limits. In Hamburg such a development began in the 1860s with the foundation of a steamship-line on the Alster. By the turn of the century the transport system (especially the tramway network) had expanded so rapidly that the city centre could be reached from virtually every point within the urban area in half an hour (Schimpff, 1903, p. 21). In Germany private expenditure on transportation was not very large in the mid-nineteenth century, averaging about 40 *Pfennige* per capita per annum. By 1913 it had climbed to 18 *Marks* per capita. In 1850 about 0.5 per cent of private consumption was spent on transportation. This had increased to 1 per cent by 1880, to 2 per cent by the turn of the century, and just before the First World War it reached 3 per cent (Hoffmann, 1965, p. 134).

The increasing separation of home and work as a result of industrialization and urbanization meant that more private households were burdened with transportation expenses. Nevertheless, the new burden may have helped simultaneously to ease living conditions in general. Instead of commuting long distances on foot, more comfortable methods of transportation offered the working class new opportunities to occupy cheap and good housing in the suburbs. This idea formed the basis for many proposals by numerous housing reformers in Germany during this period who advocated the 'decentralization' of urban housing. In practice, however, the basic assumptions of these plans proved to be misleading. According to Hamburg household budgets from 1907,[6] transportation expenses amounted to between 0.4 and 1 per cent of private expenditure in and near the town centre. Yet in the outer suburbs (*Vororte*) this rate increased to between 3 and 5 per cent. The suburbs, however, had the advantage of offering relatively cheap housing as well as better quality homes, but the decrease in rent in the outer districts in comparison with rental levels in the city's central employment area amounted to only 1 per cent of total household budgets. Thus, if one regards housing and transportation expenditures as having been related to one another, living in the outer districts of Hamburg was not a saving but an additional burden on private consumption. Living far from work and using the transportation system for inner-urban commuting still remained for a long time a privilege restricted to that part of the labour force which enjoyed favourable and fixed working hours[7] and received a regular, above-average income. This situation did not change as long as transportation costs remained high and the policy of transportation companies was based on high fares rather than on passenger volume. For the majority of the metropolitan working population, living in the suburbs brought a reduction in living costs only if they continued to cover the distance between home and work on foot. As a result, inner-urban mobility remained concentrated in the central residential districts of Hamburg despite the fact that, in general, the supply of homes in the outer suburbs was qualitatively better and relatively cheaper per unit of floorspace than in the city itself.

6 See on this point the second Sonderheft zum Reichsarbeitsblatt, *Erhebung von Wirtschaftsrech-
nungen minderbemittelter Familien im Deutschen Reiche* (Berb. im Kaiserlichen Statistischen Amte, Abteilung für Arbeiterstatistik), Berlin, 1909 and the supplement to Hamburg's *Jahresberichte der Verwaltungsbehörden der freien und Hansestadt Hamburg für das Jahr 1907* (1908).

7 Before the First World War in most of Hamburg's factories and offices an undivided, so-called 'English' working day was not known. A traditional lunch break of two hours was common, not only for most workers, but also for the majority of lower clerks. With the growing distance between home and work the purpose of the lunch hour disappeared.

An essential criterion for evaluating the housing situation is the number of vacancies. In the era of economic liberalism the urban housing market fluctuated fairly regularly between extreme housing shortage and excessive supply, a phenomenon hardly imaginable today (Wischermann, 1986; Tilly, 1991). The extreme fluctuations in the housing market are reflected by the fact that a peak number of 15,000 vacant flats was recorded in Hamburg in the mid-1890s. This was particularly obvious in 1895, a year of a significant housing surplus. Not only was there a high degree of housing mobility (Figure 9.23), but 14,000 dwellings in Hamburg (or 9.3 per cent of the existing stock) were unoccupied (Figure 9.24). The district figures also reflected a characteristic increase in both housing mobility and vacancy rates from the inner to the outer areas of the town, the only exception being the upper-class quarters. A large

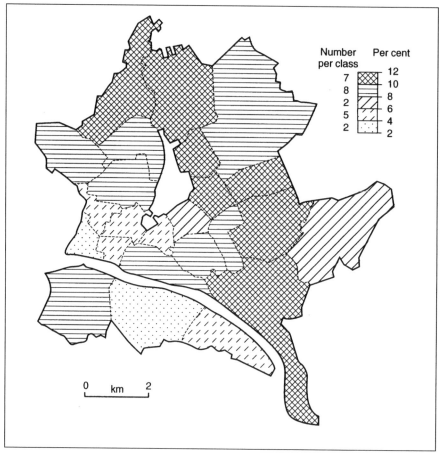

Figure 9.23: Residential mobility in Hamburg's wards in 1895 (per cent of dwellings inhabited for less than one year by current household head).

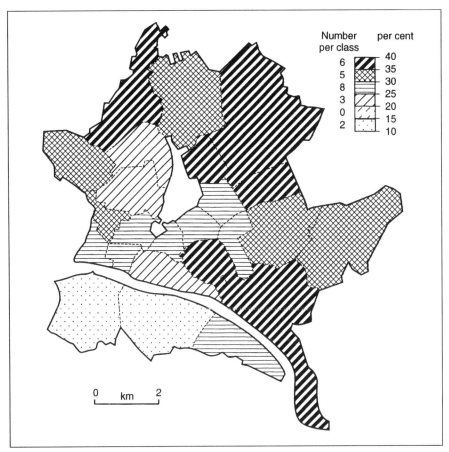

Figure 9.24: Supply of unrented housing units by ward in Hamburg in 1895 (per cent of all housing units).

proportion of the working class in Hamburg, therefore, still had to give priority to obtaining a central residential location, rather than seeking better living standards in the outer suburbs.

CONCLUSION

The most profound influence on urban development in the nineteenth century came from the adherence to liberal economic principles, especially in Prussia. Urban expansion initially was a spontaneous development with virtually no restrictions on building activity on private land and property. This unrestricted building activity was gradually curtailed in the second half of the century by regulations governing building construction in general. These restrictions, however, were not of a comprehensive nature, but were intended as a guideline for building activity necessarily generated by the process of urban expansion. Thus, official regulations did not inevitably influence urban development. Berlin was an exception in this case; the well-known Construction Plans for Berlin and the Vicinity (*Hobrechtplan*), dating from 1858–1862 and in force until 1919, exerted a decisive influence on the city's urban development. However, most of the important elements in building regulations and house construction codes were only introduced and enforced by the majority of German cities at a comparatively late date and therefore had no practical bearing on urban development up to the First World War. Despite increasing activity on the part of local authorities and a growing self-confidence within municipal administrations (Krabbe, 1989, pp. 78–98), city planning and urban growth still remained a process of 'adaptation and conformity' in the widest sense (Matzerath and Thienel, 1977, p. 175).

By the turn of the century various patterns of modern city development, as described, for example, by the Chicago School,[8] had left their mark on the inner-urban structure of Hamburg. These patterns not only reflected urban growth in terms of geographical area and population, but were also the result of increasing differentiation in urban spatial functions and living conditions.

A number of models have been put forward to explain the spatial patterns of residential districts in relation to the two key factors affecting development: the quality of housing and centrality. The well-known model of urban growth by Burgess (1925) assumes that concentric circles of residential areas develop around the commercial centre in an ascending hierarchy. The model of the urban land market developed by William Alonso (1960) extends Burgess's concept by postulating that, in general, the price of land will decrease with increasing distance from the centre. In order to carn a return comparable to that from other uses, house construction near the city centre has to be both dense and compact. One of the results of this is that the lower-income groups show a strong tendency to live near the centre because of their long working hours and high transportation costs. Thus the 'centrality' factor is more important than the 'quality of housing'. In relation to the upper classes, the importance of 'centrality' diminishes because of more favourable working conditions and transportation costs are clearly less important. The upper classes generally prioritize the 'quality of housing' which encourages them to live in suburbs with a low population density far outside the city centre.

It is impossible in the context of this chapter to provide a detailed verification of the assumptions made in these general models in relation to the historical process of urbanization in Germany as a whole. However, the continuing concentration of the lower classes in and near the centre of Hamburg, which remained most marked until the end of the nineteenth century, provides some confirmation of their general applicability. The oldest,

8 A summary of research on city development in Europe and North America has been provided by Jürgen Friedrichs (1977).

most run-down and unhealthiest tenements in Hamburg experienced an extraordinary appreciation in value during the period of industrialization due to their extremely favourable location. The specific needs of an expanding harbour and a local policy that led to a concentration of industrial settlement in the area of the free port (south of the Elbe) not only maintained, but even increased the value of the oldest residential districts.

Apart from the residential districts of the lower classes in the central area, city growth in Hamburg did not generate an ascending social hierarchy of individual districts or wards during the period of urbanization. Instead the upper classes, if they did not leave the urban environment, remained within a relatively constant area on both sides of the Alster characterized by beautiful scenery and by its close proximity to the city centre. In the course of urban growth the exclusive position of the upper classes was retained and, for example in the case of Harvestehude, was consciously regulated and maintained by specific processes of social selection.

Urbanization, however, must be understood as something more than the quantitative growth of cities and invariably involves an adaptation to an urban way of life which has increasingly influenced society in general (Reulecke, 1977). Disparities in housing conditions not only express social inequality but also generate, in turn, new social divisions. Housing and living conditions are important factors affecting development opportunities both for individuals and social groups. According to Ingrid Thienel (1977, p. 66), writing in the tradition of the older 'reformist literature':

> Class-specific income corresponded with housing conditions and helped to entrench traditional forms of segregation, creating living conditions which considerably increased the social problems in the cities and led to social depravity and crime.

Social historians have also been concerned to examine each of these factors more closely, as well as the nature and extent of their interconnectedness. They regard urban districts as being a sort of living space (*Lebensraum*) (Fritzsche, 1981), as constituting some sort of social area between the intimate form of private housing and the anonymous life of the great cities. Research has been increasingly focused on the connection between social conditions, social behaviour patterns and political movements. Bruno Fritzsche has summarized some of the results of this approach by arguing that housing conditions probably exerted a more profound influence on the emergence of workers' organizations, class consciousness and the class struggle in general than the working conditions of labourers:[9]

> The concentration of vast differences in income and wealth within one urban area effectively demonstrated the existence of classes, as well as the differences

---

9 This hypothesis is developed in detail by Bruno Fritzsche (1977).

between them; segregation in different districts, however, enhanced or at least gave rise to a feeling of solidarity within the same class. (Fritzsche, 1977, p. 461)

We shall have to wait and see to what degree these explanations will help to solve the great methodological problems facing historical research which, to begin with, must confront the fact that past, as well as present-day, municipal and administrative areas, city quarters and districts simply fail to comply with the traditional image of social homogeneity. On the whole these areas tended to be too large, too disparate and too arbitrary in their development and their structure. As a result German research has increasingly been focused on the application of a micro-statistical approach. The analysis of city districts, however, offers scholars engaged in historical research on urbanization a seldom-used method of gleaning new knowledge about emerging urban industrial societies and of analysing the development of social inequalities inherent in urban living conditions. Nevertheless, it is still debatable as to whether the analysis of individual urban districts will offer a sufficiently robust explanation for the historical emergence of certain social and political patterns of behaviour within the developing urban environment.

References

ALONSO, W. (1960), *A Model of the Urban Land Market*, University of Pennsylvania.
ARCHITEKTEN- UND INGENIEUR-VEREIN ZU HAMBURG (ed.) (1914), *Hamburg und seine Bauten unter Berücksichtigung der Nachbarstädte Altona und Wandsbeck 1914*, 2 vols, Hamburg.
ASMUS, G. (ed.) (1982), *Hinterhof, Keller und Mansarde – Einblicke in Berliner Wohnungselend*, Reinbek.
BERGER-THIMME, D. (1976), *Wohnungsfrage und Sozialstaat. Untersuchungen zu den Anfängen staatlicher Wohnungspolitik in Deutschland*, Frankfurt-am-Main and Bern.
BRUNNER, O. (1956), 'Das "ganze Haus" und die alteuropäische Okonomik', in O. Brunner, *Neue Wege der Sozialgeschichte. Vorträge und Aufsätze*, Göttingen.
BURGESS, E. W. (1925), 'The growth of the city', in R. E. Park, E. W. Burgess and R. D. McKenzie (eds), *The City*, Chicago.
DERKS, H. (1996), 'Über die Faszination des "Ganzen Hauses"', *Geschichte und Gesellschaft*, **22**, 221–42.
EVANS, R. J. (1987), *Death in Hamburg. Society and Politics in the Cholera Years 1830–1910*, Oxford.
FAULWASSER, J. (1892), *Der große Brand und der Wiederaufbau von Hamburg*, Hamburg.
FRIEDRICHS, J. (1977), *Stadtanalyse. Soziale und räumliche Organisation der Gesellschaft*, Hamburg.
FRITZSCHE, B. (1977), 'Städtisches Wachstum und soziale Konflikte', *Schweizerische Zeitschrift für Volkswirtschaft und Statistik*, **4**, 447–73.
FRITZSCHE, B. (1981), 'Das Quartier als Lebensraum', in W. Conze and U. Engelhardt (eds), *Arbeiterexistenz im 19. Jahrhundert*, Stuttgart, 92–113.
GRÜTTNER, M. (1983), 'Soziale Hygiene und soziale Kontrolle. Die Sanierung der Hamburger Gängeviertel 1892–1936', in D. Herzig, D. Langewiesche and A. Sywottek (eds), *Arbeiter in*

Hamburg. Unterschichten, Arbeiter und Arbeiterbewegung seit dem ausgehenden 18. Jahrhundert, Hamburg, 359–71.

GRÜTTNER, M. (1984), *Arbeitswelt an der Wasserkante. Sozialgeschichte der Hamburger Hafenarbeiter 1886–1914*, Göttingen.

HEIDMANN, J. H. (1891), *Hamburgs Verkehrsmittel und Wohnungsverhältnisse*, Hamburg.

HIETALA, M. (1987), *Services and Urbanisation at the Turn of the Century. The Diffusion of Innovations*, Helsinki.

HOFFMANN, W. G., with F. GRUMBACH and H. HESSE (1965), *Das Wachstum der deutschen Wirtschaft seit der Mitte des 19. Jahrhunderts*, Berlin, Heidelberg and New York.

HOWE, F. C. (1913), *European Cities at Work*, London and Leipzig.

JACKSON, J. H. Jr (1995), 'Migration in Duisburg, 1821–1914', in D. Hoerder and J. Nagler (eds), *People in Transit. German Migrations in Comparative Perspective, 1820–1930*, Cambridge, 147–76.

JAHRESBERICHTE DER VERWALTUNGSBEHÖRDEN DER FREIEN UND HANSESTADT HAMBURG FÜR DAS JAHR 1907 (1908), Hamburg.

KAISERLICHES STATISTISCHES AMT, ABTEILUNG FÜR ARBEITERSTATISTIK (1909), *Erhebung von Wirtschaftsrechnungen minderbemittelter Familien im Deutschen Reich*, (Zweiter Sonderheft zum Reichsarbeitsblatt), Berlin.

KAMPHOEFNER, W. D. (1983), 'Soziale und demographische Strukturen der Zuwanderung in deutschen Großstädte des späten 19. Jahrhunderts', in H. J. Teuteberg (ed.), *Urbanisierung im 19. und 20. Jahrhundert, Historische und Geographische Aspekte*, Cologne and Vienna, 95–116.

KÖLLMANN, W., F. HOFFMANN and A. E. MAUL (1990), 'Bevölkerungsgeschichte', in *Das Ruhrgebiet im Industriezeitalter. Geschichte und Entwicklung*, Vol. 1, Düsseldorf, 111–98.

KRABBE, W. R. (1989), *Die deutsche Stadt in 19. und 20. Jahrhundert*, Göttingen.

LANGEWIESCHE, D. (1977), 'Wanderungsbewegungen in der Hochindustrialisierungs periode. Regionale, interstädtische und innerstädtische Mobilität in Deutschland 1880–1914', *Vierteljahrschrift für Sozial- und Wirtschaftsgeschichte*, **64**, 1–40.

LANGEWIESCHE, D. and F. LENGER (1987), 'Internal migration: persistence and mobility', in K. J. Bade (ed.), *Population, Labour and Migration in 19th and 20th Century Germany*, Leamington Spa, Hamburg and New York, 87–100.

LAUX, H.-D. (1989), 'The components of population growth in Prussian cities, 1875–1905 and their influence on urban population structure', in R. Lawton and R. Lee (eds), *Urban Population Development in Western Europe from the Late-Eighteenth to the Early-Twentieth Century*, Liverpool, 120–48.

MARSCHALCK, P. (1994), 'Städtische Bevölkerungsstrukturen vor der Industrialisierung: Eheliche Fruchtbarkeit in Bremen in der ersten Hälfte des 19. Jahrhunderts', in H.-G. Haupt and P. Marschalck (eds), *Städtische Bevölkerungsentwicklung in Deutschland im 19. Jahrhundert. Soziale und demographische Aspekte der Urbanisierung*, St Katharinen, 143–72.

MATZERATH, H. (1978), 'Städtewachstum und Eingemeindungen im 19. Jahrhundert', in J. Reulecke (ed.), *Die deutsche Stadt im Industriezeitalter, Beiträge zur modernen deutschen Stadtgeschichte*, Wuppertal, 67–89.

MATZERATH, H. and I. THIENEL, (1977), 'Stadtentwicklung, Stadtplanung, Stadtentwicklungsplanung. Probleme im 19. und 20. Jahrhundert am Beispiel der Stadt Berlin', *Die Verwaltung*, **10**, 173–96.

NAHRSTEDT, W. (1972), *Die Entstehung der Freizeit, dargestellt am Beispiel Hamburgs*, Göttingen.

OLLENSCHLÄGER, G. (1940), 'Die Industrialisierung Hamburgs', unpublished PhD thesis, University of Cologne.

REIF, H. (1986), 'Arbeiter und Unternehmer in Städten des westlichen Ruhrgebiets 1850–1930. Räumliche Aspekte einer Klassenbeziehung', in J. Kocka and E. Müller-Luckner (eds), *Arbeiter und Bürger im 19. Jahrhundert. Varianten ihres Verhältnisses im europäischen Vergleich*, Munich.

REINCKE, H. (1951), 'Hamburgs Bevölkerung', in H. Reincke, *Forschungen und Skizzen zur Hamburgischen Geschichte*, Hamburg, 167–200.

REULECKE, J. (1977), 'Sozio-ökonomische Bedingungen und Folgen der Verstädterung in Deutschland', *Zeitschrift für Stadtgeschichte, Stadtsoziologie und Denkmalpflege*, **4**, 269–87.

REULECKE, J. (1985), *Geschichte der Urbanisierung in Deutschland*, Frankfurt-am-Main.

SCHIMPFF, G. (1903), *Hamburg und sein Ortsverkehr. Die städtischen Verkehrsmittel, ihre bisherige Entwicklung und künftige Gestaltung*, Berlin and Hamburg.

SCHOTT, S. (1907), *Die Citybildung in den deutschen Großstädten seit 1871*, Breslau.

SCHÜREN, R. (1989), *Soziale Mobilität. Muster, Veränderungen und Bedingungen in 19. und 20. Jahrhundert*, St Katharinen.

SEELIG, G. (1907), 'Hamburg', in Verein für Socialpolitik (ed.), *Verfassung und Verwaltungsorganization der Städte* (Heft 5, *Die Hansestädte*), Leipzig, 3–33.

Statistik des Deutschen Reichs (1884), 'Berufsstatistik nach der allgemeinen Berufszählung vom 5. Juni, 1882, Teil 2: Berufsstatistik der deutschen Großstädte', **3**, Berlin.

Statistik des Deutschen Reichs (1897), 'Berufs- und Gewerbezählung vom 14. Juni 1895, Berufsstatistik der deutschen Großstädte, Erster Theil', **107**, Berlin.

Statistik des Deutschen Reichs (1910), 'Berufs- und Bertriebszählung vom 12 Juni 1907, Abt. VI, Großstädte', **207**, Berlin, 342–50.

Statistik des Hamburgischen Staats (1867–1919), Vols. I–XXX, Hamburg.

Statistisches Handbuch für den Hamburgischen Staat (1891), Hamburg.

Statistisches Handbuch für den Hamburgischen Staat (1921), Ausgabe 1920, Hamburg.

SUTCLIFFE, A. (ed.) (1974), *Multi-Storey Living. The British Working-Class Experience*, London and New York.

TEUTEBERG, H. J. (1972), 'Die Entstehung des modernen Hamburger Hafens (1866–1896)', *Tradition. Zeitschrift für Firmengeschichte und Unternehmerbiographie*, **5/6**, 257–91.

TEUTEBERG, H. J. and C. WISCHERMANN (1992), 'Germany', in C. G. Pooley (ed.), *Housing Strategies in Europe, 1880–1930*, Leicester, 240–67.

THIENEL, I. (1977), 'Verstädterung, städtische Infrastruktur und Stadtplanung. Berlin zwischen 1850 und 1914', *Zeitschrift für Stadtgeschichte, Stadtsoziologie und Denkmalpflege*, **4**, 55–84.

TILLY, R. (1991), 'Cyclical trends and the market response: long swings in urban development in Germany', in W. R. Lee (ed.), *German Industry and German Industrialisation. Essays in German Economic and Business History in the Nineteenth and Twentieth Centuries*, London and New York, 148–84.

WISCHERMANN, C. (1983a), *Wohnen in Hamburg von dem Ersten Weltkrieg* (Studien zur Geschichte des Alltags, **2**), Münster.

WISCHERMANN, C. (1983b), 'Wohnen und Soziale Lage in der Urbanisierung. Die Wohnbedingungen hamburgischer Unter- und Mittelschichten um die Jahrhundertwende', in H. J. Teuteberg (ed.), *Urbanisierung im 19. und 20. Jahrhundert. Historische und Geographische Aspekte*, Cologne and Vienna, 309–37.

WISCHERMANN, C. (1986), 'Wohnungsmarkt, Wohnungsversorgung und Wohnmobilität in deutschen Großstädten 1870–1913', in H. J. Teuteberg (ed.), *Stadtwachstum, Industrialisierung, Sozialer Wandel*, Berlin, 101–34.

Chapter 10

DEMOGRAPHIC CHANGE AND SOCIAL STRUCTURE: THE WORKERS AND THE BOURGEOISIE IN NANTES, 1830–1848

ANGELA FAHY

INTRODUCTION

During the period of the July Monarchy the French working class was neither sociologically nor ideologically homogeneous (Magraw, 1983, p. 105). Workers in individual towns and specific industries had different grievances. Disparities in conditions led to varying responses and these responses were, in turn, informed by the economic and social histories of those communities. Magraw has pointed to the different political traditions of workers in Marseilles, Toulouse and Paris. Just as there was a geography of working-class politics and protests, likewise there were variations in the response of the middle classes to issues involving *les classes inférieurs, les ouvriers, cette classe intéressante* or *le peuple* (Magraw, 1983, p. 92).[1] The most important issues of middle-class concern were the living conditions and morality of the working class, the increase in their numbers and political activity, as well as the effect of migration from the countryside on each of these problems. The response of the middle classes to these issues was set against the background of the development of industrial production in some parts of France, especially in the areas of Paris, Lille, Lyons and Rouen. This was accompanied in places by the emergence of worker organization through the mutual aid societies and in some cases by worker protest, such as that in Lyons (Bezucha, 1974), Limoges (Merriman, 1985) and Paris (Chevalier, 1973), or in smaller towns, such as Carmaux and Lodève, dominated by traditional handicraft industries (Scott, 1974; Johnson, 1992; McPhee, 1992, p. 140). But perhaps the most important backdrop was the development of philosophical thought and social theory which increasingly infused middle-class and working-class beliefs and actions. Important influences were the ideas of Saint Simon, Fourier, Proudhon and Louis Blanc. Informed by a rationalism based on advances in scientific knowledge, society was represented as an organism in which each group had a role to play in maintaining overall harmony. Ideas of the exact nature of each group's role varied and the working classes were cast variously as ignorant and immoral, to be controlled and reformed by the philanthropy of the middle classes, or as the true producers of the nation's wealth and thus entitled to full civil and political rights.

1 Respectively, the lower classes, the workers, this interesting class or the people.

The purpose of this chapter is to examine the way in which a section of the Nantes middle class thought about and discussed the issues of industrialization and its consequences: urban growth, poverty and migration, as well as the health, morality and politics of the working classes. It will be based on an investigation of some of the institutions in which the middle classes discussed and put into practice their ideas about that relationship. Clearly such discussions and practices were in part conditioned by the information which was available about such topics as mortality, fertility and migration. For this reason the analysis will be concerned with what the Nantes middle classes knew, or chose to know, and the way in which they used such information, rather than what historical demographers might know now. The discussion which follows will examine the chronology of contemporary debate as it developed in the light of the availability of information on local and national demographic trends, as well as political and social issues. Institutions such as learned societies played an important role in the dissemination and discussion of the significant issues of the day. This contribution will therefore focus on such a society in Nantes which recorded in its journal the changing agenda of social, political and demographic issues.

HISTORICAL BACKGROUND

During the eighteenth century Nantes had developed into one of France's major ports (Leroux, 1984).[2] Located on the west coast of France at the mouth of the River Loire, it was well situated for involvement in the developing colonial trade with Africa, America and the West Indies. It became involved in the trade in textiles, sugar and slaves along with La Rochelle, Bordeaux and Rouen, and the initial profits of the slave trade were particularly high for such bourgeois families as the Deurbroucq, Montaudouin, Grou, Perrée de la Villestreux, Michel and Lauvencin (Clark, 1981; Casey, 1981; Leroux, 1984, p. 55). A wealthy mercantile élite developed which included those of noble descent, the old *haute* (upper) *bourgeoisie* and the recently rich, whose ranks included Dutch, Portuguese and Irish families. These merchants rapidly eclipsed the *propriétaire* nobles in wealth and numbers. Throughout the eighteenth century rich traders held the majority of posts as mayors and aldermen. They invested in each other's business ventures, including sugar-refining and textile manufacturing, within the Nantes area; they purchased estates and titles and married into each other's families.

The Seven Years' War, which began in 1755, brought disaster to Nantes' maritime trade as it did to many other French ports and by the time it ended many of the great family names had vanished from business. The continental blockade during the Napoleonic Wars would also take its toll. Those who

---

2 For the economic and social history of eighteenth-century Nantes, see J. Meyer, *L'ère des Negriers* (1972) and P. Bois, *L'histoire de Nantes* (1977).

remained and those who were new to commerce adopted a more cautious attitude to investment and avoided any large-scale enterprises, thus restricting the capital available for industrial ventures. This legacy of caution, based on a collective experience of the fluctuations of the mercantile economy and its vulnerability to political upheaval beyond France's own shores as well as within the country, was to distinguish the entrepreneurs of port-cities from those of the interior of France who would invest heavily in industrial projects in the mid-nineteenth century.

The politics of the Nantes bourgeoisie in the late-eighteenth century were liberal, partly for economic reasons, and they welcomed the Revolution of 1789, unlike much of Brittany which was solidly conservative. Within the city of Nantes the oligarchy of the merchant élite was never seriously threatened as they and the rest of the community were to a large extent united by common economic interests and concerns (Bois, 1977, chapter 8).

The first half of the nineteenth century saw the widening of the boundaries of wealth beyond the merchant group to include some shopkeepers, small manufacturers and the professions. This shift is evident in the electoral lists of the period which indicate an increasing number of tax payers in the lower taxation categories and a corresponding decrease in the numbers paying taxes above 1,000 francs per annum. This latter group declined from 32 per cent of the electorate in 1820 to 8 per cent by 1840, a change which cannot be explained simply by the enlargement of the franchise in 1830 when individuals paying between 200 and 300 francs in tax were admitted to the electorate. Excluding these new voters from the calculation still produces a decrease in the very wealthy of 11 per cent.[3]

The revolutionary era was clearly accompanied by urban decline and both Bordeaux and Nantes only overtook their 1790 population levels by the mid-nineteenth century (Poussou, 1989, p. 72). The population of Nantes rose from 71,739 in 1825 to 77,992 in 1830 but declined again to 75,895 by 1835. After 1835 the number of inhabitants in Nantes increased more rapidly, reaching 96,362 by 1851. At the same time, the proportion of the *département's* (or county's) population living in the city increased to 19.5 per cent (Table 10.1). This increase was due only in small part to natural growth; migration from the surrounding rural areas was the major contributor. It was also a feature of the demographic development of a number of other *départements* in this period and accounted for the disproportional increase in urban population in the period 1827 to 1846 (Table 10.2). As will be seen below, this in-migration became a major cause for middle-class concern in Nantes.

The larger part of the city's inhabitants were engaged in domestic service, workshop employment and various small enterprises. One of the largest single employers was the tinned food factory of M. Colin which had approximately

3 Archives Municipales de la ville de Nantes; Listes Electorales de la ville de Nantes, 1820, 1828, 1840.

Table 10.1: *The population of Nantes, 1801–1866.*

Year	Population of Nantes	Percentage of département's population
1801	73,900	20.0
1831	77,900	16.6
1836	75,800	16.0
1841	83,389	17.1
1846	94,200	18.2
1851	96,362	18.0
1856	108,500	19.5
1861	113,625	19.6
1866	111,900	18.7

Table 10.2: *Population change in France according to* département, *1827–1846.*

Département	Increase in département %	Urban increase %	Rural increase %
Loire Inférieure	13.2	23.2	10.9
Bouches du Rhône	26.8	34.1	19.9
Gironde	11.9	30.2	7.2
Bas Rhin	8.4	15.8	7.2
Haute Garonne	18.4	47.0	12.9
Maine et Loire	10.1	27.7	8.0
Marne	13.0	18.3	11.7
Indre et Loire	7.6	34.2	4.7
Sarthe	6.3	16.6	5.2
Var	12.4	22.1	10.2
France	11.1	13.4	10.7

100 female workers in the 1820s and the 14 ship-building yards collectively had a comparatively large workforce (Leroux, 1984, p. 154). The textile manufacturing firm of Cheguillaume, François et Cie also employed between 400 and 500 workers of whom 80 were children and 80 were women (each paid a fraction of the wages earned by the male employees). Despite this, the employers had a very good reputation for the treatment of their workers. Factory employment thus provided work for only a small proportion of Nantes' population, most manufacturing being carried out in small workshops or in the form of putting-out work carried out in the home. Both methods of

production existed in the city, while the latter predominated in the surrounding countryside. The decline of domestic craft production on the land during this period was one of the contributing factors to rural–urban migration. The manufacturing economy in Nantes was far from stable and it suffered especially from the vagaries of the textile trade. In 1827 there were 15 cotton factories or workshops; in 1838 there were 25, but by 1840 their number had declined to 13. Commentators at the time were quick to point out that this decrease was not due to the amalgamation of firms but to the general difficulties of the trade.

BOURGEOIS INSTITUTIONS AND IDEOLOGY

With the development of a well-off middle class there emerged a network of institutions which expressed their interests in the arts, science, commerce and politics. It should be noted that at this time in Nantes, as elsewhere, institutions admitted only men as members. Such institutions ranged from the informal cafés and reading rooms to learned societies—*sociétés savantes*—with quite exclusive membership. There also developed a series of charitable organizations which cared for the sick, orphaned and poor and in which women sometimes played a part as organizers. Among the learned societies, the most prominent was the *Société Académique de Nantes et du Département de la Loire Inférieure* which had originally been established under a different name in 1798. Here, new members were accepted only after they were proposed by two existing members and after they had proved their worthiness by submitting an essay which demonstrated their interest in an area of science, literature, art, commerce or philosophy. Meetings were held every three months and papers on diverse subjects were delivered and discussed. After 1830 an annual journal, the *Annales*, was published which contained reports of meetings as well as articles submitted by members for publication. In the pages of the *Annales* the thoughts of its members are recorded on both theoretical and practical aspects of industry, commerce and politics. Interests were often very topical: the issues of primary education, railway construction, penitentiary reform and industrial innovations appeared frequently. Members' preoccupations were also diverse, which was to some extent a reflection of their occupations, since within the Society's ranks there were *propriétaires* (property owners), doctors, lawyers, teachers and businessmen. Just as their interests varied, so too did their opinions, and disagreements were not uncommon.

The Society contained a cross-section of the major occupational groups which comprised the Nantes electorate (Table 10.3) and many members were active in charitable, administrative and political organizations. All its members voted and therefore paid at least 300 francs in tax per annum (200 francs after 1830). But, although they were part of a politically and economically privileged group, their politics were diverse and at times they clashed with the local

Table 10.3: *Composition of the Nantes electorate in 1820, 1828 and 1840 (per cent).*

Occupation	1820	1828	1840
Propriétaire/Rentier	37.7	29.9	28.4
Army/navy	6.7	5.8	3.2
Commerce	38.4	44.2	52.7
Professions	9.4	10.3	11.3
Civil servants	7.2	9.1	4.2
Unknown	0.6	0.7	0.2
	100.0	100.0	100.0

administration. In 1820, for example, the President was forbidden by the Prefect from giving a speech on the virtues of free trade. In 1822 a member of the Society was charged with provocation after he remonstrated with the police for arresting a workman who had shouted 'Long live Napoleon II'. Its journal thus provides a valuable insight into the views of the Society's members on a variety of contemporary issues and into the beliefs which underlay those opinions.

THE *SOCIÉTÉ ACADÉMIQUE* AND THE PEOPLE

In 1830, when the *Annales* were first published, the Society had 121 resident members. The largest single group was that of the medical profession, of whom there were 26. Together with lawyers and teachers, professional men made up half the total membership. In terms of their economic position the members were also diverse—in 1830 the annual taxes which they paid ranged from 3,348 francs to 308 francs. But all members paid at least 300 francs in taxes, the level above which one became entitled to vote in national elections. Thus, although the Society's membership represented the local diversity in wealth and occupations within the middle classes, it was far from representative of Nantes society as a whole. In addition, there were 141 corresponding members who did not live in the *département*, of whom 44 were resident in Paris. These members provided a network of communication links between sections of the middle classes within Nantes, across the country and beyond (one corresponding member was resident in London). This network was augmented by formal connections between similar societies in other towns and cities with whom the *Société Académique* exchanged journals.

The Society was also diverse in its politics, containing members who were government supporters alongside those of the liberal opposition and very occasionally those of the extreme right who supported greater power for the monarchy and the Catholic Church. In every election to the Chamber of Deputies between 1830 and 1850 at least one member of the Society stood for a place in the *département*'s deputation. Membership seems to have constituted an important preparation for political life and future candidates for election were always prominent in the Society's debates and among its officers.

The first issue of the *Annales* in this period opened with the annual address of the President, Dr Foure, who praised science, the arts, the enlightenment and progress. He went on to emphasize the importance of societies such as their own as a means by which ideas on these topics could be communicated not only among its membership, but also to other such societies. His greatest praise was reserved for education which, he stated, had a specific purpose for each social group. For the *classes inférieures* it served to increase the productivity of their work and so accustomed them to well-being and to the social order which guaranteed it. He went on to praise a type of social order in which each class had particular functions which were necessary for the harmony of the whole (*Annales*, 1830, p. 24).

Such ideas reappear many times in this issue of the *Annales*. In a discussion of the French primary education system, which was to be formalized by the Guizot Law of 1833 (Anderson, 1975; Charle, 1994, 31–32) it was declared to be satisfactory because it taught *la classe inférieure* all it needed to know for 'the career which it is destined to follow' (*Annales*, 1830, p. 69). It was in fact the education of *la classe moyenne* which gave the Society most cause for concern. The colleges were judged to be unsuitable for any but the upper classes (*les classes élevées*), since they provided no education in the subjects useful for commerce and industry. In order to remedy this the Society proposed setting up *une Athéneé publique* (a grammar school open to the public) where courses useful to the middle class would be taught free by members of the Society. The subjects were to include French, Latin, English, history and geography, physics, political economy and commerce (taught by a prominent sugar-refiner, Louis Say, brother of the leading French economist Jean-Baptiste Say), natural history, comparative anatomy, physiology and hygiene. Thus it seems that it was the position of the middle classes which was the major concern of the Society's members—perhaps an appropriate concern on the eve of the July Monarchy which is now so often described as the Bourgeois Monarchy (Price, 1981).

The *Annales* of 1831 began with an enthusiastic welcome of the July Revolution and of a monarchy and government which the Society saw as giving to the middle classes a liberty in accordance with the country's needs. But it was also quick to criticize past governments for their neglect of the provinces and urged that Brittany should receive more consideration in discussions as to how to improve France's economy. This theme was to recur in every volume of the *Annales* in this period. Memories of former economic power and of past regional autonomy in Brittany, of which Nantes was the commercial centre and largest city, created for many years a tension between a government based in Paris which was determined to centralize financial and administrative bodies and regional interests, such as those of Brittany and the

Loire, which saw themselves as neglected and denied an opportunity to participate in national economic development.

The Society's discussions in 1832 and 1833 were concerned mostly with ways of encouraging commerce and industry in the *département*. It praised the establishment of the *Société Industrielle*, which had been set up in 1830 by some of the *Société Académique*'s members. This organization was concerned with the apprenticeship and general education of the sons of workers in order that they would be able to receive training in the trades for which their fathers intended them. While involved in training they were given food, clothes, and three francs every month. Half of this sum they were obliged to save in the *Caisse d'Epargnes* which had been set up at the same time (Lepetit, 1988, pp. 349–54). This was destined to provide for them and their families in case of illness and reflected the contemporary view that the 'doctrine of savings' would encourage individual responsibility and mininize the risk of insurrection (Donzelot, 1979; Accampo, 1989, p. 150). The stated general intention of the *Société Industrielle* was to instil in the boys obedience, devotion to hard work and thrift, thus making them better workers.

It was only in 1834 that the politics of workers appeared as a topic of discussion in the *Annales*. In this year a paper was delivered on the subject of workers' coalitions and the means of preventing their re-emergence. References were made to the recent workers' protest in Lyons (see Bezucha, 1974; Strumhinger, 1979). This was clearly what gave rise to concern in Nantes, a concern which was shared by the Prefect who wrote to the Mayor (a member of the Society) that 'the existence of a Republican society in our town is beyond doubt ... we have seen from the unhappy events in Paris and Lyons that such associations bring disaster'.[4] The writer in the *Annales* was concerned more with the causes of such protest which he believed had its origins in the misery of workers' lives and the means by which the government had dealt with the uprising in the two cities. The author, Verger, condemned the government for offering nothing but armed force as a response and urged his listeners to help improve the condition of 'the poor classes' through encouraging worker-employer associations. He proposed sending a petition to the elected representatives of the *département* stating this. However, the commission which the Society set up to examine this proposal was more cautious. It concluded that workers should be taught to behave better and refused to approve the petition. Clearly the membership of the Society was not united in its view of the cause of worker unrest and the means of dealing with it. The members could afford to be divided to some extent, since there was no immediate threat of such disturbances in Nantes and thus a consensus on how to deal with such a threat was not yet required.

---

4 Archives Municipales de la ville de Nantes, Series 12, Carton 29, Dossier 1 and 2, Prefect to Mayor 18 April 1834.

By 1835 this issue had subsided from the Society's agenda and education and penitentiary reform had come to the fore, in line with their prominence in the contemporary national debate. Concern with workers' conditions, however, was being expressed elsewhere by one of its most prominent members, the doctor Ange Guépin. In this year he published, with his friend Dr Eugéne Bonamy, a substantial study of contemporary Nantes (Guépin and Bonamy, 1835). *Nantes au XIX siècle* provides a fine example of the most popular form of social analysis during this period which was often carried out by doctors armed with the new techniques of information gathering and demographic analysis. It contains a systematic investigation of all aspects of the city, which was viewed as a *corps social*, a patient whose illness could be measured, diagnosed and cured. This analysis was based on the authors' observations as doctors much involved in charitable work and discussed within the context of their belief in the social and economic philosophy of Saint Simon (Beltran and Griset, 1988, pp. 21–22). Through their revelations they hoped that readers would understand the city and set about curing its ills. They described themselves as defenders of the 'people' in the face of the rich and claimed that it was their duty to present to the better-off 'a faithful picture of the misery of the poor'. They did this by presenting a detailed description of Nantes' economy, the wages of its workers, the standard of living of each social class, as well as statistics on mortality and fertility.

Nantes au XIX siècle is full of organic metaphors, especially those derived from medicine, revealing the extent to which the authors' beliefs derived from the discourse of the day which drew heavily on such concepts of society. They condemned some popular newspapers which were being published in Nantes because their focus on suicide and murder could only produce 'a contagious imitation' (Guépin and Bonamy, 1835, p. 181). The book is most powerful in its analysis of Nantes society which the authors divided into eight categories ranging from the rich, through four types of bourgeoisie (*haute, aisé, gênés, pauvres* [respectively upper, well-off, in straitened circumstances and poor]), well-off workers, and finally those living in extreme misery. They put before their readers a vivid picture of the homes, social lives and illnesses of each social group—scenes with which they were no doubt familiar since they were themselves of prominent Nantes families and their personal and professional lives connected them with all levels of the city's life. They described the luxurious interiors of the town and country houses of the rich, their social lives at balls and concerts, the frequency of nervous disorders among women of this class; the more modest homes of the middle classes, where social life was focused on small parties in the home (especially if there were daughters of marriageable age); and the poor homes (often damp and crowded cellars) of the workers whose only recreation was to walk in the parks on Sunday (if they were allowed in). They estimated the annual household expenditure of each of these groups and concluded that it ranged from 12,000 to 300 francs. They thus spoke to their readers of a city of many different spheres, each containing a different population and a specific style of life (Guépin and Bonamy, 1835, pp. 455–92).

In order to illustrate this internal geography of urban life they spoke of the geography of death, describing each administrative area of the city in turn. In the old medieval city annual mortality was 34.8 per 1,000; in the predominantly *petit bourgeois* area it was 22.7 per 1,000 (Table 10.4). In the very poor Rue des Fumiers (Manure Street) it was 58.8 per 1,000 and the average age at death stood at 31 years. In the wealthy street Le Boulevard, on the other hand, the mortality rate was only 10.2 per 1,000. The mortality level among children under 10 was one in 32 in rich areas and one in 11 in the poorest; for infants under one year of age it was one in 11 and one in two respectively. The authors deplored the attitudes of some sections of the middle classes, such as the Society for Maternal Charity (presided over by middle-class women) which gave assistance only to mothers who could produce a marriage certificate and swear that they had good morals. The local administration also was not spared criticism for putting up signs during the recent cholera epidemic advising the public to be well-housed, well-fed, well-clothed and not to go out into the cold when sweating.[5] Guépin retorted that this was of little use to the many poor who could not read, worked for 14 hours (for as little as two francs per day), lived in a damp cellar and ate whatever they could find. He added that they could hardly be blamed for turning to alcohol.

To those men and women of Nantes who read this book such revelations were perhaps shocking, but the discussions by the Society did not lead to any immediate raising of its social conscience. Despite, or perhaps because of, this publication and a severe cholera epidemic in 1832–1834 (Bourdelais and Raulot, 1987, p. 73; Bourdelais, 1991), the *Annales* of the Society in 1836 published discussions on the theatre, horses and art. Even the Prefect's anxiety in 1837 concerning a report of 40 radical workers' cafés in the city did not

Table 10.4: *Guépin's classification of the population of Nantes by canton and urban mortality in 1829 (per 1,000).*

Canton	Social classification	Mortality in 1829 (per 1,000)
1	Poor	34.8
2	Rich/petit bourgeois	25.4
3	Petit bourgeois	22.7
4	Poor	30.2
5	Very rich/very poor	25.3
6	Comfortable workers	24.5

5 For a general discussion of the incidence of cholera in France, see Bourdelais and Raulot (1987).

impinge on the Society's immediate concerns.[6] But by 1838 the pathological view of an ailing society had re-emerged. The President, Dr Foure, advocated the payment of a decent wage to workers and the protection of the family as the basis of the social order. In the same year an 'Essay on hygiene, contemplated in its relationship with philosophy and political economy' relied heavily on images of corruption, contagion and disorder in discussing the plight of the urban poor. Pauperism was deplored because it was a symptom of the disorder of morals, ignorance, intemperance and debauchery among the poor. At no point was it suggested that pauperism could be the product of anything other than weaknesses believed to be inherent in this social group (*Annales*, 1837, p. 230). This increasing anxiety concerning the corruption of parts of the *corps social* no doubt owed a great deal to Dr Guépin's revelations, but it was also part of a national middle-class anxiety, articulated in books, newspapers and learned journals, which increasingly regarded the poor as 'the dangerous classes' (Chevalier, 1973).

In 1837 the city archivist presented a summary of important statistics for the city, among them a table of its population divided by occupational groups (Table 10.5). It should be noted that women were only classified separately in the case of domestic servants; in all other cases they were included with men. The absence of a category for married women who did not work, and the fact that the total added up to the official census figure, suggests that married women were included in their husbands' occupational group. This implies that some of the figures given are not accurate, since the inclusion of wives leads to an over-estimation. But the fact that the information was presented in this way is equally interesting, since it reveals the priorities which were current at this time—the only female role which merited separate consideration was that of the domestic servant (*Annales*, 1837, p. 462).

Table 10.5: *Population of Nantes in 1837 by occupation.*

Civil servants	150	Soldiers	400
Clergy	525	Workers	17,120
Rentier	3,500	Domestics (male)	1,150
Clerks	900	Domestics (female)	5,430
Office/shop employees	700	No occupation	1,500
Traders	450	Indigent	1,171
Shopkeepers	5,550	Hospital patients	2,078
Industrialists	425	Children	1,600
Architects/artists	170	Old people	8,000
Lawyers/doctors/chemists	310	Unknown	9,895
Teachers (male and female)	189	Floating	10,000
Students	200		

6 Archives Municipales de la ville de Nantes, Series 12, Carton 28, Dossier 1.

In 1838 women were present during the Society's proceedings for the first time, although they had frequently appeared as the topic of discussion in the medical section of its proceedings where middle-class female neuroses were particularly popular as subjects of debate. However, their presence was brief and decorative—two ladies dutifully performed a piano duet at the beginning of the annual general meeting. The issue of worker protest, however, did reappear on this occasion within the context of a discussion of the usefulness of charitable institutions operating in Nantes. The local *Société de Secours Mutuel*, established in 1830 by the *Société Industrielle*, was praised for bringing workers together and for encouraging them to save money (Sibalis, 1989). In doing so it was believed to be exerting an influence of great social importance on the working class. Evidence of the depth of this influence was given in an account of how a potential protest was defused by the intervention of the middle-class organizers of the *Société de Secours Mutuel*. Recent technological innovations in a local wood-cutting factory had led to the dismissal of 90 workers, all members of the same *Société*. They had responded by protesting and threatening to damage the building. At this point they were persuaded that property was sacred and that the use of force was contrary to the spirit of liberty. So moved were the workers that they left the factory 'with tears in their eyes' (*Annales*, 1838, p. 340). The *Société de Secours Mutuel* thus acted in this instance as an effective means of controlling worker protest. It is not revealed whether the workers' tears were due to frustration or repentance.

Faith in such societies was not universal among the middle classes. In the *Annales* of 1839 Dr Guépin, now the Secretary General of the *Société Académique*, condemned men who mistook them for workers' coalitions and who feared more for the employer than the worker (*Annales*, 1839, p. 453). By 1840 the ailing economy of the city was again a cause of the *Société Académique*'s concern. In his presidential address the printer Camille Mellinet called for an investigation of the important question as to whether Nantes should become an industrial city or not and, if so, what its principal products should be. But he did not look on industrial progress with unqualified optimism, expressing instead concern for its influence on the moral state of the workers. He warned that the decline of rural industry would lead to an influx of workers into Nantes and asked if that might not lead to events such as those in Lyons. He even suggested that it would be of 'moral interest' to encourage migrants to return to the countryside (*Annales*, 1840, p. 38).

Eugéne Bonamy, Guépin's co-author, had a more hopeful outlook and urged that the Society's members devote themselves to ensuring the moral improvement of all citizens and especially of *le peuple*. This was in accordance with his faith in the philosophy of Saint Simon which advocated a sort of religion of industrial progress based on Christian fraternalism. Guépin declared that 'the people' needed to be loved and assisted because 'they cannot escape unaided from their miserable condition'. He also appealed for the better supervision of children in factories so that their health would not deteriorate, nor their morals become perverted. But he did not argue against child employment (*Annales*, 1840, p. 38). The Society decided to set up a series of committees to investigate the trends in births, marriages and deaths, public morality and crime. Some of the resulting reports are discussed later.

In 1841 Mellinet praised *ces hommes du peuple* upon whom France's industry depended, exhorting the Society's members to look upon them with 'fraternal sympathy in those workshops where fetid odours shorten the lives of the workers' (*Annales*, 1841, p. 438). In 1843 the 'precarious condition' of the working classes in Nantes was a cause of concern to the President, himself a factory owner, who attributed it to ignorance, intemperance and the absence of religious principles. He added that it was also due to the seasonality of work and the closure of workshops (*Annales*, 1843, p. 419). The threat of worker coalitions was also recognized and charitable associations for promoting workers' care were stated to be preferable since they, unlike the coalitions, did not distract them from their 'modest destiny'. But alternative voices continued to speak through the pages of the *Annales*: a civil engineer, for example, spoke of the dignity of human labour and the horror of its abuses by 'the capitalist system'. He proposed that the unrest which might arise could be averted by allowing workers to participate in the system and, in doing so, to share the interests of the capitalist class (*Annales*, 1843, p. 487). In this year a lively discussion also took place on the subject of utopian socialism which was dismissed by some members as 'existing only in the more or less fertile brains of a few economists in the capital' (*Annales*, 1843, p. 19). But this concept also had its supporters in the ranks of the Society and they urged members to consider its usefulness.

In 1845 the debate on the virtues of industrialization continued, with some members painting a picture of potential widespread prosperity which would allow workers the comfort and leisure to 'accomplish their religious duties, attend to their domestic tasks and supervise their childrens' education' (*Annales*, 1845, p. 13). The discussion of economic theory also continued with a paper in 1847 on 'The effects of the equal division of land among all the citizens'. This proposal, however, was condemned and charity was advocated as the way to overcome poverty. In the same year a lengthy paper reviewed the work of a number of economists including Adam Smith, Say, Godwin, Blanqui and Malthus. Each was considered from the point of view of his contribution to the 'solution of the social problems of poverty and overpopulation'. Malthus was criticized for his failure to look at all aspects of the population problem, especially the fact that improvements in living conditions would lead to a fall in fertility. Only Blanqui was praised as 'having the good fortune not to be a utopian' (*Annales*, 1847, pp. 331–54).

The annual address of the President in 1847 expressed the growing concern of the Society's members on the subject of the adverse effects of industrialization and the vagaries of the industrial economy. The state of Nantes' industry at this time must have contributed largely to this concern, as most factories were struggling and had a reduced workforce. The local *Comptoir d'Escompte* also reported on this in 1848. Fears of the creation of *la mendicité armée* were expressed by the President who urged an improvement in the conditions of the 'labouring classes' as a way of averting the danger. Since migration was seen as one of the major causes of contemporary urban problems, the Society had organized an essay competition on the subject of 'The causes of migration to towns and ways of halting this movement'. There were 49 entries and the winner was a lawyer from Angers who condemned the romantic notion of the countryside as a bucolic paradise (''this only exists in the gardens of country mansions', *Annales*, 1847, p. 488) and deplored the failure of individuals and the government to invest in agricultural improvements. Until this was done, he claimed, the city would always seem a more attractive place, even with its perceptible miseries.

By 1848 a very dark view of the evils of the industrial system was being presented to the Society. Colombel related a meeting with an Englishman, with 'a cold, dry, calculating heart', who spoke of the misery of the English worker. There the miner and factory worker suffered not only the dreadful physical effects of their work but also the 'most hideous vices', including drunkenness, prostitution and 'villainous debauchery', to which such misery led. Colombel urged his listeners to consider seriously the dangers to French society if it followed England's 'fatal path' (*Annales*, 1848, p. 474). Thus innate caution among the middle class of Nantes with regard to speculative investment may now have been reinforced by serious doubts about the morality of the factory system in general.

For another member of the Society the evils of industrial progress lay not in its essence but in its tendency to concentrate in towns where rootless workers became susceptible to agitation. The speaker, a pharmacist, suggested that factories should be moved to the countryside, that female labour should be used, and that the men should be employed in agricultural work (*Annales*, 1848, p. 485). Although he cited several economists in support of this idea, his fellow members were horrified. The Secretary General of the Society replied emphatically:

> No! No! Do not tear women away from the sacred mission with which they have been entrusted ... consider woman's supple figure, see her delicate hands and arms ... listen to her soft voice ... do not condemn her to the life of the workshop which disturbs her body, destroys her health, at the same time corrupting her heart and spirit. (*Annales*, 1848, p. 488)

Yet to such a life the male worker was consigned without hesitation, blessed with the fraternal sympathy of the middle classes. Outrage at the suggestion that women should take over industrial work at a time when working-class women in Nantes and elsewhere were exploited as domestic servants, piece-workers in factories and in the home, and as prostitutes, underlines the confusion which arose in middle-class philosophies when issues of gender and class intersected. In this example the ideal of a woman as a dutiful wife and gentle mother, which was rigorously promoted within the middle class, was also automatically applied to *le peuple* (DeGroat, 1997, p. 34). Working-class women were already employed in activities and jobs which were low-paid, exhausting and often degrading, but this type of work seems to have been acceptable to the middle classes as long as it was invisible behind the doors of attics, kitchens and brothels (McMillan, 1981, p. 1).

The Secretary General's remarks also reveal another gender-based prejudice prevalent at the time, namely the unsuitability of women for work in any form of mechanized production. This exclusion of women from the scientific world also transcended class boundaries. Whether educated at home or in school, middle- or working-class girls were taught needlework while their brothers were taught mathematics, metalwork and mechanical drawing (Heywood, 1991).

The application of these principles by both the middle and working class of Nantes was evident in the operation of the charitable institutions known as the *Salles d'Asile* (Refuge Rooms) which had been established in 1833. In this context, the male directors (all members of the Society) took charge of the accounts and the maintenance of the buildings: the women's committee regulated the internal order of the institution (supervising the teachers, directing the children's work, etc.). This division of tasks replicated that of the middle-class home. The children who attended the *Salles d'Asile* were to be cared for while their parents worked, but they were also allocated roles that were thought to be appropriate. The girls knitted stockings, which were then given to the poorest children in attendance, while the boys learned to use looms and gave the finished cloth to their parents to make the family's clothes. Thus girls were taught domestic skills and the virtue of charity; the boys were taught mechanical skills and encouraged to help support their families.[7]

Up to this point, the only substantial examination of the demography of Nantes was that of Dr Guépin. Discussions on such topics as the misery of the working classes and the problem of migration did not claim any scientific basis; that is, writers did not use numerical data nor statistical analysis to support their assertions. However, in 1850 the first substantial study of the city's demography appeared in the *Annales* and this was a result of the appeal for such a study which had originally been made in 1840. In it the author first of all reminded his readers of the essay competition of 1848 on the subject of migration and agreed with the winning entry that migration was 'a burden for the towns and even a danger to their safety' (*Annales*, 1850). He then proposed to use the official documents to determine the answers to two important questions—was the movement of country dwellers to the towns real and how significant was it?

---

7 A similar gender-specific approach to charitable provision and training was evident in Saint Chamond as well as in Lancashire during the cotton famine: see Accampo (1989, p. 147); Evans (1990).

First of all the population trends for France as a whole were examined and it was established that the rate of population increase had been 11.1 per cent in the period 1827 to 1846. The rate of increase in towns had been 13.4 per cent and that in rural areas 10.7 per cent. Therefore, he concluded that migration was a primary cause of the registered increase in urban population. Having thus answered the first question, the specific case of the *département* of Loire Inférieure (in which Nantes is situated) was examined and it was found that the rural population had increased in the same period by 10.9 per cent whereas the urban population had grown by 23.2 per cent. This result was compared with trends in other *départements* (Table 10.2) and it was concluded that the Loire Inférieur ranked twenty-fourth in overall population growth, with an increase in population of 13.2 per cent. Some urban areas clearly suffered more seriously than others from migration. Growth in the urban population of the Loire Inférieure was less than that of Haute Garonne, Bouches du Rhône (containing Marseilles), Gironde (containing Bordeaux) or Indre et Loire. But Nantes itself ranked thirteenth among provincial cities in terms of its population increase (Table 10.6). Having studied the statistics for births and deaths for many of these cities, the author then stated that the observed growth could not be attributed solely to natural increase. He concluded by arguing that although it was known that migration took place, it was only after such a study that its relative importance could be appreciated. Finally, he called on the government to find an urgent solution to the growing migration problem (*Annales*, 1850, pp. 407–39).[8]

In 1852 a detailed study of the population of Nantes was presented. It was based on census data from 1791 onwards (Table 10.7), although the author warned of the questionable reliability of the pre-1819 material. The local administration, it was argued, had been in the habit of over-estimating total

Table 10.6: *Population increase of the most rapidly growing French provincial cities, 1827–1846 (per cent).*

City	Population increase	City	Population increase
Toulouse	56.6	Bordeaux	28.5
Marseilles	44.8	La Rochelle	27.6
Blois	40.2	Nîmes	26.5
Angers	35.5	Strasbourg	24.9
Nancy	33.2	Le Mans	24.0
Limoges	33.4	Nantes	23.0
Tours	29.7		

8 For an analysis of the scale and significance of migration, see Moch (1983).

Table 10.7: *The population of Nantes, 1791–1851.**

Year	Total		Year	Total
1791	77,671		1830	83,681
1802	77,356		1836	85,895
1809	68,434		1841	78,146
1814	67,067		1847	88,937
1819	64,053		1851	96,362
1825	77,025			

* Discrepancies between this and Table 10.1 are due to inconsistencies in the inclusion of the non-resident section of the population.

Table 10.8: *Population change in cantons 1–6 in Nantes, 1809–1851 (per cent).*

Period	Canton					
	1	*2*	*3*	*4*	*5*	*6*
1809–1814	+ 5.8	+ 6.6	+ 4.0	− 5.8	− 12.8	− 7.9
1814–1819	+ 6.5	+ 7.8	− 2.9	− 9.1	+ 4.2	+ 11.3
1819–1825	+ 9.6	+ 22.7	+ 11.3	+ 23.3	+ 26.1	+ 25.0
1825–1830	+ 10.7	+ 1.8	− 5.5	+ 8.1	− 1.3	+ 7.3
1830–1841	− 1.8	+ 12.9	− 7.1	+ 8.0	− 14.9	+ 5.9
1841–1847	+ 21.3	+ 12.7	+ 3.9	+ 7.1	+ 13.7	+ 24.0
1847–1851*	+ 4.5	− 14.5	+ 7.7	− 9.1	− 1.5	− 0.5

* Excluding a total non-resident population of 5,059.

population, particularly if the figures were to be used to calculate taxation assessments or conscription levels for the army. Since data are available after 1809 for the different districts of Nantes, a table of population change at the cantonal level can therefore be created (Table 10.8). This reveals a virtually continuous growth in population in most cantons, but there were variations in both scale and timing. The first canton contained the old city centre and Guépin had described it in 1835 as being the worst in the city (with a mortality rate of 34.8 per 1,000). The fourth canton was also described as very poor in 1835, while the others were mixed in character. The first canton experienced its largest population increase in the period 1841–1847; the second, third, fourth, fifth and sixth cantons in 1819–1825. The substantial population increase in the first canton (already known for its reputation for extreme poverty and high mortality) in the 1840s coincided with the appearance of a great anxiety concerning the dangers of migration and pauperism among the middle-class members of the Society.

Table 10.9: *Total births and deaths in Nantes, 1810–1850.*

	1810–1820	*1820–1830*	*1830–1840*	*1840–1850*
Births	19,576	24,040	25,808	28,278
Deaths	17,942	22,589	25,169	26,150
Surplus of births (+)/ deaths (−)	+ 1,634	+ 1,451	+ 639	+ 2,128

This section of the demographic study was followed by an analysis of births and deaths in the period 1810 to 1850 (Table 10.9), which confirmed that the increase in the population of Nantes was indeed due to in-migration. Throughout this period net in-migration accounted for approximately 70 per cent of the registered growth in total population. The period 1830 to 1840 was exceptional, both for its small excess of births over deaths (due largely to the cholera epidemics of this period) and to the decrease in total population (suggesting that in-migration was not common during those years). Both the periods 1820–1830 and 1840–1850 showed large increases due to in-migration. Although the rate of in-migration in the earlier period was higher at 22.3 per cent, it was the later increase of 15.5 per cent which caused the greater alarm.

CONCLUSION

Nantes did not become an industrial city like Lille or Lyons in this period, perhaps as a result of a spirit of cautious innovation that prevailed within the middle classes. Their experiences of the economic fluctuations of the eighteenth and early-nineteenth centuries, together with the failure of successive governments to take any real interest in the city's development, ensured that capital was used carefully and risks minimized. Many enterprises remained small, retaining the character of eighteenth-century production in terms of their scale, although some technological innovations were in fact introduced. Maritime trade, however, remained an important part of the city's economy.

Although divided in economic interests and occupations, some worker protests did take place. Weavers went on strike in 1833 and carpenters in 1836 (Guin, 1976). But because their organization was not cohesive, their demands were easily refused by their employers. Those political groups which workers did join, such as the *Société des Droits de l'Homme*, were often organized by, or closely linked to, bourgeois reformers such as Guépin. Thus a liberal, even socialist, but not a revolutionary philosophy prevailed in the port-city— communicated to those workers who were politicized by elements in the middle classes. Such philosophies had prevailed in Nantes for several generations within a middle class whose politics during the Restoration and much of the

July Monarchy were of moderate opposition. The works of Voltaire and Rousseau were often prominent on their bookshelves.

The thoughts of the *Société Académique*'s members undoubtedly reveal aspects of such a philosophy. Up to 1837 any references to the working classes invariably allocated to them an inferior role which was believed by the middle classes to be necessary in order to maintain the existing social order. The working class was seen only as a group to whom they had a philanthropic responsibility. Even when the fear of worker protest raised its head, it was viewed either sympathetically or with calm disapproval, since it was never a serious threat in Nantes during this period. It was not until 1838, however, that the working-class poor were portrayed as corrupt and immoral, and in this case attention was focused on France as a whole rather than Nantes itself. By 1840 the morality of industrial progress was itself being called into question. Many pages of the *Annales* were devoted to careful and often heated consideration of the effects of industry on the health and morals of the British and French working classes.[9]

In the *Annales* several views of society and the role of the working classes ran side by side with those derived from national political and philosophical debates, those based on an observation of events in France and elsewhere, as well as those drawn from the experience of Nantes itself. Interest in the demography of the city emerged on only two occasions. In 1835 Guépin's study of the *corps social* of Nantes was published, the purpose of which was to reveal the illnesses which needed to be cured. Debate within the Society, however, seems to have been little affected by these revelations and it continued to be influenced more by national political and social issues rather than those specific to Nantes. Interest in the details of Nantes' own demographic development did not become an important topic until 1850 when a study of migration and population trends was undertaken in order to provide proof that a serious problem now existed. Thus the papers published in 1850 and 1852 provided the quantitative data which largely confirmed anxieties that were already firmly in place. The results were used to sharpen contemporary anxieties and to justify theories as to how the resultant problems could be dealt with. It is interesting to note that even though Nantes' population grew more rapidly in the 1820s than in the 1840s, it was the latter period which provoked the most concern in Nantes. Combined with increasing anxiety about social unrest, workers' political activity in the 1840s and the upheaval of the 1848 revolution, the demographic studies of the early 1850s provided popular scientific evidence that legitimated middle-class concerns and identified sinister causes behind contemporary social problems.

9 See Stearns (1978, chapter 5) for a general discussion of bourgeois attitudes to the working class and the effects of industrialization and urbanization. In 1848 Dr Guépin assured the working class of Nantes that class violence was unnecessary and that the established élites would not resist reform (Magraw, 1983, p. 126).

References

ACCAMPO, E. (1989), *Industrialization, Family Life and Class Relations. Saint Chamond, 1815–1914*, Berkeley, Los Angeles and London.

ANDERSON, R. D. (1975), *Education in France 1848–1870*, Oxford.

Annales de la Société Académique de Nantes et du Département de la Loire Inférieure (1830–1850), Nantes.

BELTRAN, A. and P. GRISET (1988), *La Croissance économique de la France 1815–1814*, Paris.

BEZUCHA, R. J. (1974), *The Lyon Uprising of 1834: Social and Political Conflict in the Early July Monarchy*, Cambridge, Mass.

BOIS, P. (1977), *Histoire de Nantes*, Toulouse.

BOURDELAIS, P. (1991), 'Choléra des villes et choléra des champs. Fait et représentations', in R. Leboutte et al. (eds), *Historiens et populations. Liber Amicorum Etienne Hélin*, Louvain-la-Neuve, 219–30.

BOURDELAIS, P. and J.-Y. RAULOT (1987), *Une Peur Bleue. Histoire du Cholera en France 1832–1854*, Paris.

CASEY, J. D. (1981), *Bordeaux, Colonial Port of Nineteenth-Century France*, New York.

CHARLE, C. (1994), *A Social History of France in the 19th Century*, Oxford and Providence.

CHEVALIER, L. (1973), *Labouring Classes and Dangerous Classes in Paris During the First Half of the Nineteenth Century*, London.

CLARK, J. G. (1981), *La Rochelle and the Atlantic Economy during the Eighteenth Century*, Baltimore and London.

DEGROAT, J. A. (1997), 'The public nature of women's work: definitions and debates during the revolution of 1848', *French Historical Studies*, **20**(1), 31–47.

DONZELOT, J. (1979), *The Policing of Families: Welfare versus the State*, London.

EVANS, C. (1990), 'Unemployment and the making of the feminine during the Lancashire cotton famine', in P. Hudson and W. R. Lee (eds), *Women's Work and the Family Economy in Historical Perspective*, Manchester, 248–70.

GUÉPIN, A. and E. BONAMY (1835), *Nantes au XIX siècle: statistique topographique, industrielle et morale*, Nantes (reprinted 1981 with a foreword by P. Le Pichon and A. Supiot).

GUIN, Y. (1976), *Le mouvement ouvrier nantais: essai sur le syndicalisme d'action directe à Nantes et à Saint-Nazaire*, Paris.

HEYWOOD, C. (1991), 'On learning gender roles during childhood in nineteenth-century France', *French History*, **5**(4), 451–66.

JOHNSON, C. H. (1992), 'Patterns of proletarianization', in L. R. Berlanstein (ed.), *The Industrial Revolution and Work in Nineteenth-Century Europe*, London and New York, 81–101.

LEPETIT, B. (1988), *Les villes dans la France Moderne (1740–1840)*, Paris.

LEROUX, E. (1984), *Histoire d'une Ville et de ses Habitants, Nantes, Des Origines à 1914*, Nantes.

MAGRAW, R. (1983), *France 1815–1914: The Bourgeois Century*, London.

McMILLAN, J. F. (1981), *Housewife or Harlot: The Place of Women in French Society 1870–1940*, London.

McPHEE, P. (1992), *A Social History of France 1780–1880*, London and New York.

MERRIMAN, J. M. (1985), *The Red City. Limoges and the French Nineteenth Century*, London.

MEYER, J. (1972), *L'Ere des Negriers*, Paris.

MOCH, L. P. (1983), *Paths to the City: Regional Migration in Nineteenth-Century France*, Beverley Hills.

POUSSOU, J.-P. (1989), 'The population increase of French towns between 1750 and 1914, and its demographic consequences', in R. Lawton and R. Lee (eds), *Urban Population Development in Western Europe from the Late-Eighteenth to the Early-Twentieth Century*, Liverpool, 68–92.

PRICE, R. (1981), *An Economic History of Modern France 1730–1914*, London.

SCOTT, J. W. (1974), *The Glassworkers of Carmaux: French Craftsmen and Political Action in a Nineteenth Century City*, Cambridge, Mass.

SIBALIS, M. D. (1989), 'The mutual aid societies of Paris, 1789–1848', *French History*, **3**(1), 1–30.

STEARNS, P. N. (1978), *Paths to Authority. The Middle Class and the Industrial Labour Force in France, 1820–48*, Urbana, Chicago and London.

STRUMHINGER, L. S. (1979), *Women and the Making of the Working Class: Lyon 1830–70*, St Albans.

Chapter 11

POPULATION, SOCIETY AND POLITICS IN CORK FROM THE LATE-EIGHTEENTH CENTURY TO 1900

JOHN B. O'BRIEN

INTRODUCTION

There was no significant change in Cork's population between 1821, the year of the first census, and the end of the century (Connell, 1950): it oscillated around 80,000, rising in the 1840s and again in the 1880s but, even then, the increases were not spectacular (Table 11.1). This was in stark contrast to the striking 250 per cent increase during the eighteenth century.[1] Still, in the national context, Cork more than held its own in the nineteenth century. While Irish population dropped by more than 40 per cent between 1841 and 1891, Cork's declined by only 6 per cent. In fact it was still ahead of Belfast until 1841 but, of course, was far outstripped by the latter city in the second half of the century when, against the national trend, the population of Belfast more than trebled between 1841 and 1891 (*Report from the Select Committee*, 1891, p. 535). However, the apparent stability of Cork's population throughout the nineteenth century conceals the fact that, in terms of natural increase, Cork was declining from at least 1841 onwards and, had it not been for the influx of people from elsewhere in Ireland and abroad, it undoubtedly would have registered a substantial fall in population during the second half of the century. Unfortunately, the census enumerators did not distinguish between Cork city and Cork county, so that we do not know the extent of migration from the county into the city. In the light of the consolidation of rural holdings in County Cork, where the percentage of those over 30 acres by 1841 was nearly double that of the national average (Donnelly, 1975, p. 15), and due to the extensive expansion of grazing that accompanied structural change in the primary sector, there is no reason to doubt that a substantial number of dispossessed country people found their way into the city. For many, it would have been an alternative to emigration. In the city they would have joined those born elsewhere, both in Ireland and abroad, who numbered 5,224 in 1841 rising to 10,930 by 1901, representing 6.47 per cent and 14.35 per cent of the population respectively (*Censuses of Ireland*, 1841; 1901).

---

1 Dr David Dickson's revised estimates for Cork's eighteenth-century population produce a figure in 1706 of 17,595 and in 1796 of 57,033. See Appendix Table XXII of his unpublished PhD thesis (Dickson, 1977): for nineteenth-century data see *Censuses of Ireland* (1821–1891).

Table 11.1: *Population size and density in Cork city parishes, 1841–1891.*

Parish	1841		1851		1861		1871		1881		1891	
	No.	*Per acre*	*No.*	*Per acre*	*No.*	*Per acre*	*No.*	*Per acre*	*No.*	*Per acre*	*No.*	*Per acre*
Holy Trinity	8,338	102	10,920	133	8,687	106	8,090	99	7,104	86	6,198	75
St Anne's Shandon	23,087	18	24,560	19	25,600	20	25,793	20	27,113	21	26,698	21
St Finbar's	6,207	32	6,119	32	5,678	30	6,090	32	7,057	37	6,986	37
St Mary's Shandon	14,149	52	14,212	52	12,893	48	12,106	45	13,488	50	11,331	42
St Nicholas	16,273	44	13,860	37	14,622	39	15,326	41	15,247	41	15,228	41
St Paul's	4,563	207	4,468	203	4,147	188	3,752	170	2,967	134	2,245	102
St Peter's	8,103	219	8,809	238	7,966	215	7,482	202	7,148	193	6,659	179
Total	80,720		82,948		79,593		78,639		80,124		75,345	

Source: *Censuses of Ireland*, 1841–1891; see also Cronin, 1994, p. 3 (Table 1) for a breakdown of Cork's population by sex.

Migration into Cork during the nineteenth century owed less to the city's economic prospects than it did to the depressed rural situation which forced people to leave. In the eighteenth century the situation was different: for one thing, Cork did not depend on rural migrants for its demographic development; its population growth was adequately sustained by its own rates of natural increase, in part a reflection of high and possibly rising marital fertility typical of Ireland as a whole (Mokyr and O'Gráda, 1984; Schellekens, 1993). Further, because of the prevailing prosperity within the city, especially inthe second half of the century and up until the 1820s, Cork was attractive for prospective migrants. David Dickson (1977, p. 638), the historian of eighteenth-century Cork, concluded that the:

> most plausible explanation of the region's demographic transformation is that a traditionally high birth rate was accompanied by a fairly low death rate over long periods of time. The rarity of subsistence crises in the eighteenth century does not mean that the general level of health was particularly satisfactory or that the adult life expectancy was great, only that with one exception major reverses were absent.

Cork crossed de Vries's 20,000 threshold in the 1680s, having captured a significant share of the new Atlantic trade in barrelled meat and butter (Dickson, 1989, p. 179; de Vries, 1984). From around 17,500 in 1706, Cork's population had grown to 41,000 in 1750 and then to a striking 80,000 by 1821 (Dickson, 1977, p. 420; Census of Ireland, 1821). While such a rate of population growth was a major influence on Cork's development, the indigenous inhabitants, in turn, also benefited from the city's growing prosperity, especially in the later-eighteenth century.

Cork city is not blessed with natural resources; it has no coal, no iron ore, nor has it ever been an administrative centre of any consequence. For these reasons, it has had to rely on its harbour and on its hinterland for its economic momentum, although once growth was under way, the city's prosperity was enhanced by the range of the commercial and professional services which it then provided. Indeed it was fortunate for Cork that its commercial development in the eighteenth century, especially the growth of external trade, was matched by a corresponding expansion in domestic production. It was this feature which distinguished Cork from its northern rival, Belfast, and from its southern neighbour, Waterford. While Waterford averaged 38,302 tons of shipping per annum through its port between 1776 and 1800, Cork averaged 96,680 tons during the same period.[2] Cork's population, as a result, was more than treble that of Waterford's by 1821 when comparable figures for both cities become available (Report from the Select Committee, 1891, p. 555).

But these factors do not in themselves explain the dramatic improvement in Cork's fortunes relative to Waterford from the middle of the eighteenth

2 Public Record Office, London, Customs 15: figures derived by the author from a table cited in Dickson (1975).

century. It could be argued that Waterford, with its excellent harbour and its fertile hinterland, should have prospered equally; it also had the advantage of being closer to Britain, of possessing an extensive estuary, stretching far inland due to the confluence of the rivers Suir and Barrow, while in medieval times it had been the second city in the country (Walton, 1981, p. 1; Power, 1993, p. 46). Why the difference, then, between the two cities?

TRADE AND THE ECONOMIC DEVELOPMENT OF CORK

Cork's ascendancy was due to a combination of factors: human, institutional, geographical and traditional. Waterford may have been closer to Great Britain, but its proximity to Dublin, equally close to Britain, placed a formidable competitor in the way of its development. Cork had little to fear from that quarter—it was further away and, because of the nature of its hinterland, it was shielded from Dublin's competition. Cork's agricultural catchment area was more geared to pasture than to tillage. Being deep-soiled and well suited for grass, it was ideal for cattle-rearing, both dry and dairying, whereas the light-soiled lands adjacent to Waterford, both in that county and in Wexford, were best tilled. Admittedly, corn prices were buoyant in the second half of the eighteenth century but, because of transport difficulties, much of the corn grown in Waterford's hinterland was milled in rural flour mills, ultimately finding its way to Dublin bakeries. It was otherwise with Cork's agricultural staples: cattle could be moved even on foot, despite the bad roads, allowing Cork abattoirs to draw supplies from as far north as Tipperary, as far west as Limerick and also from parts of County Kerry. The dairy herds of the Lee and the Bandon valleys ensured a steady supply of butter for the Cork butter market, as well as an ample supply of pigs for Cork pork butchers. In the course of the eighteenth century Cork merchants recognized these natural advantages and were not slow in exploiting them. The Cork Butter Market, a traditional dealing market, was reorganized in 1769 in response to complaints about the quality of Cork butter and a Committee of Merchants was established which for a hundred years maintained strict control over the running of the market, especially the grading of its products (Donnelly, 1971). By 1789 the Cork market accounted for nearly 50 per cent of all Irish butter exports, in contrast to only 35 per cent in the late 1760s (O'Sullivan, 1937, p. 334; Dickson, 1993, p. 373). In the case of beef, exports through Cork reached a peak of 58.6 per cent of the Irish total in 1789, although the decline after that date, especially in the late 1790s, conceals the fact that the provisioning of the British fleet in Cork harbour was not recorded in the export figures (O'Sullivan, 1937, Appendix 31, p. 326). Pork exports reached their peak in 1784, with 59.1 per cent of Irish exports passing through Cork in that year (O'Sullivan, 1937, Appendix 33, p. 341), but, as in the case of beef, the decline in pork exports in the 1790s may well be attributed to the provisioning demands of the fleet in Cork harbour which meant that output most likely was well maintained.

However striking the advances made in the provisioning trade and in exports, it was Cork's eminence in textiles which especially distinguished the city from its southern neighbour Waterford in the last quarter of the eighteenth century. The employment opportunities provided in the textile industry were increasingly the main outlets for Cork's growing population. Food processing, in this context, had less employment potential. Dickson (1977, p. 563) has calculated that, in the yarn-spinning sector of the industry, between 15,000 and 20,000 spinners were employed in the Cork region, catering primarily for the export market, and that another 4–5,000 were working for the home market. Developments in the textile industry at the end of the eighteenth century were able to build on experience and tradition in the Cork region extending back into the seventeenth century or even earlier. It was a feature of the genius of Cork businessmen, at least until the end of the eighteenth century, that they were able to move from one production line to another, depending on the state of the market; in the early-eighteenth century the emphasis was on the production of frieze and worsted yarn, but when that trade declined 'some of the displaced wool spinners became hand spinners for cotton, others found more enduring employment as cotton weavers and former combers were able to work in jenny-shops instead' (Dickson, 1977, p. 597). The same was true of the linen industry, which found a ready outlet in the sail cloth required by visiting vessels in need of an overhaul but also catered for other markets. Exports of linen cloth rose dramatically at the end of the eighteenth century, from 280,000 yards by 1780 to 1,540,000 yards in 1816 (Dickson, 1977, Appendix Table XIX).

These spectacular developments cannot, however, be isolated from the impact which foreign trade had on the port of Cork. Custom receipts grew from about £50,000 per annum in the 1750s to over £200,000 by the end of the century (Dickson, 1977, Appendix Table VIII). But, paradoxically, the local agents engaged in the export trade were far less active than their domestically-orientated counterparts. Exporters responded to demand; they seldom created it, nor for that matter did they risk their capital in foreign ventures. Unlike their fellow merchants catering for the local market, who were prepared to lend money to their agricultural suppliers during the growing season, the exporters were invariably commission agents engaged by principals in England, France or even further afield. Their most important client was the British government, in particular the Admiralty and the Treasury. Up until 1782 Cork was the sole centre for provisioning navy and army supply ships and even after that concession was withdrawn the city still supplied nearly two-thirds of the wet provisions for the navy. Dickson (1977, p. 488) attributes that monopoly to the fact 'that Cork absentee landowners—the Southwells and the second Earl of Egmont—held high office in the Admiralty'. In fact, the Navy Board opposed the lobby by other Irish ports to become supplementary provisioning agents (Dickson, 1977, p. 488). But Cork was not entirely dependent on military provisioning; its worldwide export trade, built up in the course of the eighteenth century, ensured that Cork had alternative outlets for its products should its Admiralty contracts fail. The success of that business can be attributed to Cork's strategic location for ships employed in the Atlantic trade, especially with America. In 1794, Cork exported 80 per cent, or 22,500 tons, of all Irish beef going to America (O'Sullivan, 1937, Appendix 31, p. 333). In 1795 it supplied the countries on the American continent with 91.5 per cent of their Irish butter, or 20,101 tons, while in 1799 Cork provided nearly 100 per cent of all Irish pork going to America, or 15,000 tons (O'Sullivan, 1937, Appendix 32 and 33, pp. 340, 347). In addition, it had a lucrative trade in butter with Portugal, amounting to an average of 24,000 tons per annum between 1783 and 1800 (O'Sullivan, 1937, Appendix 32, p. 337). It is therefore apparent that Cork's prosperity, especially in the last quarter of the eighteenth century, was one of the main factors in the city's spectacular population increase; a rapid rate of natural increase within the city itself combined with an influx of migrants from its hinterland in search of work were the results.

But it was not to last. The future which had looked so assured at the turn of the nineteenth century was soon to give way to one of the most depressed periods in Cork's history. Factories were to close, trading was to decline, unemployment was to rise, living conditions were to deteriorate, disease was to become rampant, with one major outbreak of cholera in 1832 sweeping away hundreds of Cork's inhabitants. The bonanza of the late-eighteenth century was to prove ephemeral.

A number of reasons can be cited for this decline, any of which would have had adverse effects on its own but their combined influence in so short a time was to prove disastrous. Perhaps the most important of these was the depression which beset Cork's agricultural hinterland after 1818, when prices in Britain for agricultural produce dropped sharply. Between 1818 and 1822 grain prices were halved (Mitchell and Deane, 1962, p. 488), while the price of beef and pork fell by about one-third between 1812–1815 and 1821–1825 (Crotty, 1966, p. 284). A depressed agricultural hinterland inevitably had adverse repercussions for Cork; the fall in rural demand led to a contraction of the textile, leather and even liquor industries. But this was compounded by the collapse of British demand, especially for Cork provisions. With the ending of the Napoleonic Wars and the dispersal of the British navy, the provision trade of Cork declined, with serious consequences for the city's coopers (Cronin, 1993, p. 734). The growing export trade in live cattle was slight compensation as it contributed little to the local urban economy; while the sales yards may have been throbbing with life, the butchers, the packagers, the provision merchants and even the coopers suffered because of the demise of the meat trade. These also suffered from the return to gold in 1819 and the re-establishment of the convertibility of Irish bank notes into gold. A contraction of credit ensued, especially among those banks that had over-extended themselves during the heady days of the Napoleonic Wars. The banks that were unable to adjust to changing conditions invariably failed, with 7 of the 14

Munster and Kilkenny banks closing their doors during those years. According to Cullen (1972, p. 103), 'from a peak of between £1.3 to £1.5 million in 1813, the circulation of private bank notes in the south fell to between £400,000 to £500,000 in 1823'. When the Irish pound was raised to parity with the pound sterling in 1826, the impact was exceptionally deflationary because of the apparent 20 per cent over-valuation of the Irish currency. The final blow fell in 1824 when, after a respite of 24 years, Irish industry was at last exposed to the full brunt of the commercial clauses of the Act of Union. It then experienced the direct blast of British competition and, as this unfortunately coincided with a sharp and severe slump in Britain following the repeal of the Bubble Act in 1825, more than the usual quota of British manufactured goods were dumped on the Irish market at ruinous prices.

The overall impact of these developments on Cork was devastating. The textile industry suffered most; in fact it was all but decimated and many small masters were effectively reduced to the level of journeymen (Bielenberg, 1991; Cronin, 1994, p. 39). In the suburbs of Blackpool and Glasheen destitution was endemic (Fahy, 1993, p. 794). By 1833 there was only one manufacturer of woollens and only two worsted-spinning and stuff manufacturers of any consequence in the city (*The Parliamentary Gazetteer*, 1846, p. 528). Evidence presented to the Poor Law Enquiry in 1836 indicated that between 4,000 and 5,000 weavers had left Cork for England since 1810 (Cullen, 1972, p. 119). This rout had particularly serious repercussions for Blackpool, the traditional textile centre in Cork. It led to an era of unprecedented poverty and destitution in that area of the city and eventually to the clearing of many of the insanitary hovels located there. The linen industry also suffered from the reduced number of fleet vessels using Cork harbour. Soap manufacturers were hit by the decrease in the slaughtering of cattle, while the manufacturers of candles were adversely affected for the same reason (Lewis, 1837, p. 417).

Of the industries to survive, by far the most significant was tanning. Cork leather was of high quality and was readily exported. In 1835 there were possibly 46 tan yards in various parts of the city, the most extensive being located in the North Gate vicinity where there were 615 tanners in constant employment (Lewis, 1837, p. 416). The average number of hides tanned annually amounted to 110,000 and from 1835 onwards tanners found it necessary to import hides from as far afield as Montevideo and Gibraltar in order to supplement local supplies (Lewis, 1837, p. 416).

Brewing and distilling could still call on the abundant corn crops from Cork's hinterland for their raw materials and, like the leather industry, these sectors of the local economy continued to prosper, as yet unhampered by Father Mathew's temperance campaign. In 1835 Cork city distillers were producing 1,400,000 gallons of whiskey annually and were processing 268,000 barrels of corn and employing about 1,000 men; the quantity of whiskey shipped through the port in that year was 1,279 puncheons. Among the 28 breweries found in the city and county of Cork in 1835 by far the largest was

Messrs Beamish and Crawford; the brewery had in fact been the leading one in Ireland up until 1833. Henry Inglis (1834), who visited Cork city in 1834, wrote that 'of the concerns of Beamish and Crawford, in breweries and flour mills, some idea may be formed from the circumstance that one-eighth of the whole rate of the city of Cork is paid by that firm'. However, the advent of Father Mathew severely damaged the prosperity of the drink industry and also that of barley growers (Walsh, 1956–57; Kerrigan, 1992). According to J. S. Donnelly Jr (1975, p. 35):

> Brewing was less hard hit than distilling, but during the decade following the start of the temperance campaign in 1838, the number of bushels of malt upon which the required duty was paid fell from over 2,000,000 to only about 1.5 million or by about 25 per cent.

In fact in Ireland as a whole domestic consumption of grain spirits fell from nearly 12.3 million gallons in 1838 to only about 6 million gallons in 1848, or by more than 50 per cent.

Ship-building was an industry which also played a prominent part in Cork's local economy (O Mahony, 1989); the first paddle steamer made in Ireland was built in Cork in 1812, while the Cork and Waterford yards were the pioneers in the 1840s of iron ship-building in Ireland. In 1836 there were 302 ships, of 21,514 tons, registered in the port of Cork. The two local ship-building yards, each with a patent slip for hauling up and repairing vessels of up to 500 tons, also provided valuable employment—at least 1,600 men were employed in the local ship-building industry. While obviously not as busy as during the heyday of the Napoleonic Wars, Cork harbour in the first half of the nineteenth century still bustled. In 1835, for example, 141 vessels of 27,571 tons left the harbour for foreign ports, while 167 vessels of 30,1921 tons arrived; coastal trading was even more extensive with 1,844 vessels of 235,912 tons arriving and 1,422 vessels of 138,767 tons departing. In addition to the passage of the merchant fleets of the world through its port, Cork had its own line of packets by 1825 owned by the St Georges Company which traded on a regular basis between Cork and Liverpool and afterwards between Cork and Bristol. In the 1840s the capital of that company according to Lewis (1837, p. 415) amounted to £300,000 subscribed in shares, of which one-third were held by Cork proprietors. It employed seven vessels of about 500 tons burden and 250 horse power each; two of these plied to Bristol, one to Liverpool, three to London and one to Dublin, and all carried passengers, goods and cattle.

The impact of the depression was unevenly spread; manufacturing suffered most and, except for tanning, brewing, distilling and ship-building, it was nearly wiped out. Regrettably, the new industries were not yet capable of absorbing the employment fall-out of the traditional textile-based concerns, with the result that for most of the first half of the nineteenth century unemployment was excessively high in Cork. It was stated in evidence before the Select Committee on Irish and Scottish Vagrants in 1829, for example, that Cork had the highest unemployment of all contemporary Irish towns, with over 80 per cent of men out of work.[3] Trading was far less affected by the slump and, in fact, the port on this occasion came to the rescue of the city and its hinterland: but, because of the shift in exports from beef to cattle on the hoof, it was no substitute, especially in employment terms, for the collapse of the local textile industry.

The selective nature of the depression was also evident in the fact that Cork's primary commercial activity, butter marketing, continued to prosper during those years—the average annual number of firkins passing through the weigh-houses of the Butter Market rose from 209,000 between 1800 and 1809 to 260,000 between 1830 and 1839 (Gibson, 1861, pp. 379–80). As already noted, shipping activity also increased during this period, while the range of the city's imports is indicative of the wealth of the fortunate few still in employment in the surviving industries or engaged in commerce: for example, wine imports still remained high despite the challenge from home-distilled spirits and the quantity of tobacco on which duty was paid at the Customs House in 1835 was 647,000 lbs (Lewis, 1837, p. 414). Herrings, linseed oil, raw sugar and many other such items were all imported in large quantities. Thus it is apparent that certain sections of Cork society continued to enjoy a relatively high standard of living, despite the fact that the economic situation of their less fortunate neighbours had deteriorated sharply.

POPULATION AND POLITICS IN CORK

However, despite these oscillations in Cork's economic fortunes, its inhabitants were reluctant to change their life-styles. This may have been due to the city's origins on a group of marshy islands in the lower reaches of the River Lee. Until 1750 the present main street was still a channel of the river, and not until the beginning of the nineteenth century were all the little channels that criss-crossed the main island (Morrison's Island) filled in or bridged over. This meant that even when Cork's population began to grow rapidly in the eighteenth century access to and from the main island was confined to two bridges, Northgate and Southgate. Movement was accordingly restricted; people stayed put, ignorant of the surrounding countryside, but apparently content with their circumscribed horizons. This left an enduring mark on popular attitudes in Cork, because even when seven more bridges, including a major one leading off Patrick Street, were constructed during the 50 years after 1774 the people were slow to move from the congested original island to the more spacious liberties.

The first available figures from the 1841 census point to an average population density of 35.66 persons per acre for the seven parishes of the city—

3 Minutes of Evidence before the Select Committee on Irish and Scottish Vagrants, 1829, **IV**, p. 14.

with a range of 18 persons per acre in St Anne's Shandon to 219 in St Peter's (*Census of Ireland*, 1841) (Table 11.1). There was little change until the late-nineteenth century, despite the exodus which took place during the Famine; it would appear that vacated tenements were promptly filled by recently arrived migrants in the city.

The persistence of residential congestion was to have disastrous results on the many occasions during the nineteenth century when Cork was ravaged by disease. The 1832 cholera epidemic resulted in 4,457 cases being admitted to the temporary hospitals opened for that purpose and of these 1,385 died, a mortality rate of 31 per cent. While the 1849 cholera outbreak was less severe, nevertheless 1,329 died out of the total number of those admitted to local hospitals and Cork's mortality rate of 41.8 per cent was well above that of other Irish cities. For example, Dublin, with three times Cork's population, had only 3,813 cases, of whom 1,664 died. The impact of typhus, while less fatal, was more far-reaching: as many as 18,000 cases of typhus fever were admitted to Cork's three fever hospitals in 1818, although it was estimated that 10,000 more were probably infected—in all, approximately 33 per cent of the population. Typhus struck again in 1835–1837, with 9,422 admissions to the fever hospitals; in the following year, of the 4,941 typhus cases in Cork, 281 died. During the Famine six temporary fever hospitals were opened and these registered 14,805 admissions, of whom 583 died; the cholera outbreak was compounded by smallpox in 1849 and of the 2,596 cases reported, 115 died.

Even with a less congested population and a gradual improvement in living standards, there were still outbreaks of disease, especially smallpox, in the second half of the nineteenth century. Vaccination was almost certainly less extensive in Ireland than in England and Wales and smallpox remained an important cause of infant and child deaths (Mokyr and O'Gráda, 1984, p. 485). In 1871–1872, for example, a major smallpox epidemic killed 1,000 of the 4,000 admissions to the Cork Fever Hospital and the Cork Union Work House. Typhus in 1863–1865 resulted in 249 deaths from the 2,655 cases reported, while minor outbreaks of cholera in 1853–1854 and in 1866 led to 45 deaths (Cummins, 1957).

The extent to which Cork was characterized by residential concentration during this period is also apparent from the occupancy of houses where, on average, there were two families per house both in 1832 and 1841 (*Census of Ireland*, 1841). Murphy (1980, p. 27) has calculated from census returns that 72.25 per cent of all families were living in slum accommodation in 1841 and almost 11,000 families still lived in slums in 1871: there was no appreciable change in this situation until the 1890s (Hourihan, 1993, p. 953). Even in the 1870s when the Corporation, acting under Cross's Act, embarked on a systematic scheme for slum clearances and rehousing, substantial resistance was encountered from those who were not prepared to move the one mile from the city centre to the new houses (Murphy, 1980, p. 30). The absence of any form of public transport in Cork before the 1850s also meant that the suburbs were slow to develop (Fahy, 1993, p. 802). In fact the Liberties, containing 42,621 acres in 1831, had only 22,000 inhabitants, or approximately 0.51 per acre (*Census of Ireland*, 1841). This persistent concentration of population in the central areas of Cork is all the more remarkable when placed in the context of the evolution of European cities. Roger Mols (1954–56) has shown how the population densities of towns in Europe before the industrial revolution were particularly low: for example, Rome in 1526, with a population of nearly 54,000, averaged only 15.5 people per acre, while the range over its vast surface of 5.27 square miles varied from approximately 125 persons in its most crowded area of Rioni to no more than 3 or 4 persons per acre in its least crowded district. Although Cork could never be described as an industrial city, it remained an exception; its 70,000 poverty-stricken inhabitants were located within very narrow spatial limits. Even at the peak of the late-eighteenth-century industrial boom, trading was still the dominant activity and this remained the case into the nineteenth century. It is all the more surprising, then, that its population should have remained so concentrated for so long.

The high population density of Cork also provides some explanation for the bitterness of urban politics before the development of the suburbs, as well as in the later-nineteenth century. In pre-Famine Cork people of all classes lived out their lives in close proximity to one another, without much privacy and in an atmosphere bordering on the claustrophobic, which left an indelible stamp on their social relationships, power struggles and cultural pursuits. As the Commission on Municipal Corporation Boundaries observed:

> It is difficult to particularise on any quarter of the city; St. Patrick's Street, the Grand Parade, the South Mall, Great George Street, St. Patrick's Hill etc., are inhabited by persons of wealth and respectability or occupied by ware houses, but many of the streets, and nearly all the lanes branching off from these main streets and places, are occupied by numerous families of the lower classes and many apparently in the lowest state of destitution.[4]

Thus, within the confines of the city centre all social classes shared the limited space available: merchants rubbed shoulders with artisans, artisans with labourers, Protestants with Catholics; and all these groups were directly confronted with the vast army of destitutes who, impervious to the fading employment opportunities in the nineteenth century, squatted in central Cork.

The wealthy were, of course, outflanked by the poverty stricken; even in 1832 the propertied classes did not account for more than 7,000 of the city's 80,000 citizens (O'Brien, 1980, p. 4). But it was a measure of the former's

4 See also Fahy (1986).

astuteness that, even within that confined space, they successfully contained the masses. This was no mean feat because, as a police official reporting to Dublin Castle in 1870 observed, 'the Cork masses can be collected in an incredibly short time—ripe and ready for mischief—perhaps in no other part of the country is there so formidable and so disaffected a mob as that of Cork'.[5] However, success in this respect masks the existence of deep animosities within the propertied classes that were barely concealed. Cork's middle-class cohesion was deceptive: they closed ranks when confronted by the masses or when their own economic well-being was at stake; on all other occasions internal divisions were openly manifest and, on balance, the fissures within their own ranks were greater than those between themselves and the poorer classes. The fact that before the Famine most of Cork's propertied classes of all religious persuasions lived, worked and socialized within the city centre only served to accentuate the differences that divided them, especially in the political arena.

The main focus for discontent was the Corporation from which most Catholic merchants were excluded before 1841 (d'Alton, 1980); of course, the 73,000 citizens disenfranchised at Parliamentary elections were also debarred from the Corporation, but in pre-Famine Cork they voiced few objections—they apparently knew their place! With the Catholic merchants it was different; these were at least the equals, economically, of their Protestant counterparts and also there were far more of them (O'Brien, 1980). After 1841 the composition of the Corporation was to mirror closely the balance of wealth in Cork with merchants dominating proceedings throughout, winning an average of 23 of the 25 seats, and with manufacturers gaining a declining number of seats in accordance with their diminishing importance (Murphy, 1986). Both Catholics and Protestants were included among these groupings, but now in proportion to their numbers and standing in Cork society, although Protestant wealth still ensured that the latter obtained a higher proportion of the seats than their numbers warranted (Table 11.2). Because Catholic wealth failed to achieve similar representation before the Famine, due to the skill with which the Protestant clique manipulated an undemocratic system to their own advantage, the Catholics were understandably aggrieved. In pre-Famine Cork the political and the economic élites did not overlap at a time when the franchise was property-orientated. That disjunction accounts for the bitterness of the struggle between the two groups for political ascendency in the 1830s. It also heightened social tensions.

In the claustrophobic atmosphere of pre-Famine Cork few occurrences went unnoticed, not least the provocative displays of exclusiveness by the Corporation clique. The glittering receptions in the Mansion House, the civic balls on royal occasions, the ceremonial opening of the Corporation and a host of other semi-private functions obliquely linked with public office, reinforced

CSORP, 1870: 12819, 12956, 13023, 16317.

Table 11.2: *The political and religious composition of Cork Corporation, 1841–1899.*

	Roman Catholic/ Liberal members		Established Church, Dissenters/Unionist members	
	No.	%	No.	%
1841	44	69	20	31
1853	29	52	27	48
1863	33	59	25	41
1871	38	68	18	32
1883	39	70	17	30
1891	38	68	18	32
1899	36	64	20	36

* The Corporation membership was cut from 64 to 56 in 1852.
Source: Murphy, 1986, p. 6.

the barriers between the Protestant merchants and their Catholic rivals who were directly confronted with manifestations of their own ostracism (O'Brien, 1980). Chamber of Commerce dinners and parades for the Liberator, William of Orange, were no substitute for the panache associated with the trappings of state—albeit at the local level. It also meant that the many business dealings of the two communities could not allay the resentment of the Catholics at their political isolation.

The enactment of the Municipal Reform Act in 1840 changed all that: now both merchant communities had equal access to local power and, as a result, the close correlation between creed and politics no longer evoked the same animosities. While the Protestants, in general, still held to their Unionist commitments and the Catholics to their repeal aspirations, they were quite prepared to co-operate on local issues, ensuring that between them they retained a monopoly of power. Membership of the Corporation was still restricted mainly to merchants, manufacturers and professionals, while Cork's representatives at Westminster were also confined to merchants, preferably native-born, although with the arrival of C. S. Parnell, MP for Cork from 1880 to 1890, outsiders finally obtained a foothold. However, all the elected representatives were expected to place local issues before national and imperial concerns.

This continuity in the character of the membership of Cork Corporation tends to conceal the frequent changes which occurred in the composition both of that body and also of the merchant community itself. In general, these closely paralleled changes in Cork's economy. Few of the merchants cited by Dickson as being prominent in the 1780s were still in business in the 1840s, although they were largely from families who had owned much of the city and administered trade and society before 1641 (O'Brien, 1984, p. 11; 1985b, pp. 155–56; Dickson, 1977, p. 153). Change was clearly much more rapid in the nineteenth century, with many of these general merchants disappearing and their place being taken either by the butter merchants, or by textile manufacturers, meat processors and, later, by the tanners. The Goulds, the Roches, the Terrys, the Meades, and the Coppingers had to give way to the Murphys, the Lyons, the Hacketts and the Beamishes. Some of these were to survive into the twentieth century, especially those associated with brewing and distilling, but for the rest their fortunes were to ebb like those of their respective industries in the last quarter of the nineteenth century. Cork's Butter Market succumbed in the 1870s to continental competition in the British market, as well as to the growing popularity of butterine and the increasing number of fresh butter outlets in the Munster region before finally closing its doors in 1884 (Donnelly, 1971, pp. 154, 160). In the case of tanning the 1870s heralded its decline because of a failure to innovate technologically in the face of competition from more highly merchandized British leather products, especially purpose-made footwear (Cronin, 1994, p. 39). Many families engaged in that trade went out of business, the only remaining testament to the former prowess of local tanners and butter merchants being the substantial monuments erected in better times to their memories in St Joseph's cemetery (O'Brien, 1980, p. 8). From an examination of the Cork trade directories at approximately ten-yearly intervals beginning in 1824 and continuing to the end of the century, Murphy (1981, p. 132) has concluded that 'though certain large city business concerns like the brewers, distillers and provision stores remained in the same families for generations, the smaller concerns remained in individual families for much shorter periods, that is, from one to three generations'. She also found that the same pattern was reflected in the composition of the Corporation in the latter decades of the century. In the 1880s and 1890s the former merchants of the Butter Market and of the leather industry had their places taken by retailers and vendors and those generally classified as dealers—still men of property, but whose forebears would have been associated with the excluded Burgesses Association of the 1840s. They are certainly not in the same category as the dethroned merchant princes (Murphy, 1986, Table 6). Nevertheless, they shared the socially conservative attitudes of their more wealthy predecessors.

The response of the local authorities and in particular the Cork middle classes which dominated these institutions to contemporary economic and social problems was predictable. For the most part, the middle class operated within the constraints of the existing system, seldom questioning the wisdom of the prevailing orthodoxy. They responded to acute urban distress with piecemeal palliatives, without ever ascertaining the causes of these problems. In 1831 they made no provision for the cholera epidemic that was sweeping Europe and which reached Cork in April 1832 (O'Brien, 1985a); in the first few months of that epidemic they moved the sick and the dying from one improvised hospital to another in response to a public anxious to distance themselves from the infected. As a remedy for the ensuing depression they merely campaigned for the promotion of Irish manufacturers or a 'buy Cork' campaign, without ever considering the level of wages, the wider market for Cork goods, or even the living and working conditions of their operatives (O'Brien, 1984, pp. 17, 28). Their criteria were essentially parsimonious, so that even in the economic sphere they were not prepared to spend more than they had to on the city: instead, they pressed Westminster to create a suitable environment in which Cork business would flourish. In 1836, for example, they sought to convince the British government that they should purchase Portuguese wines in order to prevent the Portuguese from raising duties on Irish butter.[6] In 1839 30 Protestant and 11 Catholic merchants combined to oppose the Poor Law Commissioners' plan to build a new poor house for the city (*Cork Constitution*, 4 July 1839), nor did the reformed town council as a body give any aid to the Irish manufacture movement of the early 1840s, even after a deputation of tradesmen had especially requested the council to help in the establishment of an Irish manufacture market on North Main Street (*Cork Examiner*, 20 December 1841; 3 January 1842). In the early 1850s, under the Act for the Improvement of the Borough of Cork (15 and 16 Victoria C145), the Corporation built a number of new streets and houses but 'the changes were geared to improving the appearance of the city rather than bettering the conditions of the slum dweller' (Murphy, 1980, pp. 30–80).

THE CONTROL AND SUPPRESSION OF RADICALISM

The surprising feature of Cork in the nineteenth century is not that the propertied classes held these views, but rather that these were shared, on the whole, by many of the distressed majority of the city's population. These had far less to be complacent about, especially the unemployed and those living in sub-human conditions. Still, in the course of the nineteenth century, in spite of their proclivities to riotous behaviour, their demands were essentially for more bread and more work, seldom for a reconstruction of the system of production.

As has been noted already, the distress of the bulk of the city's population stemmed mainly from the collapse of the textile industry in the 1820s and from the contraction of the provisioning trade after the Napoleonic Wars. Those employed in the leather industry, in brewing and distilling and especially in the Butter Market could still count on secure employment and a living wage. However, these openings fell far short of Cork's employment requirements. Even in the second half of the century, when new textile factories were built utilizing more modern equipment (*Cork Examiner*, 5 August 1850;

---

6 George Atkins, Secretary of Merchants, To All Members of Parliament for Cork, 8 February 1836, in *Committee of Merchants' Records*, held in Cork Museum.

17 November 1850) and when the transport and building sectors of the local economy prospered,[7] there was still high unemployment.[8] Because of falling prices and stable or even rising wages in some sectors (O'Brien, 1977, p. 9), those in employment actually experienced an improvement in their standard of living but, even in such cases, the seasonality of much of their work, the existence of a large residual labour force only too willing to take their places, and the blurring of the distinctions between skilled and unskilled which was effected by the introduction of new machinery, especially in textiles, only served to emphasize the precariousness of their situation. Why, then, did they conform?

The lower classes of Cork conformed because they believed that they had no other choice. They were also encouraged in that belief by those who considered that they themselves had much to lose from changes in the social structure and the economic system. These included not only the propertied élite, but also workers in gainful employment who were not prepared to risk their precarious positions for an economic or a social unknown. By skilful manipulation these social groups deflected the hungry masses from radical or revolutionary agitation, holding out the possibility of a better future within the existing system that might be jeopardized by precipitate action. But if such an appeal did not convince, they invariably embellished it by invoking repeal of the Union as a panacea for all Cork's troubles. The Catholic clergy and the local press were welcome allies in that deception.

Until the end of the nineteenth century the masses and, in particular, Cork's general or unskilled workers lacked any type of organization through which they could articulate their economic and social grievances. In the 1830s local workers may have swelled the ranks of the Trades Associations' parades in Cork, but these were controlled from the very beginning by the Catholic merchants (O'Brien, 1984, pp. 17–18) and, even as late as the 1890s, according to Murphy (1980, p. 42), 'perhaps only about three in every ten unskilled labourers in Cork were unionized'. The craftsmen were better organized (Cronin, 1994) but, as elsewhere, they were loath to share this advantage with others; they resented the presence of skilled labourers from outside Cork entering the city and were particularly suspicious of talented general labourers, the so-called 'handymen', who might threaten their own exclusiveness. They were not prepared to risk their own security, either by opening their ranks to

7 In 1841 there were approximately 8,000 men engaged in manufacture in Cork, but by 1901 there were a little over 4,000. The number of skilled men in the building trade rose from approximately 1,400 in 1841 to over 1,600 in 1901 and the rise in the transport sector was particularly striking, with the number of men employed rising from 315 in 1841 to 3,423 in 1901: see *Censuses of Ireland* (1841–1901) and Murphy (1981).

8 During the nineteenth century as a whole between 40 and 70 per cent of Cork's male population was normally engaged in gainful employment. Among females the proportion employed varied between 34 and 40 per cent, with domestic service the most important area of employment: see Murphy (1981, p. 128).

others or by engaging in unacceptable public agitation. The irony was that, in spite of their best efforts, they too found themselves by the 1870s with a skeleton organization because of the decimation of many of the trades due to the collapse of local industries. In the 1830s as many as 40 separate trade societies marched behind their colourful banners in public demonstrations, but by 1900 the maximum number participating was only 19 (*Cork Mercantile Chronicle*, 21 March 1832; 9 June 1832; *Cork Examiner*, 8 October 1898). By then, the survivors identified more with political groups like the Fenians than with their traditional craft organizations.

The merchant classes capitalized on these deficiencies by the unusual expedient of encouraging the masses in their belief that the root cause of all their troubles was British misrule in Ireland rather than the propertied classes' own economic shortcomings. They therefore successfully erected a political smokescreen around a conflagration that was essentially economic in origin. A Cork ballad of the 1830s succinctly captured this strategy:

> The tradesmen and labourer that's now in poverty
> Will sit in their parlour and sing melodiously
> We'll have mutton, beef and bacon with butter, eggs and veal,
> And religion will come again to welcome the Repeal.[9]

As a result, the unemployed and the unskilled channelled their discontent through nationalist rather than through working-class organizations: for example, the mobs gave vocal support to nationalist candidates in the 1832, 1835 and 1841 elections (O'Brien, 1980, pp. 16–17). The latter was the most violent election in nineteenth-century Cork, when men and their womenfolk conducted a campaign of open violence against the Conservative voters. In the election of 1852 similar scenes took place. It is not surprising, therefore, that the ever vigilant *Cork Constitution* (14 June 1852), the local Tory paper, should have observed that:

> while men anxiously search for the means of employing the industrial tradesman, it is not seemly that others should labour to turn him into a party tool, to be employed for ends that will ever be contested while attempted by a party.

By the 1860s the disenfranchised were swelling the ranks of the Fenians. As Table 11.3 indicates, the Cork Fenian movement was drawn from among the lower ranks of Cork society, in contrast to O'Connell's movements of the 1830s and 1840s when merchants, manufacturers and professionals had dominated events. Nevertheless, even with the Fenians, it was still the small shopkeepers and small masters that supplied the leaders (for example, Brian Dillon was a publican and William O'Carroll was a master baker).

But the appeal of nationalism does not completely explain why peculiarly

---

9 Quoted in Murphy (1981, p. 146).

Table 11.3: *Social composition of the Cork Fenian movement, 1865–1870.**

Occupational group	% of rank-and-file	% of leadership
Artisans	46	32
Unskilled labourers	20	–
Drapers' assistants	8	7
Clerks	3.5	14
Publicans, shopkeepers	3	3.5
Merchants, dealers	3	–
Other occupations	5.5	–

* Excluding unidentified individuals.
Source: Murphy, 1980, p. 47.

working-class movements had such little support in the depressed conditions of nineteenth-century Cork. For example, the Chartists and the Fabian Society had few adherents in Cork, while trade unions were dominated by craftsmen, whose conservatism ensured that these remained firmly within the existing structures and reflected prevailing values that were essentially bourgeois. Even though Fergus O'Connor was born near Cork, his movement generated no enthusiasm in his native county. It was likewise in the case of the Fabians. An English coach-maker who came to Cork failed in his attempt to establish a branch of that society in the city. He concluded that the Cork tradesmen were 'far from fit subjects for a Fabian society … scratch them, and you find a conservative of the crudest type' (Murphy, 1980, p. 44). The Internationale in 1872 met a similar reception, while Connolly's Republican and Socialist Party in the early 1900s evoked much the same response. A possible explanation of this conservatism is to be found in the general structure of Cork's industry and trade throughout the nineteenth century. In contrast to many British cities dominated by a single industry, there was a far greater degree of occupational fragmentation and diffusion in Cork. Furthermore, production and trading units were on the whole small, ensuring close contact between the employer and dependent labour with the result that conservatism percolated through the ranks of the local workforce. Apart from the ship-building sector, where between 300 and 800 men were employed in each of the two local ship-yards in the 1850s and 1860s, the average workforce was comparatively small (*Cork Examiner*, 8 October 1852; 28 April 1854; 29 February 1860; 8 October 1864). Among the bigger tailoring establishments, up to 50 men worked together on the employers' premises, but smaller firms seldom employed centrally more than 10 or 15 men, and a large part of the work was done by male and female outworkers in their own homes (*Cork Examiner*, 28 August 1892; 3, 4, 8 April, 31 May, 25 August 1893). In the case of the printers, between 20 and 40 men worked in each of the newspaper offices, while among coopers individual workshops could accommodate between 10 and 40 men (*Cork Examiner*, 4 September 1885).

Two influences militating against the growth of radicalism in Cork came from outside the working classes: from the press and the clergy. The local press, liberal as well as Tory, adamantly opposed any movement seeking social change and successfully blocked any pressure for radical change by the simple expedient of ignoring its existence. Thus the short-lived Irish Democratic Association of 1849–1850 was simply not reported by the *Cork Examiner*, the local liberal newspaper. But perhaps more powerful than the press in discouraging the development of social radicalism was the influence of the Catholic clergy. The Democrats, the supporters of the Internationale of 1872 and the Irish Republic and Socialist Party of the early 1900s all came under the lash of clerical opposition, with a consequent decimation of their membership (Murphy, 1981, p. 153).

The clearest indication of the absence of any desire for social change was the reluctance of the Labour Party to enter local government before 1898 or to group behind a merchant with socialist commitments. In 1898, in the election for the Corporation under the Local Government Act of that year which increased the municipal electorate four-fold, Labour candidates won 7 of the 56 seats but, true to form, not one of these was a skilled labourer (*Cork Constitution*, 18 January 1899). Moreover, they entered the town council without any social or political programme whatsoever. They appear to have made no pre-election pledges and were obviously more anxious to prove the strength of their nationalism than their 'Labourism'.

CONCLUSION

While demographic change was a significant factor in determining the course of social and economic development in Cork, it was not the dominant one. In the eighteenth century, when economic progress was rapid, the strategic situation of Cork harbour, the character of the city's hinterland and the quality of its entrepreneurs were as important in that respect. However, in the nineteenth century the size of the population bore little relation to the level of economic activity, mainly because of the alacrity with which migrants moved into the city to fill the places of the voluntary and involuntary emigrants. In fact, the presence of a surplus population and the ensuing high level of unemployment may well have impeded the emergence in Cork of a distinctive working-class consciousness and of working-class policies. The employed were intimidated by the existence of a reservoir of potential workers from criticizing overtly the existing system in case they might also find themselves redundant. As a result, the sights of the unemployed did not rise above the occasional riot and they certainly never demanded any radical restructuring of the existing social and economic system. The lower classes of Cork were duped by the expectation of a repeal of the Union which the property owners and craftsmen did nothing to dampen; if anything, they encouraged such fallacious beliefs. In one respect, however, population did play a positive role in nineteenth-century Cork. Because of residential concentration within narrow confines, high population density tended to sharpen divisions between the local people and especially within the merchant classes. The ensuing clashes may not have been concerned primarily with economic fundamentals and in most respects were far removed from Cork's real problems: nevertheless, because of the claustrophobic atmosphere in which they took place, such disputes were very bitter and perhaps even deflected the conflicting parties from addressing Cork's real needs. Thus, while the process of population change in the eighteenth century undoubtedly contributed to economic development, in the nineteenth century demographic factors had a greater impact on the town's social attitudes and on local politics.

References

BIELENBERG, A. (1991), *Cork's Industrial Revolution 1780–1880: Development or Decline?*, Cork.

Census of Ireland (1821–1901), London.

CONNELL, K. H. (1950), *The Population of Ireland, 1750–1845*, Oxford.

Cork Constitution (1839–1899), Cork.

Cork Examiner (1841–1898), Cork.

Cork Mercantile Chronicle (1832), Cork.

CRONIN, M. (1993), 'Work and workers in Cork City and County 1800–1900', in P. O'Flanagan and C. G. Buttimer (eds), *Cork History and Society. Interdisciplinary Essays on the History of an Irish County*, Dublin, 721–55.

CRONIN, M. (1994), *Country, Class or Craft? The Politicisation of the Skilled Artisan in Nineteenth-Century Cork*, Cork.

CROTTY, R. D. (1966), *Irish Agricultural Production, its Volume and Structure*, Cork.

CULLEN, L. M. (1972), *An Economic History of Ireland since 1660*, London.

CUMMINS, N. M. (1957), *Some Chapters of Cork Medical History*, Cork.

d'ALTON, I. (1980), *Protestant Society and Politics in Cork 1812–1844*, Cork.

de VRIES, J. (1984), *European Urbanization 1500–1800*, London.

DICKSON, D. (1975), 'The growth of Irish cities in the 18th century', unpublished conference paper.

DICKSON, D. (1977), 'An economic history of the Cork region in the 18th century', unpublished PhD thesis, University of Dublin.

DICKSON, D. (1989), 'The demographic implications of Dublin's growth, 1650–1850', in R. Lawton and R. Lee (eds), *Urban Population Development in Western Europe from the Late-Eighteenth to the Early-Twentieth Century*, Liverpool, 178–89.

DICKSON, D. (1993), 'Butter comes to market: the origins of commercial dairying in County Cork', in P. O'Flanagan and C. G. Buttimer (eds), *Cork History and Society. Interdisciplinary Essays on the History of an Irish County*, Dublin, 367–90.

DONNELLY, J. S. Jr (1971), 'Cork market: its role in the 19th century Irish butter trade', *Studia Hibernica*, **11**, 136–63.

DONNELLY, J. S. Jr (1975), *The Land and the People of Nineteenth-Century Cork*, London.

FAHY, A. M. (1986), 'Residence, workforce and patterns of change: Cork 1778–1863', in L. M.

Cullen and P. Butel (eds), *Cities and Merchants: French and Irish Perspectives on Urban Development 1500–1900*, Dublin.

FAHY, A. M. (1993), 'Place and class in Cork', in P. O'Flanagan and C. G. Buttimer (eds), *Cork History and Society. Interdisciplinary Essays on the History of an Irish County*, Dublin, 793–812.

GIBSON, C. B. (1861), *The History of the County and City of Cork*, **2**, London.

HOURIHAN, K. (1993), 'The evolution and influence of town planning in Cork', in P. O'Flanagan and C. G. Buttimer (eds), *Cork History and Society. Interdisciplinary Essays on the History of an Irish County*, Dublin, 941–62.

INGLIS, H. (1834), *A Journey through Ireland during the Spring, Summer and Autumn of 1834*, London.

KERRIGAN, C. (1992), *Father Mathew and the Irish Temperance Movement 1838–1849*, Cork.

LEWIS, S. (1837), *Topographical Dictionary of Ireland*, **1**, London.

MITCHELL, B. R. and P. DEANE (1962), *Abstract of British Historical Statistics*, Cambridge.

MOKYR, J. and C. O'GRADA (1984), 'New developments in Irish population history, 1700–1850', *Economic History Review*, **XXXVII**(4), 473–488.

MOLS, R. (1954–56), *Introduction à la démographie historique des villes d'Europe du XIV au XVIIIe siècle*, Louvain.

MURPHY, M. (1980), 'The working classes of nineteenth-century Ireland', *Journal of the Cork Archaeological and Historical Society*, **LXXXV**(241–42), 26–51.

MURPHY, M. (1981), 'The economic and social structure of nineteenth-century Cork', in D. Harkness and M. O'Dowd (eds), *The Town in Ireland*, Belfast, 125–54.

MURPHY, M. (1986), 'Cork commercial society, 1850–1899: politics and problems', in L. M. Cullen and P. Butel (eds), *Cities and Merchants: French and Irish Perspectives on Urban Development 1500–1900*, Dublin, 233–44.

O'BRIEN, J. B. (1977), 'Agricultural prices and living costs in pre-famine Ireland', *Journal of the Cork Historical and Archaeological Society*, **LXXXII**(235), 1–10.

O'BRIEN, J. B. (1980), *The Catholic Middle Classes in Pre-Famine Cork*, National University of Ireland.

O'BRIEN, J. B. (1984), 'Merchant classes in Cork before the famine', unpublished conference paper.

O'BRIEN, J. B. (1985a), 'Cork, its people and environments, 1800–45', *Cork Examiner*, May.

O'BRIEN, J. B. (1985b), 'The Hacketts: glimpses of entrepreneurial life in Cork 1800–70', *Journal of the Cork Historical and Archaeological Society*, **XC**(249), 150–57.

O MAHONY, C. (1989), 'Shipbuilding and repairing in nineteenth-century Cork', *Journal of the Cork Historical and Archaeological Society*, **XCIV**(253), 74–87.

O'SULLIVAN, W. (1937), *The Economic History of Cork from the Earliest Times to the Act of Union*, London.

POWER, T. P. (1993), *Land, Politics and Society in Eighteenth-Century Tipperary*, Oxford.

Report from the Select Committee on the Financial Relations (England, Scotland and Ireland) (1891), London (reprinted by Irish University Press, 1970).

SCHELLEKENS, J. (1993), 'The role of marital fertility in Irish population history, 1750–1840', *Economic History Review*, **XLVI**(2), 369–78.

The Parliamentary Gazetteer of Ireland, 1844–45 (1846), London.

WALSH, Fr T. J. (1956–57), 'Father Mathew in Cork', in *The Capuchin Annual*, 116–24.

WALTON, J. C. (1981), 'The merchant community of Waterford in the 16th and 17th centuries', unpublished conference paper.

INDEX

Note: page numbers in **bold** denote lists of references; those in *italic* denote collaborators not listed in the text.